UNIVERSITY CASEBOOK SERIES®

2016 SUPPLEMENT TO

CONSTITUTIONAL LAW

CASES AND MATERIALS

FOURTEENTH EDITION

JONATHAN D. VARAT
Professor of Law Emeritus and Former Dean
University of California, Los Angeles

VIKRAM D. AMAR
Dean and Iwan Foundation Professor of Law
University of Illinois College of Law

FOUNDATION
PRESS

University Casebook Series is a trademark registered in the U.S. Patent and Trademark Office.

© 2013 LEG, Inc. d/b/a West Academic Publishing
© 2014, 2015 LEG, Inc. d/b/a West Academic
© 2016 LEG, Inc. d/b/a West Academic
    444 Cedar Street, Suite 700
    St. Paul, MN 55101
    1-877-888-1330

Printed in the United States of America

ISBN: 978-1-63460-704-9

PREFACE

Perhaps the most noteworthy occurrence at the Supreme Court during the October 2015 Term was the sudden death of Associate Justice Antonin Scalia on February 13, 2016. Justice Scalia's passing left a vacancy on the Court that has not yet been filled. Although President Obama on March 16 nominated Merrick Garland, the Chief Judge of the United States Court of Appeals for the District of Columbia Circuit, to replace Justice Scalia, the Senate's Republican leadership has taken the position that the vacancy should not be filled until after the presidential election in November and that no hearings on the nomination should be held before then, and perhaps not until a new President takes office.

With the short-handed Court perceived—in a rough sense—to be evenly divided methodologically and jurisprudentially, and with four of the remaining eight Justices having been appointed by Republican Presidents and four by Democratic Presidents, the replacement of Justice Scalia quickly became a campaign issue in the 2016 Presidential race. Moreover, two of the potentially most notable cases this Term ended up without opinions as 4–4 affirmances of the lower court's judgment by an equally divided Court. The first was *Friedrichs v. California Teachers Association*, which raised the question of whether *Abood v. Detroit Board of Education* should be overruled and, specifically, whether it violates the First Amendment to require that public employees affirmatively object to subsidizing nonchargeable speech by public-sector unions, rather than requiring that employees affirmatively consent to subsidizing such speech. The case also might have been a vehicle to reconsider whether nonunion workers could be required to pay for any union expenses—even those ostensibly tied to bargaining over working conditions that affect all employees. The affirmance left in place a Ninth Circuit ruling in favor of the union. The second was *United States v. Texas*, which raised questions of the standing of States to contest the President's authority to adopt policies concerning immigration enforcement deferrals, and, if standing were found, of the statutory and constitutional authority of the President to adopt those policies. The affirmance left in place a Fifth Circuit ruling in favor of Texas.

Major decisions regarding affirmative action in university admissions and abortion restrictions were rendered by the eight-Justice Court, however, and those decisions are reflected in this Supplement. So are some First Amendment and reapportionment decisions, among others.

JONATHAN D. VARAT
VIKRAM D. AMAR

July 2016

TABLE OF CONTENTS

PART 4. CONSTITUTIONAL PROTECTION OF EXPRESSION AND CONSCIENCE

TABLE OF CASES

The principal cases are in bold type.

UNIVERSITY CASEBOOK SERIES®

2016 SUPPLEMENT TO

CONSTITUTIONAL LAW

CASES AND MATERIALS

FOURTEENTH EDITION

PART 1

THE CONSTITUTION AND THE COURTS: THE JUDICIAL FUNCTION IN CONSTITUTIONAL CASES

CHAPTER 3

THE JURISDICTION OF FEDERAL COURTS IN CONSTITUTIONAL CASES

3. CASES AND CONTROVERSIES AND JUSTICIABILITY

B. STANDING

1. "CONVENTIONAL" STANDING

Page 68. Add after Texas v. Lesage:

Clapper v. Amnesty International, 570 U.S. ___, 133 S.Ct. 1138 (2013). A group of American attorneys and human rights, labor, legal and media organizations lacked standing to challenge the FISA Amendments Act of 2008, which permits the U.S. Attorney General and the Director of National Intelligence to seek approval from the Foreign Intelligence Surveillance Court (FISC) to obtain foreign intelligence information through surveillance of individuals who are not "United States persons." The plaintiffs' allegations that they engage in sensitive international communications with foreign individuals who, plaintiffs believe, are likely targets of federal surveillance were inadequate, because there was not a strong enough likelihood that: (1) the federal government would imminently target persons with whom plaintiffs communicated; (2) even if such persons were targeted, the federal government would make use of the FISA Amendments Act rather than other surveillance methods; (3) even if FISC permission were sought, it would be granted; and (4) even if FISC permission were sought and obtained, the federal government would successfully intercept particular communications to which plaintiffs were parties.

3. TAXPAYER AND CITIZEN STANDING

Page 76. Add after Raines v. Byrd:

Arizona State Legislature v. Arizona Independent Redistricting Commission, 576 U.S. ___, 135 S.Ct. 2652 (2015). In 2000 the voters of Arizona enacted Proposition 106, an initiative creating the Arizona Independent Redistricting Commission (AIRC) and giving it the exclusive power to draw congressional district lines, a function previously exercised by the elected state legislature. In early 2012, based on the 2010 census, the AIRC formulated redistricting maps to be used in federal elections. The elected legislature then filed suit in federal court, alleging that Proposition 106 impermissibly divested authority from the elected representative body in violation of the so-called Elections Clause, Article I § 4, which provides in part:

"The Times, Places and Manner of holding Elections for Senators and Representatives shall be prescribed in each State by the Legislature thereof. . . . " A three-judge district court rejected the challenge on the merits, and the Supreme Court affirmed on appeal by a 5–4 vote. On the question of whether the elected legislature had standing, five Justices explicitly found standing to exist, two Justices rejected standing, and two others dissented on the merits without mentioning standing.

Justice Ginsburg's opinion for the Court began by reiterating the requirements of "an injury in the form of 'invasion of a legally protected interest' that is 'concrete and particularized' and 'actual or imminent,'" and that the injury "also . . . be 'fairly traceable to the challenged action.'" The majority continued:

"The Arizona Legislature maintains that the Elections Clause vests in it 'primary responsibility' for redistricting. . . . To exercise that responsibility, the Legislature urges, it must have at least the opportunity to engage (or decline to engage) in redistricting before the State may involve other actors in the redistricting process. . . . Proposition 106, which gives the AIRC binding authority over redistricting, regardless of the Legislature's action or inaction, strips the Legislature of its alleged prerogative to initiate redistricting. That asserted deprivation would be remedied by a court order enjoining the enforcement of Proposition 106. Although we conclude that the Arizona Legislature does not have the exclusive, constitutionally guarded role it asserts, . . . , one must not 'confus[e] weakness on the merits with absence of Article III standing.' . . .

"The AIRC argues that the Legislature's alleged injury is insufficiently concrete to meet the standing requirement absent some 'specific legislative act that would have taken effect but for Proposition 106.' The United States, as *amicus curiae*, urges that even more is needed: the Legislature's injury will remain speculative, the United States contends, unless and until the Arizona Secretary of State refuses to implement a competing redistricting plan passed by the Legislature. . . . In our view, the Arizona Legislature's suit is not premature, nor is its alleged injury too 'conjectural' or 'hypothetical' to establish standing.

"Two prescriptions of Arizona's Constitution would render the Legislature's passage of a competing plan and submission of that plan to the Secretary of State unavailing. Indeed, those actions would directly and immediately conflict with the regime Arizona's Constitution establishes. Cf. Sporhase v. Nebraska ex rel. Douglas, 458 U. S. 941, 944, n. 2 (1982) (failure to apply for permit which 'would not have been granted' under existing law did not deprive plaintiffs of standing to challenge permitting regime). First, the Arizona Constitution instructs that the Legislature 'shall not have the power to adopt any measure that supersedes [an initiative], in whole or in part, . . . unless the superseding measure furthers the purposes' of the initiative. Art. IV, pt. 1, § 1(14). Any redistricting map passed by the Legislature in an effort to supersede the AIRC's map surely would not 'furthe[r] the purposes' of Proposition 106. Second, once the AIRC certifies its redistricting plan to the Secretary of State, Arizona's Constitution requires the Secretary to implement that plan and no other. See Art. IV, pt. 2, § 1(17); . . . . To establish standing, the Legislature need not violate the Arizona Constitution and show that the Secretary of State would similarly disregard the State's fundamental instrument of government.

"Raines v. Byrd, 521 U. S. 811 (1997), does not aid AIRC's argument that there is no standing here. In *Raines*, this Court held that six *individual Members* of Congress lacked standing to challenge the Line Item Veto Act. *Id.*, at 813–814, 829–830 (holding specifically and only that 'individual members of Congress [lack] Article III standing'). The Act, which gave the President authority to cancel certain spending and tax benefit measures after signing them into law, allegedly diluted the efficacy of the Congressmembers' votes. . . . The 'institutional injury' at issue, we reasoned, scarcely zeroed in on any individual Member. . . . '[W]idely dispersed,' the alleged injury 'necessarily [impacted] all Members of Congress and both Houses . . . equally.' . . . None of the plaintiffs, therefore, could tenably claim a 'personal stake' in the suit. . . .

"In concluding that the individual Members lacked standing, the Court 'attach[ed] some importance to the fact that [the *Raines* plaintiffs had] not been authorized to represent their respective Houses of Congress.' . . . '[I]ndeed,' the Court observed, 'both houses actively oppose[d] their suit.' . . . Having failed to prevail in their own Houses, the suitors could not repair to the Judiciary to complain. The Arizona Legislature, in contrast, is an institutional plaintiff asserting an institutional injury, and it commenced this action after authorizing votes in both of its chambers, . . . That 'different . . . circumstanc[e],' . . . was not *sub judice* in *Raines*.

"Closer to the mark is this Court's decision in Coleman v. Miller, 307 U. S. 433 (1939). There, plaintiffs were 20 (of 40) Kansas State Senators, whose votes 'would have been sufficient to defeat [a] resolution ratifying [a] proposed [federal] constitutional amendment.' . . . We held they had standing to challenge, as impermissible under Article V of the Federal Constitution, the State Lieutenant Governor's tie-breaking vote for the amendment. . . . *Coleman*, as we later explained in *Raines*, stood 'for the proposition that legislators whose votes would have been sufficient to defeat (or enact) a specific legislative Act have standing to sue if that legislative action goes into effect (or does not go into effect), on the ground that their votes have been completely nullified.' . . . Our conclusion that the Arizona Legislature has standing fits that bill. Proposition 106, together with the Arizona Constitution's ban on efforts to undermine the purposes of an initiative, . . . would 'completely nullif[y]' any vote by the Legislature, now or 'in the future,' purporting to adopt a redistricting plan. . . ."

The Court added that "[t]he case before us does not touch or concern the question whether Congress has standing to bring a suit against the President. There is no federal analogue to Arizona's initiative power, and a suit between Congress and the President would raise separation-of-powers concerns absent here." Chief Justice Roberts, joined by Justices Scalia, Thomas and Alito, wrote a dissent on the merits that did not discuss standing. Justices Scalia and Thomas each wrote a dissent, joined only by the other, arguing that the elected legislature lacked standing.

Page 77. Add the following footnote (a) to the end of the opinion of the Court excerpt in Federal Election Commission v. Akins:

ª   In Spokeo, Inc. v. Robins, 577 U.S. ___, 136 S. Ct. 1540 (2016), the Court reiterated that "the injury-in-fact requirement requires a plaintiff to allege an injury that is both 'concrete *and* particularized,'" and that particularity can be satisfied even if concreteness is not. As a result, lower courts must analyze both aspects of injury-in-fact to ensure that each is present.

Page 77. Add after Clinton v. New York:

4.   STANDING TO REPRESENT THE INTERESTS OF A STATE

Hollingsworth v. Perry

570 U.S. ___, 133 S.Ct. 2652, 186 L.Ed.2d 768 (2013).

Chief Justice Roberts delivered the opinion of the Court.

The public is currently engaged in an active political debate over whether same-sex couples should be allowed to marry. That question has also given rise to litigation. . . .

Federal courts have authority under the Constitution to answer such questions only if necessary to do so in the course of deciding an actual "case" or "controversy." As used in the Constitution, those words do not include every sort of dispute, but only those "historically viewed as capable of resolution through the judicial process." *Flast v. Cohen*, 392 U.S. 83, 95 (1968). This is an essential limit on our power: It ensures that we act as *judges*, and do not engage in policymaking properly left to elected representatives.

For there to be such a case or controversy, it is not enough that the party invoking the power of the court have a keen interest in the issue. That party must also have "standing," which requires, among other things, that it have suffered a concrete and particularized injury. Because we find that petitioners do not have standing, we have no authority to decide this case on the merits, and neither did the Ninth Circuit.

I

In 2008, the California Supreme Court held that limiting the official designation of marriage to opposite-sex couples violated the equal protection clause of the California Constitution. . . . Later that year, California voters passed the ballot initiative at the center of this dispute, known as Proposition 8. That proposition amended the California Constitution to provide that "[o]nly marriage between a man and a woman is valid or recognized in California." Cal. Const., Art. I, § 7.5. . . .

. . .

Respondents, two same-sex couples who wish to marry, filed suit in federal court, challenging Proposition 8 under the Due Process and Equal Protection Clauses of the Fourteenth Amendment to the Federal Constitution. The complaint named as defendants California's Governor, attorney general, and various other state and local officials responsible for enforcing California's marriage laws. Those officials refused to defend the law, although they have continued to enforce it throughout this litigation. The District Court allowed petitioners—the official proponents of the initiative, see Cal. Elec.Code Ann. § 342—to intervene to defend it. After a 12-day bench trial, the District Court declared Proposition 8 unconstitutional, permanently enjoining the California officials named as defendants from enforcing the law, and "directing the official defendants that all persons under their control or supervision" shall not enforce it. *Perry v. Schwarzenegger*, 704 F.Supp.2d 921, 1004 (N.D.Cal.2010).

Those officials elected not to appeal the District Court order. When petitioners did, the Ninth Circuit asked them to address "why this appeal should not be dismissed for lack of Article III standing.". . . After briefing and argument, the Ninth Circuit certified a question to the California Supreme Court:

> "Whether under Article II, Section 8 of the California Constitution, or otherwise under California law, the official proponents of an initiative measure possess either a particularized interest in the initiative's validity or the authority to assert the State's interest in the initiative's validity, which would enable them to defend the constitutionality of the initiative upon its adoption or appeal a judgment invalidating the initiative, when the public officials charged with that duty refuse to do so." *Perry v. Schwarzenegger*, 628 F.3d 1191, 1193 (2011).

The California Supreme Court agreed to decide the certified question, and answered in the affirmative. Without addressing whether the proponents have a particularized interest of their own in an initiative's validity, the court concluded that "[i]n a postelection challenge to a voter-approved initiative measure, the official proponents of the initiative are authorized under California law to appear and assert the state's interest in the initiative's validity and to appeal a judgment invalidating the measure when the public officials who ordinarily defend the measure or appeal such a judgment decline to do so." *Perry v. Brown*, 52 Cal.4th 1116, 1127 (2011).

Relying on that answer, the Ninth Circuit concluded that petitioners had standing under federal law to defend the constitutionality of Proposition 8. California, it reasoned, " 'has standing to defend the constitutionality of its [laws],' " and States have the "prerogative, as independent sovereigns, to decide for themselves who may assert their interests." *Perry v. Brown*, 671 F.3d 1052, 1070, 1071 (2012) (quoting *Diamond v. Charles*, 476 U.S. 54, 62 (1986)). "All a federal court need determine is that the state has suffered a harm sufficient to confer standing and that the party seeking to invoke the jurisdiction of the court is authorized by the state to represent its interest in remedying that harm." 671 F.3d, at 1072.

On the merits, the Ninth Circuit affirmed the District Court. . . .

We granted certiorari to review that determination, and directed that the parties also brief and argue "Whether petitioners have standing under Article III, § 2, of the Constitution in this case." 568 U.S. ___ (2012).

II

Article III of the Constitution confines the judicial power of federal courts to deciding actual "Cases" or "Controversies." § 2. One essential aspect of this requirement is that any person invoking the power of a federal court must demonstrate standing to do so. This requires the litigant to prove that he has suffered a concrete and particularized injury that is fairly traceable to the challenged conduct, and is likely to be redressed by a favorable judicial decision. *Lujan v. Defenders of Wildlife*, 504 U.S. 555, 560–561 (1992). In other words, for a federal court to have authority under the Constitution to settle a dispute, the party before it must seek a remedy for a personal and tangible harm. "The presence of a disagreement, however sharp and acrimonious it may be, is insufficient by itself to meet Art. III's requirements." *Diamond, supra*, at 62.

The doctrine of standing, we recently explained, "serves to prevent the judicial process from being used to usurp the powers of the political branches." *Clapper v. Amnesty Int'l USA*, 568 U.S. ___, ___ (2013). In light of this "overriding and time-honored concern about keeping the Judiciary's power within its proper constitutional sphere, we must put aside the natural urge to proceed directly to the merits of [an] important dispute and to 'settle' it for the sake of convenience and efficiency." *Raines v. Byrd*, 521 U.S. 811, 820 (1997).

Most standing cases consider whether a plaintiff has satisfied the requirement when filing suit, but Article III demands that an "actual controversy" persist throughout all stages of litigation. *Already, LLC v. Nike, Inc.*, 568 U.S. ___, ___ (2013). That means that standing "must be met by persons seeking appellate review, just as it must be met by persons appearing in courts of first instance." *Arizonans for Official English v. Arizona*, 520 U.S. 43, 64 (1997). We therefore must decide whether petitioners had standing to appeal the District Court's order.

Respondents initiated this case in the District Court against the California officials responsible for enforcing Proposition 8. The parties do not contest that respondents had Article III standing to do so. Each couple expressed a desire to marry and obtain "official sanction" from the State, which was unavailable to them given the declaration in Proposition 8 that "marriage" in California is solely between a man and a woman. App. 59.

After the District Court declared Proposition 8 unconstitutional and enjoined the state officials named as defendants from enforcing it, however, the inquiry under Article III changed. Respondents no longer had any injury to redress—they had won—and the state officials chose not to appeal.

The only individuals who sought to appeal that order were petitioners, who had intervened in the District Court. But the District Court had not ordered them to do or refrain from doing anything. To have standing, a litigant must seek relief for an injury that affects him in a "personal and individual way." *Defenders of Wildlife, supra*, at 560, n. 1. He must possess a "direct stake in the outcome" of the case. *Arizonans for Official English, supra*, at 64. Here, however, petitioners had no "direct stake" in the outcome of their appeal. Their only interest in having the District Court order reversed was to vindicate the constitutional validity of a generally applicable California law.

We have repeatedly held that such a "generalized grievance," no matter how sincere, is insufficient to confer standing. A litigant "raising only a generally available grievance about government—claiming only harm to his and every citizen's interest in proper application of the Constitution and laws, and seeking relief that no more directly and tangibly benefits him than it does the public at large—does not state an Article III case or controversy." *Defenders of Wildlife, supra,* at 573–574. . . .

Petitioners argue that the California Constitution and its election laws give them a " 'unique,' 'special,' and 'distinct' role in the initiative process—one 'involving both authority and responsibilities that differ from other supporters of the measure.' " Reply Brief 5 (quoting 52 Cal.4th, at 1126, 1142, 1160). . . .

But once Proposition 8 was approved by the voters, the measure became "a duly enacted constitutional amendment or statute." 52 Cal.4th, at 1147. Petitioners have no role—special or otherwise—in the enforcement of Proposition 8. See *id.,* at 1159 (petitioners do not "possess any official authority . . . to directly enforce the initiative measure in question"). They therefore have no "personal stake" in defending its enforcement that is distinguishable from the general interest of every citizen of California. *Defenders of Wildlife, supra,* at 560–561.

Article III standing "is not to be placed in the hands of 'concerned bystanders,' who will use it simply as a 'vehicle for the vindication of value interests.' " *Diamond,* 476 U.S., at 62. . . . [S]ee *Arizonans for Official English,* 520 U.S., at 65 ("Nor has this Court ever identified initiative proponents as Article-III-qualified defenders of the measures they advocated."); *Don't Bankrupt Washington Committee v. Continental Ill. Nat. Bank & Trust Co. of Chicago,* 460 U.S. 1077 (1983) (summarily dismissing, for lack of standing, appeal by an initiative proponent from a decision holding the initiative unconstitutional).

III

A

Without a judicially cognizable interest of their own, petitioners attempt to invoke that of someone else. They assert that even if they have no cognizable interest in appealing the District Court's judgment, the State of California does, and they may assert that interest on the State's behalf. It is, however, a "fundamental restriction on our authority" that "[i]n the ordinary course, a litigant must assert his or her own legal rights and interests, and cannot rest a claim to relief on the legal rights or interests of third parties." *Powers v. Ohio,* 499 U.S. 400, 410 (1991). There are "certain, limited exceptions" to that rule. *Ibid.* But even when we have allowed litigants to assert the interests of others, the litigants themselves still "must have suffered an injury in fact, thus giving [them] a sufficiently concrete interest in the outcome of the issue in dispute." *Id.,* at 411.

. . .

B

Petitioners contend that this case is different, because the California Supreme Court has determined that they are "authorized under California law to appear and assert the state's interest" in the validity of Proposition 8. 52 Cal.4th, at 1127. The court below agreed: "All a federal court need determine is that the state has suffered a harm sufficient to confer standing and that the party seeking to invoke the jurisdiction of the court is authorized by the state to represent its interest in remedying that harm." 671 F.3d, at 1072. As petitioners put it, they "need no more show a personal injury, separate from the State's indisputable interest in the validity of its law, than would California's Attorney General or did the legislative leaders held to have standing in *Karcher v. May*, 484 U.S. 72 (1987)." Reply Brief 6.

In *Karcher*, we held that two New Jersey state legislators—Speaker of the General Assembly Alan Karcher and President of the Senate Carmen Orechio—could intervene in a suit against the State to defend the constitutionality of a New Jersey law, after the New Jersey attorney general had declined to do so. 484 U.S., at 75. "Since the New Jersey Legislature had authority under state law to represent the State's interests in both the District Court and the Court of Appeals," we held that the Speaker and the President, in their official capacities, could vindicate that interest in federal court on the legislature's behalf. *Id.*, at 82.

Far from supporting petitioners' standing, however, *Karcher* is compelling precedent against it. The legislators in that case intervened in their official capacities as Speaker and President of the legislature. No one doubts that a State has a cognizable interest "in the continued enforceability" of its laws that is harmed by a judicial decision declaring a state law unconstitutional. *Maine v. Taylor*, 477 U.S. 131, 137 (1986). To vindicate that interest or any other, a State must be able to designate agents to represent it in federal court. See *Poindexter v. Greenhow*, 114 U.S. 270, 288 (1885) ("The State is a political corporate body [that] can act only through agents"). That agent is typically the State's attorney general. But state law may provide for other officials to speak for the State in federal court, as New Jersey law did for the State's presiding legislative officers in *Karcher*. See 484 U.S., at 81–82.

What is significant about *Karcher* is what happened after the Court of Appeals decision in that case. Karcher and Orechio lost their positions as Speaker and President, but nevertheless sought to appeal to this Court. We held that they could not do so. We explained that while they were able to participate in the lawsuit in their official capacities as presiding officers of the incumbent legislature, "since they no longer hold those offices, they lack authority to pursue this appeal." *Id.*, at 81.

The point of *Karcher* is not that a State could authorize private parties to represent its interests; Karcher and Orechio were permitted to proceed only because they were state officers, acting in an official capacity. As soon as they lost that capacity, they lost standing. Petitioners here hold no office and have always participated in this litigation solely as private parties.

. . .

C

Both petitioners and respondents seek support from dicta in *Arizonans for Official English v. Arizona*, 520 U.S. 43. The plaintiff in *Arizonans for Official English* filed a constitutional challenge to an Arizona ballot initiative declaring English " 'the official language of the State of Arizona.' " *Id.*, at 48. After the District Court declared the initiative unconstitutional, Arizona's Governor announced that she would not pursue an appeal. Instead, the principal sponsor of the ballot initiative—the Arizonans for Official English Committee—sought to defend the measure in the Ninth Circuit. *Id.*, at 55–56. Analogizing the sponsors to the Arizona Legislature, the Ninth Circuit held that the Committee was "qualified to defend [the initiative] on appeal," and affirmed the District Court. *Id.*, at 58, 61.

Before finding the case mooted by other events, this Court expressed "grave doubts" about the Ninth Circuit's standing analysis. *Id.*, at 66. We reiterated that "[s]tanding to defend on appeal in the place of an original defendant . . . demands that the litigant possess 'a direct stake in the outcome.' " *Id.*, at 64 (quoting *Diamond*, 476 U.S., at 62). We recognized that a legislator authorized by state law to represent the State's interest may satisfy standing requirements, as in *Karcher*, *supra*, at 82, but noted that the Arizona committee and its members were "not elected representatives, and we [we]re aware of no Arizona law appointing initiative sponsors as agents of the people of Arizona to defend, in lieu of public officials, the constitutionality of initiatives made law of the State." *Arizonans for Official English*, *supra*, at 65.

Petitioners argue that, by virtue of the California Supreme Court's decision, they are authorized to act " 'as agents of the people' of California." Brief for Petitioners 15 (quoting *Arizonans for Official English*, *supra*, at 65). But that Court never described petitioners as "agents of the people," or of anyone else. Nor did the Ninth Circuit. The Ninth Circuit asked—and the California Supreme Court answered—only whether petitioners had "the authority to assert the State's interest in the initiative's validity." 628 F.3d, at 1193; 52 Cal.4th, at 1124. All that the California Supreme Court decision stands for is that, so far as California is concerned, petitioners may argue in defense of Proposition 8. This "does not mean that the proponents become de facto public officials"; the authority they enjoy is "simply the authority to participate as parties in a court action and to assert legal arguments in defense of the state's interest in the validity of the initiative measure." *Id.*, at 1159. That interest is by definition a generalized one, and it is precisely because proponents assert such an interest that they lack standing under our precedents.

And petitioners are plainly not agents of the State—"formal" or otherwise. . . .

. . . [T]he most basic features of an agency relationship are missing here. Agency requires more than mere authorization to assert a particular interest. "An essential element of agency is the principal's right to control the agent's actions." 1 Restatement (Third) of Agency § 1.01, Comment f (2005) (hereinafter Restatement). Yet petitioners answer to no one; they decide for themselves, with no review, what arguments to make and how to make them. Unlike California's attorney general, they are not elected at regular intervals—or elected at all. See Cal. Const., Art. V, § 11. No provision provides for their removal. As one amicus explains, "the proponents apparently have an unelected appointment for an unspecified period of time as defenders of the initiative, however and to whatever extent they choose to defend it." Brief for Walter Dellinger 23.

"If the relationship between two persons is one of agency . . . , the agent owes a fiduciary obligation to the principal." 1 Restatement § 1.01, Comment e. But petitioners owe nothing of the sort to the people of California. Unlike California's elected officials, they have taken no oath of office. *E.g.*, Cal. Const., Art. XX, § 3 (prescribing the oath for "all public officers and employees, executive, legislative, and judicial"). As the California Supreme Court explained, petitioners are bound simply by "the same ethical constraints that apply to all other parties in a legal proceeding." 52 Cal.4th, at 1159. They are free to pursue a purely ideological commitment to the law's constitutionality without the need to take cognizance of resource constraints, changes in public opinion, or potential ramifications for other state priorities.

Finally, the California Supreme Court stated that "[t]he question of who should bear responsibility for any attorney fee award . . . is entirely distinct from the question" before it. *Id.*, at 1161 (emphasis added). But it is hornbook law that "a principal has a duty to indemnify the agent against expenses and other losses incurred by the agent in defending against actions brought by third parties if the agent acted with actual authority in taking the action challenged by the third party's suit." 2 Restatement § 8.14, Comment d. If the issue of fees is entirely distinct from the authority question, then authority cannot be based on agency.

Neither the California Supreme Court nor the Ninth Circuit ever described the proponents as agents of the State, and they plainly do not qualify as such.

IV

The dissent eloquently recounts the California Supreme Court's reasons for deciding that state law authorizes petitioners to defend Proposition 8. We do not "disrespect[ ]" or "disparage[ ]" those reasons. . . . Nor do we question California's sovereign right to maintain an initiative process, or the right of initiative proponents to defend their initiatives in California courts, where Article III does not apply. But as the dissent acknowledges, . . . standing in federal court is a question of federal law, not state law. And no matter its reasons, the fact that a State thinks a private party should have standing to seek relief for a generalized grievance cannot override our settled law to the contrary.

    . . .

* * *

We have never before upheld the standing of a private party to defend the constitutionality of a state statute when state officials have chosen not to. We decline to do so for the first time here.

Because petitioners have not satisfied their burden to demonstrate standing to appeal the judgment of the District Court, the Ninth Circuit was without jurisdiction to consider the appeal. The judgment of the Ninth Circuit is vacated, and the case is remanded with instructions to dismiss the appeal for lack of jurisdiction.

It is so ordered.

Justice Kennedy, with whom Justice Thomas, Justice Alito, and Justice Sotomayor join, dissenting.

. . .

In my view Article III does not require California, when deciding who may appear in court to defend an initiative on its behalf, to comply with the Restatement of Agency or with this Court's view of how a State should make its laws or structure its government. The Court's reasoning does not take into account the fundamental principles or the practical dynamics of the initiative system in California, which uses this mechanism to control and to bypass public officials—the same officials who would not defend the initiative, an injury the Court now leaves unremedied. The Court's decision also has implications for the 26 other States that use an initiative or popular referendum system and which, like California, may choose to have initiative proponents stand in for the State when public officials decline to defend an initiative in litigation. See M. Waters, Initiative and Referendum Almanac 12 (2003). In my submission, the Article III requirement for a justiciable case or controversy does not prevent proponents from having their day in court.

. . .

I

. . .

This Court, in determining the substance of state law, is "bound by a state court's construction of a state statute." *Wisconsin v. Mitchell*, 508 U.S. 476, 483 (1993). And the Supreme Court of California, in response to the certified question submitted to it in this case, has determined that State Elections Code provisions directed to initiative proponents do inform and instruct state law respecting the rights and status of proponents in postelection judicial proceedings. Here, in reliance on these statutes and the California Constitution, the State Supreme Court has held that proponents do have authority "under California law to appear and assert the state's interest in the initiative's validity and appeal a judgment invalidating the measure when the public officials who ordinarily defend the measure or appeal such a judgment decline to do so." *Perry v. Brown*, 52 Cal.4th 1116, 1127 (2011).

The reasons the Supreme Court of California gave for its holding have special relevance in the context of determining whether proponents have the authority to seek a federal-court remedy for the State's concrete, substantial, and continuing injury. As a class, official proponents are a small, identifiable group. See Cal. Elec.Code Ann. § 9001(a) (West Cum.Supp. 2013). Because many of their decisions must be unanimous, see §§ 9001(b)(1), 9002(b), they are necessarily few in number. Their identities are public. § 9001(b)(2). Their commitment is substantial. See §§ 9607–9609 (West Cum.Supp. 2013) (obtaining petition signatures); § 9001(c) (monetary fee); §§ 9065(d), 9067, 9069 (West 2003) (drafting arguments for official ballot pamphlet). They know and understand the purpose and operation of the proposed law, an important requisite in defending initiatives on complex matters such as taxation and insurance. Having gone to great lengths to convince voters to enact an initiative, they have a stake in the outcome and the necessary commitment to provide zealous advocacy.

Thus, in California, proponents play a "unique role . . . in the initiative process." 52 Cal.4th, at 1152. They "have a unique relationship to the voter-approved measure that makes them especially likely to be reliable and vigorous advocates for the measure and to be so viewed by those whose votes secured the initiative's enactment into law." *Ibid.*; see also *id.*, at 1160 (because of "their special relationship to the initiative measure," proponents are "the most obvious and logical private individuals to ably and vigorously defend the validity of the challenged measure on behalf of the interests of the voters who adopted the initiative into law"). Proponents' authority under state law is not a contrivance. It is not a fictional construct. It is the product of the California Constitution and the California Elections Code. There is no basis for this Court to set aside the California Supreme Court's determination of state law.

. . .

II

A

The Court concludes that proponents lack sufficient ties to the state government. It notes that they "are not elected," "answer to no one," and lack " 'a fiduciary obligation' " to the State. . . . But what the Court deems deficiencies in the proponents' connection to the State government, the State Supreme Court saw as essential qualifications to defend the initiative system. The very object of the initiative system is to establish a lawmaking process that does not depend upon state officials. In California, the popular initiative is necessary to implement "the theory that all power of government ultimately resides in the people." 52 Cal.4th, at 1140. The right to adopt initiatives has been described by the California courts as "one of the most precious rights of [the State's] democratic process." *Ibid.* That historic role for the initiative system "grew out of dissatisfaction with the then governing public officials and a widespread belief that the people had lost control of the political process." *Ibid.* The initiative's "primary purpose," then, "was to afford the people the ability to propose and to adopt constitutional amendments or statutory provisions that their elected public officials had refused or declined to adopt." *Ibid.*

The California Supreme Court has determined that this purpose is undermined if the very officials the initiative process seeks to circumvent are the only parties who can defend an enacted initiative when it is challenged in a legal proceeding. . . .

Yet today the Court demands that the State follow the Restatement of Agency. . . . There are reasons, however, why California might conclude that a conventional agency relationship is inconsistent with the history, design, and purpose of the initiative process. The State may not wish to associate itself with proponents or their views outside of the "extremely narrow and limited" context of this litigation, 52 Cal.4th, at 1159, or to bear the cost of proponents' legal fees. The State may also wish to avoid the odd conflict of having a formal agent of the State (the initiative's proponent) arguing in favor of a law's validity while state officials (e.g., the attorney general) contend in the same proceeding that it should be found invalid.

Furthermore, it is not clear who the principal in an agency relationship would be. It would make little sense if it were the Governor or attorney general, for that would frustrate the initiative system's purpose of circumventing elected officials who fail or refuse to effect the public will. . . . If there is to be a principal, then, it must be the people of California, as the ultimate sovereign in the State. See *ibid.*(quoting Cal. Const., Art. II, § 1) (" 'All political power is inherent in the people' "). But the Restatement may offer no workable example of an agent representing a principal composed of nearly 40 million residents of a State. Cf. 1 Restatement (Second) of Agency, p. 2, Scope Note (1957) (noting that the Restatement "does not state the special rules applicable to public officers"); 1 Restatement (First) of Agency, p. 4, Scope Note (1933) (same).

And if the Court's concern is that the proponents are unaccountable, that fear is neither well founded nor sufficient to overcome the contrary judgment of the State Supreme Court. It must be remembered that both elected officials and initiative proponents receive their authority to speak for the State of California directly from the people. The Court apparently believes that elected officials are acceptable "agents" of the State, but they are no more subject to ongoing supervision of their principal—i.e., the people of the State—than are initiative proponents. At most, a Governor or attorney general can be recalled or voted out of office in a subsequent election, but proponents, too, can have their authority terminated or their initiative overridden by a subsequent ballot measure. Finally, proponents and their attorneys, like all other litigants and counsel who appear before a federal court, are subject to duties of candor, decorum, and respect for the tribunal and co-parties alike, all of which guard against the possibility that initiative proponents will somehow fall short of the appropriate standards for federal litigation.

B

Contrary to the Court's suggestion, this Court's precedents do not indicate that a formal agency relationship is necessary. . . .

. . .

III

There is much irony in the Court's approach to justiciability in this case. A prime purpose of justiciability is to ensure vigorous advocacy, yet the Court insists upon litigation conducted by state officials whose preference is to lose the case. The doctrine is meant to ensure that courts are responsible and constrained in their power, but the Court's opinion today means that a single district court can make a decision with far-reaching effects that cannot be reviewed. And rather than honor the principle that justiciability exists to allow disputes of public policy to be resolved by the political process rather than the courts, . . . here the Court refuses to allow a State's authorized representatives to defend the outcome of a democratic election.

The Court's opinion disrespects and disparages both the political process in California and the well-stated opinion of the California Supreme Court in this case. The California Supreme Court, not this Court, expresses concern for vigorous representation; the California Supreme Court, not this Court, recognizes the necessity to avoid conflicts of interest; the California Supreme Court, not this Court, comprehends the real interest at stake in this litigation and identifies the most proper party to defend that interest. The California Supreme Court's opinion reflects a better understanding of the dynamics and principles of Article III than does this Court's opinion.

. . . [a]

C. MOOTNESS

Page 79. Add before note on Capable of Repetition Yet Evading Review:

In **Campbell-Ewald Co. v. Gomez**, 577 U.S. ___, 136 S.Ct. 663 (2016), the Court by a 6–3 vote held that an unaccepted offer to satisfy the named plaintiff's individual claim in a case where the complaint seeks relief on behalf of the plaintiff and a class of persons similarly situated did not render the individual's claim or the case moot under Article III. The claim was brought under the Telephone Consumer Protection Act against an advertising and marketing agency for sending allegedly unwanted and unlawful texts to the plaintiff. Defendant offered to pay the plaintiff an amount of money equal to the maximum damage award available under the statute for his individual claims, but did not offer any money for the class. Nor did it admit liability or provide money for attorney's fees. After the plaintiff failed to accept the offer, defendant moved to dismiss the case under Federal Rule of Civil Procedure 12(b)(1) for lack of subject matter jurisdiction, reasoning that the settlement

---

[a] The same day it decided *Perry*, the Court decided *United States v. Windsor*, in which the Court reached the merits of a challenge to the federal Defense of Marriage Act (DOMA) (which, like Proposition 8, limited marriage to a union between a man and a woman), notwithstanding the fact that the President and the U.S Attorney General, like the California Governor and California Attorney General in *Perry*, agreed with the challengers to the enactment. But unlike the Governor and the California Attorney General, the U.S. officials in *Windsor* appealed the lower court rulings striking down the DOMA, even though the federal officials agreed with those rulings, to the higher federal courts. The opinions in *Windsor*, which include a discussion of justiciability there, are reported infra, page 63.

offer rendered the plaintiff's claim and thus the dispute moot. Writing an opinion for the Court joined by Justices Kennedy, Breyer, Sotomayor and Kagan, Justice Ginsburg rejected this notion, observing that under Rule 68 of the Federal Rules of Civil Procedure, an unaccepted settlement offer by a defendant is deemed withdrawn and lacking in any legal force after 14 days. Like other unaccepted contract offers, it creates no lasting right or obligation. Because the settlement offer was not accepted, the parties remained sufficiently adverse.

Justice Thomas concurred in the judgment but would have relied on the common-law history of "tender"—in which, he said, a defendant's offer to pay, without more, was deemed insufficient to end a case—rather than on the modern law of contract. Chief Justice Roberts, joined by Justices Scalia and Alito, dissented, reasoning that when "the defendant *agrees* to fully redress [the] injury [that plaintiff alleges], there is no longer a case or controversy for purposes of Article III." The approach adopted by the majority, argued the Chief Justice, "takes [the] important responsibility [to determine whether the plaintiff has the requisite personal stake under Article III] away from the federal courts and hands it to the plaintiff [who can invoke federal judicial power simply by refusing to accept an offer that fully satisfies his claim]."

D. RIPENESS

Page 81. Add before City of Los Angeles v. Lyons:

Susan B. Anthony List v. Driehaus, 573 U.S. ___, 134 S.Ct. 2334 (2014). Along with another organization, the Susan B. Anthony List (SBA), a "pro-life advocacy organization," sued to challenge an Ohio law that criminalizes the making of "a false statement concerning a candidate [for any public office] knowing the same to be false or with reckless disregard of whether it is false or not, if the statement is designed to promote the election, nomination or defeat of the candidate." Under the Ohio law, if anyone complains that somebody has made a false statement within the meaning of the statute during an election campaign, a panel of the Ohio Elections Commission (Commission) must make a prompt, preliminary determination of whether there is probable cause to believe a statutory violation has occurred. If and only if a panel concludes that probable cause exists, the case is referred to the full Commission, which then is charged with determining whether "clear and convincing" evidence supports the conclusion that a violation has in fact taken place. If it so finds, the Commission can refer the case to the state prosecutors, who then have ordinary prosecutorial discretion (possibly overseen by the State Attorney General) to initiate a prosecution or not. In the 2010 election, SBA publicly stated that democratic Congressman and candidate Steve Driehaus had voted for "taxpayer-funded abortion" because of his support for the Affordable Care Act (ACA). Driehaus complained, and a Commission panel found probable cause that a violation had been committed. Although the case never went further than that, and although Driehaus has not announced a candidacy for any future office, SBA nonetheless sought an injunction against the law's enforcement because of its desire to engage in "substantially similar activity" in upcoming elections.

A unanimous Court (with Justice Thomas writing) held that SBA was suffering an Article III injury that could be redressed in federal court, because SBA had alleged " 'an intention to engage in a course of conduct arguably affected with a constitutional interest, but proscribed by a statute, and there exists a credible threat of enforcement thereunder.' " The fact that SBA does not concede that its past or planned future statements are indeed false "misses the point[,]" because the question is not whether SBA's speech is actually false, but whether Ohio officials may try to prove that the speech runs afoul of the statute, just as the Commission began to try to do so in 2010: "There is reason to think that similar speech in the future will result in similar proceedings, notwithstanding SBA's belief in the truth of its allegations. Nothing in this Court's decisions requires a plaintiff who wishes to challenge the constitutionality of a law to confess that he will in fact violate that law." As to the relevance, vel non, of Driehaus being a candidate, the Court reasoned: "Petitioners' speech focuses on the broader issue of support for the ACA, not on the voting record of a single candidate. See Reply Brief 4–5 (identifying other elected officials who plan to seek reelection as potential objects of SBA's criticisms). Because petitioners' alleged future speech is not directed exclusively at Driehaus, it does not matter whether he " 'may run for office again.' " Finally, the Court observed: "Although the threat of Commission proceedings is a substantial one, we need not decide whether that threat standing alone gives rise to an Article III injury. The burdensome Commission proceedings here are backed by the additional threat of criminal prosecution. We conclude that the combination of those two threats suffices to create an Article III injury under the circumstances of this case."

PART 2

ALLOCATION OF GOVERNMENTAL POWERS: THE NATION AND THE STATES; THE PRESIDENT, THE CONGRESS, AND THE COURTS

CHAPTER 4

THE SCOPE OF NATIONAL POWER

2. SOURCES OF NATIONAL POWER: EARLY DEVELOPMENTS

A. THE MARSHALL COURT'S VIEW

Page 123. Add before note (4) the following, and change note (4) to note (5):

(4) **United States v. Kebodeaux,** 570 U.S. ___, 133 S.Ct. 2496 (2013). The Court, by a 7–2 vote, invoked the "Necessary and Proper" Clause to uphold the Sex Offender Registration and Notification Act (SORNA), 120 Stat. 590, 42 U.S.C. § 16901 et seq.—a federal statute requiring persons convicted of federal sex offenses to register in the States where they live and work—as applied to a former member of the United States Air Force who was court-martialed in 1999 for a sex offense, served three months in prison, and suffered a bad-conduct discharge. Congress passed SORNA in 2006, and the federal government made clear by regulation that SORNA's registration requirements apply to federal sex offenders who had already completed their sentences when SORNA was enacted. When Kebodeaux failed to comply with SORNA in 2007 by neglecting to re-register after changing residences within the State of Texas, he was federally prosecuted and convicted. A divided en banc panel of the Fifth Circuit reversed his conviction, reasoning that, having fully served his sentence, Kebodeaux was, at the time SORNA was adopted, "no longer in federal custody, in the military, under any sort of supervised release or parole, or in any other special relationship with the federal government." For this reason, the lower court ruled, the federal Government lacked power under the "Necessary and Proper" Clause to regulate Kebodeaux's intrastate movements.

The Supreme Court reversed. Justice Breyer's majority opinion, joined by Justices Kennedy, Ginsburg, Sotomayor and Kagan, relied in part on an earlier federal statute that, like SORNA, required federal sex offenders to register in the States in which they locate after their sentences are complete, but that, unlike SORNA, was in effect at the time Kebodeaux's offense was committed. Justice Breyer explained:

"We do not agree with the Circuit's conclusion. And, in explaining our reasons, we need not go much further than the Circuit's critical assumption that Kebodeaux's release was 'unconditional,' i.e., that after Kebodeaux's release, he was not in 'any . . . special relationship with the federal government.' 687 F.3d, at 234. To the contrary, the Solicitor General, tracing through a complex set of statutory cross-references, has pointed out that at the time of his offense and conviction Kebodeaux was subject to the federal

Wetterling Act, an Act that imposed upon him registration requirements very similar to those that SORNA later mandated. . . .

"Congress enacted the Wetterling Act in 1994 and updated it several times prior to Kebodeaux's offense. Like SORNA, it used the federal spending power to encourage States to adopt sex offender registration laws. 42 U.S.C. § 14071(i) (2000 ed.). . . . Like SORNA, it applied to those who committed federal sex crimes. § 14071(b)(7)(A). And like SORNA, it imposed federal penalties upon federal sex offenders who failed to register in the States in which they lived, worked, and studied. §§ 14072(i)(3)–(4).

" . . .

"We are not aware of any plausible counterargument to the obvious conclusion, namely that as of the time of Kebodeaux's offense, conviction and release from federal custody, these Wetterling Act provisions applied to Kebodeaux and imposed upon him registration requirements very similar to those that SORNA later imposed. Contrary to what the Court of Appeals may have believed, the fact that the federal law's requirements in part involved compliance with state-law requirements made them no less requirements of federal law. See generally *United States v. Sharpnack*, 355 U.S. 286, 293–294 (1958) (Congress has the power to adopt as federal law the laws of a State and to apply them in federal enclaves); *Gibbons v. Ogden*, 9 Wheat. 1, 207–208 (1824) ('Although Congress cannot enable a State to legislate, Congress may adopt the provisions of a State on any subject. . . . The act [adopts state systems for regulation of pilots] and gives [them] the same validity as if its provisions had been specially made by Congress').

"Both the Court of Appeals and Kebodeaux come close to conceding that if, as of the time of Kebodeaux's offense, he was subject to a federal registration requirement, then the Necessary and Proper Clause authorized Congress to modify the requirement as in SORNA and to apply the modified requirement to Kebodeaux. See 687 F.3d, at 234–235, and n. 4; Tr. of Oral Arg. 38–39. And we believe they would be right to make this concession.

"No one here claims that the Wetterling Act, as applied to military sex offenders like Kebodeaux, falls outside the scope of the Necessary and Proper Clause. And it is difficult to see how anyone could persuasively do so. The Constitution explicitly grants Congress the power to 'make Rules for the . . . Regulation of the land and naval Forces.' Art. I, § 8, cl. 14. And, in the Necessary and Proper Clause itself, it grants Congress the power to 'make all Laws which shall be necessary and proper for carrying into Execution the foregoing Powers' and 'all other Powers' that the Constitution vests 'in the Government of the United States, or in any Department or Officer thereof.' Id., cl. 18.

"The scope of the Necessary and Proper Clause is broad. In words that have come to define that scope Chief Justice Marshall long ago wrote:

'Let the end be legitimate, let it be within the scope of the constitution, and all means which are appropriate, which are plainly adapted to that end, which are not prohibited, but consist with the letter and spirit of the constitution, are constitutional.' *McCulloch v. Maryland*, 4 Wheat. 316, 421 (1819).

"As we have come to understand these words and the provision they explain, they 'leav[e] to Congress a large discretion as to the means that may be employed in executing a given power.' *Lottery Case*, 188 U.S. 321, 355 (1903). . . . The Clause allows Congress to 'adopt any means, appearing to it most eligible and appropriate, which are adapted to the end to be accomplished and consistent with the letter and spirit of the Constitution.' *James Everard's Breweries v. Day*, 265 U.S. 545, 559 (1924).

"The Constitution, for example, makes few explicit references to federal criminal law, but the Necessary and Proper Clause nonetheless authorizes Congress, in the implementation of other explicit powers, to create federal crimes, to confine offenders to prison, to hire guards and other prison personnel, to provide prisoners with medical care and educational training, to ensure the safety of those who may come into contact with prisoners, to ensure the public's safety through systems of parole and supervised release, and, where a federal prisoner's mental condition so requires, to confine that prisoner civilly after the expiration of his or her term of imprisonment. See *United States v. Comstock*, 560 U.S. 126, 136–137 (2010).

"Here, under the authority granted to it by the Military Regulation and Necessary and Proper Clauses, Congress could promulgate the Uniform Code of Military Justice. It could specify that the sex offense of which Kebodeaux was convicted was a military crime under that Code. It could punish that crime through imprisonment and by placing conditions upon Kebodeaux's release. And it could make the civil registration requirement at issue here a consequence of Kebodeaux's offense and conviction. This civil requirement, while not a specific condition of Kebodeaux's release, was in place at the time Kebodeaux committed his offense, and was a consequence of his violation of federal law.

"And Congress' decision to impose such a civil requirement that would apply upon the release of an offender like Kebodeaux is eminently reasonable. Congress could reasonably conclude that registration requirements applied to federal sex offenders after their release can help protect the public from those federal sex offenders and alleviate public safety concerns. . . . There is evidence that recidivism rates among sex offenders are higher than the average for other types of criminals. See Dept. of Justice, Bureau of Justice Statistics, P. Langan, E. Schmitt, & M. Durose, Recidivism of Sex Offenders Released in 1994, p. 1 (Nov. 2003) (reporting that compared to non-sex offenders, released sex offenders were four times more likely to be rearrested for a sex crime, and that within the first three years following release 5.3% of released sex offenders were rearrested for a sex crime). There is also conflicting evidence on the point. Cf. R. Tewsbury, W. Jennings, & K. Zgoba, Final Report on Sex Offenders: Recidivism and Collateral Consequences (Sept. 2011) (concluding that sex offenders have relatively low rates of recidivism, and that registration requirements have limited observable benefits regarding recidivism). But the Clause gives Congress the power to weigh the evidence and to reach a rational conclusion, for example, that safety needs justify postrelease registration rules. See *Lambert v. Yellowley*, 272 U.S. 581, 594–595 (1926) (upholding congressional statute limiting the amount of spirituous liquor that may be prescribed by a physician, and noting that Congress' "finding [regarding the appropriate amount], in the presence of the well-known diverging opinions of physicians, cannot be regarded as arbitrary or without a reasonable basis"). See also *Gonzales v. Raich*, 545 U.S. 1, 22 (2005) ('In assessing the scope of Congress' authority under the Commerce Clause, we stress that the task before us is a modest one. We need not determine whether respondents' activities, taken in the aggregate, substantially affect interstate commerce in fact, but only whether a "rational basis" exists for so concluding'). See also H.R.Rep. No. 109–218, pt. 1, pp. 22, 23 (2005) (House Report) (citing statistics compiled by the Justice Department as support for SORNA's sex offender registration regime).

"....

"The upshot is that here Congress did not apply SORNA to an individual who had, prior to SORNA's enactment, been 'unconditionally released,' i.e., a person who was not in 'any ... special relationship with the federal government,' but rather to an individual already subject to federal registration requirements that were themselves a valid exercise of federal power under the Military Regulation and Necessary and Proper Clauses. . . .

"SORNA, enacted after Kebodeaux's release, somewhat modified the applicable registration requirements. In general, SORNA provided more detailed definitions of sex offenses, described in greater detail the nature of the information registrants must provide, and imposed somewhat different limits upon the length of time that registration must continue and the frequency with which offenders must update their registration. 42 U.S.C. §§ 16911, 16913–16916 (2006 ed. and Supp. V). . . .

"As applied to an individual already subject to the Wetterling Act like Kebodeaux, SORNA makes few changes. In particular, SORNA modified the time limitations for a sex offender who moves to update his registration to within three business days of the move from both seven days before and seven days after the move, as required by the Texas law enforced under the Wetterling Act. . . . SORNA also increased the federal penalty for a federal offender's registration violation to a maximum of 10 years from a maximum of 1 year for a first offense. Compare 18 U.S.C. § 2250(a) with 42 U.S.C. § 14072(i) (2000 ed.). Kebodeaux was sentenced to one year and one day of imprisonment. For purposes of federal law, SORNA reduced the duration of Kebodeaux's registration requirement to 25 years from the lifetime requirement imposed by Texas law, . . . and reduced the frequency with which Kebodeaux must update his registration to every six months from every 90 days as imposed by Texas law . . . . And as far as we can tell, while SORNA punishes violations of its requirements (instead of violations of state law), the Federal Government has prosecuted a sex offender for violating SORNA only when that offender also violated state-registration requirements.

"SORNA's general changes were designed to make more uniform what had remained 'a patchwork of federal and 50 individual state registration systems,' *Reynolds v. United States*, 565 U.S. ___, ___, 132 S.Ct. 975 (2012), with 'loopholes and deficiencies' that had resulted in an estimated 100,000 sex offenders becoming 'missing' or 'lost,' House Report 20, 26. See S.Rep. No. 109–369, pp. 16–17 (2006). . . . SORNA's more specific changes reflect Congress' determination that the statute, changed in respect to frequency, penalties, and other details, will keep track of more offenders and will encourage States themselves to adopt its uniform standards. No one here claims that these changes are unreasonable or that Congress could not reasonably have found them 'necessary and proper' means for furthering its pre-existing registration ends.

"We conclude that the SORNA changes as applied to Kebodeaux fall within the scope Congress' authority under the Military Regulation and Necessary and Proper Clauses."

Chief Justice Roberts and Justice Alito each wrote a concurring opinion. Chief Justice Roberts "agree[d] with the Court that Congress had the power, under the Military Regulation and Necessary and Proper Clauses of Article I, to require Anthony Kebodeaux to register as a sex offender." In particular, he observed that a "servicemember will be less likely to violate a relevant military regulation if he knows that, having done so, he will be required to register as a sex offender years into the future." But the Chief Justice was troubled by the fact that the majority, "having established that premise and thus resolved the case before us, nevertheless [went] on to discuss the general public safety benefits of the registration requirement." Because he found that analysis to be "beside the point" and might lead "incautious readers [to] think they have found in the majority opinion something they would not find in either the Constitution or any prior decision of ours: a federal police power," he concurred in the judgment only. Justice Alito's opinion concurring in the judgment rested "solely on the ground that the registration requirement at issue is necessary and proper to execute Congress' power '[t]o make Rules for the Government and Regulation of the land and naval Forces[,]' " and the fact that, because a State might defer to federal enforcement of the federal sex offender registration system, "the offender, if convicted, may fall through the cracks of a state registration system."

Justice Scalia and Justice Thomas each wrote dissenting opinions. Justice Scalia joined most of Justice Thomas' dissent, which challenged Congress' ability to enact the Wetterling Act's registration requirement in the first place. Justice Scalia disagreed, however, with Justice Thomas's view that "what is necessary and proper to enforce a statute validly enacted pursuant to an enumerated power is not itself necessary and proper to the execution of an enumerated power." In Justice Scalia's view, if "SORNA's registration requirement were ' "reasonably adapted," '. . . . to carrying into execution some other, valid enactment," he would sustain it. For Justice Scalia, then, the key questions were whether "the Wetterling Act's registration requirement was itself a valid exercise of any federal power, [and whether] SORNA is designed to carry the Wetterling Act into execution." He found "the former proposition [to be] dubious, [and] the latter obviously untrue."

Page 126. Add the following, before State Power to Administer Presidential Elections:

Arizona State Legislature v. Arizona Independent Redistricting Commission, 576 U.S. ___, 135 S.Ct. 2652 (2015). In 2000 the voters of Arizona enacted Proposition 106, an initiative creating the Arizona

Independent Redistricting Commission (AIRC) and giving it the exclusive power to draw congressional district lines in the State, a function previously exercised by the elected state legislature. In early 2012, based on the 2010 census, the AIRC formulated redistricting maps to be used in federal elections. The elected state legislature then filed suit in federal court, alleging that Proposition 106 impermissibly divested authority from the elected representative body in violation of the so-called Elections Clause, Article I § 4, which provides: "The Times, Places and Manner of holding Elections for Senators and Representatives shall be prescribed in each State by the Legislature thereof; but Congress may at any time by Law make or alter such Regulations." A three-judge district court rejected the challenge on the merits, and the Supreme Court affirmed on appeal by a 5–4 vote.

Justice Ginsburg's opinion for the Court, joined by Justices Kennedy, Breyer, Sotomayor and Kagan, held that the term "legislature" in Article I § 4 does not require that federal redistricting be done by a state's representative body, but instead permits the people of a state to provide for redistricting by an independent commission. The Court, recognizing that the framers may not have envisioned the full scope of the initiative process in place in many states today, relied on the general history and purpose of the Clause, and also on prior cases in which the Court had upheld, respectively, the use of the referendum process and the gubernatorial veto in rejecting the districts drawn by elected state legislatures. Ohio Ex. Rel. Davis v. Hildebrant, 241 U.S. 565 (1916); Smiley v. Holm, 285 U.S. 355 (1932). The Court also relied on a federal statute, 2 U.S.C. § 2(a(c), which the Court interpreted as expressing Congress' desire that so long as a state has redistricted in a manner consistent with its own state laws, the resulting districting plan should become the presumptively governing map. Noting that "there can be no dispute that Congress itself may draw a State's congressional-district boundaries" and has "plenary authority to 'make or alter' [a] State's plan," the majority rejected as "wooden" the idea, advanced by the elected Arizona legislature, that Congress is "preclude[d] from allowing a State to redistrict without the involvement of its representative body, even if Congress could enact the same redistricting plan" itself. But any uncertainty about the "import" of the Congressional authorization was "resolved" by the Court's clear holding that the Elections Clause itself, even in the absence of Congressional authorization, "permits regulation of congressional districts by initiative."

Chief Justice Roberts wrote a dissent, joined by Justices Scalia, Thomas and Alito, arguing that the text of the Elections Clause, and that of other provisions of the Constitution that refer to the "Legislature" of a state, along with the history underlying and the cases interpreting these provisions, cut against the constitutionality of Proposition 106.

3. THE SCOPE OF NATIONAL POWER TODAY

A. THE COMMERCE POWER

Page 173. Add the following footnote (a) to the end of the opinion of the Court excerpt in Gonzales v. Raich:

^a In Taylor v. United States, 577 U.S. ___, ___ S.Ct. ___ (2016), a 7–1 majority of the Court invoked *Raich* to resolve a criminal dispute under the Hobbs Act, which makes it a federal crime to use robbery to affect, or attempt to affect, "commerce"—a term defined broadly as interstate commerce "and all other commerce over which the United States has jurisdiction." Taylor was accused of targeting for robbery a marijuana dealer's drugs or drug proceeds, and the Court had little difficulty in concluding that such a robbery fell within the Hobbs Act because under *Raich* "the Commerce Clause gives Congress authority to regulate the national market for marijuana, including the authority to proscribe the purely intrastate production, possession, and sale of this controlled substance. Because Congress may regulate these intrastate activities based on their aggregate effect on interstate commerce, it follows that Congress may [as it has chosen to in the Hobbs Act] also regulate intrastate drug *theft*." Justice Thomas dissented.

CHAPTER 6

THE SCOPE OF STATE POWER

4. IMPLIED RESTRICTIONS OF THE COMMERCE CLAUSE—PRODUCTION AND TRADE

B. REQUIRING BUSINESS OPERATIONS TO BE PERFORMED IN THE HOME STATE

Page 281. Add after Department of Revenue of Kentucky v. Davis:

Comptroller of Treasury of Maryland v. Wynne, 576 U.S. ___, 135 S.Ct. 1787 (2015). Maryland's personal income tax on residents of the state includes a "state" income tax as well as a "county" income tax. Maryland residents who are subject to income tax in other states for income earned in those other states are given a credit (for the taxes paid to those other states) against the "state" but not the "county" component of Maryland's tax.

The Court held by a 5–4 vote that this scheme violated dormant Commerce Clause principles by treating Maryland residents who earn all their income in Maryland more favorably than residents who earn some or all of their income through interstate commerce. Like other tax laws that had been struck down in prior cases, Maryland's scheme "had the potential to result in the discriminatory double taxation of income earned out of state and created a powerful incentive to engage in intrastate rather than interstate economic activity." Applying a test that requires "internal consistency," the Court looked to "the structure of the tax at issue to see whether its identical application by every State in the Union would place interstate commerce at a disadvantage as compared with commerce intrastate." Under this test, the Court concluded:

> "Maryland's income tax scheme fails.... A simple example illustrates the point. Assume that every State imposed the following taxes, which are similar to Maryland's "county" and "special nonresident" taxes: (1) a 1.25% tax on income that residents earn in State, (2) a 1.25% tax on income that residents earn in other jurisdictions, and (3) a 1.25% tax on income that nonresidents earn in State. Assume further that two taxpayers, April and Bob, both live in State A, but that April earns her income in State A whereas Bob earns his income in State B. In this circumstance, Bob will pay more income tax than April solely because he earns income interstate. Specifically, April will have to pay a 1.25% tax only once, to State A. But Bob will have to pay a 1.25% tax twice: once to State A, where he resides, and once to State B, where he earns the income.

> "Critically—and this dispels a central argument made by petitioner and the principal dissent—the Maryland scheme's discriminatory treatment of interstate commerce is not simply the

result of its interaction with the taxing schemes of other States. Instead, the internal consistency test reveals what the undisputed economic analysis shows: Maryland's tax scheme is inherently discriminatory and operates as a tariff."

Justice Alito wrote the majority opinion, in which Chief Justice Roberts and Justices Kennedy, Breyer and Sotomayor joined. Justices Scalia and Thomas each wrote a dissenting opinion in which the other joined in part. Justice Ginsburg also wrote a dissenting opinion, in which Justices Scalia and Kagan joined.

CHAPTER 7

SEPARATION OF POWERS

1. THE PRESIDENT'S POWER TO DETERMINE NATIONAL POLICY

B. INTERNATIONAL RELATIONS

Page 345. Add after Medellin v. Texas:

Recognition of Foreign Sovereignty

Zivotofsky v. Kerry

576 U.S. ___, 135 S.Ct. 2076, 192 L.Ed.2d 83 (2015).

Justice Kennedy delivered the opinion of the Court.

A delicate subject lies in the background of this case. That subject is Jerusalem. Questions touching upon the history of the ancient city and its present legal and international status are among the most difficult and complex in international affairs. In our constitutional system these matters are committed to the Legislature and the Executive, not the Judiciary. As a result, in this opinion the Court does no more, and must do no more, than note the existence of international debate and tensions respecting Jerusalem. Those matters are for Congress and the President to discuss and consider as they seek to shape the Nation's foreign policies.

The Court addresses two questions to resolve the inter-branch dispute now before it. First, it must determine whether the President has the exclusive power to grant formal recognition to a foreign sovereign. Second, if he has that power, the Court must determine whether Congress can command the President and his Secretary of State to issue a formal statement that contradicts the earlier recognition. The statement in question here is a congressional mandate that allows a United States citizen born in Jerusalem to direct the President and Secretary of State, when issuing his passport, to state that his place of birth is "Israel."

I

A

Jerusalem's political standing has long been, and remains, one of the most sensitive issues in American foreign policy, and indeed it is one of the most delicate issues in current international affairs. In 1948, President Truman formally recognized Israel in a signed statement of "recognition." See Statement by the President Announcing Recognition of the State of Israel, Public Papers of the Presidents, May 14, 1948, p. 258 (1964). That statement did not recognize Israeli sovereignty over Jerusalem. Over the last 60 years, various actors have sought to assert full or partial sovereignty over the city, including Israel, Jordan, and the Palestinians. Yet, in contrast to a consistent policy of formal recognition of Israel, neither President Truman nor any later United States President has issued an official statement or declaration acknowledging any country's sovereignty over Jerusalem. Instead, the Executive Branch has maintained that " 'the status of Jerusalem . . . should be decided not unilaterally but in consultation with all concerned.' " United Nations Gen. Assembly Official Records, 5th Emergency Sess., 1554th Plenary Meetings, United Nations Doc. No. 1 A/PV.1554, p. 10 (July 14, 1967); see, *e.g.,* Remarks by President Obama in Address to the United Nations Gen. Assembly (Sept. 21, 2011), 2011 Daily Comp. of Pres. Doc. No. 00661, p. 4 ("Ultimately, it is the Israelis and the Palestinians, not us, who must reach agreement on the issues that divide them," including "Jerusalem"). In a letter to Congress then-Secretary of State Warren Christopher expressed the Executive's concern that "[t]here is no issue related to the Arab-Israeli negotiations that is more sensitive than Jerusalem." See 141 Cong. Rec. 28967 (1995) (letter to Robert Dole, Majority Leader, (June 20, 1995)). He further noted the Executive's opinion that "any effort . . . to bring it to the forefront" could be "very damaging to the success of the peace process." *Ibid.*

The President's position on Jerusalem is reflected in State Department policy regarding passports and consular reports of birth abroad. Understanding that passports will be construed as reflections of American policy, the State Department's Foreign Affairs Manual instructs its employees, in general, to record the place of birth on a passport as the "country [having] present sovereignty over the actual area of birth." Dept. of State, 7 Foreign Affairs Manual (FAM) § 1383.4 (1987). If a citizen objects to the country listed as sovereign by the State Department, he or she may list the city or town of birth rather than the country. . . . The FAM, however, does not allow citizens to list a sovereign that conflicts with Executive Branch policy. . . . Because the United States does not recognize any country as having sovereignty over Jerusalem, the FAM instructs employees to record the place of birth for citizens born there as "Jerusalem."

In 2002, Congress passed the Act at issue here, the Foreign Relations Authorization Act. . . . Section 214 of the Act is titled "United States Policy with Respect to Jerusalem as the Capital of Israel.". . . The subsection that lies at the heart of this case, § 214(d), addresses passports. That subsection seeks to override the FAM by allowing citizens born in Jerusalem to list their place of birth as "Israel." Titled "Record of Place of Birth as Israel for Passport Purposes," § 214(d) states "[f]or purposes of the registration of birth, certification of nationality, or issuance of a passport of a United States citizen born in the city of Jerusalem, the Secretary shall, upon the request of the citizen or the citizen's legal guardian, record the place of birth as Israel.". . .

When he signed the Act into law, President George W. Bush issued a statement declaring his position that § 214 would, "if construed as mandatory rather than advisory, impermissibly interfere with the President's constitutional authority to formulate the position of the United States, speak for the Nation in international affairs, and determine the terms on which recognition is given to foreign states." Statement on Signing the Foreign Relations Authorization Act, Fiscal Year 2003, Public Papers of the Presidents, George W. Bush, Vol. 2, Sept. 30, 2002, p. 1698 (2005). The President concluded, "U. S. policy regarding Jerusalem has not changed." *Ibid.*

Some parties were not reassured by the President's statement. A cable from the United States Consulate in Jerusalem noted that the Palestine Liberation Organization Executive Committee, Fatah Central Committee, and the Palestinian Authority Cabinet had all issued statements claiming that the Act " 'undermines the role of the U. S. as a sponsor of the peace process.' " . . . In the Gaza Strip and elsewhere residents marched in protest. See The Associated Press and Reuters, Palestinians Stone Police Guarding Western Wall, The Seattle Times, Oct. 5,2002, p. A7.

In response the Secretary of State advised diplomats to express their understanding of "Jerusalem's importance to both sides and to many others around the world.". . . He noted his belief that America's "policy towards Jerusalem" had not changed. . . .

B

In 2002, petitioner Menachem Binyamin Zivotofsky was born to United States citizens living in Jerusalem. . . . In December 2002, Zivotofsky's mother visited the American Embassy in Tel Aviv to request both a passport and a consular report of birth abroad for her son. . . . She asked that his place of birth be listed as " 'Jerusalem, Israel.' " . . . The Embassy clerks explained that, pursuant to State Department policy, the passport would list only "Jerusalem.". . . Zivotofsky's parents objected and, as his guardians, brought suit on his behalf in the United States District Court for the District of Columbia, seeking to enforce § 214(d).

Pursuant to § 214(d), Zivotofsky claims the right to have "Israel" recorded as his place of birth in his passport. . . . The arguments in Zivotofsky's brief center on his passport claim, as opposed to the consular report of birth abroad. Indeed, in the court below, Zivotofsky waived any argument that his consular report of birth abroad should be treated differently than his passport. . . . He has also waived the issue here by failing to differentiate between the two documents. As a result, the Court addresses Zivotofsky's passport arguments and need not engage in a separate analysis of the validity of § 214(d) as applied to consular reports of birth abroad.

After Zivotofsky brought suit, the District Court dismissed his case, reasoning that it presented a nonjusticiable political question and that Zivotofsky lacked standing. . . . The Court of Appeals for the District of Columbia Circuit reversed on the standing issue, . . . but later affirmed the District Court's political question determination. . . .

This Court granted certiorari, vacated the judgment, and remanded the case. Whether § 214(d) is constitutional, the Court held, is not a question reserved for the political branches. . . .

On remand the Court of Appeals held the statute unconstitutional. It determined that "the President exclusively holds the power to determine whether to recognize a foreign sovereign," . . . and that "section 214(d) directly contradicts a carefully considered exercise of the Executive branch's recognition power.". . .

This Court again granted certiorari. . . .

II

In considering claims of Presidential power this Court refers to Justice Jackson's familiar tripartite framework from *Youngstown Sheet & Tube Co.* v. *Sawyer*, 343 U. S. 579, 635–638 (1952) (concurring opinion). The framework divides exercises of Presidential power into three categories: First, when "the President acts pursuant to an express or implied authorization of Congress, his authority is at its maximum, for it includes all that he possesses in his own right plus all that Congress can delegate.". . . Second, "in absence of either a congressional grant or denial of authority" there is a "zone of twilight in which he and Congress may have concurrent authority," and where "congressional inertia, indifference or quiescence may" invite the exercise of executive power. . . . Finally, when "the President takes measures incompatible with the expressed or implied will of Congress . . . he can rely only upon his own constitutional powers minus any constitutional powers of Congress over the matter.". . . To succeed in this third category, the President's asserted power must be both "exclusive" and "conclusive" on the issue. . . .

In this case the Secretary contends that § 214(d) infringes on the President's exclusive recognition power by "requiring the President to contradict his recognition position regarding Jerusalem in official communications with foreign sovereigns.". . . In so doing the Secretary acknowledges the President's power is "at its lowest ebb.". . . Because the President's refusal to implement § 214(d) falls into Justice Jackson's third category, his claim must be "scrutinized with caution," and he may rely solely on powers the Constitution grants to him alone. . . .

To determine whether the President possesses the exclusive power of recognition the Court examines the Constitution's text and structure, as well as precedent and history bearing on the question.

A

Recognition is a "formal acknowledgement" that a particular "entity possesses the qualifications for statehood" or "that a particular regime is the effective government of a state." Restatement (Third) of Foreign Relations Law of the United States § 203, Comment *a*, p. 84 (1986). It may also involve the determination of a state's territorial bounds. See 2 M. Whiteman, Digest of International Law § 1, p. 1 (1963) (Whiteman) ("[S]tates may recognize or decline to recognize territory as belonging to, or under the sovereignty of, or having been acquired or lost by, other states"). Recognition is often effected by an express "written or oral declaration." 1 J. Moore, Digest of International Law § 27, p. 73 (1906) (Moore). It may also be implied— for example, by concluding a bilateral treaty or by sending or receiving diplomatic agents. *Ibid.*; I. Brownlie, Principles of Public International Law 93 (7th ed. 2008) (Brownlie).

Legal consequences follow formal recognition. Recognized sovereigns may sue in United States courts, . . . and may benefit from sovereign immunity when they are sued. . . . The actions of a recognized sovereign committed within its own territory also receive deference in domestic courts under the act of state doctrine. . . .

Recognition at international law, furthermore, is a precondition of regular diplomatic relations. 1 Moore § 27, at 72. Recognition is thus "useful, even necessary," to the existence of a state. . . .

Despite the importance of the recognition power in foreign relations, the Constitution does not use the term "recognition," either in Article II or elsewhere. The Secretary asserts that the President exercises the recognition power based on the Reception Clause, which directs that the President "shall receive Ambassadors and other public Ministers." Art. II, § 3. As Zivotofsky notes, the Reception Clause received little attention at the Constitutional Convention. See Reinstein, Recognition: A Case Study on the Original Understanding of Executive Power, 45 U.Rich. L. Rev. 801, 860–862 (2011). In fact, during the ratification debates, Alexander Hamilton claimed that the power to receive ambassadors was "more a matter of dignity than of authority," a ministerial duty largely "without consequence." The Federalist No. 69, p. 420 (C. Rossiter ed. 1961).

At the time of the founding, however, prominent international scholars suggested that receiving an ambassador was tantamount to recognizing the sovereignty of the sending state. See E. de Vattel, The Law of Nations § 78, p. 461 (1758) (J. Chitty ed. 1853) ("[E]very state, truly possessed of sovereignty, has a right to send ambassadors" and "to contest their right in this instance" is equivalent to "contesting their sovereign dignity"); see also 2 C. van Bynkershoek, On Questions of Public Law 156–157 (1737) (T. Frank ed. 1930) ("Among writers on public law it is usually agreed that only a sovereign power has a right to send ambassadors"); 2 H. Grotius, On the Law of War and Peace 440–441 (1625) (F. Kelsey ed. 1925) (discussing the duty to admit ambassadors of sovereign powers). It is a logical and proper inference, then, that a Clause directing the President alone to receive ambassadors would be understood to acknowledge his power to recognize other nations.

This in fact occurred early in the Nation's history when President Washington recognized the French Revolutionary Government by receiving its ambassador. See A. Hamilton, Pacificus No. 1, in The Letters of Pacificus and Helvidius 5, 13–14 (1845) (reprint 1976) (President "acknowledged the republic of France, by the reception of its minister"). After this incident the import of the Reception Clause became clear—causing Hamilton to change his earlier view. He wrote that the Reception Clause "includes th[e power] of judging, in the case of a revolution of government in a foreign country, whether the new rulers are competent organs of the national will, and ought to be recognised, or not." See *id.*, at 12; see also 3 J. Story, Commentaries on the Constitution of the United States § 1560, p. 416 (1833) ("If the executive receives an ambassador, or other minister, as the representative of a new nation . . . it is an acknowledgment of the sovereign authority *de facto* of such new nation, or party"). As a result, the

Reception Clause provides support, although not the sole authority, for the President's power to recognize other nations.

The inference that the President exercises the recognition power is further supported by his additional Article II powers. It is for the President, "by and with the Advice and Consent of the Senate," to "make Treaties, provided two thirds of the Senators present concur." Art. II, § 2, cl.2. In addition, "he shall nominate, and by and with the Advice and Consent of the Senate, shall appoint Ambassadors" as well as "other public Ministers and Consuls." *Ibid.*

As a matter of constitutional structure, these additional powers give the President control over recognition decisions. At international law, recognition may be effected by different means, but each means is dependent upon Presidential power. In addition to receiving an ambassador, recognition may occur on "the conclusion of a bilateral treaty," or the "formal initiation of diplomatic relations," including the dispatch of an ambassador. Brownlie 93; see also 1 Moore § 27, at 73. The President has the sole power to negotiate treaties, see *United States* v. *Curtiss-Wright Export Corp.*, 299 U. S. 304, 319 (1936), and the Senate may not conclude or ratify a treaty without Presidential action. The President, too, nominates the Nation's ambassadors and dispatches other diplomatic agents. Congress may not send an ambassador without his involvement. Beyond that, the President himself has the power to open diplomatic channels simply by engaging in direct diplomacy with foreign heads of state and their ministers. The Constitution thus assigns the President means to effect recognition on his own initiative. Congress, by contrast, has no constitutional power that would enable it to initiate diplomatic relations with a foreign nation. Because these specific Clauses confer the recognition power on the President, the Court need not consider whether or to what extent the Vesting Clause, which provides that the "executive Power" shall be vested in the President, provides further support for the President's action here. Art. II, § 1, cl. 1.

The text and structure of the Constitution grant the President the power to recognize foreign nations and governments. The question then becomes whether that power is exclusive. The various ways in which the President may unilaterally effect recognition—and the lack of any similar power vested in Congress—suggest that it is. So, too, do functional considerations. Put simply, the Nation must have a single policy regarding which governments are legitimate in the eyes of the United States and which are not. Foreign countries need to know, before entering into diplomatic relations or commerce with the United States, whether their ambassadors will be received; whether their officials will be immune from suit in federal court; and whether they may initiate lawsuits here to vindicate their rights. These assurances cannot be equivocal.

Recognition is a topic on which the Nation must " 'speak . . . with one voice.' " *American Ins. Assn.* v. *Garamendi*, 539 U. S. 396, 424 (2003) (quoting *Crosby* v. *National Foreign Trade Council*, 530 U. S. 363, 381 (2000)). That voice must be the President's. Between the two political branches, only the Executive has the characteristic of unity at all times. And with unity comes the ability to exercise, to a greater degree, "[d]ecision, activity, secrecy, and dispatch." The Federalist No. 70, p. 424 (A. Hamilton). The President is capable, in ways Congress is not, of engaging in the delicate and often secret diplomatic contacts that may lead to a decision on recognition. . . . He is also better positioned to take the decisive, unequivocal action necessary to recognize other states at international law. 1 Oppenheim's International Law § 50, p. 169 (R. Jennings & A. Watts eds., 9th ed. 1992) (act of recognition must "leave no doubt as to the intention to grant it").These qualities explain why the Framers listed the traditional avenues of recognition—receiving ambassadors, making treaties, and sending ambassadors—as among the President's Article II powers.

. . . [T]he President since the founding has exercised this unilateral power to recognize new states—and the Court has endorsed the practice. . . . Texts and treatises on international law treat the President's word as the final word on recognition. See, *e.g.*, Restatement (Third) of Foreign Relations Law § 204, at 89 ("Under the Constitution of the United States the President has exclusive authority to recognize or not to recognize a foreign state or government"); see also L. Henkin, Foreign Affairs and the U. S. Constitution 43 (2d ed. 1996) ("It is no longer questioned that the President does not merely perform the ceremony of receiving foreign ambassadors but also determines whether the United States should recognize or refuse to recognize a foreign government"). In light of this authority all six judges who considered this case in the Court of Appeals agreed that the President holds the exclusive recognition power. . . .

It remains true, of course, that many decisions affecting foreign relations—including decisions that may determine the course of our relations with recognized countries—require congressional action. Congress may "regulate Commerce with foreign Nations," "establish an uniform Rule of Naturalization," "define and punish Piracies and Felonies committed on the high Seas, and Offences against the Law of Nations," "declare War," "grant Letters of Marque and Reprisal," and "make Rules for the Government and Regulation of the land and naval Forces." U. S. Const., Art. I, § 8. In addition, the President cannot make a treaty or appoint an ambassador without the approval of the Senate. Art. II, § 2, cl. 2. The President, furthermore, could not build an American Embassy abroad without congressional appropriation of the necessary funds. Art. I, § 8, cl. 1. Under basic separation-of-powers principles, it is for the Congress to enact the laws, including "all Laws which shall be necessary and proper for carrying into Execution" the powers of the Federal Government. § 8, cl. 18.

In foreign affairs, as in the domestic realm, the Constitution "enjoins upon its branches separateness but interdependence, autonomy but reciprocity." *Youngstown*, 343 U. S., at 635 (Jackson, J., concurring). Although the President alone effects the formal act of recognition, Congress' powers, and its central role in making laws, give it substantial authority regarding many of the policy determinations that precede and follow the act of recognition itself. If Congress disagrees with the President's recognition policy, there may be consequences. Formal recognition may seem a hollow act if it is not accompanied by the dispatch of an ambassador, the easing of trade restrictions, and the conclusion of treaties. And those decisions require action by the Senate or the whole Congress.

In practice, then, the President's recognition determination is just one part of a political process that may require Congress to make laws. The President's exclusive recognition power encompasses the authority to acknowledge, in a formal sense, the legitimacy of other states and governments, including their territorial bounds. Albeit limited, the exclusive recognition power is essential to the conduct of Presidential duties. The formal act of recognition is an executive power that Congress may not qualify. If the President is to be effective in negotiations over a formal recognition determination, it must be evident to his counterparts abroad that he speaks for the Nation on that precise question.

A clear rule that the formal power to recognize a foreign government subsists in the President therefore serves a necessary purpose in diplomatic relations. All this, of course, underscores that Congress has an important role in other aspects of foreign policy, and the President may be bound by any number of laws Congress enacts. In this way ambition counters ambition, ensuring that the democratic will of the people is observed and respected in foreign affairs as in the domestic realm. See The Federalist No. 51, p. 322 (J. Madison).

B

No single precedent resolves the question whether the President has exclusive recognition authority and, if so, how far that power extends. In part that is because, until today, the political branches have resolved their disputes over questions of recognition. The relevant cases, though providing important instruction, address the division of recognition power between the Federal Government and the States, see, *e.g., Pink*, 315 U. S. 203, or between the courts and the political branches, see, *e.g., Banco Nacional de Cuba*, 376 U. S., at 410—not between the President and Congress. As the parties acknowledge, some isolated statements in those cases lend support to the position that Congress has a role in the recognition process. In the end, however, a fair reading of the cases shows that the President's role in the recognition process is both central and exclusive. During the administration of President Van Buren, in a case involving a dispute over the status of the Falkland Islands, the Court noted that "when the executive branch of the government" assumes "a fact in regard to the sovereignty of any island or country, it is conclusive on the judicial department." *Williams*, 13 Pet., at 420. Once the President has made his determination, it "is enough to know, that in the exercise of his constitutional functions, he has decided the question. Having done this under the responsibilities which belong to him, it is obligatory on the people and government of the Union." *Ibid.*

Later, during the 1930's and 1940's, the Court addressed issues surrounding President Roosevelt's decision to recognize the Soviet Government of Russia. In *United States* v. *Belmont,* 301 U. S. 324 (1937), and *Pink*, 315 U. S. 203, New York state courts declined to give full effect to the terms of executive agreements the President had concluded in negotiations over recognition of the Soviet regime. In particular the state courts, based on New York public policy, did not treat assets that had been seized by the Soviet Government as property of Russia and declined to turn those assets over to the United States. The Court stated that it "may not be doubted" that "recognition, establishment of diplomatic relations, . . . and agreements with respect thereto" are "within the competence of the President." *Belmont*, 301 U. S., at 330. In these matters, "the Executive ha[s] authority to speak as the sole organ of th[e] government." *Ibid.* The Court added that the President's authority "is not limited to a determination of the government to be recognized. It includes the power to determine the policy which is to govern the question of recognition." *Pink, supra*, at 229; see also *Guaranty Trust Co.*, 304 U. S., at 137–138 (The "political department['s] . . . action in recognizing a foreign government and in receiving its diplomatic representatives is conclusive on all domestic courts"). Thus, New York state courts were required to respect the executive agreements.

It is true, of course, that *Belmont* and *Pink* are not direct holdings that the recognition power is exclusive. Those cases considered the validity of executive agreements, not the initial act of recognition. The President's determination in those cases did not contradict an Act of Congress. And the primary issue was whether the executive agreements could supersede state law. Still, the language in *Pink* and *Belmont*, which confirms the President's competence to determine questions of recognition, is strong support for the conclusion that it is for the President alone to determine which foreign governments are legitimate.

Banco Nacional de Cuba contains even stronger statements regarding the President's authority over recognition. There, the status of Cuba's Government and its acts as a sovereign were at issue. As the Court explained, "Political recognition is exclusively a function of the Executive." 376 U. S., at 410. Because the Executive had recognized the Cuban Government, the Court held that it should be treated as sovereign and could benefit from the "act of state" doctrine. See also *Baker* v. *Carr*, 369 U. S. 186, 213 (1962) ("[I]t is the executive that determines a person's status as representative of a foreign government"); *National City Bank of N. Y.*, 348 U. S., at 358 ("The status of the Republic of China in our courts is a matter for determination by the Executive and is outside the competence of this Court"). As these cases illustrate, the Court has long considered recognition to be the exclusive prerogative of the Executive.

The Secretary now urges the Court to define the executive power over foreign relations in even broader terms. He contends that under the Court's precedent the President has "exclusive authority to conduct diplomatic relations," along with "the bulk of foreign-affairs powers.". . . In support of his submission that the President has broad, undefined powers over foreign affairs, the Secretary quotes *United States* v. *Curtiss-Wright Export Corp.*, which described the President as "the sole organ of the federal government in the field of international relations." 299 U. S., at 320. This Court declines to acknowledge that unbounded power. A formulation broader than the rule that the President alone determines what nations to formally recognize as legitimate—and that he consequently controls his statements on matters of recognition—presents different issues and is unnecessary to the resolution of this case.

The *Curtiss-Wright* case does not extend so far as the Secretary suggests. In *Curtiss-Wright*, the Court considered whether a congressional delegation of power to the President was constitutional. Congress had passed a joint resolution giving the President the discretion to prohibit arms sales to certain militant powers in South America. The resolution provided criminal penalties for violation of those orders. *Id.,* at 311–312. The Court held that the delegation was constitutional, reasoning that Congress may grant the President substantial authority and discretion in the field of foreign affairs. *Id.,* at 315–329. Describing why such broad delegation may be appropriate, the opinion stated:

> "In this vast external realm, with its important, complicated, delicate and manifold problems, the President alone has the power to speak or listen as a representative of the nation. He *makes* treaties with the advice and consent of the Senate; but he alone negotiates. Into the field of negotiation the Senate cannot intrude; and Congress itself is powerless to invade it. As Marshall said in his great argument of March 7, 1800, in the House of Representatives, 'The President is the sole organ of the nation in its external relations, and its sole representative with foreign nations.' [10 Annals of Cong.] 613." *Id.,* at 319.

This description of the President's exclusive power was not necessary to the holding of *Curtiss-Wright*—which, after all, dealt with congressionally authorized action, not a unilateral Presidential determination. Indeed, *Curtiss-Wright* did not hold that the President is free from Congress' lawmaking power in the field of international relations. The President does have a unique role in communicating with foreign governments, as then-Congressman John Marshall acknowledged. See 10 Annals of Cong. 613 (1800) (cited in *Curtiss-Wright, supra,* at 319). But whether the realm is foreign or domestic, it is still the Legislative Branch, not the Executive Branch, that makes the law.

In a world that is ever more compressed and interdependent, it is essential the congressional role in foreign affairs be understood and respected. For it is Congress that makes laws, and in countless ways its laws will and should shape the Nation's course. The Executive is not free from the ordinary controls and checks of Congress merely because foreign affairs are at issue. See, *e.g., Medellín* v. *Texas,* 552 U. S. 491, 523–532 (2008); *Youngstown,* 343 U. S., at 589; *Little* v. *Barreme,* 2 Cranch 170, 177–179 (1804); Glennon, Two Views of Presidential Foreign Affairs Power: *Little* v. *Barreme* or *Curtiss-Wright?* 13 Yale J. Int'l L. 5, 19–20 (1988); cf. *Dames & Moore* v. *Regan,* 453 U. S. 654, 680–681 (1981). It is not for the President alone to determine the whole content of the Nation's foreign policy.

That said, judicial precedent and historical practice teach that it is for the President alone to make the specific decision of what foreign power he will recognize as legitimate, both for the Nation as a whole and for the purpose of making his own position clear within the context of recognition in discussions and negotiations with foreign nations. Recognition is an act with immediate and powerful significance for international relations, so the President's position must be clear. Congress cannot require him to contradict his own statement regarding a determination of formal recognition. Zivotofsky's contrary arguments are unconvincing. The decisions he relies upon are largely inapposite. This Court's cases do not hold that the recognition power is shared. *Jones* v. *United States*, 137 U. S. 202 (1890), and *Boumediene* v. *Bush*, 553 U. S. 723 (2008), each addressed the status of territories controlled or acquired by the United States—not whether a province ought to be recognized as part of a foreign country. See also *Vermilya-Brown Co.* v. *Connell*, 335 U. S. 377, 380 (1948) ("[D]etermination of [American] sovereignty over an area is for the legislative and executive departments"). And no one disputes that Congress has a role in determining the status of United States territories. See U. S. Const., Art. IV, § 3, cl. 2 (Congress may "dispose of and make all needful Rules and Regulations respecting the Territory or other Property belonging to the United States"). Other cases describing a shared power address the recognition of Indian tribes—which is, similarly, a distinct issue from the recognition of foreign countries. See *Cherokee Nation* v. *Georgia*, 5 Pet. 1 (1831).

To be sure, the Court has mentioned both of the political branches in discussing international recognition, but it has done so primarily in affirming that the Judiciary is not responsible for recognizing foreign nations. See *Oetjen*, 246 U. S., at 302 (" 'Who is the sovereign, *de jure* or *de facto*, of a territory is not a judicial, but is a political question, the determination of which by the legislative and executive departments of any government conclusively binds the judges' " (quoting *Jones, supra,* at 212)); *United States* v. *Palmer*, 3 Wheat. 610, 643 (1818) ("[T]he courts of the union must view [a] newly constituted government as it is viewed by the legislative and executive departments of the government of the United States"). This is consistent with the fact that Congress, in the ordinary course, does support the President's recognition policy, for instance by confirming an ambassador to the recognized foreign government. Those cases do not cast doubt on the view that the Executive Branch determines whether the United States will recognize foreign states and governments and their territorial bounds.

C

Having examined the Constitution's text and this Court's precedent, it is appropriate to turn to accepted understandings and practice. In separation-of-powers cases this Court has often "put significant weight upon historical practice." *NLRB* v. *Noel Canning*, 573 U. S. ___, ___ (2014) (slip op., at 6) (emphasis deleted). Here, history is not all on one side, but on balance it provides strong support for the conclusion that the recognition power is the President's alone. As Zivotofsky argues, certain historical incidents can be interpreted to support the position that recognition is a shared power. But the weight of historical evidence supports the opposite view, which is that the formal determination of recognition is a power to be exercised only by the President. The briefs of the parties and *amici*, which have been of considerable assistance to the Court, give a more complete account of the relevant history, as do the works of scholars in this field. See, *e.g.,* Brief for Respondent 26–39; Brief for Petitioner 34–57; Brief for American Jewish Committee as *Amicus Curiae* 6–24; J. Goebel, The Recognition Policy of the United States 97–170 (1915) (Goebel); 1Moore §§ 28–58, 74–164; Reinstein, Is the President's Recognition Power Exclusive? 86 Temp. L. Rev. 1, 3–50 (2013). But even a brief survey of the major historical examples, with an emphasis on those said to favor Zivotofsky, establishes no more than that some Presidents have chosen to cooperate with Congress, not that Congress itself has exercised the recognition power. From the first Administration forward, the President has claimed unilateral authority to recognize foreign sovereigns. For the most part, Congress has acquiesced in the Executive's exercise of the recognition power. On occasion, the President has chosen, as may often be prudent, to consult and coordinate with Congress. As Judge Tatel noted in this case, however, "the most striking thing" about the history of recognition "is what is absent from it: a situation like this one," where Congress has enacted a statute contrary to the President's formal and considered statement concerning recognition. . . .

. . .

III

As the power to recognize foreign states resides in the President alone, the question becomes whether § 214(d) infringes on the Executive's consistent decision to withhold recognition with respect to Jerusalem. See *Nixon* v. *Administrator of General Services*, 433 U. S. 425, 443 (1977) (action unlawful when it "prevents the Executive Branch from accomplishing its constitutionally assigned functions"). Section 214(d) requires that, in a passport or consular report of birth abroad, "the Secretary shall, upon the request of the citizen or the citizen's legal guardian, record the place of birth as Israel" for a "United States citizen born in the city of Jerusalem." 116 Stat. 1366. That is, § 214(d) requires the President, through the Secretary, to identify citizens born in Jerusalem who so request as being born in Israel. But according to the President, those citizens were not born in Israel. As a matter of United States policy, neither Israel nor any other country is acknowledged as having sovereignty over Jerusalem. In this way, § 214(d) "directly contradicts" the "carefully calibrated and longstanding Executive branch policy of neutrality toward Jerusalem.". . . If the power over recognition is to mean anything, it must mean that the President not only makes the initial, formal recognition determination but also that he may maintain that determination in his and his agent's statements. This conclusion is a matter of both common sense and necessity. If Congress could command the President to state a recognition position inconsistent with his own, Congress could override the President's recognition determination. Under international law, recognition may be effected by "written or oral declaration of the recognizing state." 1 Moore § 27, at 73. In addition an act of recognition must "leave no doubt as to the intention to grant it."1 Oppenheim's International Law § 50, at 169. Thus, if Congress could alter the President's statements on matters of recognition or force him to contradict them, Congress in effect would exercise the recognition power.

As Justice Jackson wrote in *Youngstown*, when a Presidential power is "exclusive," it "disabl[es] the Congress from acting upon the subject." 343 U. S., at 637–638 (concurring opinion). Here, the subject is quite narrow: The Executive's exclusive power extends no further than his formal recognition determination. But as to that determination, Congress may not enact a law that directly contradicts it. This is not to say Congress may not express its disagreement with the President in myriad ways. For example, it may enact an embargo, decline to confirm an ambassador, or even declare war. But none of these acts would alter the President's recognition decision.

If Congress may not pass a law, speaking in its own voice, that effects formal recognition, then it follows that it may not force the President himself to contradict his earlier statement. That congressional command would not only prevent the Nation from speaking with one voice but also prevent the Executive itself from doing so in conducting foreign relations.

Although the statement required by § 214(d) would not itself constitute a formal act of recognition, it is a mandate that the Executive contradict his prior recognition determination in an official document issued by the Secretary of State. See *Urtetiqui* v. *D'Arcy*, 9 Pet. 692, 699 (1835) (a passport "from its nature and object, is addressed to foreign powers" and "is to be considered . . . in the character of a political document"). As a result, it is unconstitutional. This is all the more clear in light of the longstanding treatment of a passport's place-of-birth section as an official executive statement implicating recognition. . . . The Secretary's position on this point has been consistent: He will not place information in the place-of-birth section of a passport that contradicts the President's recognition policy. See 7 FAM § 1383. If a citizen objects to the country listed as sovereign over his place of birth, then the Secretary will accommodate him by listing the city or town of birth rather than the country. See *id.,* § 1383.6. But the Secretary will not list a sovereign that contradicts the President's recognition policy in a passport. Thus, the Secretary will not list "Israel" in a passport as the country containing Jerusalem.

The flaw in § 214(d) is further underscored by the undoubted fact that the purpose of the statute was to infringe on the recognition power—a power the Court now holds is the sole prerogative of the President. The statute is titled "United States Policy with Respect to Jerusalem as the Capital of Israel." § 214. . . . The House Conference Report proclaimed that § 214 "contains four provisions related to the recognition of Jerusalem as Israel's capital." H. R. Conf. Rep. No. 107–671, p. 123 (2002). And, indeed, observers interpreted § 214 as altering United States policy regarding Jerusalem—which led to protests across the region. . . . From the face of § 214, from the legislative history, and from its reception, it is clear that Congress wanted to express its displeasure with the President's policy by, among other things, commanding the Executive to contradict his own, earlier stated position on Jerusalem. This Congress may not do.

It is true, as Zivotofsky notes, that Congress has substantial authority over passports. See *Haig* v. *Agee*, 453; U. S. 280 (1981); *Zemel* v. *Rusk*, 381 U. S. 1 (1965); *Kent* v. *Dulles*, 357 U. S. 116 (1958). The Court does not question the power of Congress to enact passport legislation of wide scope. In *Kent* v. *Dulles*, for example, the Court held that if a person's " 'liberty' " to travel "is to be regulated" through a passport, "it must be pursuant to the lawmaking functions of the Congress." See *id.*, at 129. Later cases, such as *Zemel* v. *Rusk* and *Haig* v. *Agee*, also proceeded on the assumption that Congress must authorize the grounds on which passports may be approved or denied. See *Zemel, supra*, at 7–13; *Haig, supra*, at 289–306. This is consistent with the extensive lawmaking power the Constitution vests in Congress over the Nation's foreign affairs.

The problem with § 214(d), however, lies in how Congress exercised its authority over passports. It was an improper act for Congress to "aggrandiz[e] its power at the expense of another branch" by requiring the President to contradict an earlier recognition determination in an official document issued by the Executive Branch. *Freytag* v. *Commissioner*, 501 U. S. 868, 878 (1991). To allow Congress to control the President's communication in the context of a formal recognition determination is to allow Congress to exercise that exclusive power itself. As a result, the statute is unconstitutional.

* * *

In holding § 214(d) invalid the Court does not question the substantial powers of Congress over foreign affairs in general or passports in particular. This case is confined solely to the exclusive power of the President to control recognition determinations, including formal statements by the Executive Branch acknowledging the legitimacy of a state or government and its territorial bounds. Congress cannot command the President to contradict an earlier recognition determination in the issuance of passports. The judgment of the Court of Appeals for the District of Columbia Circuit is

Affirmed.

Justice Breyer, concurring.

I continue to believe that this case presents a political question inappropriate for judicial resolution. . . . But because precedent precludes resolving this case on political question grounds, . . . , I join the Court's opinion.

Justice Thomas, concurring in the judgment in part and dissenting in part.

Our Constitution allocates the powers of the Federal Government over foreign affairs in two ways. First, it expressly identifies certain foreign affairs powers and vests them in particular branches, either individually or jointly. Second, it vests the residual foreign affairs powers of the Federal Government—*i.e.,* those not specifically enumerated in the Constitution—in the President by way of Article II's Vesting Clause.

Section 214(d) of the Foreign Relations Authorization Act, Fiscal Year 2003, ignores that constitutional allocation of power insofar as it directs the President, contrary to his wishes, to list "Israel" as the place of birth of Jerusalem-born citizens on their passports. The President has long regulated passports under his residual foreign affairs power, and this portion of § 214(d) does not fall within any of Congress' enumerated powers.

By contrast, § 214(d) poses no such problem insofar as it regulates consular reports of birth abroad. Unlike passports, these reports were developed to effectuate the naturalization laws, and they continue to serve the role of identifying persons who need not be naturalized to obtain U. S. citizenship. The regulation of these reports does not fall within the President's foreign affairs powers, but within Congress' enumerated powers under the Naturalization and Necessary and Proper Clauses.

Rather than adhere to the Constitution's division of powers, the Court relies on a distortion of the President's recognition power to hold both of these parts of § 214(d) unconstitutional. Because I cannot join this faulty analysis, I concur only in the portion of the Court's judgment holding § 214(d) unconstitutional as applied to passports. I respectfully dissent from the remainder of the Court's judgment.

. . .

Chief Justice Roberts, with whom Justice Alito joins, dissenting.

Today's decision is a first: Never before has this Court accepted a President's direct defiance of an Act of Congress in the field of foreign affairs. We have instead stressed that the President's power reaches "its lowest ebb" when he contravenes the express will of Congress, "for what is at stake is the equilibrium established by our constitutional system." *Youngstown Sheet & Tube Co.* v. *Sawyer*, 343 U. S. 579, 637–638 (1952) (Jackson, J., concurring).

. . .

The first principles in this area are firmly established. The Constitution allocates some foreign policy powers to the Executive, grants some to the Legislature, and enjoins the President to "take Care that the Laws be faithfully executed." Art. II, § 3. The Executive may disregard "the expressed or implied will of Congress" only if the Constitution grants him a power "at once so conclusive and preclusive" as to "disabl[e] the Congress from acting upon the subject." *Youngstown*, 343 U. S., at 637–638 (Jackson, J., concurring).

Assertions of exclusive and preclusive power leave the Executive "in the least favorable of possible constitutional postures," and such claims have been "scrutinized with caution" throughout this Court's history. *Id.*, at 640, 638; see *Dames & Moore* v. *Regan*, 453 U. S. 654, 668–669 (1981). For our first 225 years, no President prevailed when contradicting a statute in the field of foreign affairs. See *Medellín* v. *Texas*, 552 U. S. 491, 524–532 (2008); *Hamdan* v. *Rumsfeld*, 548 U. S. 557, 590–595, 613–625 (2006); *Youngstown*, 343 U. S., at 587–589 (majority opinion); *Little* v. *Barreme*, 2 Cranch 170, 177–179 (1804).

In this case, the President claims the exclusive and preclusive power to recognize foreign sovereigns. The Court devotes much of its analysis to accepting the Executive's contention. . . . I have serious doubts about that position. The majority places great weight on the Reception Clause, which directs that the Executive "shall receive Ambassadors and other public

Ministers." Art. II, § 3. But that provision, framed as an obligation rather than an authorization, appears alongside the *duties* imposed on the President by Article II, Section 3, not the *powers* granted to him by Article II, Section 2. Indeed, the People ratified the Constitution with Alexander Hamilton's assurance that executive reception of ambassadors "is more a matter of dignity than of authority" and "will be without consequence in the administration of the government." The Federalist No. 69, p. 420 (C. Rossiter ed. 1961). In short, at the time of the founding, "there was no reason to view the reception clause as a source of discretionary authority for the president." Adler, The President's Recognition Power: Ministerial or Discretionary? 25Presidential Studies Q. 267, 269 (1995).

The majority's other asserted textual bases are even more tenuous. The President does have power to make treaties and appoint ambassadors. Art. II, § 2. But those authorities are *shared* with Congress, *ibid.*, so they hardly support an inference that the recognition power is *exclusive.*

Precedent and history lend no more weight to the Court's position. The majority cites dicta suggesting an exclusive executive recognition power, but acknowledges contrary dicta suggesting that the power is shared. See, *e.g.*, *United States* v. *Palmer*, 3 Wheat. 610, 643 (1818) ("the courts of the union must view [a] newly constituted government as it is viewed by *the legislative and executive departments* of the government of the United States" (emphasis added)). When the best you can muster is conflicting dicta, precedent can hardly be said to support your side.

As for history, the majority admits that it too points in both directions. Some Presidents have claimed an exclusive recognition power, but others have expressed uncertainty about whether such preclusive authority exists. Those in the skeptical camp include Andrew Jackson and Abraham Lincoln, leaders not generally known for their cramped conceptions of Presidential power. Congress has also asserted its authority over recognition determinations at numerous points in history. The majority therefore falls short of demonstrating that "Congress has accepted" the President's exclusive recognition power. In any event, we have held that congressional acquiescence is only "pertinent" when the President acts in the absence of express congressional authorization, not when he asserts power to disregard a statute, as the Executive does here. *Medellín*, 552 U. S., at 528; see *Dames & Moore*, 453 U. S., at 678–679.

In sum, although the President has authority over recognition, I am not convinced that the Constitution provides the "conclusive and preclusive" power required to justify defiance of an express legislative mandate. *Youngstown*, 343 U. S., at 638 (Jackson, J., concurring). As the leading scholar on this issue has concluded, the "text, original understanding, post-ratification history, and structure of the Constitution do not support the . . . expansive claim that this executive power is plenary." Reinstein, Is the President's Recognition Power Exclusive? 86 Temp. L. Rev. 1, 60 (2013).

But even if the President does have exclusive recognition power, he still cannot prevail in this case, because the statute at issue *does not implicate recognition.* . . . The relevant provision, § 214(d), simply gives an American citizen born in Jerusalem the option to designate his place of birth as Israel "[f]or purposes of" passports and other documents. Foreign Relations Authorization Act, Fiscal Year 2003. . . . The State Department itself has explained that "identification"—not recognition—"is the principal reason that U. S. passports require 'place of birth.' " App. 42. Congress has not disputed the Executive's assurances that § 214(d) does not alter the longstanding United States position on Jerusalem. And the annals of diplomatic history record no examples of official recognition accomplished via optional passport designation.

. . .

Justice Scalia, with whom the Chief Justice and Justice Alito join, dissenting.

Before this country declared independence, the law of England entrusted the King with the exclusive care of his kingdom's foreign affairs. The royal prerogative included the "sole power of sending ambassadors to foreign states, and receiving them at home," the sole authority to "make treaties, leagues, and alliances with foreign states and princes," "the sole prerogative of making war and peace," and the "sole power of raising and regulating fleets and armies." 1 W. Blackstone, Commentaries *253, *257, *262. The People of the United States had other ideas when they organized our Government. They considered a sound structure of balanced powers essential to the preservation of just government, and international relations formed no exception to that principle.

The People therefore adopted a Constitution that divides responsibility for the Nation's foreign concerns between the legislative and executive departments. The Constitution gave the President the "executive Power," authority to send and responsibility to receive ambassadors, power to make treaties, and command of the Army and Navy—though they qualified some of these powers by requiring consent of the Senate. Art. II, §§ 1–3. At the same time, they gave Congress powers over war, foreign commerce, naturalization, and more. Art. I, § 8. "Fully eleven of the powers that Article I, § 8 grants Congress deal in some way with foreign affairs." L. Tribe, American Constitutional Law, § 5–18, p. 965.

This case arises out of a dispute between the Executive and Legislative Branches about whether the United States should treat Jerusalem as a part of Israel. The Constitution contemplates that the political branches will make policy about the territorial claims of foreign nations the same way they make policy about other international matters: The President will exercise his powers on the basis of his views, Congress its powers on the basis of its views. That is just what has happened here.

I

The political branches of our Government agree on the real-world fact that Israel controls the city of Jerusalem. . . . They disagree, however, about how official documents should record the birthplace of an American citizen born in Jerusalem. The Executive does not accept any state's claim to sovereignty over Jerusalem, and it maintains that the birthplace designation "Israel" would clash with this stance of neutrality. But the National Legislature has enacted a statute that provides: "For purposes of the registration of birth, certification of nationality, or issuance of a passport of a United States citizen born in the city of Jerusalem, the Secretary [of State] shall, upon the request of the citizen or the citizen's legal guardian, record the place of birth as Israel." Foreign Relations Authorization Act, Fiscal Year 2003, § 214(d). . . . Menachem Zivotofsky's parents seek enforcement of this statutory right in the issuance of their son's passport and consular report of birth abroad. They regard their son's birthplace as a part of Israel and insist as "a matter of conscience" that his Israeli nativity "not be erased" from his identity documents. App. 26.

Before turning to Presidential power under Article II, I think it well to establish the statute's basis in congressional power under Article I. Congress's power to "establish an uniform Rule of Naturalization," Art. I, § 8, cl. 4, enables it to grant American citizenship to someone born abroad. *United States* v. *Wong Kim Ark*, 169 U. S. 649, 702–703 (1898). The naturalization power also enables Congress to furnish the people it makes citizens with papers verifying their citizenship—say a consular report of birth abroad (which certifies citizenship of an American born outside the United States) or a passport (which certifies citizenship for purposes of international travel). As the Necessary and Proper Clause confirms, every congressional power "carries with it all those incidental powers which are necessary to its complete and effectual execution." *Cohens* v. *Virginia*, 6 Wheat. 264, 429 (1821). Even on a miserly understanding of Congress's incidental authority, Congress may make grants of citizenship "effectual" by providing for the issuance of certificates authenticating them.

One would think that if Congress may grant Zivotofsky a passport and a birth report, it may also require these papers to record his birthplace as "Israel." The birthplace specification promotes the document's citizenship-authenticating function by identifying the bearer, distinguishing people with similar names but different birthplaces from each other, helping authorities uncover identity fraud, and facilitating retrieval of the Government's citizenship records. See App. 70. To be sure, recording Zivotovsky's birthplace as "Jerusalem" rather than "Israel" would fulfill these objectives, but when faced with alternative ways to carry its powers into execution, Congress has the "discretion" to choose the one it deems "most beneficial to the people." *McCulloch* v. *Maryland*, 4 Wheat. 316, 421 (1819). It thus has the right to decide that recording birthplaces as "Israel" makes for better foreign policy. Or that regardless of international politics, a passport or birth report should respect its bearer's conscientious belief that Jerusalem belongs to Israel.

No doubt congressional discretion in executing legislative powers has its limits; Congress's chosen approach must be not only "necessary" to carrying its powers into execution, but also "proper." Congress thus may not transcend boundaries upon legislative authority stated or implied elsewhere in the Constitution. But as we shall see, § 214(d) does not transgress any such restriction.

II

The Court frames this case as a debate about recognition. Recognition is a sovereign's official acceptance of a status under international law. A sovereign might recognize a foreign entity as a state, a regime as the other state's government, a place as part of the other state's territory, rebel forces in the other state as a belligerent power, and so on. 2 M. Whiteman, Digest of International Law § 1 (1963) (hereinafter Whiteman). President Truman recognized Israel as a state in 1948, but Presidents have consistently declined to recognize Jerusalem as a part of Israel's (or any other state's) sovereign territory.

The Court holds that the Constitution makes the President alone responsible for recognition and that § 214(d) invades this exclusive power. I agree that the Constitution *empowers* the President to extend recognition on behalf of the United States, but I find it a much harder question whether it makes that power exclusive. The Court tells us that "the weight of historical evidence" supports exclusive executive authority over "the formal determination of recognition.". . . But even with its attention confined to formal recognition, the Court is forced to admit that "history is not all on one side.". . . To take a stark example, Congress legislated in 1934 to grant independence to the Philippines, which were then an American colony. . . . In the course of doing so, Congress directed the President to "recognize the independence of the Philippine Islands as a separate and self-governing nation" and to "acknowledge the authority and control over the same of the government instituted by the people thereof.". . . Constitutional? And if Congress may control recognition when exercising its power "to dispose of . . . the Territory or other Property belonging to the United States," Art. IV, § 3, cl. 2, why not when exercising other enumerated powers? Neither text nor history nor precedent yields a clear answer to these questions. Fortunately, I have no need to confront these matters today—nor does the Court—because § 214(d) plainly does not concern recognition.

Recognition is more than an announcement of a policy. Like the ratification of an international agreement or the termination of a treaty, it is a formal legal act with effects under international law. It signifies acceptance of an international status, and it makes a commitment to continued acceptance of that status and respect for any attendant rights. See, *e.g.,* Convention on the Rights and Duties of States, Art. 6, Dec. 26, 1933, . . . "Its legal effect is to create an estoppel. By granting recognition, [states] debar themselves from challenging in future whatever they have previously acknowledged." 1 G. Schwarzenberger, International Law 127 (3d ed. 1957). In order to extend recognition, a state must perform an act that unequivocally manifests that intention. Whiteman § 3. That act can consist of an express conferral of recognition, or one of a handful of acts that by international custom imply recognition—chiefly, entering into a bilateral treaty, and sending or receiving an ambassador. *Ibid.*

To know all this is to realize at once that § 214(d) has nothing to do with recognition. Section 214(d) does not require the Secretary to make a formal declaration about Israel's sovereignty over Jerusalem. And nobody suggests that international custom infers acceptance of sovereignty from the birthplace designation on a passport or birth report, as it does from bilateral treaties or exchanges of ambassadors. Recognition would preclude the United States (as a matter of international law) from later contesting Israeli sovereignty over Jerusalem. But making a notation in a passport or birth report does not encumber the Republic with any international obligations. It leaves the Nation free (so far as international law is concerned) to change its mind in the future. That would be true even if the statute required *all* passports to list "Israel." But in fact it requires only those passports to list "Israel" for which the citizen (or his guardian) *requests* "Israel"; all the rest, under the Secretary's policy, list "Jerusalem." It is utterly impossible for this deference to private requests to constitute an act that unequivocally manifests an intention to grant recognition.

Section 214(d) performs a more prosaic function than extending recognition. Just as foreign countries care about what our Government has to say about their borders, so too American citizens often care about what our Government has to say about their identities. Cf. *Bowen* v. *Roy*, 476 U. S. 693 (1986). The State Department does not grant or deny recognition in order to accommodate these individuals, but it does make exceptions to its rules about how it records birthplaces. Although normal protocol requires specifying the bearer's country of birth in his passport, Dept. of State, 7 Foreign Affairs Manual (FAM) § 1300, App. D, § 1330(a) (2014), the State Department will, if the bearer protests, specify the city of birth instead—so that an Irish nationalist may have his birthplace recorded as "Belfast" rather than "United Kingdom," *id.,* § 1380(a). And although normal protocol requires specifying the country with *present* sovereignty over the bearer's place of birth, *id.,* § 1330(b), a special exception allows a bearer born before 1948 in what was then Palestine to have his birthplace listed as "Palestine," *id.,* § 1360(g). Section 214(d) requires the State Department to make a further accommodation. Even though the Department normally refuses to specify a country that lacks recognized sovereignty over the bearer's birthplace, it must suspend that policy upon the request of an American citizen born in Jerusalem. Granting a request to specify "Israel" rather than "Jerusalem" does not recognize Israel's sovereignty over Jerusalem, just as granting a request to specify "Belfast" rather than "United Kingdom" does not derecognize the United Kingdom's sovereignty over Northern Ireland.

The best indication that § 214(d) does not concern recognition comes from the State Department's policies concerning Taiwan. According to the Solicitor General, the United States "acknowledges the Chinese position" that Taiwan is a part of China, but "does not take a position" of its own on that issue. . . . Even so, the State Department has for a long time recorded the birthplace of a citizen born in Taiwan as "China." It indeed *insisted* on doing so until Congress passed a law (on which § 214(d) was modeled) giving citizens the option to have their birthplaces recorded as "Taiwan.". . . The Solicitor General explains that the designation "China" "involves a geographic description, not an assertion that Taiwan is . . . part of sovereign China.". . . Quite so. Section 214(d) likewise calls for nothing beyond a "geographic description"; it does not require the Executive even to assert, never mind formally recognize, that Jerusalem is a part of sovereign Israel. Since birthplace specifications in citizenship documents are matters within Congress's control, Congress may treat Jerusalem as a part of Israel when regulating the recording of birthplaces, even if the President does not do so when extending recognition. Section 214(d), by the way, expressly directs the Secretary to "record the place of birth as Israel" "*[f]or purposes of* the registration of birth, certification of nationality, or issuance of a passport." (Emphasis added.) And the law bears the caption, "Record of Place of Birth as Israel *for Passport Purposes.*" (Emphasis added.) Finding recognition in this provision is rather like finding admission to the Union in a provision that treats American Samoa as a State for purposes of a federal highway safety program, 23 U. S. C. § 401.

III

The Court complains that § 214(d) requires the Secretary of State to issue official documents implying that Jerusalem is a part of Israel; that it appears in a section of the statute bearing the title "United States Policy with Respect to Jerusalem as the Capital of Israel"; and that foreign "observers interpreted [it] as altering United States policy regarding Jerusalem." But these features do not show that § 214(d) recognizes Israel's sovereignty over Jerusalem. They show only that the law displays symbolic support for Israel's territorial claim. That symbolism may have tremendous significance as a matter of international diplomacy, but it makes no difference as a matter of constitutional law. Even if the Constitution gives the President sole power to extend recognition, it does not give him sole power to make all decisions relating to foreign disputes over sovereignty. To the contrary, a fair reading of Article I allows Congress to decide for itself how its laws should handle these controversies. Read naturally, power to "regulate Commerce with foreign Nations," § 8, cl. 3, includes power to regulate imports from Gibraltar as British goods or as Spanish goods. Read naturally, power to "regulate the Value . . . of foreign Coin," § 8, cl. 5, includes power to honor (or not) currency issued by Taiwan. And so on for the other enumerated powers. These are not airy hypotheticals. A trade statute from 1800, for example, provided that "the whole of the island of Hispaniola"—whose status was then in controversy—"shall for purposes of [the] act be considered as a dependency of the French Republic." § 7, . . . In 1938, Congress allowed admission of the Vatican City's public records in federal courts, decades before the United States extended formal recognition. . . . Whiteman § 68. The Taiwan Relations Act of 1979 grants Taiwan capacity to sue and be sued, even though the United States does not recognize it as a state. 22 U. S. C. § 3303(b)(7). Section 214(d) continues in the same tradition.

The Constitution likewise does not give the President exclusive power to determine which claims to statehood and territory "are legitimate in the eyes of the United States,". . . . Congress may express its own views about these matters by declaring war, restricting trade, denying foreign aid, and much else besides. To take just one example, in 1991, Congress responded to Iraq's invasion of Kuwait by enacting a resolution authorizing use of military force. . . . No doubt the resolution reflected Congress's views about the legitimacy of Iraq's territorial claim. The preamble referred to Iraq's "illegal occupation" and stated that "the international community has demanded . . . that Kuwait's independence and legitimate government be restored.". . . These statements are far more categorical than the caption "United States Policy with Respect to Jerusalem as the Capital of Israel." Does it follow that the authorization of the use of military force invaded the President's exclusive powers? Or that it would have done so had the President recognized Iraqi sovereignty over Kuwait?

History does not even support an exclusive Presidential power to make what the Court calls "formal statements" about "the legitimacy of a state or government and its territorial bounds,". . . . For a long time, the Houses of Congress have made formal statements announcing their own positions on these issues, again without provoking constitutional objections. A recent resolution expressed the House of Representatives' "strong support for the legitimate, democratically-elected Government of Lebanon" and condemned an "illegitimate" and "unjustifiable" insurrection by "the terrorist group Hizballah." H. Res. 1194, 110th Cong, 2d Sess., 1, 4 (2008). An earlier enactment declared "the sense of the Congress that . . . Tibet . . . is an occupied country under the established principles of international law" and that "Tibet's true representatives are the Dalai Lama and the Tibetan Government in exile." § 355, . . . (1991). After Texas won independence from Mexico, the Senate resolved that "the State of Texas having established and maintained an independent Government, . . . it is expedient and proper . . . that the independent political existence of the said State be acknowledged by the Government of the United States." Cong. Globe, 24th Cong., 2d Sess., 83 (1837); see *id.*, at 270.

In the final analysis, the Constitution may well deny Congress power to recognize—the power to make an international commitment accepting a foreign entity as a state, a regime as its government, a place as a part of its territory, and so on. But whatever else § 214(d) may do, it plainly does not make (or require the President to make) a commitment accepting Israel's sovereignty over Jerusalem.

. . .

2. CONGRESSIONAL INTERFERENCE WITH PRESIDENTIAL PREROGATIVES

B. APPOINTMENT, DISCHARGE, AND SUPERVISION OF "OFFICERS OF THE UNITED STATES"

Page 395. Add the following before Section 3:

National Labor Relations Board v. Noel Canning
573 U.S. ___, 134 S.Ct. 2550, 189 L.Ed.2d 538 (2014).

Justice Breyer delivered the opinion of the Court.

Ordinarily the President must obtain "the Advice and Consent of the Senate" before appointing an "Office[r] of the United States." U.S. Const., Art.

II, § 2, cl. 2. But the Recess Appointments Clause creates an exception. It gives the President alone the power "to fill up all Vacancies that may happen during the Recess of the Senate, by granting Commissions which shall expire at the End of their next Session." Art. II, § 2, cl. 3. We here consider three questions about the application of this Clause.

The first concerns the scope of the words "recess of the Senate." Does that phrase refer only to an inter-session recess (*i.e.,* a break between formal sessions of Congress), or does it also include an intra-session recess, such as a summer recess in the midst of a session? We conclude that the Clause applies to both kinds of recess.

The second question concerns the scope of the words "vacancies that may happen." Does that phrase refer only to vacancies that first come into existence during a recess, or does it also include vacancies that arise prior to a recess but continue to exist during the recess? We conclude that the Clause applies to both kinds of vacancy. The third question concerns calculation of the length of a "recess." The President made the appointments here at issue on January 4, 2012. At that time the Senate was in recess pursuant to a December 17, 2011, resolution providing for a series of brief recesses punctuated by "*pro forma* session[s]," with "no business . . . transacted," every Tuesday and Friday through January 20, 2012. S. J., 112th Cong., 1st Sess., 923 (2011) (hereinafter 2011 S. J.). In calculating the length of a recess are we to ignore the *pro forma* sessions, thereby treating the series of brief recesses as a single, month-long recess? We conclude that we cannot ignore these *pro forma* sessions. Our answer to the third question means that, when the appointments before us took place, the Senate was in the midst of a 3-day recess. Three days is too short a time to bring a recess within the scope of the Clause. Thus we conclude that the President lacked the power to make the recess appointments here at issue.

I

The case before us arises out of a labor dispute. The National Labor Relations Board (NLRB) found that a Pepsi-Cola distributor, Noel Canning, had unlawfully refused to reduce to writing and execute a collective-bargaining agreement with a labor union. The Board ordered the distributor to execute the agreement and to make employees whole for any losses. . . . The Pepsi-Cola distributor subsequently asked the Court of Appeals for the District of Columbia Circuit to set the Board's order aside. It claimed that three of the five Board members had been invalidly appointed, leaving the Board without the three lawfully appointed members necessary for it to act. . . .

The three members in question were Sharon Block, Richard Griffin, and Terence Flynn. In 2011 the President had nominated each of them to the Board. As of January 2012, Flynn's nomination had been pending in the Senate awaiting confirmation for approximately a year. The nominations of each of the other two had been pending for a few weeks. On January 4, 2012, the President, invoking the Recess Appointments Clause, appointed all three to the Board.

The distributor argued that the Recess Appointments Clause did not authorize those appointments. It pointed out that on December 17, 2011, the Senate, by unanimous consent, had adopted a resolution providing that it would take a series of brief recesses beginning the following day. See 2011 S. J. 923. Pursuant to that resolution, the Senate held *pro forma* sessions every Tuesday and Friday until it returned for ordinary business on January 23, 2012. . . . The President's January 4 appointments were made between the January 3 and January 6 *pro forma* sessions. In the distributor's view, each *pro forma* session terminated the immediately preceding recess. Accordingly, the appointments were made during a 3-day adjournment, which is not long enough to trigger the Recess Appointments Clause.

The Court of Appeals agreed that the appointments fell outside the scope of the Clause. But the court set forth different reasons. It held that the Clause's words "the recess of the Senate" do not include recesses that occur *within* a formal session of Congress, *i.e.*, intra-session recesses. Rather those words apply only to recesses *between* those formal sessions, *i.e.*, inter-session recesses. Since the second session of the 112th Congress began on January 3, 2012, the day before the President's appointments, those appointments occurred during an intra-session recess, and the appointments consequently fell outside the scope of the Clause. . . . The Court of Appeals added that, in any event, the phrase "vacancies that may happen during the recess" applies only to vacancies that come into existence during a recess. . . . The vacancies that Members Block, Griffin, and Flynn were appointed to fill had arisen before the beginning of the recess during which they were appointed. For this reason too the President's appointments were invalid. And, because the Board lacked a quorum of validly appointed members when it issued its order, the order was invalid. . . . We recognize that the President has nominated others to fill the positions once occupied by Members Block, Griffin, and Flynn, and that the Senate has confirmed these successors. But, as the parties recognize, the fact that the Board now unquestionably has a quorum does not moot the controversy about the validity of the previously entered Board order. And there are pending before us petitions from decisions in other cases involving challenges to the appointment of Board Member Craig Becker. The President appointed Member Becker during an intra-session recess that was not punctuated by *pro forma* sessions, and the vacancy Becker filled had come into existence prior to the recess. . . . Other cases involving similar challenges are also pending in the Courts of Appeals. . . . Thus, we believe it is important to answer all three questions that this case presents.

II

Before turning to the specific questions presented, we shall mention two background considerations that we find relevant to all three. First, *the Recess Appointments Clause sets forth a subsidiary, not a primary, method for appointing officers of the United States.* The immediately preceding Clause— Article II, Section 2, Clause 2—provides the primary method of appointment. It says that the President "shall nominate, *and by and with the Advice and Consent of the Senate*, shall appoint Ambassadors, other public Ministers and

Consuls, Judges of the supreme Court, and all other Officers of the United States" (emphasis added).

The Federalist Papers make clear that the Founders intended this method of appointment, requiring Senate approval, to be the norm (at least for principal officers). Alexander Hamilton wrote that the Constitution vests the power of *nomination* in the President alone because "one man of discernment is better fitted to analise and estimate the peculiar qualities adapted to particular offices, than a body of men of equal, or perhaps even of superior discernment." The Federalist No. 76, p. 510 (J. Cooke ed. 1961). At the same time, the need to secure Senate approval provides "an excellent check upon a spirit of favoritism in the President, and would tend greatly to preventing the appointment of unfit characters from State prejudice, from family connection, from personal attachment, or from a view to popularity." *Id.,* at 513. Hamilton further explained

> that the "ordinary power of appointment is confided to the President and Senate *jointly,* and can therefore only be exercised during the session of the Senate; but as it would have been improper to oblige this body to be continually in session for the appointment of officers; and as vacancies might happen *in their recess,* which it might be necessary for the public service to fill without delay, the succeeding clause is evidently intended to authorise the President *singly* to make temporary appointments." *Id.,* No. 67, at 455.

Thus the Recess Appointments Clause reflects the tension between, on the one hand, the President's continuous need for "the assistance of subordinates," *Myers* v. *United States,* 272 U.S. 52, 117 (1926), and, on the other, the Senate's practice, particularly during the Republic's early years, of meeting for a single brief session each year. . . . We seek to interpret the Clause as granting the President the power to make appointments during a recess but not offering the President the authority routinely to avoid the need for Senate confirmation.

Second, *in interpreting the Clause, we put significant weight upon historical practice.* For one thing, the interpretive questions before us concern the allocation of power between two elected branches of Government. Long ago Chief Justice Marshall wrote that

> a doubtful question, one on which human reason may pause, and the human judgment be suspended, in the decision of which the great principles of liberty are not concerned, but the respective powers of those who are equally the representatives of the people, are to be adjusted; if not put at rest by the practice of the government, ought to receive a considerable impression from that practice." *McCulloch* v. *Maryland,* 4 Wheat. 316, 401 (1819).

And we later confirmed that "[l]ong settled and established practice is a consideration of great weight in a proper interpretation of constitutional provisions" regulating the relationship between Congress and the President. *The Pocket Veto Case,* 279 U.S. 655, 689 (1929); see also *id.,* at 690 ("[A] practice of at least twenty years duration 'on the part of the executive department, acquiesced in by the legislative department, . . . is entitled to great regard in determining the true construction of a constitutional provision the phraseology of which is in any respect of doubtful meaning' ". . . .

We recognize, of course, that the separation of powers can serve to safeguard individual liberty, *Clinton* v. *City of New York*, 524 U.S. 417, 449–450 (1998) (Kennedy, J., concurring), and that it is the "duty of the judicial department"—in a separation-of-powers case as in any other—"to say what the law is," *Marbury* v. *Madison*, 1 Cranch 137, 177 (1803). But it is equally true that the longstanding "practice of the government," *McCulloch, supra,* at 401, can inform our determination of "what the law is," *Marbury, supra,* at 177.

That principle is neither new nor controversial. As James Madison wrote, it "was foreseen at the birth of the Constitution, that difficulties and differences of opinion might occasionally arise in expounding terms & phrases necessarily used in such a charter . . . and that it might require a regular course of practice to liquidate & settle the meaning of some of them.". . . And our cases have continually confirmed Madison's view. *E.g., Mistretta* v. *United States*, 488 U.S. 361, 401 (1989); *Dames & Moore* v. *Regan*, 453 U.S. 654, 686 (1981); *Youngstown Sheet & Tube Co.* v. *Sawyer*, 343 U.S. 579, 610–611 (1952) (Frankfurter, J., concurring); *The Pocket Veto Case, supra,* at 689–690; *Ex parte Grossman*, 267 U.S. 87, 118–119 (1925); *United States* v. *Midwest Oil Co.*, 236 U.S. 459, 472–474 (1915); *McPherson* v. *Blacker*, 146 U.S. 1, 27 (1892); *McCulloch, supra; Stuart* v. *Laird*, 1 Cranch 299 (1803). These precedents show that this Court has treated practice as an important interpretive factor even when the nature or longevity of that practice is subject to dispute, and even when that practice began after the founding era. . . . There is a great deal of history to consider here. Presidents have made recess appointments since the beginning of the Republic. Their frequency suggests that the Senate and President have recognized that recess appointments can be both necessary and appropriate in certain circumstances. We have not previously interpreted the Clause, and, when doing so for the first time in more than 200 years, we must hesitate to upset the compromises and working arrangements that the elected branches of Government themselves have reached.

III

The first question concerns the scope of the phrase *"the recess* of the Senate." Art. II, § 2, cl. 3 (emphasis added). The Constitution provides for congressional elections every two years. And the 2-year life of each elected Congress typically consists of two formal 1-year sessions, each separated from the next by an "inter-session recess.". . . The Senate or the House of Representatives announces an inter-session recess by approving a resolution stating that it will "adjourn *sine die*," i.e., without specifying a date to return (in which case Congress will reconvene when the next formal session is scheduled to begin).

The Senate and the House also take breaks in the midst of a session. The Senate or the House announces any such "intra-session recess" by adopting a resolution stating that it will "adjourn" to a fixed date, a few days or weeks or even months later. All agree that the phrase "the recess of the Senate" covers inter-session recesses. The question is whether it includes intra-session recesses as well.

In our view, the phrase "the recess" includes an intra-session recess of substantial length. Its words taken literally can refer to both types of recess. Founding-era dictionaries define the word "recess," much as we do today, simply as "a period of cessation from usual work." 13 The Oxford English Dictionary 322–323 (2d ed. 1989) (hereinafter OED) (citing 18th-and 19th-century sources for that definition of "recess"); 2 N. Webster, An American Dictionary of the English Language (1828) ("[r]emission or suspension of business or procedure"); 2 S. Johnson, A Dictionary of the English Language 1602–1603 (4th ed. 1773) (hereinafter Johnson) (same). The Founders themselves used the word to refer to intra-session, as well as to inter- session, breaks. See, *e.g.,* 3 Records of the Federal Convention of 1787, p. 76 (M. Farrand rev. 1966) . . . ; *id.,* at 191 . . . ; 1 T. Jefferson, A Manual of Parliamentary Practice §LI, p. 165 (2d ed. 1812) (describing a "recess by adjournment" which did *not* end a session).

We recognize that the word "the" in "*the* recess" might suggest that the phrase refers to the single break separating formal sessions of Congress. That is because the word "the" frequently (but not always) indicates "a particular thing." 2 Johnson 2003. But the word can also refer "to a term used generically or universally." 17 OED 879. The Constitution, for example, directs the Senate to choose a President *pro tempore* "in *the* Absence of the Vice- President." Art. I, § 3, cl. 5 (emphasis added). And the Federalist Papers refer to the chief magistrate of an ancient Achaean league who "administered the government in *the* recess of the Senate." The Federalist No. 18, at 113 (J. Madison) (emphasis added). Reading "the" generically in this way, there is no linguistic problem applying the Clause's phrase to both kinds of recess. And, in fact, the phrase "the recess" was used to refer to intra-session recesses at the time of the founding. . . .

The constitutional text is thus ambiguous. And we believe the Clause's purpose demands the broader interpretation. The Clause gives the President authority to make appointments during "the recess of the Senate" so that the President can ensure the continued functioning of the Federal Government when the Senate is away. The Senate is equally away during both an inter-session and an intra-session recess, and its capacity to participate in the appointments process has nothing to do with the words it uses to signal its departure.

History also offers strong support for the broad interpretation. We concede that pre-Civil War history is not helpful. But it shows only that Congress generally took long breaks between sessions, while taking no significant intra-session breaks at all (five times it took a break of a week or so at Christmas). . . . Obviously, if there are no significant intra-session recesses, there will be no intra-session recess appointments. In 1867 and 1868, Congress for the first time took substantial, non-holiday intra-session breaks, and President Andrew Johnson made dozens of recess appointments. The Federal Court of Claims upheld one of those specific appointments, writing "[w]e have *no doubt* that a vacancy occurring while the Senate was thus temporarily adjourned" during the "first session of the Fortieth Congress" was "legally filled by appointment of the President alone." *Gould* v. *United States*, 19 Ct. Cl. 593, 595–596 (1884) (emphasis added). Attorney General Evarts also issued three opinions concerning the constitutionality of President Johnson's appointments, and it apparently did not occur to him that the distinction between intra-session and inter-session recesses was significant. . . . Similarly, though the 40th Congress impeached President Johnson on charges relating to his appointment power, he was not accused of violating the Constitution by making intra-session recess appointments. . . . In all, between the founding and the Great Depression, Congress took substantial intra-session breaks (other than holiday breaks) in four years: 1867, 1868, 1921, and 1929. . . . And in each of those years the President made intra-session recess appointments. . . . Since 1929, and particularly since the end of World War II, Congress has shortened its inter-session breaks as it has taken longer and more frequent intra-session breaks; Presidents have correspondingly made more intra-session recess appointments. Indeed, if we include military appointments, Presidents have made thousands of intra-session recess appointments. . . .

President Franklin Roosevelt, for example, commissioned Dwight Eisenhower as a permanent Major General during an intra-session recess; President Truman made Dean Acheson Under Secretary of State; and President George H. W. Bush reappointed Alan Greenspan as Chairman of the Federal Reserve Board. . . . Justice Scalia does not dispute any of these facts. Not surprisingly, the publicly available opinions of Presidential legal advisers that we have found are nearly unanimous in determining that the Clause authorizes these appointments. In 1921, for example, Attorney General Daugherty advised President Harding that he could make intra-session recess appointments. He reasoned: "If the President's power of appointment is to be defeated because the Senate takes an adjournment to a specified date, the painful and inevitable result will be measurably to prevent the exercise of governmental functions. I cannot bring myself to believe that the framers of the Constitution ever intended such a catastrophe to happen." 33 Op. Atty. Gen. 20, 23. We have found memoranda offering similar advice to President Eisenhower and to every President from Carter to the present. . . .

We must note one contrary opinion authored by President Theodore Roosevelt's Attorney General Philander Knox. Knox advised the President that the Clause did not cover a 19-day intra-session Christmas recess. 23 Op. Atty. Gen. 599 (1901). But in doing so he relied heavily upon the use of the word "the," a linguistic point that we do not find determinative. . . . And Knox all but confessed that his interpretation ran contrary to the basic purpose of the Clause. . . . Moreover, only three days before Knox gave his opinion, the Solicitor of the Treasury came to the opposite conclusion. . . . We therefore do not think Knox's isolated opinion can disturb the consensus advice within the Executive Branch taking the opposite position.

What about the Senate? Since Presidents began making intra-session recess appointments, individual Senators have taken differing views about the proper definition of "the recess.". . . But neither the Senate considered as a body nor its committees, despite opportunities to express opposition to the practice of intra-session recess appointments, has done so. Rather, to the extent that the Senate or a Senate committee has expressed a view, that view has favored a functional definition of "recess," and a functional definition encompasses intra-session recesses. Most notably, in 1905 the Senate Committee on the Judiciary objected strongly to President Theodore Roosevelt's use of the Clause to make more than 160 recess appointments during a "fictitious" inter-session recess. . . . The Judiciary Committee, when stating its strong objection, defined "recess" in functional terms as

> "the period of time when the Senate is not sitting in regular or extraordinary session as a branch of the Congress . . . ; when its members owe no duty of attendance; when its Chamber is empty; when, because of its absence, it cannot receive communications from the President or participate as a body in making appointments." 1905 Senate Report, at 2 (emphasis deleted). That functional definition encompasses intra-session, as well as inter-session, recesses. . . .

. . .

We recognize that the Senate cannot easily register opposition as a body to every governmental action that many, perhaps most, Senators oppose. But the Senate has not been silent or passive regarding the meaning of the Clause: A Senate Committee did register opposition to President Theodore Roosevelt's use of the Clause, and the Senate as a whole has legislated in an effort to discourage certain kinds of recess appointments. And yet we are not aware of any formal action it has taken to call into question the broad and functional definition of "recess" first set out in the 1905 Senate Report and followed by the Executive Branch since at least 1921. Nor has Justice Scalia identified any. All the while, the President has made countless recess appointments during intra-session recesses.

The upshot is that restricting the Clause to inter-session recesses would frustrate its purpose. It would make the President's recess-appointment power dependent on a formalistic distinction of Senate procedure. Moreover, the President has consistently and frequently interpreted the word "recess" to apply to intra-session recesses, and has acted on that interpretation. The Senate as a body has done nothing to deny the validity of this practice for at least three-quarters of a century. And three-quarters of a century of settled practice is long enough to entitle a practice to "great weight in a proper interpretation" of the constitutional provision. . . .

We are aware of, but we are not persuaded by, three important arguments to the contrary. First, some argue that the Founders would likely have intended the Clause to apply only to inter-session recesses, for they hardly knew any other. See, *e.g.,* Brief for Originalist Scholars as *Amici Curiae* 27–29. Indeed, from the founding until the Civil War inter-session recesses were the only kind of significant recesses that Congress took. The problem with this argument, however, is that it does not fully describe the relevant founding intent. The question is not: Did the Founders at the time think about intra-session recesses? Perhaps they did not. The question is: Did the Founders intend to restrict the scope of the Clause to the form of congressional recess then prevalent, or did they intend a broader scope permitting the Clause to apply, where appropriate, to somewhat changed circumstances? The Founders knew they were writing a document designed to apply to ever-changing circumstances over centuries. After all, a Constitution is "intended to endure for ages to come," and must adapt itself to a future that can only be "seen dimly," if at all. *McCulloch*, 4 Wheat., at 415. We therefore think the Framers likely did intend the Clause to apply to a new circumstance that so clearly falls within its essential purposes, where doing so is consistent with the Clause's language.

Second, some argue that the intra-session interpretation permits the President to make "illogic[ally]" long recess appointments. . . . A recess appointment made between Congress' annual sessions would permit the appointee to serve for about a year, *i.e.,* until the "end" of the "next" Senate "session." Art. II, § 2, cl. 3. But an intra-session appointment made at the beginning or in the middle of a formal session could permit the appointee to serve for 1½ or almost 2 years (until the end of the following formal session).

We agree that the intra-session interpretation permits somewhat longer recess appointments, but we do not agree that this consequence is "illogical.". . . A recess appointment that lasts somewhat longer than a year will ensure the President the continued assistance of subordinates that the Clause permits him to obtain while he and the Senate select a regular appointee. An appointment should last until the Senate has "an opportunity to act on the subject," Story, § 1551, at 410, and the Clause embodies a determination that a full session is needed to select and vet a replacement.

Third, the Court of Appeals believed that application of the Clause to intra-session recesses would introduce "vagueness" into a Clause that was otherwise clear. . . . One can find problems of uncertainty, however, either way. In 1867, for example, President Andrew Johnson called a special session of Congress, which took place during a lengthy intra-session recess. Consider the period of time that fell just after the conclusion of that special session. Did that period remain an intra-session recess, or did it become an inter-session recess? Historians disagree about the answer. . . .

Or suppose that Congress adjourns *sine die*, but it does so conditionally, so that the leadership can call the members back into session when "the public interest shall warrant it.". . . If the Senate Majority Leader were to reconvene the Senate, how would we characterize the preceding recess? Is it still inter-session? On the narrower interpretation the label matters; on the broader it does not.

The greater interpretive problem is determining how long a recess must be in order to fall within the Clause. Is a break of a week, or a day, or an hour too short to count as a "recess"? The Clause itself does not say. And Justice Scalia claims that this silence itself shows that the Framers intended the Clause to apply only to an inter-session recess. . . .

We disagree. For one thing, the most likely reason the Framers did not place a textual floor underneath the word "recess" is that they did not foresee the *need* for one. . . .

Moreover, the lack of a textual floor raises a problem that plagues *both* interpretations—Justice Scalia's and ours. Today a brief inter-session recess is just as possible as a brief intra-session recess. And though Justice Scalia says that the "notion that the Constitution empowers the President to make unilateral appointments every time the Senate takes a half-hour lunch break is *so absurd as to be self-refuting*," he must immediately concede (in a footnote) that the President "can make recess appointments during any break *between* sessions, *no matter how short*.". . .

Even the Solicitor General, arguing for a broader interpretation, acknowledges that there is a lower limit applicable to both kinds of recess. He argues that the lower limit should be three days by analogy to the Adjournments Clause of the Constitution. . . . That Clause says: "Neither House, during the Session of Congress, shall, without the Consent of the other, adjourn for more than three days." Art. I, § 5, cl. 4.

We agree with the Solicitor General that a 3-day recess would be too short. . . . The Adjournments Clause reflects the fact that a 3-day break is not a significant interruption of legislative business. As the Solicitor General says, it is constitutionally *de minimis*. . . . A Senate recess that is so short that it does not require the consent of the House is not long enough to trigger the President's recess-appointment power. That is not to say that the President may make recess appointments during any recess that is "more than three days." Art. I, § 5, cl. 4. The Recess Appointments Clause seeks to permit the Executive Branch to function smoothly when Congress is unavailable. And though Congress has taken short breaks for almost 200 years, and there have been many thousands of recess appointments in that time, we have not found a single example of a recess appointment made during an intra-session recess that was shorter than 10 days. Nor has the Solicitor General. . . . There are a few historical examples of recess appointments made during inter-session recesses shorter than 10 days. . . . But when considered against 200 years of settled practice, we regard these few scattered examples as anomalies. We therefore conclude, in light of historical practice, that a recess of more than 3 days but less than 10 days is presumptively too short to fall within the Clause. We add the word "presumptively" to leave open the possibility that some very unusual circumstance—a national catastrophe, for instance, that renders the Senate unavailable but calls for an urgent response—could demand the exercise of the recess-appointment power during a shorter break. (It should go without saying—except that Justice Scalia compels us to say it—that political opposition in the Senate would not qualify as an unusual circumstance.)

In sum, we conclude that the phrase "the recess" applies to both intra-session and inter-session recesses. If a Senate recess is so short that it does not require the consent of the House, it is too short to trigger the Recess Appointments Clause. See Art. I, § 5, cl. 4. And a recess lasting less than 10 days is presumptively too short as well.

IV

The second question concerns the scope of the phrase "vacancies *that may happen* during the recess of the Senate." Art. II, § 2, cl. 3 (emphasis added). All agree that the phrase applies to vacancies that initially occur during a recess. But does it also apply to vacancies that initially occur before a recess and continue to exist during the recess? In our view the phrase applies to both kinds of vacancy. We believe that the Clause's language, read literally, permits, though it does not naturally favor, our broader interpretation. We concede that the most natural meaning of "happens" as applied to a "vacancy" (at least to a modern ear) is that the vacancy "happens" when it initially occurs. See 1 Johnson 913 (defining "happen" in relevant part as meaning "[t]o fall out; to chance; to come to pass"). But that is not the only possible way to use the word. Thomas Jefferson wrote that the Clause is "certainly susceptible of [two] constructions.". . . It "may mean 'vacancies that may happen to be' or 'may happen to fall' " during a recess. . . .

. . .

In any event, the linguistic question here is not whether the phrase can be, but whether it must be, read more narrowly. The question is whether the Clause is ambiguous. *The Pocket Veto Case*, 279 U.S., at 690. And the broader reading, we believe, is at least a permissible reading of a " 'doubtful' " phrase. *Ibid.* We consequently go on to consider the Clause's purpose and historical practice.

The Clause's purpose strongly supports the broader interpretation. That purpose is to permit the President to obtain the assistance of subordinate officers when the Senate, due to its recess, cannot confirm them. Attorney General Wirt clearly described how the narrower interpretation would undermine this purpose:

> "Put the case of a vacancy occurring in an office, held in a distant part of the country, on the last day of the Senate's session. Before the vacancy is made known to the President, the Senate rises. The office may be an important one; the vacancy may paralyze a whole line of action in some essential branch of our internal police; the public interests may imperiously demand that it shall be immediately filled. But the vacancy happened to occur during the session of the Senate; and if the President's power is to be limited to such vacancies only as happen to occur during the recess of the Senate, the vacancy in the case put must continue, however ruinous the consequences may be to the public." 1 Op. Atty. Gen., at 632.

Examples are not difficult to imagine: An ambassadorial post falls vacant too soon before the recess begins for the President to appoint a replacement; the Senate rejects a President's nominee just before a recess, too late to select another. . . . Thus the broader construction, encompassing vacancies that initially occur before the beginning of a recess, is the "only construction of the constitution which is compatible with its spirit, reason, and purposes; while, at the same time, it offers no violence to its language." *Id.*, at 633. . . .

. . .

Historical practice over the past 200 years strongly favors the broader interpretation. The tradition of applying the Clause to pre-recess vacancies dates at least to President James Madison. There is no undisputed record of Presidents George Washington, John Adams, or Thomas Jefferson making such an appointment, though the Solicitor General believes he has found records showing that Presidents Washington and Jefferson did so. . . .

President Adams seemed to endorse the broader view of the Clause in writing, though we are not aware of any appointments he made in keeping with that view. . . .

. . . [President James Monroe] received and presumably acted upon Attorney General Wirt's advice, namely that "all vacancies which, from any casualty, happen to exist at a time when the Senate cannot be consulted as to filling them, may be temporarily filled by the President." 1 Op. Atty. Gen., at 633. Nearly every subsequent Attorney General to consider the question throughout the Nation's history has thought the same. *E.g.,* 2 Op. Atty. Gen. 525, 528 (1832); 7 Op. Atty. Gen. 186, 223 (1855); 10 Op. Atty. Gen. 356, 356–357 (1862);12 Op. Atty. Gen. 32, 33 (1866); 12 Op. Atty. Gen., at 452; 14 Op. Atty. Gen. 562, 564 (1875); 15 Op. Atty. Gen. 207 (1877); 16 Op. Atty. Gen. 522, 524 (1880); 17 Op. Atty. Gen. 521 (1883); 18 Op. Atty. Gen. 29, 29–30 (1884); 19 Op. Atty. Gen. 261, 262 (1889); 26 Op. Atty. Gen. 234, 234–235 (1907); 30 Op. Atty. Gen. 314, 315 (1914); 41 Op. Atty. Gen. 463, 465 (1960); 3 Op. OLC 314 (1979); 6 Op. OLC 585, 586 (1982); 20 Op. OLC 124, 161 (1996); 36 Op. OLC ___ (2012). . . . Moreover, the Solicitor General has compiled a list of 102 (mostly uncontested) recess appointments made by Presidents going back to the founding. . . . Given the difficulty of finding accurate information about vacancy dates, that list is undoubtedly far smaller than the actual number. No one disputes that every President since James Buchanan has made recess appointments to preexisting vacancies.

Common sense also suggests that many recess appointees filled vacancies that arose before the recess began. [W]ith research assistance from the Supreme Court Library, we have examined a random sample of the recess appointments made by our two most recent Presidents, and have found that almost all of those appointments filled pre-recess vacancies: Of a sample of 21 recess appointments, 18 filled pre-recess vacancies and only 1 filled a vacancy that arose during the recess in which he was appointed. The precise date on which 2 of the vacancies arose could not be determined. . . .Taken together, we think it is a fair inference that a large proportion of the recess appointments in the history of the Nation have filled pre-existing vacancies.

Did the Senate object? Early on, there was some sporadic disagreement with the broad interpretation. . . . In any event, by 1862 Attorney General Bates could still refer to "the unbroken acquiescence of the Senate" in support of the broad interpretation. . . .

. . .

In light of some linguistic ambiguity, the basic purpose of the Clause, and the historical practice we have described, we conclude that the phrase "all vacancies" includes vacancies that come into existence while the Senate is in session.

V

The third question concerns the calculation of the length of the Senate's "recess." On December 17, 2011, the Senate by unanimous consent adopted a resolution to convene "*pro forma* session[s]" only, with "no business . . . transacted," on every Tuesday and Friday from December 20,2011, through January 20, 2012. 2011 S. J. 923. At the end of each *pro forma* session, the Senate would "adjourn until" the following *pro forma* session. *Ibid.* During that period, the Senate convened and adjourned as agreed. It held *pro forma* sessions on December 20, 23, 27, and 30, and on January 3, 6, 10, 13, 17, and 20; and at the end of each *pro forma* session, it adjourned until the time and date of the next. *Id.,* at 923–924; . . . . The President made the recess appointments before us on January 4, 2012, in between the January 3 and the January 6 *pro forma* sessions. We must determine the significance of these sessions—that is, whether, for purposes of the Clause, we should treat them as periods when the Senate was in session or as periods when it was in recess. If the former, the period between January 3 and January 6 was a 3-day recess, which is too short to trigger the President's recess-appointment power. . . . If the latter, however, then the 3-day period was part of a much longer recess during which the President did have the power to make recess appointments. . . .

In our view, however, the *pro forma* sessions count as sessions, not as periods of recess. We hold that, for purposes of the Recess Appointments Clause, the Senate is in session when it says it is, provided that, under its own rules, it retains the capacity to transact Senate business. The Senate met that standard here.

The standard we apply is consistent with the Constitution's broad delegation of authority to the Senate to determine how and when to conduct its business. The Constitution explicitly empowers the Senate to "determine the Rules of its Proceedings." Art. I, § 5, cl. 2. And we have held that "all matters of method are open to the determination" of the Senate, as long as there is "a reasonable relation between the mode or method of proceeding established by the rule and the result which is sought to be attained" and the rule does not "ignore constitutional restraints or violate fundamental rights." *United States v. Ballin*, 144 U.S. 1, 5 (1892).

In addition, the Constitution provides the Senate with extensive control over its schedule. There are only limited exceptions. See Amdt. 20, § 2 (Congress must meet once a year on January 3, unless it specifies another day by law); Art. II, § 3 (Senate must meet if the President calls it into special session); Art. I, § 5, cl. 4 (neither House may adjourn for more than three days without consent of the other). See also Art. II, § 3 ("[I]n Case of Disagreement between [the Houses], with Respect to the Time of Adjournment, [the President] may adjourn them to such Time as he shall think proper"). The

Constitution thus gives the Senate wide latitude to determine whether and when to have a session, as well as how to conduct the session. This suggests that the Senate's determination about what constitutes a session should merit great respect.

Furthermore, this Court's precedents reflect the breadth of the power constitutionally delegated to the Senate. We generally take at face value the Senate's own report of its actions. When, for example, "the presiding officers" of the House and Senate sign an enrolled bill (and the President "approve[s]" it), "its authentication as a bill that has passed Congress should be deemed complete and unimpeachable." *Marshall Field & Co. v. Clark*, 143 U.S. 649, 672 (1892). By the same principle, when the Journal of the Senate indicates that a quorum was present, under a valid Senate rule, at the time the Senate passed a bill, we will not consider an argument that a quorum was not, in fact, present. *Ballin, supra,* at 9. The Constitution requires the Senate to keep its Journal, Art. I, § 5, cl. 3 ("Each House shall keep a Journal of its proceedings . . . "), and "if reference may be had to" it, "it must be assumed to speak the truth," *Ballin, supra,* at 4.

For these reasons, we conclude that we must give great weight to the Senate's own determination of when it is and when it is not in session. But our deference to the Senate cannot be absolute. When the Senate is without the *capacity* to act, under its own rules, it is not in session even if it so declares. See Tr. of Oral Arg. 69 (acknowledgment by counsel for *amici* Senators that if the Senate had left the Capitol and "effectively given up . . . the business of legislating" then it might be in recess, even if it said it was not). In that circumstance, the Senate is not simply unlikely or unwilling to act upon nominations of the President. It is *unable* to do so. The purpose of the Clause is to ensure the continued functioning of the Federal Government while the Senate is unavailable. . . . This purpose would count for little were we to treat the Senate as though it were in session even when it lacks the ability to provide its "advice and consent." Art. II, § 2, cl. 2. Accordingly, we conclude that when the Senate declares that it is in session and possesses the capacity, under its own rules, to conduct business, it is in session for purposes of the Clause.

Applying this standard, we find that the *pro forma* sessions were sessions for purposes of the Clause. First, the Senate said it was in session. . . . Second, the Senate's rules make clear that during its *pro forma* sessions, despite its resolution that it would conduct no business, the Senate retained the power to conduct business. During any *pro forma* session, the Senate could have conducted business simply by passing a unanimous consent agreement. . . .

By way of contrast, we do not see how the Senate could conduct business during a recess. It could terminate the recess and then, when in session, pass a bill. But in that case, of course, the Senate would no longer be in recess. It would be in session. And that is the crucial point. Senate rules make clear that, once in session, the Senate can act even if it has earlier said that it would not.

. . .

Finally, the Solicitor General warns that our holding may " 'disrup[t] the proper balance between the coordinate branches by preventing the Executive Branch from accomplishing its constitutionally assigned functions.' " . . . We do not see, however, how our holding could significantly alter the constitutional balance. Most appointments are not controversial and do not produce friction between the branches. Where political controversy is serious, the Senate unquestionably has other methods of preventing recess appointments. As the Solicitor General concedes, the Senate could preclude the President from making recess appointments by holding a series of twice-a-week *ordinary* (not *pro forma*) sessions. And the nature of the business conducted at those ordinary sessions—whether, for example, Senators must vote on nominations, or may return to their home States to meet with their constituents—is a matter for the Senate to decide. The Constitution also gives the President (if he has enough allies in Congress) away to force a recess. Art. II, § 3 ("[I]n Case of Disagreement between [the Houses], with Respect to the Time of Adjournment, [the President] may adjourn them to such Time as he shall think proper"). Moreover, the President and Senators engage with each other in many different ways and have a variety of methods of encouraging each other to accept their points of view.

Regardless, the Recess Appointments Clause is not designed to overcome serious institutional friction. It simply provides a subsidiary method for appointing officials when the Senate is away during a recess. Here, as in other contexts, friction between the branches is an inevitable consequence of our constitutional structure. See *Myers*, 272 U.S., at 293 (Brandeis, J., dissenting). That structure foresees resolution not only through judicial interpretation and compromise among the branches but also by the ballot box.

VI

The Recess Appointments Clause responds to a structural difference between the Executive and Legislative Branches: The Executive Branch is perpetually in operation, while the Legislature only acts in intervals separated by recesses. The purpose of the Clause is to allow the Executive to continue operating while the Senate is unavailable. We believe that the Clause's text, standing alone, is ambiguous. It does not resolve whether the President may make appointments during intra-session recesses, or whether he may fill pre-recess vacancies. But the broader reading better serves the Clause's structural function. Moreover, that broader reading is reinforced by centuries of history, which we are hesitant to disturb. We thus hold that the Constitution empowers the President to fill any existing vacancy during any recess—intra-session or inter-session—of sufficient length. Justice Scalia would render illegitimate thousands of recess appointments reaching all the way back to the founding era. More than that: Calling the Clause an "anachronism," he would basically read it out of the Constitution. . . . He performs this act of judicial excision in the name of liberty. We fail to see how excising the Recess Appointments Clause preserves freedom. . . .

. . .

Given our answer to the last question before us, we conclude that the Recess Appointments Clause does not give the President the constitutional authority to make the appointments here at issue. Because the Court of Appeals reached the same ultimate conclusion (though for reasons we reject), its judgment is affirmed.

Justice Scalia, with whom Chief Justice Roberts, Justice Thomas and Justice Alito join, concurring in the judgment.

Except where the Constitution or a valid federal law provides otherwise, all "Officers of the United States" must be appointed by the President "by and with the Advice and Consent of the Senate." U.S. Const., Art. II, § 2, cl. 2. That general rule is subject to an exception: "The President shall have Power to fill up all Vacancies that may happen during the Recess of the Senate, by granting Commissions which shall expire at the End of their next Session." *Id.*, § 2, cl. 3. This case requires us to decide whether the Recess Appointments Clause authorized three appointments made by President Obama to the National Labor Relations Board in January 2012 without the Senate's consent.

To prevent the President's recess-appointment power from nullifying the Senate's role in the appointment process, the Constitution cabins that power in two significant ways. First, it may be exercised only in "the Recess of the Senate," that is, the intermission between two formal legislative sessions. Second, it may be used to fill only those vacancies that "happen during the Recess," that is, offices that become vacant during that intermission. Both conditions are clear from the Constitution's text and structure, and both were well understood at the founding. The Court of Appeals correctly held that the appointments here at issue are invalid because they did not meet either condition.

Today's Court agrees that the appointments were invalid, but for the far narrower reason that they were made during a 3-day break in the Senate's session. On its way to that result, the majority sweeps away the key textual limitations on the recess-appointment power. It holds, first, that the President can make appointments without the Senate's participation even during short breaks in the middle of the Senate's session, and second, that those appointments can fill offices that became vacant long before the break in which they were filled. The majority justifies those atextual results on an adverse-possession theory of executive authority: Presidents have long claimed the powers in question, and the Senate has not disputed those claims with sufficient vigor, so the Court should not "upset the compromises and working arrangements that the elected branches of Government themselves have reached.". . .

The Court's decision transforms the recess-appointment power from a tool carefully designed to fill a narrow and specific need into a weapon to be wielded by future Presidents against future Senates. To reach that result, the majority casts aside the plain, original meaning of the constitutional text in deference to late-arising historical practices that are ambiguous at best. The majority's insistence on deferring to the Executive's untenably broad interpretation of the power is in clear conflict with our precedent and forebodes a diminution of this

Court's role in controversies involving the separation of powers and the structure of government. I concur in the judgment only.

I.   Our Responsibility

Today's majority disregards two overarching principles that ought to guide our consideration of the questions presented here. First, the Constitution's core, government-structuring provisions are no less critical to preserving liberty than are the later adopted provisions of the Bill of Rights. Indeed, "[s]o convinced were the Framers that liberty of the person inheres in structure that at first they did not consider a Bill of Rights necessary." *Clinton v. City of New York*, 524 U.S. 417, 450 (1998) (Kennedy, J., concurring). Those structural provisions reflect the founding generation's deep conviction that "checks and balances were the foundation of a structure of government that would protect liberty." *Bowsher v. Synar*, 478 U.S. 714, 722 (1986). It is for that reason that "the claims of individuals—not of Government departments—have been the principal source of judicial decisions concerning separation of powers and checks and balances.". . . Those decisions all rest on the bedrock principle that "the constitutional structure of our Government" is designed first and foremost not to look after the interests of the respective branches, but to "protec[t] individual liberty.". . .

Second and relatedly, when questions involving the Constitution's government-structuring provisions are presented in a justiciable case, it is the solemn responsibility of the Judicial Branch " 'to say what the law is.' " . . . This Court does not defer to the other branches' resolution of such controversies; as Justice Kennedy has previously written, our role is in no way "lessened" because it might be said that "the two political branches are adjusting their own powers between themselves." *Clinton*, at 449 (concurring opinion). Since the separation of powers exists for the protection of individual liberty, its vitality "does not depend" on "whether 'the encroached-upon branch approves the encroachment.' " *Free Enterprise Fund*, *supra*, at 497 (quoting *New York v. United States*, 505 U.S. 144, 182 (1992)); see also *Freytag* v. *Commissioner*, 501 U.S. 868, 879–880 (1991); *Metropolitan Washington Airports Authority v. Citizens for Abatement of Aircraft Noise, Inc.*, 501 U.S. 252, 276–277 (1991). Rather, policing the "enduring structure" of constitutional government when the political branches fail to do so is "one of the most vital functions of this Court." *Public Citizen v. Department of Justice*, 491 U.S. 440, 468 (1989) (Kennedy, J., concurring in judgment).

Our decision in [*INS v.*] *Chadha* [462 U.S. 919 (1984)] illustrates that principle. There, we held that a statutory provision authorizing one House of Congress to cancel an executive action taken pursuant to statutory authority— a so-called "legislative veto"—exceeded the bounds of Congress's authority under the Constitution. . . . We did not hesitate to hold the legislative veto unconstitutional even though Congress had enacted, and the President had signed, nearly 300 similar provisions over the course of 50 years. . . . Just the opposite: We said the other branches' enthusiasm for the legislative veto "sharpened rather than blunted" our review. . . . Likewise, when the charge is made that a practice "enhances the President's powers beyond" what the

Constitution permits, "[i]t is no answer . . . to say that Congress surrendered its authority by its own hand." *Clinton*, 524 U.S., at 451 (Kennedy, J., concurring). "[O]ne Congress cannot yield up its own powers, much less those of other Congresses to follow. Abdication of responsibility is not part of the constitutional design.". . .

Of course, where a governmental practice has been open, widespread, and unchallenged since the early days of the Republic, the practice should guide our interpretation of an ambiguous constitutional provision. See, *e.g., Alden v. Maine*, 527 U.S. 706, 743–744 (1999); *Bowsher, supra,* at 723–724; *Myers v. United States*, 272 U.S. 52, 174–175 (1926); see also *Youngstown Sheet & Tube Co. v. Sawyer*, 343 U.S. 579, 610 (1952) (Frankfurter, J., concurring) (arguing that "a systematic, unbroken, executive practice, long pursued to the knowledge of the Congress and never before questioned" should inform interpretation of the "Executive Power" vested in the President); *Rutan v. Republican Party of Ill.*, 497 U.S. 62, 95, and n. 1 (1990) (Scalia, J., dissenting). But " '[p]ast practice does not, by itself, create power.' " *Medellín v. Texas*, 552 U.S. 491, 532 (2008) (quoting *Dames & Moore v. Regan*, 453 U.S. 654, 686 (1981)). That is a necessary corollary of the principle that the political branches cannot by agreement alter the constitutional structure. Plainly, then, a self-aggrandizing practice adopted by one branch well after the founding, often challenged, and never before blessed by this Court—in other words, the sort of practice on which the majority relies in this case—does not relieve us of our duty to interpret the Constitution in light of its text, structure, and original understanding.

Ignoring our more recent precedent in this area, which is extensive, the majority relies on *The Pocket Veto Case*, 279 U.S. 655, 689 (1929), for the proposition that when interpreting a constitutional provision "regulating the relationship between Congress and the President," we must defer to the settled practice of the political branches if the provision is " 'in any respect of doubtful meaning.' " . . . The language the majority quotes from that case was pure dictum. The *Pocket Veto* Court had to decide whether a bill passed by the House and Senate and presented to the President less than 10 days before the adjournment of the first session of a particular Congress, but neither signed nor vetoed by the President, became a law. Most of the opinion analyzed that issue like any other legal question and concluded that treating the bill as a law would have been inconsistent with the text and structure of the Constitution. Only near the end of the opinion did the Court add that its conclusion was "confirmed" by longstanding Presidential practice in which Congress appeared to have acquiesced. 279 U.S., at 688–689. We did not suggest that the case would have come out differently had the longstanding practice been otherwise.[1]

---

[1]   The other cases cited by the majority in which we have afforded significant weight to historical practice . . . are consistent with the principles described above. Nearly all involved venerable and unchallenged practices, and constitutional provisions that were either deeply ambiguous or plainly supportive of the practice.

II.   Intra-Session Breaks

The first question presented is whether "the Recess of the Senate," during which the President's recess appointment power is active, is (a) the period between two of the Senate's formal sessions, or (b) any break in the Senate's proceedings. I would hold that "the Recess" is the gap between sessions and that the appointments at issue here are invalid because they undisputedly were made *during* the Senate's session. The Court's contrary conclusion—that "the Recess" includes "breaks in the midst of a session," . . . —is inconsistent with the Constitution's text and structure, and it requires judicial fabrication of vague, unadministrable limits on the recess-appointment power (thus defined) that overstep the judicial role. And although the majority relies heavily on "historical practice," no practice worthy of our deference supports the majority's conclusion on this issue.

A.   Plain Meaning

A sensible interpretation of the Recess Appointments Clause should start by recognizing that the Clause uses the term "Recess" in contradistinction to the term "Session." As Alexander Hamilton wrote: "The time within which the power is to operate 'during the recess of the Senate' and the duration of the appointments 'to the end of the next session' of that body, conspire to elucidate the sense of the provision." The Federalist No. 67, p. 455 (J. Cooke ed. 1961).

In the founding era, the terms "recess" and "session" had well-understood meanings in the marking-out of legislative time. The life of each elected Congress typically consisted (as it still does) of two or more formal sessions separated by adjournments "*sine die,*" that is, without a specified return date. . . . The period *between* two sessions was known as "the recess." See 26 Annals of Cong. 748 (1814) (Sen. Gore) ("The time of the Senate consists of two periods, viz: their session and their recess"). As one scholar has thoroughly demonstrated, "in government practice the phrase 'the Recess' *always* referred to the gap between sessions.". . . By contrast, other provisions of the Constitution use the verb "adjourn" rather than "recess" to refer to the commencement of breaks *during* a formal legislative session. See, *e.g.,* Art. I, § 5, cl. 1; *id.,* § 5, cl. 4.

To be sure, in colloquial usage both words, "recess" and "session," could take on alternative, less precise meanings. A session could include any short period when a legislature's members were "assembled for business," and a recess could refer to any brief "suspension" of legislative "business." 2 N. Webster, American Dictionary of the English Language (1828). So the Continental Congress could complain of the noise from passing carriages disrupting its "daily Session," 29 Journals of the Continental Congress 1774–1789, p. 561 (1785) (J. Fitzpatrick ed.1933), and the House could "take a recess" from 4 o'clock to 6 o'clock, Journal of the House of Representatives, 17th Cong., 2d Sess., p. 259 (1823). But as even the majority acknowledges, the Constitution's use of "the word 'the' in '*the* [R]ecess' " tends to suggest "that the phrase refers to the single break separating formal sessions.". . .

More importantly, neither the Solicitor General nor the majority argues that the Clause uses "session" in its loose, colloquial sense. And if "the next Session" denotes a *formal* session, then "the Recess" must mean the break *between* formal sessions. As every commentator on the Clause until the 20th century seems to have understood, the "Recess" and the "Session" to which the Clause refers are mutually exclusive, alternating states. See, *e.g.,* The Federalist No. 67, at 455 (explaining that appointments would require Senatorial consent "during the session of the Senate" and would be made by the President alone "*in their recess*"); 1 Op. Atty. Gen. 631 (1823) (contrasting vacancies occurring "during the recess of the Senate" with those occurring "during the session of the Senate"); 2 Op. Atty Gen. 525, 527 (1832) (discussing a vacancy that "took place while the Senate was in session, and not during the recess"). It is linguistically implausible to suppose—as the majority does—that the Clause uses one of those terms ("Recess") informally and the other ("Session") formally in a single sentence, with the result that an event can occur during *both* the "Recess" *and* the "Session."

Besides being linguistically unsound, the majority's reading yields the strange result that an appointment made during a short break near the beginning of one official session will not terminate until the end of the *following* official session, enabling the appointment to last for up to two years. The majority justifies that result by observing that the process of confirming a nominee "may take several months.". . . But the average duration of the confirmation process is irrelevant. The Clause's self-evident design is to have the President's unilateral appointment last only until the Senate has "had an *opportunity* to act on the subject." 3 J. Story, Commentaries on the Constitution of the United States § 1551, p. 410 (1833) (emphasis added).

. . .

To avoid the absurd results that follow from its colloquial reading of "the Recess," the majority is forced to declare that some intra-session breaks— though undisputedly within the phrase's colloquial meaning—are simply "too short to trigger the Recess Appointments Clause.". . . But it identifies no textual basis whatsoever for limiting the length of "the Recess," nor does it point to any clear standard for determining how short is too short. It is inconceivable that the Framers would have left the circumstances in which the President could exercise such a significant and potentially dangerous power so utterly indeterminate. Other structural provisions of the Constitution that turn on duration are quite specific: Neither House can adjourn "for more than three days" without the other's consent. Art. I, § 5, cl. 4. The President must return a passed bill to Congress "within ten Days (Sundays excepted)," lest it become a law. *Id.,* § 7, cl. 2. Yet on the majority's view, when the first Senate considered taking a 1-month break, a 3-day weekend, or a half-hour siesta, it had no way of knowing whether the President would be constitutionally authorized to appoint officers in its absence. And any officers appointed in those circumstances would have served under a cloud, unable to determine with any degree of confidence whether their appointments were valid.

Fumbling for some textually grounded standard, the majority seizes on the Adjournments Clause, which bars either House from adjourning for more than three days without the other's consent. . . . It goes without saying that nothing in the constitutional text supports that disposition. . . .

And what about breaks longer than three days? The majority says that a break of four to nine days is "presumptively too short" but that the presumption may be rebutted in an "unusual circumstance," such as a "national catastrophe . . . that renders the Senate unavailable but calls for an urgent response.". . . The majority must hope that the *in terrorem* effect of its "presumptively too short" pronouncement will deter future Presidents from making any recess appointments during 4-to-9-day breaks and thus save us from the absurd spectacle of unelected judges evaluating (after an evidentiary hearing?) whether an alleged "catastrophe" was sufficiently "urgent" to trigger the recess-appointment power. . . .

As for breaks of 10 or more days: We are presumably to infer that such breaks do not trigger any "presumpt[ion]"against recess appointments, but does that mean the President has an utterly free hand? . . . Who knows? The majority does not say, and neither does the Constitution.

Even if the many questions raised by the majority's failure to articulate a standard could be answered, a larger question would remain: If the Constitution's text empowers the President to make appointments during any break in the Senate's proceedings, by what right does the majority subject the President's exercise of that power to vague, court-crafted limitations with no textual basis? The majority claims its temporal guideposts are informed by executive practice, but a President's self-restraint cannot "bind his successors by diminishing their powers." *Free Enterprise Fund*, 561 U.S., at 497; cf. *Clinton* v. *Jones*, 520 U.S. 681, 718 (1997) (Breyer, J., concurring in judgment) ("voluntary actions" by past Presidents "tel[l] us little about what the Constitution commands").

An interpretation that calls for this kind of judicial adventurism cannot be correct. Indeed, if the Clause really did use "Recess" in its colloquial sense, then there would be no "judicially discoverable and manageable standard for resolving" whether a particular break was long enough to trigger the recess-appointment power, making that a nonjusticiable political question. . . .

B.   Historical Practice

For the foregoing reasons, the Constitution's text and structure unambiguously refute the majority's freewheeling interpretation of "the Recess." It is not plausible that the Constitution uses that term in a sense that authorizes the President to make unilateral appointments during *any* break in Senate proceedings, subject only to hazy, atextual limits crafted by this Court centuries after ratification.

The majority, however, insists that history "offers strong support" for its interpretation. The historical practice of the political branches is, of course, irrelevant when the Constitution is clear. But even if the Constitution were thought ambiguous on this point, history does not support the majority's interpretation.

. . .

* * *

What does all this amount to? In short: Intra-session recess appointments were virtually unheard of for the first 130 years of the Republic, were deemed unconstitutional by the first Attorney General to address them, were not openly defended by the Executive until 1921, were not made in significant numbers until after World War II, and have been repeatedly criticized as unconstitutional by Senators of both parties. It is astonishing for the majority to assert that this history lends "strong support," . . . to its interpretation of the Recess Appointments Clause. And the majority's contention that recent executive practice in this area merits deference because the Senate has not done more to oppose it is utterly divorced from our precedent. "The structural interests protected by the Appointments Clause are not those of any one branch of Government but of the entire Republic," *Freytag*, 501 U.S., at 880, and the Senate could not give away those protections even if it wanted to. See *Chadha*, 462 U.S., at 957–958; *Clinton*, 524 U.S., at 451–452 (Kennedy, J., concurring).

Moreover, the majority's insistence that the Senate gainsay an executive practice "as a body" in order to prevent the Executive from acquiring power by adverse possession . . . will systematically favor the expansion of executive power at the expense of Congress. In any controversy between the political branches over a separation of-powers question, staking out a position and defending it over time is far easier for the Executive Branch than for the Legislative Branch. . . .

III. Pre-Recess Vacancies

The second question presented is whether vacancies that "happen during the Recess of the Senate," which the President is empowered to fill with recess appointments, are (a) vacancies that *arise* during the recess, or (b) all vacancies that *exist* during the recess, regardless of when they arose. I would hold that the recess-appointment power is limited to vacancies that arise during the recess in which they are filled, and I would hold that the appointments at issue here—which undisputedly filled pre-recess vacancies—are invalid for that reason as well as for the reason that they were made during the session. The Court's contrary conclusion is inconsistent with the Constitution's text and structure, and it further undermines the balance the Framers struck between Presidential and Senatorial power. Historical practice also fails to support the majority's conclusion on this issue.

C. Plain Meaning

As the majority concedes, "the most natural meaning of 'happens' as applied to a 'vacancy' . . . is that the vacancy 'happens' when it initially occurs.". . . The majority adds that this meaning is most natural "to a modern ear," . . . , but it fails to show that founding-era ears heard it differently. "Happen" meant then, as it does now," [t]o fall out; to chance; to come to pass." 1 Johnson, Dictionary of the English Language 913. Thus, a vacancy that *happened* during the Recess was most reasonably understood as one that *arose* during the recess. It was, of course, possible in certain contexts for the word "happen" to mean "happen to be" rather than "happen to occur," as in the idiom "it so happens." But that meaning is not at all natural when the subject is a vacancy, a state of affairs that comes into existence at a particular moment in time.

In any event, no reasonable reader would have understood the Recess Appointments Clause to use the word "happen" in the majority's "happen to be" sense, and thus to empower the President to fill all vacancies that might *exist* during a recess, regardless of when they arose. For one thing, the Clause's language would have been a surpassingly odd way of giving the President that power. The Clause easily could have been written to convey that meaning clearly: It could have referred to "all Vacancies that may exist during the Recess," or it could have omitted the qualifying phrase entirely and simply authorized the President to "fill up all Vacancies during the Recess.". . .

For another thing, the majority's reading not only strains the Clause's language but distorts its constitutional role, which was meant to be subordinate. As Hamilton explained, appointment with the advice and consent of the Senate was to be "the general mode of appointing officers of the United States." The Federalist No. 67, at 455. The Senate's check on the President's appointment power was seen as vital because " 'manipulation of official appointments' had long been one of the American revolutionary generation's greatest grievances against executive power." *Freytag*, 501 U.S., at 883. The unilateral power conferred on the President by the Recess Appointments Clause was therefore understood to be "nothing more than a supplement" to the "general method" of advice and consent. The Federalist No. 67, at 455.

If, however, the Clause had allowed the President to fill *all* pre-existing vacancies during the recess by granting commissions that would last throughout the following session, it would have been impossible to regard it—as the Framers plainly did—as a mere codicil to the Constitution's principal, power-sharing scheme for filling federal offices. On the majority's reading, the President would have had no need *ever* to seek the Senate's advice and consent for his appointments: Whenever there was a fair prospect of the Senate's rejecting his preferred nominee, the President could have appointed that individual unilaterally during the recess, allowed the appointment to expire at the end of the next session, renewed the appointment the following day, and so on *ad infinitum*. (Circumvention would have been especially easy if, as the majority also concludes, the President was authorized to make such appointments during any intra-session break of more than a few days.) It is unthinkable that such an obvious means for the Executive to expand its power would have been overlooked during the ratification debates.

. . .

D.   Historical Practice

For the reasons just given, it is clear that the Constitution authorizes the President to fill unilaterally only those vacancies that arise during a recess, not every vacancy that happens to exist during a recess. Again, however, the majority says "[h]istorical practice" requires the broader interpretation. . . . And again the majority is mistaken. Even if the Constitution were wrongly thought to be ambiguous on this point, a fair recounting of the relevant history does not support the majority's interpretation.

. . .

The majority correctly admits that there is "no undisputed record of Presidents George Washington, John Adams, or Thomas Jefferson" using a recess appointment to fill a pre-recess vacancy. . . .

James Madison's administration seems to have rejected the majority's reading as well. . . .

. . .

If Madison or his predecessors made any appointments in reliance on the broader reading, those appointments must have escaped general notice. . . .

The Executive Branch did not openly depart from [a narrower] interpretation until 1823, when Wirt issued the opinion discussed earlier. Even within that branch, Wirt's view was hotly contested. . . . Wirt's analysis nonetheless gained ground in the Executive Branch over the next four decades; but it did so slowly and fitfully.

. . .

The tide seemed to turn—as far as the Executive Branch was concerned— in the mid-19th century: Attorney General Cushing in 1855 and Attorney General Bates in 1862 both treated Wirt's position as settled without subjecting it to additional analysis. . . . The Solicitor General identifies only 10 recess appointments made between 1823 and 1863 that filled pre-recess vacancies— about one every four years. . . . That is hardly an impressive number, and most of the appointments were to minor offices . . . unlikely to have gotten the Senate's attention. But the Senate did notice when, in 1862, President Lincoln recess-appointed David Davis to fill a seat on this Court that had become vacant before the recess . . . —and it reacted with vigor.

. . .

Two months after Lincoln's recess appointment of Davis, the Senate directed the Judiciary Committee "to inquire whether the practice . . . of appointing officers to fill vacancies which have not occurred during the recess of Congress, but which existed at the preceding session of Congress, is in accordance with the Constitution; and if not, what remedy shall be applied.". . . The committee responded with a report denouncing Wirt's interpretation of the Clause as "artificial," "forced and unnatural," "unfounded," and a "perversion of language." S. Rep. No. 80, 37th Cong., 3d Sess., pp. 4–6 (1863). . . .

. . .

The majority, . . . , finds it significant that in two small "random sample[s]" of contemporary recess appointments—24 since 1981 and 21 since 2000—the bulk of the appointments appear to have filled pre-existing vacancies. . . . Based on that evidence, the majority thinks it "a fair inference that a large proportion of the recess appointments in the history of the Nation have filled pre-existing vacancies.". . . The extrapolation of that sweeping conclusion from a small set of recent data does not bear even the slightest scrutiny.

. . .

IV. Conclusion

What the majority needs to sustain its judgment is an ambiguous text and a clear historical practice. What it has is a clear text and an at-best-ambiguous historical practice. Even if the Executive could accumulate power through adverse possession by engaging in a *consistent* and *unchallenged* practice over a long period of time, the oft-disputed practices at issue here would not meet that standard. Nor have those practices created any justifiable expectations that could be disappointed by enforcing the Constitution's original meaning. There is thus no ground for the majority's deference to the unconstitutional recess appointment practices of the Executive Branch.

The majority replaces the Constitution's text with a new set of judge-made rules to govern recess appointments. . . . How this new regime will work in practice remains to be seen. . . .

The real tragedy of today's decision is not simply the abolition of the Constitution's limits on the recess appointment power and the substitution of a novel framework invented by this Court. It is the damage done to our separation-of-powers jurisprudence more generally. It is not every day that we encounter a proper case or controversy requiring interpretation of the Constitution's structural provisions. Most of the time, the interpretation of those provisions is left to the political branches—which, in deciding how much respect to afford the constitutional text, often take their cues from this Court. We should therefore take every opportunity to affirm the primacy of the Constitution's enduring principles over the politics of the moment. Our failure to do so today will resonate well beyond the particular dispute at hand. Sad, but true: The Court's embrace of the adverse-possession theory of executive power (a characterization the majority resists but does not refute) will be cited in diverse contexts, including those presently unimagined, and will have the effect of aggrandizing the Presidency beyond its constitutional bounds and undermining respect for the separation of powers.

I concur in the judgment only.

PART 3

GOVERNMENT AND THE INDIVIDUAL: THE PROTECTION OF LIBERTY AND PROPERTY UNDER THE DUE PROCESS AND EQUAL PROTECTION CLAUSES

CHAPTER 9

THE DUE PROCESS, CONTRACT, AND JUST COMPENSATION CLAUSES AND THE REVIEW OF THE REASONABLENESS OF LEGISLATION

1. ECONOMIC REGULATORY LEGISLATION

C. THE JUST COMPENSATION CLAUSE OF THE FIFTH AMENDMENT—WHAT DOES IT ADD TO DUE PROCESS?

1. RESTRICTIONS ON PROPERTY USE

Page 518. Add before Lingle v. Chevron U.S.A. Inc.:

Horne v. Department of Agriculture, 576 U.S. ___, 135 S.Ct. 2419 (2015). With only Justice Sotomayor dissenting on this point, the Court upheld a *per se* taking claim under Loretto v. Teleprompter Manhattan CATV Corp. The claim was asserted by raisin growers required to set aside a portion of their crop for the Government, free of charge ("reserve raisins"), as part of a "marketing order" designed to help stabilize prices under the Agricultural Marketing Act of 1937. The "required allocation" was "determined by the Raisin Administrative Committee, a Government entity composed largely of growers and others in the raisin business appointed by the Secretary of Agriculture." Chief Justice Roberts wrote for the Court and provided this description:

" . . . The Raisin Committee acquires title to the reserve raisins . . . and decides how to dispose of them in its discretion. It sells them in noncompetitive markets, for example to exporters, federal agencies, or foreign governments; donates them to charitable causes; releases them to growers who agree to reduce their raisin production; or disposes of them by 'any other means' consistent with the purposes of the raisin program. 7 CFR § 989.67(b)(5) (2015). Proceeds from Committee sales are principally used to subsidize handlers who sell raisins for export (not including the Hornes, who are not raisin exporters). Raisin growers retain an interest in any net proceeds from sales the Raisin Committee makes, after deductions for the export subsidies and the Committee's administrative expenses. In the years at issue in this case, those proceeds were less than the cost of producing the crop one year, and nothing at all the next."

When the Hornes refused to set aside any raisins for the Government, they were fined "the market value of the missing raisins—some $480,000—as well as an additional civil penalty of just over $200,000 for disobeying the order to turn them over." Their defense that the reserve requirement "was an unconstitutional taking of their property under the Fifth Amendment" was rejected by the Ninth Circuit, which viewed it as a permissible "use restriction." The Court reversed, holding first that personal property is as "protected against physical appropriation" as is real property, and that the reserve requirement "is a clear physical taking":

"Actual raisins are transferred from the growers to the Government. Title to the raisins passes to the Raisin Committee. . . . The Committee's raisins must be physically segregated from free-tonnage raisins. 7 CFR § 989.66(b)(2). Reserve raisins are sometimes left on the premises of handlers, but they are held 'for the account' of the Government. § 989.66(a). The Committee disposes of what become its raisins as it wishes, to promote the purposes of the raisin marketing order.

"Raisin growers subject to the reserve requirement thus lose the entire 'bundle' of property rights in the appropriated raisins—'the rights to possess, use and dispose of' them, *Loretto*, . . . —with the exception of the speculative hope that some residual proceeds may be left when the Government is done with the raisins and has deducted the expenses of implementing all aspects of the marketing order."

Chief Justice Roberts emphasized "the settled difference in our takings jurisprudence between appropriation and regulation. A physical taking of raisins and a regulatory limit on production may have the same economic impact on a grower. The Constitution, however, is concerned with means as well as ends. The Government has broad powers, but the means it uses to achieve its ends must be 'consist[ent] with the letter and spirit of the constitution.' *McCulloch v. Maryland*, 4 Wheat. 316, 421 (1819)."

Second, the Court held, the "fact that the growers retain a contingent interest of indeterminate value does not mean there has been no physical taking, particularly since the value of the interest depends on the discretion of the taker, and may be worthless, as it was for one of the two years at issue here." The Chief Justice said that the "Government and dissent . . . confuse our inquiry concerning *per se* takings with our analysis for regulatory takings": "[O]nce there is a taking, as in the case of a physical appropriation, any payment from the Government in connection with that action goes, at most, to the question of just compensation. . . . That is not an issue here: The Hornes did not receive any net proceeds from Raisin Committee sales for the years at issue, because they had not set aside any reserve raisins in those years (and, in any event, there were no net proceeds in one of them)."

Third, the Court rejected the Government's contention "that the reserve requirement is not a taking because raisin growers voluntarily choose to participate in the raisin market." Instead, "[s]elling produce in interstate commerce, although certainly subject to reasonable government regulation, is . . . not a special governmental benefit that the Government may hold hostage, to be ransomed by the waiver of constitutional protection." Raisins "are private property—the fruit of the growers' labor[, and a]ny physical taking of them for public use must be accompanied by just compensation."

Finally, the Court rejected the Government's request for a remand if the Court concluded, as it did, that there had been a taking. The Government contended that in order to calculate what compensation would be due "the calculation must consider what the value of the reserve raisins would have been without the price support program, as well as 'other benefits . . . from the regulatory program, such as higher consumer demand for raisins spurred by enforcement of quality standards and promotional activities.'" The Court, however, insisted that the proper measure of compensation was the market value of the raisins at the time of the taking, finding "no support" for the Government's "hypothetical-based approach, or its notion that general regulatory activity such as enforcement of quality standards can constitute just compensation for a specific physical taking." The Government had "already calculated the amount of just compensation in this case, when it fined the Hornes the fair market value of the raisins: $483,843.53 [and could not] now disavow that valuation. . . . There is accordingly no need for a remand; the Hornes should simply be relieved of the obligation to pay the fine and associated civil penalty they were assessed when they resisted the Government's effort to take their raisins."

Although agreeing that there had been a taking, Justice Breyer, in his opinion concurring in part and dissenting in part, joined by Justices Ginsburg and Kagan, would have remanded the case to allow the lower courts "to consider argument on the question of just compensation." To him, "[t]he marketing order may afford just compensation for the takings of raisins that it imposes. If that is correct, then the reserve requirement does not violate the Takings Clause." He wrote in part:

" . . . When the Government takes as reserve raisins a percentage of the annual crop, the raisin owners retain the remaining . . . raisins. The reserve requirement is intended, at least in part, to enhance the price that free-tonnage raisins will fetch on the open market. . . . And any such enhancement matters. This Court's precedents indicate that, when calculating the just compensation that the Fifth Amendment requires, a court should deduct from the value of the taken (reserve) raisins any enhancement caused by the taking to the value of the remaining (free-tonnage) raisins.

" . . .

" . . . The value of the raisins taken might exceed the value of the benefit conferred. In that case, the reserve requirement effects a taking without just compensation, and the Hornes' decision not to comply with the requirement was justified. On the other hand, the benefit might equal or exceed the value of the raisins taken. In that case, the California Raisin Marketing Order does not effect a taking without just compensation."

Justice Sotomayor's lone dissent urged that "*Loretto*—when properly understood—does not encompass the circumstances of this case because it only applies where all property rights have been destroyed by governmental action." She viewed "a claim of a *Loretto* taking" as "a bold accusation that carries with it a heavy burden. To qualify as a *per se* taking under *Loretto*, the governmental action must be so completely destructive to the property owner's rights—all of them—as to render the ordinary, generally applicable protections of the *Penn Central* framework either a foregone conclusion or unequal to the task. Simply put, the retention of even one property right that is not destroyed is sufficient to defeat a claim of a *per se* taking under *Loretto*." Because the Hornes "retain at least one meaningful property interest in the reserve raisins: the right to receive some money for their disposition[,]" she argued that "this case does not fall within the narrow confines of *Loretto*."

Moreover, "another line of cases . . . , when viewed together, teach that the government may require certain property rights to be given up as a condition of entry into a regulated market without effecting a *per se* taking." She elaborated in part:

" . . . [I]nsofar as the Hornes wish to sell some raisins in a market regulated by the Government and at a price supported by governmental intervention, the Order requires that they give up the right to sell a portion of those raisins at that price and instead accept disposal of them at a lower price. Given that we have held that the Government may impose a price on the privilege of engaging in a particular business without effecting a taking—which is all that the Order does—it follows that the Order at the very least does not run afoul of our *per se* takings jurisprudence. Under a different takings test, one might reach a different conclusion. But the Hornes have advanced only this narrow *per se* takings claim, and that claim fails."

Justice Sotomayor criticized the Court for "unsettl[ing] an important area of our jurisprudence[,] . . . stretching the otherwise strict *Loretto* test into an unadministrable one, and deeming regulatory takings jurisprudence irrelevant in some undefined set of cases involving government regulation of property rights." She found this "intervention" especially "baffling [in] that it ultimately instructs the Government that it can permissibly achieve its market control goals by imposing a quota without offering raisin producers a way of reaping any return whatsoever on the raisins they cannot sell. I have trouble understanding why anyone would prefer that."

2.   MANDATED ACCESS TO PROPERTY

Page 529. Add after City of Monterey v. Del Monte Dunes:

Koontz v. St. Johns River Water Management District, 570 U.S. __, 133 S.Ct. 2586 (2013). A developer who sought a permit to build on the 3.7-acre northern portion of his 14.9-acre parcel that was largely classified as wetlands subject to regulation offered a conservation easement on the 11-acre southern portion in exchange for the permit, as mitigation for the environmental effects of the development. The District considered that "inadequate" and offered to "approve construction only if he agreed to one of two concessions"—either "reduce the . . . development to 1 acre and deed to the District a conservation easement on the remaining 13.9 acres[,]" or "proceed [to] build[ ] on 3.7 acres and deed[ ] a conservation easement to the government on the remainder of the property, if he also agreed to hire contractors to make improvements to . . . enhance [about] 50 acres of District-owned wetlands" several miles away. The District also "said that it 'would . . . favorably consider' alternatives to its suggested offsite mitigation projects if petitioner proposed something 'equivalent.' " The developer sued under a Florida statute "allow[ing] owners to recover 'monetary damages' if a state agency's action is 'an unreasonable exercise of the state's police power constituting a taking without just compensation.' " Given the developer's offer and its finding "that the property's northern section had already been 'seriously degraded' by extensive construction on the surrounding parcels[,] . . . the trial court concluded that any further mitigation in the form of payment for offsite improvements to District property lacked both a nexus and rough proportionality to the environmental impact of the proposed construction" in violation of *Nollan* and *Dolan*. The intermediate appellate court affirmed, but the Florida Supreme Court reversed, distinguishing *Nollan* and *Dolan* first because the District denied the application due to the developer's refusal to make concessions rather than approve the application on condition of meeting the District's demands, and second because the District did not demand an interest in real property, but demanded money instead. The Supreme Court reversed, 5–4, holding "that the government's demand for property from a land-use permit applicant must satisfy the requirements of *Nollan* and *Dolan* even when the government denies the permit and even when its demand is for money." The Court remanded the case, however, "express[ing] no view on the merits of petitioner's claim that respondent's actions here failed to comply with the principles set forth in this opinion and those two cases."

Justice Alito's majority opinion rested on "an overarching principle, known as the unconstitutional conditions doctrine, that vindicates the Constitution's enumerated rights by preventing the government from coercing people into giving them up." As applied here, he wrote in part:

"*Nollan* and *Dolan* 'involve a special application' of this doctrine that protects the Fifth Amendment right to just compensation for property the government takes when owners apply for land-use permits. . . . Our decisions in those cases reflect two realities of the permitting process. The first is that land-use permit applicants are especially vulnerable to the type of coercion that the unconstitutional conditions doctrine prohibits because the government often has broad discretion to deny a permit that is worth far more than property it would like to take. . . . Extortionate demands of this sort frustrate the Fifth Amendment right to just compensation, and the unconstitutional conditions doctrine prohibits them.

"A second reality of the permitting process is that many proposed land uses threaten to impose costs on the public that dedications of property can offset. . . . Insisting that landowners internalize the negative externalities of their conduct is a hallmark of responsible land-use policy, and we have long sustained such regulations against constitutional attack. . . .

"*Nollan* and *Dolan* accommodate both realities. . . . Under *Nollan* and *Dolan* the government may choose whether and how a permit applicant is required to mitigate the impacts of a proposed development, but it may not leverage its legitimate interest in mitigation to pursue governmental ends that lack an essential nexus and rough proportionality to those impacts."

Justice Alito said that the principles undergirding *Nollan* and *Dolan* "do not change depending on whether the government *approves* a permit on the condition that the applicant turn over property or *denies* a permit because the applicant refuses to do so." Rather, "[o]ur unconstitutional conditions cases have long refused to attach significance to the distinction between conditions precedent and conditions subsequent." He elaborated that "[e]xtortionate demands for property in the land use permitting context run afoul of the Takings Clause not because they take property but because they impermissibly burden the right not to have property taken without just compensation." And he declared that "we have repeatedly rejected the argument that if the government need not confer a benefit at all, it can withhold the benefit because someone refuses to give up constitutional rights." Hence, "[e]ven if respondent would have been entirely within its rights in denying the permit for some other reason, that greater authority does not imply a lesser power to condition permit approval on petitioner's forfeiture of his constitutional rights." He added this caveat, however:

"That is not to say, however, that there is *no* relevant difference between a consummated taking and the denial of a permit based on an unconstitutionally extortionate demand. Where the permit is denied and the condition is never imposed, nothing has been taken. While the unconstitutional conditions doctrine recognizes that this *burdens* a constitutional right, the Fifth Amendment mandates a particular *remedy*—just compensation—only for takings. In cases where there is an excessive demand but no taking, whether money damages are available is not a question of federal constitutional law but of the cause of action—whether state or federal—on which the landowner relies. Because petitioner brought his claim pursuant to a state law cause of action, the Court has no occasion to discuss what remedies might be available for a *Nollan/Dolan* unconstitutional conditions violation either here or in other cases."

The Court's additional holding "that so-called 'monetary exactions' must satisfy the nexus and rough proportionality requirements of *Nollan* and *Dolan*" was premised on several grounds. First, it would otherwise be "very easy for land-use permitting officials to evade the limitations of *Nollan* and *Dolan*. Because the government need only provide a permit applicant with one alternative that satisfies the nexus and rough proportionality standards, a permitting authority wishing to exact an easement could simply give the owner a choice of either surrendering an easement or making a payment equal to the easement's value." Second, the "fulcrum this case turns on is the direct link between the government's demand and a specific parcel of real property. Because of that direct link, this case implicates the central concern of *Nollan* and *Dolan*: the risk that the government may use its substantial power and discretion in land-use permitting to pursue governmental ends that lack an essential nexus and rough proportionality to the effects of the proposed new use of the specific property at issue, thereby diminishing without justification the value of the property." Third, rather than claiming "that the government can commit a *regulatory* taking by directing someone to spend money[,] . . . petitioner's claim rests on the more limited proposition that when the government commands the relinquishment of funds linked to a specific, identifiable property interest such as a bank account or parcel of real property, a *'per se* [takings] approach' is the proper mode of analysis under the Court's precedent." Finally, "to order a landowner to make improvements to public lands that are nearby . . . would transfer an interest in property from the landowner to the government. For that reason, any such demand would amount to a *per se* taking similar to the taking of an easement or a lien."

Although the majority acknowledged that taxes and user fees are not "takings," it concluded that the Court had "had little trouble distinguishing between the two." And it "disagree[d] with the dissent's forecast that our decision will work a revolution in land use law by depriving local governments of the ability to charge reasonable permitting fees."

Justice Kagan's dissent, joined by Justices Ginsburg, Breyer, and Sotomayor, agreed with the majority that the "*Nollan-Dolan* standard applies not only when the government approves a development permit conditioned on the owner's conveyance of a property interest (*i.e.*, imposes a condition subsequent), but also when the government denies a permit until the owner meets the condition (*i.e.*, imposes a condition precedent)." But "extend[ing] *Nollan* and *Dolan* to cases in which the government conditions a permit not on the transfer of real property, but instead on the payment or expenditure of money[,] . . . [unwisely] threatens to subject a vast array of land-use regulations, applied daily in States and localities throughout the country, to heightened constitutional scrutiny." Also, the District in any event "never demanded *anything* (including money) in exchange for a permit[,]" and "no taking occurred in this case because Koontz never acceded to a demand (even had there been one), and so no property changed hands[, and thus] Koontz . . . cannot claim just compensation under the Fifth Amendment."

The dissent elaborated in part:

"[T]he *Nollan-Dolan* test applies only when the property the government demands during the permitting process is the kind it otherwise would have to pay for—or, put differently, when the appropriation of that property, outside the permitting process, would constitute a taking. . . . Even the majority acknowledges this basic point about *Nollan* and *Dolan*. . . .

"Here, Koontz claims that the District demanded that he spend money to improve public wetlands, not that he hand over a real property interest. . . . The key question then is: Independent of the permitting process, does requiring a person to pay money to the government, or spend money on its behalf, constitute a taking requiring just compensation? Only if the answer is yes does the *Nollan-Dolan* test apply.

"But we have already answered that question no. . . .

"Thus, a requirement that a person pay money to repair public wetlands is not a taking. . . . Because the government is merely imposing a 'general liability' to pay money, . . . the order to repair wetlands, viewed independent of the permitting process, does not constitute a taking. And that means the order does not trigger the *Nollan-Dolan* test, because it does not force Koontz to relinquish a constitutional right.

. . .

"The majority . . . falls back on the sole way the District's alleged demand related to a property interest: The demand arose out of the permitting process for Koontz's land. But under the analytic framework that *Nollan* and *Dolan* established, that connection alone is insufficient to trigger heightened scrutiny. . . .

"The majority's approach, on top of its analytic flaws, threatens significant practical harm. By applying *Nollan* and *Dolan* to permit conditions requiring monetary payments—with no express limitation except as to taxes—the majority extends the Takings Clause, with its notoriously 'difficult' and 'perplexing' standards, into the very heart of local land-use regulation and service delivery. . . . Cities and towns across the nation impose many kinds of permitting fees every day. Some enable a government to mitigate a new development's impact on the community, like increased traffic or pollution—or destruction of wetlands. . . . Others cover the direct costs of providing services like sewage or water to the development. . . . Still others are meant to limit the number of landowners who engage in a certain activity, as fees for liquor licenses do. . . . All now must meet *Nollan* and *Dolan*'s nexus and proportionality tests. The Federal Constitution thus will decide whether one town is overcharging for sewage, or another is setting the price to sell liquor too high. And the flexibility of state and local governments to take the most routine actions to enhance their communities will diminish accordingly.

"That problem becomes still worse because the majority's distinction between monetary 'exactions' and taxes is so hard to apply. . . . Nor does the majority's opinion provide any help with that issue: Perhaps its most striking feature is its refusal to say even a word about how to make the distinction that will now determine whether a given fee is subject to heightened scrutiny.

"Perhaps the Court means in the future to curb the intrusion into local affairs that its holding will accomplish. . . . At the least, the majority's refusal "to say more" about the scope of its new rule now casts a cloud on every decision by every local government to require a person seeking a permit to pay or spend money.

. . .

"In sum, *Nollan* and *Dolan* restrain governments from using the permitting process to do what the Takings Clause would otherwise prevent—*i.e.*, take a specific property interest without just compensation. Those cases have no application when governments impose a general financial obligation as part of the permitting process. . . . I would keep *Nollan* and *Dolan* in their intended sphere and affirm the Florida Supreme Court."

Justice Kagan also would have "affirm[ed] the judgment below for two independent reasons." First:

"[T]he District never made a demand or set a condition—not to cede an identifiable property interest, not to undertake a particular mitigation project, not even to write a check to the government. Instead, the District suggested to Koontz several non-exclusive ways to make his applications conform to state law. The District's only hard-and-fast requirement was that Koontz do something—anything—to satisfy the relevant permitting criteria. Koontz's failure to obtain the permits therefore did not result from his refusal to accede to an allegedly extortionate demand or condition; rather, it arose from the legal deficiencies of his applications, combined with his unwillingness to correct them *by any means. Nollan* and *Dolan* were never meant to address such a run-of-the-mill denial of a land-use permit. As applications of the unconstitutional conditions doctrine, those decisions require a condition; and here, there was none."

Second, since "Koontz never paid a cent, so the District took nothing from him[,]" and all the Justices agree that he thus "is not entitled to just compensation under the Takings Clause[,]" there was no reason for a remand to the Florida Supreme Court, because the Florida statute allows "damages only for 'an unreasonable exercise of the state's police power constituting a taking without just compensation.' " Justice Kagan then asked:

" . . . In what legal universe could a law authorizing damages only for a 'taking' also provide damages when (as all agree) no taking has occurred? I doubt that inside-out, upside-down universe is the State of Florida. Certainly, none of the Florida courts in this case suggested that the majority's hypothesized remedy actually exists; rather, the trial and appellate courts imposed a damages remedy on the mistaken theory that there *had* been a taking (although of exactly what neither was clear). . . ."

2. PROTECTION OF PERSONAL LIBERTIES

B. FAMILY AND MARITAL RELATIONSHIPS

Page 553. Add after Zablocki v. Redhail:

Obergefell v. Hodges

576 U.S. ___, 135 S.Ct. 2584, 192 L.Ed.2d 609 (2015).

Justice Kennedy delivered the opinion of the Court.

The Constitution promises liberty to all within its reach, a liberty that includes certain specific rights that allow persons, within a lawful realm, to define and express their identity. The petitioners in these cases seek to find that liberty by marrying someone of the same sex and having their marriages deemed lawful on the same terms and conditions as marriages between persons of the opposite sex.

I

These cases come from Michigan, Kentucky, Ohio, and Tennessee, States that define marriage as a union between one man and one woman. [Fourteen same-sex couples, and two men whose same-sex partners are deceased, claimed in different actions that denying them the right to marry or to have their marriages, lawfully performed in another State, given full recognition, violated the Fourteenth Amendment. Judgments in their favor in various district courts were reversed by the Sixth Circuit in consolidated cases.]

. . . This Court granted review, limited to two questions. . . . The first, presented by the cases from Michigan and Kentucky, is whether the Fourteenth Amendment requires a State to license a marriage between two people of the same sex. The second, presented by the cases from Ohio, Tennessee, and, again, Kentucky, is whether the Fourteenth Amendment requires a State to recognize a same-sex marriage licensed and performed in a State which does grant that right.

II

Before addressing the principles and precedents that govern these cases, it is appropriate to note the history of the subject now before the Court.

A

From their beginning to their most recent page, the annals of human history reveal the transcendent importance of marriage. The lifelong union of a man and a woman always has promised nobility and dignity to all persons, without regard to their station in life. Marriage is sacred to those who live by their religions and offers unique fulfillment to those who find meaning in the secular realm. Its dynamic allows two people to find a life that could not be found alone, for a marriage becomes greater than just the two persons. Rising from the most basic human needs, marriage is essential to our most profound hopes and aspirations.

The centrality of marriage to the human condition makes it unsurprising that the institution has existed for millennia and across civilizations. . . . It is fair and necessary to say these references were based on the understanding that marriage is a union between two persons of the opposite sex.

That history is the beginning of these cases. The respondents say it should be the end as well. To them, it would demean a timeless institution if the concept and lawful status of marriage were extended to two persons of the same sex. Marriage, in their view, is by its nature a gender-differentiated union of man and woman. This view long has been held—and continues to be held—in good faith by reasonable and sincere people here and throughout the world.

The petitioners acknowledge this history but contend that these cases cannot end there. Were their intent to demean the revered idea and reality of marriage, the petitioners' claims would be of a different order. But that is neither their purpose nor their submission. To the contrary, it is the enduring importance of marriage that underlies the[ir] contentions. . . . Far from seeking to devalue marriage, the petitioners seek it for themselves because of their respect—and need—for its privileges and responsibilities. And their immutable nature dictates that same-sex marriage is their only real path to this profound commitment.

Recounting the circumstances of three of these cases illustrates the urgency of the petitioners' cause from their perspective. [Obergefell and his partner of over two decades had a "lasting, committed relation" in Ohio and chose to marry in Maryland after the latter was diagnosed with the progressive, debilitating, and incurable disease of ALS. He died three months later, but] Ohio law does not permit Obergefell to be listed as the surviving spouse on [his] death certificate. By statute, they must remain strangers even in death, a state-imposed separation Obergefell deems "hurtful for the rest of time.". . . He brought suit to be shown as the surviving spouse on [his partner's] death certificate.

[Two female nurses from Michigan, also in a committed relationship, are raising three adopted children together, one of whom needed "around-the-clock care" and another with special needs.] Michigan, however, permits only opposite-sex married couples or single individuals to adopt, so each child can have only one woman as his or her legal parent. If an emergency were to arise, schools and hospitals may treat the three children as if they had only one parent. And, were tragedy to befall either [woman], the other would have no legal rights over the children she had not been permitted to adopt. This couple seeks relief from the continuing uncertainty their unmarried status creates in their lives.

[A soldier married his partner in New York before being deployed to Afghanistan, and they settled in Tennessee on his return to work for the Army there.] Their lawful marriage is stripped from them whenever they reside in Tennessee, returning and disappearing as they travel across state lines. . . .

The[se] cases . . . involve other petitioners as well. . . . Their stories reveal that they seek not to denigrate marriage but rather to live their lives, or honor their spouses' memory, joined by its bond.

B

. . . The history of marriage is one of both continuity and change. That institution—even as confined to opposite-sex relations—has evolved over time.

For example, marriage was once viewed as an arrangement by the couple's parents based on political, religious, and financial concerns; but by the time of the Nation's founding it was understood to be a voluntary contract between a man and a woman. . . . As the role and status of women changed, the institution further evolved. Under the centuries-old doctrine of coverture, a married man and woman were treated by the State as a single, male-dominated legal entity. . . . As women gained legal, political, and property rights, and as society began to understand that women have their own equal dignity, the law of coverture was abandoned. . . . These . . . developments in the institution of marriage . . . worked deep transformations in its structure, affecting aspects of marriage long viewed by many as essential. . . .

These new insights have strengthened, not weakened, the institution of marriage. Indeed, changed understandings of marriage are characteristic of a Nation where new dimensions of freedom become apparent to new generations, often through perspectives that begin in pleas or protests and then are considered in the political sphere and the judicial process.

This dynamic can be seen in the Nation's experiences with the rights of gays and lesbians. Until the mid-20th century, same-sex intimacy long had been condemned as immoral by the state itself in most Western nations, a belief often embodied in the criminal law. For this reason, among others, many persons did not deem homosexuals to have dignity in their own distinct identity. . . . Even when a greater awareness of the humanity and integrity of homosexual persons came in the period after World War II, the argument that gays and lesbians had a just claim to dignity was in conflict with both law and widespread social conventions. . . .

For much of the 20th century, moreover, homosexuality was treated as an illness. . . . Only in more recent years have psychiatrists and others recognized that sexual orientation is both a normal expression of human sexuality and immutable. . . .

In the late 20th century, following substantial cultural and political developments, same-sex couples began to lead more open and public lives and to establish families. This development was followed by a quite extensive discussion of the issue in both governmental and private sectors and by a shift in public attitudes toward greater tolerance. As a result, questions about the rights of gays and lesbians soon reached the courts, where the issue could be discussed in the formal discourse of the law.

[Justice Kennedy recounted legal developments, including Bowers v. Hardwick, 478 U. S. 186 (1986), Romer v. Evans, 517 U. S. 620 (1996), and Lawrence v. Texas, 539 U. S. 558 (2003), as well as state court decisions and laws on both sides of the question, and the 1996 Defense of Marriage Act (DOMA), defining marriage for all federal-law purposes as "only a legal union between one man and one woman as husband and wife." He then continued:]

. . . Two Terms ago, in United States v. Windsor, 570 U. S. ___ (2013), this Court invalidated DOMA to the extent it barred the Federal Government from treating same-sex marriages as valid even when they were lawful in the State where they were licensed. DOMA, the Court held, impermissibly disparaged those same-sex couples "who wanted to affirm their commitment to one another before their children, their family, their friends, and their community.". . .

. . .

After years of litigation, legislation, referenda, and the discussions that attended these public acts, the States are now divided on the issue of same-sex marriage. . . .

III

. . .

The identification and protection of fundamental rights is an enduring part of the judicial duty to interpret the Constitution. That responsibility, however, "has not been reduced to any formula." Poe v. Ullman, 367 U. S. 497, 542 (1961) (Harlan, J., dissenting). Rather, it requires courts to exercise reasoned judgment in identifying interests of the person so fundamental that the State must accord them its respect. . . . History and tradition guide and discipline this inquiry but do not set its outer boundaries. . . . That method respects our history and learns from it without allowing the past alone to rule the present.

The nature of injustice is that we may not always see it in our own times. The generations that wrote and ratified the Bill of Rights and the Fourteenth Amendment did not presume to know the extent of freedom in all of its dimensions, and so they entrusted to future generations a charter protecting the right of all persons to enjoy liberty as we learn its meaning. When new insight reveals discord between the Constitution's central protections and a received legal stricture, a claim to liberty must be addressed.

Applying these established tenets, the Court has long held the right to marry is protected by the Constitution. . . . Loving v. Virginia, 388 U. S. 1, 12 (1967), . . . Zablocki v. Redhail, 434 U. S. 374, 384 (1978), . . . [and] Turner v. Safley, 482 U. S. 78, 95 (1987), which held the right to marry was abridged by regulations limiting the privilege of prison inmates to marry. Over time and in other contexts, the Court has reiterated that the right to marry is fundamental under the Due Process Clause. . . .

It cannot be denied that this Court's cases describing the right to marry presumed a relationship involving opposite-sex partners. The Court, like many institutions, has made assumptions defined by the world and time of which it is a part. This was evident in Baker v. Nelson, 409 U. S. 810, a one-line summary decision issued in 1972, holding the exclusion of same-sex couples from marriage did not present a substantial federal question.

Still, . . . in assessing whether the force and rationale of its cases apply to same-sex couples, the Court must respect the basic reasons why the right to marry has been long protected. . . .

This analysis compels the conclusion that same-sex couples may exercise the right to marry. The four principles and traditions to be discussed demonstrate that the reasons marriage is fundamental under the Constitution apply with equal force to same-sex couples.

A first premise of the Court's relevant precedents is that the right to personal choice regarding marriage is inherent in the concept of individual autonomy. . . .

Choices about marriage shape an individual's destiny. . . .

The nature of marriage is that, through its enduring bond, two persons together can find other freedoms, such as expression, intimacy, and spirituality. This is true for all persons, whatever their sexual orientation. . . . There is dignity in the bond between two men or two women who seek to marry and in their autonomy to make such profound choices. . . .

A second principle in this Court's jurisprudence is that the right to marry is fundamental because it supports a two-person union unlike any other in its importance to the committed individuals. This point was central to Griswold v. Connecticut. . . . And in *Turner*, the Court again acknowledged the intimate association protected by this right, holding prisoners could not be denied the right to marry because their committed relationships satisfied the basic reasons why marriage is a fundamental right. . . . The right to marry thus dignifies couples who "wish to define themselves by their commitment to each other." *Windsor*, . . . Marriage responds to the universal fear that a lonely person might call out only to find no one there. It offers the hope of companionship and understanding and assurance that while both still live there will be someone to care for the other.

As this Court held in *Lawrence*, same-sex couples have the same right as opposite-sex couples to enjoy intimate association. *Lawrence* invalidated laws that made same-sex intimacy a criminal act. . . . But while *Lawrence* confirmed a dimension of freedom that allows individuals to engage in intimate association without criminal liability, it does not follow that freedom stops there. Outlaw to outcast may be a step forward, but it does not achieve the full promise of liberty.

A third basis for protecting the right to marry is that it safeguards children and families and thus draws meaning from related rights of childrearing, procreation, and education. . . . By giving recognition and legal structure to their parents' relationship, marriage allows children "to understand the integrity and closeness of their own family and its concord with other families in their community and in their daily lives." *Windsor* . . . Marriage also affords the permanency and stability important to children's best interests. . . .

As all parties agree, many same-sex couples provide loving and nurturing homes to their children, whether biological or adopted. And hundreds of thousands of children are presently being raised by such couples. . . . Most States have allowed gays and lesbians to adopt, either as individuals or as couples, and many adopted and foster children have same-sex parents. . . . This provides powerful confirmation from the law itself that gays and lesbians can create loving, supportive families.

Excluding same-sex couples from marriage thus conflicts with a central premise of the right to marry. Without the recognition, stability, and predictability marriage offers, their children suffer the stigma of knowing their families are somehow lesser. They also suffer the significant material costs of being raised by unmarried parents, relegated through no fault of their own to a more difficult and uncertain family life. The marriage laws at issue here thus harm and humiliate the children of same-sex couples. See *Windsor* . . .

That is not to say the right to marry is less meaningful for those who do not or cannot have children. An ability, desire, or promise to procreate is not and has not been a prerequisite for a valid marriage in any State. . . . The constitutional marriage right has many aspects, of which childbearing is only one.

Fourth and finally, this Court's cases and the Nation's traditions make clear that marriage is a keystone of our social order. . . . Marriage remains a building block of our national community.

. . . [W]hile the States are in general free to vary the benefits they confer on all married couples, they have throughout our history made marriage the basis for an expanding list of governmental rights, benefits, and responsibilities. These aspects of marital status include: taxation; inheritance and property rights; rules of intestate succession; spousal privilege in the law of evidence; hospital access; medical decisionmaking authority; adoption rights; the rights and benefits of survivors; birth and death certificates; professional ethics rules; campaign finance restrictions; workers' compensation benefits; health insurance; and child custody, support, and visitation rules. See Brief for United States as Amicus Curiae 6–9; Brief for American Bar Association as Amicus Curiae 8–29. Valid marriage under state law is also a significant status for over a thousand provisions of federal law. See *Windsor* . . . The States have contributed to the fundamental character of the marriage right by placing that institution at the center of so many facets of the legal and social order.

There is no difference between same- and opposite-sex couples with respect to this principle. Yet by virtue of their exclusion from that institution, same-sex couples are denied the constellation of benefits that the States have linked to marriage. This harm results in more than just material burdens. Same-sex couples are consigned to an instability many opposite-sex couples would deem intolerable in their own lives. As the State itself makes marriage all the more precious by the significance it attaches to it, exclusion from that status has the effect of teaching that gays and lesbians are unequal in important respects. It demeans gays and lesbians for the State to lock them out of a central institution of the Nation's society. Same-sex couples, too, may aspire to the transcendent purposes of marriage and seek fulfillment in its highest meaning.

The limitation of marriage to opposite-sex couples may long have seemed natural and just, but its inconsistency with the central meaning of the fundamental right to marry is now manifest. With that knowledge must come the recognition that laws excluding same-sex couples from the marriage right impose stigma and injury of the kind prohibited by our basic charter.

. . . [R]espondents refer to Washington v. Glucksberg, 521 U. S. 702, 721 (1997), which called for a " 'careful description' " of fundamental rights[, and] assert the petitioners do not seek to exercise the right to marry but rather a new and nonexistent "right to same-sex marriage.". . . *Glucksberg* did insist that liberty under the Due Process Clause must be defined in a most circumscribed manner, with central reference to specific historical practices. Yet while that approach may have been appropriate for the asserted right there involved (physician-assisted suicide), it is inconsistent with the approach this Court has used in discussing other fundamental rights, including marriage and intimacy. *Loving* did not ask about a "right to interracial marriage"; *Turner* did not ask about a "right of inmates to marry"; and *Zablocki* did not ask about a "right of fathers with unpaid child support duties to marry." Rather, each case inquired about the right to marry in its comprehensive sense, asking if there was a sufficient justification for excluding the relevant class from the right. . . .

That principle applies here. If rights were defined by who exercised them in the past, then received practices could serve as their own continued justification and new groups could not invoke rights once denied. This Court has rejected that approach, both with respect to the right to marry and the rights of gays and lesbians. See *Loving*, 388 U. S., at 12; *Lawrence*, 539 U. S., at 566–567.

The right to marry is fundamental as a matter of history and tradition, but rights come not from ancient sources alone. They rise, too, from a better informed understanding of how constitutional imperatives define a liberty that remains urgent in our own era. Many who deem same-sex marriage to be wrong reach that conclusion based on decent and honorable religious or philosophical premises, and neither they nor their beliefs are disparaged here. But when that sincere, personal opposition becomes enacted law and public policy, the necessary consequence is to put the imprimatur of the State itself on an exclusion that soon demeans or stigmatizes those whose own liberty is then denied. Under the Constitution, same-sex couples seek in marriage the same legal treatment as opposite-sex couples, and it would disparage their choices and diminish their personhood to deny them this right.

The right of same-sex couples to marry that is part of the liberty promised by the Fourteenth Amendment is derived, too, from that Amendment's guarantee of the equal protection of the laws. The Due Process Clause and the Equal Protection Clause are connected in a profound way, though they set forth independent principles. Rights implicit in liberty and rights secured by equal protection may rest on different precepts and are not always coextensive, yet in some instances each may be instructive as to the meaning and reach of the other. In any particular case one Clause may be thought to capture the essence of the right in a more accurate and comprehensive way, even as the two Clauses may converge in the identification and definition of the right. . . .

The Court's cases touching upon the right to marry reflect this dynamic. In *Loving* the Court invalidated a prohibition on interracial marriage under both the Equal Protection Clause and the Due Process Clause. . . . The reasons why marriage is a fundamental right became more clear and compelling from a full awareness and understanding of the hurt that resulted from laws barring interracial unions.

The synergy between the two protections is illustrated further in *Zablocki*[, where] . . . the essential nature of the marriage right . . . made apparent the law's incompatibility with requirements of equality. Each concept—liberty and equal protection—leads to a stronger understanding of the other.

. . . [I]nvidious sex-based classifications in marriage remained common through the mid-20th century [and t]hese classifications denied the equal dignity of men and women. . . . Responding to a new awareness, the Court invoked equal protection principles to invalidate laws imposing sex-based inequality on marriage. . . . Like *Loving* and *Zablocki*, these precedents show the Equal Protection Clause can help to identify and correct inequalities in the institution of marriage, vindicating precepts of liberty and equality under the Constitution.

. . .

In *Lawrence* the Court acknowledged the interlocking nature of these constitutional safeguards . . . [, drawing] upon principles of liberty and equality to define and protect the rights of gays and lesbians, holding the State "cannot demean their existence or control their destiny by making their private sexual conduct a crime.". . .

This dynamic also applies to same-sex marriage. It is now clear that the challenged laws burden the liberty of same-sex couples, and it must be further acknowledged that they abridge central precepts of equality. Here the marriage laws enforced by the respondents are in essence unequal: same-sex couples are denied all the benefits afforded to opposite-sex couples and are barred from exercising a fundamental right. Especially against a long history of disapproval of their relationships, this denial to same-sex couples of the right to marry works a grave and continuing harm. The imposition of this disability on gays and lesbians serves to disrespect and subordinate them. And the Equal Protection Clause, like the Due Process Clause, prohibits this unjustified infringement of the fundamental right to marry. . . .

These considerations lead to the conclusion that the right to marry is a fundamental right inherent in the liberty of the person, and under the Due Process and Equal Protection Clauses of the Fourteenth Amendment couples of the same-sex may not be deprived of that right and that liberty. The Court now holds that same-sex couples may exercise the fundamental right to marry. . . .

Baker v. Nelson must be and now is overruled, and the State laws challenged by Petitioners in these cases are now held invalid to the extent they exclude same-sex couples from civil marriage on the same terms and conditions as opposite-sex couples.

IV

There may be an initial inclination in these cases to proceed with caution—to await further legislation, litigation, and debate. . . .

Yet there has been far more deliberation than this argument acknowledges. There have been referenda, legislative debates, and grassroots campaigns, as well as countless studies, papers, books, and other popular and scholarly writings. There has been extensive litigation in state and federal courts. . . .

. . .

The dynamic of our constitutional system is that individuals need not await legislative action before asserting a fundamental right. . . . It is of no moment whether advocates of same-sex marriage now enjoy or lack momentum in the democratic process. The issue before the Court here is the legal question whether the Constitution protects the right of same-sex couples to marry.

This is not the first time the Court has been asked to adopt a cautious approach to recognizing and protecting fundamental rights. In *Bowers*, a bare majority upheld a law criminalizing same-sex intimacy. . . . Although *Bowers* was eventually repudiated in *Lawrence*, men and women were harmed in the interim, and the substantial effects of these injuries no doubt lingered long after *Bowers* was overruled. Dignitary wounds cannot always be healed with the stroke of a pen.

A ruling against same-sex couples would have the same effect—and, like *Bowers*, would be unjustified under the Fourteenth Amendment. The petitioners' stories make clear the urgency of the issue they present to the Court. James Obergefell now asks whether Ohio can erase his marriage . . . for all time. April DeBoer and Jayne Rowse now ask whether Michigan may continue to deny them the certainty and stability all mothers desire to protect their children, and for them and their children the childhood years will pass all too soon. Ijpe DeKoe and Thomas Kostura now ask whether Tennessee can deny to one who has served this Nation the basic dignity of recognizing his New York marriage. Properly presented with the petitioners' cases, the Court has a duty to address these claims and answer these questions.

. . .

The respondents also argue allowing same-sex couples to wed will harm marriage as an institution by leading to fewer opposite-sex marriages. . . . Decisions about whether to marry and raise children are based on many personal, romantic, and practical considerations; and it is unrealistic to conclude that an opposite-sex couple would choose not to marry simply because same-sex couples may do so. . . . The respondents have not shown a foundation for the conclusion that allowing same-sex marriage will cause the harmful outcomes they describe. Indeed, with respect to this asserted basis for excluding same-sex couples from the right to marry, it is appropriate to observe these cases involve only the rights of two consenting adults whose marriages would pose no risk of harm to themselves or third parties.

. . .

V

These cases also present the question whether the Constitution requires States to recognize same-sex marriages validly performed out of State. As made clear by the case of Obergefell and Arthur, and by that of DeKoe and Kostura, the recognition bans inflict substantial and continuing harm on same-sex couples.

. . . In light of the fact that many States already allow same-sex marriage—and hundreds of thousands of these marriages already have occurred—the disruption caused by the recognition bans is significant and ever-growing.

. . . The Court, in this decision, holds same-sex couples may exercise the fundamental right to marry in all States. It follows that the Court also must hold—and it now does hold—that there is no lawful basis for a State to refuse to recognize a lawful same-sex marriage performed in another State on the ground of its same-sex character.

* * *

. . . [Petitioners] ask for equal dignity in the eyes of the law. The Constitution grants them that right.

The judgment . . . is reversed.

Chief Justice Roberts, with whom Justice Scalia and Justice Thomas join, dissenting.

Petitioners make strong arguments rooted in social policy and considerations of fairness. . . .

But this Court is not a legislature. Whether same-sex marriage is a good idea should be of no concern to us. Under the Constitution, judges have power to say what the law is, not what it should be. . . .

Although the policy arguments for extending marriage to same-sex couples may be compelling, the legal arguments for requiring such an extension are not. The fundamental right to marry does not include a right to make a State change its definition of marriage. And a State's decision to maintain the meaning of marriage that has persisted in every culture throughout human history can hardly be called irrational. In short, our Constitution does not enact any one theory of marriage. The people of a State are free to expand marriage to include same-sex couples, or to retain the historic definition.

. . . Many people will rejoice at this decision, and I begrudge none their celebration. But for those who believe in a government of laws, not of men, the majority's approach is deeply disheartening. Supporters of same-sex marriage have achieved considerable success persuading their fellow citizens—through the democratic process—to adopt their view. That ends today. Five lawyers have closed the debate and enacted their own vision of marriage as a matter of constitutional law. Stealing this issue from the people will for many cast a cloud over same-sex marriage, making a dramatic social change that much more difficult to accept.

The majority's decision is an act of will, not legal judgment. The right it announces has no basis in the Constitution or this Court's precedent. . . . [T]he Court invalidates the marriage laws of more than half the States and orders the transformation of a social institution that has formed the basis of human society for millennia, for the Kalahari Bushmen and the Han Chinese, the Carthaginians and the Aztecs. Just who do we think we are?

It can be tempting for judges to confuse our own preferences with the requirements of the law. But as this Court has been reminded throughout our history, the Constitution "is made for people of fundamentally differing views."

Lochner v. New York, 198 U. S. 45, 76 (1905) (Holmes, J., dissenting). . . . The majority today[, however,] . . . seizes for itself a question the Constitution leaves to the people, at a time when the people are engaged in a vibrant debate on that question. And it answers that question based not on neutral principles of constitutional law, but on its own "understanding of what freedom is and must become." I have no choice but to dissent.

. . .

I

. . . There is no serious dispute that, under our precedents, the Constitution protects a right to marry and requires States to apply their marriage laws equally. The real question in these cases is what constitutes "marriage," or—more precisely—who decides what constitutes "marriage"?

. . .

A

As the majority acknowledges, marriage "has existed for millennia and across civilizations." For all those millennia, across all those civilizations, "marriage" referred to only one relationship: the union of a man and a woman. . . .

This universal definition of marriage . . . is no historical coincidence. . . . It arose in the nature of things to meet a vital need: ensuring that children are conceived by a mother and father committed to raising them in the stable conditions of a lifelong relationship. . . .

. . .

. . . [B]y bestowing a respected status and material benefits on married couples, society encourages men and women to conduct sexual relations within marriage rather than without. . . .

This singular understanding of marriage has prevailed in the United States throughout our history. . . .

The Constitution itself says nothing about marriage, and the Framers thereby entrusted the States with "[t]he whole subject of the domestic relations of husband and wife." *Windsor*. . . . There is no dispute that every State at the founding—and every State throughout our history until a dozen years ago—defined marriage in the traditional, biologically rooted way. . . .

. . .

This Court's precedents have repeatedly described marriage in ways that are consistent only with its traditional meaning. Early cases on the subject referred to marriage as "the union for life of one man and one woman," Murphy v. Ramsey, 114 U. S. 15, 45 (1885), which forms "the foundation of the family and of society, without which there would be neither civilization nor progress," Maynard v. Hill, 125 U. S. 190, 211 (1888). We later described marriage as "fundamental to our very existence and survival," an understanding that necessarily implies a procreative component. Loving v. Virginia, 388 U. S. 1, 12 (1967); see Skinner v. Oklahoma ex rel. Williamson, 316 U. S. 535, 541 (1942).

More recent cases have directly connected the right to marry with the "right to procreate." Zablocki v. Redhail, 434 U. S. 374, 386 (1978).

As the majority notes, some aspects of marriage have changed over time. . . .

. . . [T]hese developments . . . did not, however, work any transformation in the core structure of marriage as the union between a man and a woman. . . .

. . .

II

Petitioners first contend that the marriage laws of their States violate the Due Process Clause. The Solicitor General of the United States, appearing in support of petitioners, expressly disowned that position before this Court. . . . The majority nevertheless resolves these cases for petitioners based almost entirely on the Due Process Clause.

. . . [T]he majority's approach has no basis in principle or tradition, except for the unprincipled tradition of judicial policymaking that characterized discredited decisions such as Lochner v. New York. . . .

A

. . .

The need for restraint in administering the strong medicine of substantive due process is a lesson this Court has learned the hard way. The Court first applied substantive due process to strike down a statute in Dred Scott v. Sandford, 19 How. 393 (1857)[, which] invalidated the Missouri Compromise on the ground that legislation restricting the institution of slavery violated the implied rights of slaveholders. The Court relied on its own conception of liberty and property in doing so. . . . In a dissent that has outlasted the majority opinion, Justice Curtis explained that when the "fixed rules which govern the interpretation of laws [are] abandoned, and the theoretical opinions of individuals are allowed to control" the Constitution's meaning, "we have no longer a Constitution; we are under the government of individual men, who for the time being have power to declare what the Constitution is, according to their own views of what it ought to mean." Id., at 621.

. . .

[After recounting the history of *Lochner* and its progeny, and the Court's eventual recognition of "its error," Chief Justice Roberts continued:]

Rejecting *Lochner* does not require disavowing the doctrine of implied fundamental rights, and this Court has not done so. But to avoid repeating *Lochner*'s error of converting personal preferences into constitutional mandates, our modern substantive due process cases have stressed the need for "judicial self-restraint." . . . Our precedents have required that implied fundamental rights be "objectively, deeply rooted in this Nation's history and tradition," and "implicit in the concept of ordered liberty, such that neither liberty nor justice would exist if they were sacrificed." *Glucksberg* . . .

. . .

Proper reliance on history and tradition of course requires looking beyond the individual law being challenged, so that every restriction on liberty does not supply its own constitutional justification. The Court is right about that. But given the few "guideposts for responsible decisionmaking in this unchartered area," . . . "an approach grounded in history imposes limits on the judiciary that are more meaningful than any based on [an] abstract formula,". . . . Expanding a right suddenly and dramatically is likely to require tearing it up from its roots. . . . The only way to ensure restraint in this delicate enterprise is "continual insistence upon respect for the teachings of history, solid recognition of the basic values that underlie our society, and wise appreciation of the great roles [of] the doctrines of federalism and separation of powers." Griswold v. Connecticut, 381 U. S. 479, 501 (1965) (Harlan, J., concurring in judgment).

B

. . .

1

. . . As a matter of constitutional law, . . . the sincerity of petitioners' wishes is not relevant.

When the majority turns to the law, it relies primarily on precedents discussing the fundamental "right to marry." Turner v. Safley, 482 U. S. 78, 95 (1987); Zablocki, 434 U. S., at 383; see Loving, 388 U. S., at 12. . . .

None of the laws at issue in those cases purported to change the core definition of marriage as the union of a man and a woman. . . . As the majority admits, the institution of "marriage" discussed in every one of these cases "presumed a relationship involving opposite-sex partners."

In short, the "right to marry" cases stand for the important but limited proposition that particular restrictions on access to marriage *as traditionally defined* violate due process. These precedents say nothing at all about a right to make a State change its definition of marriage, which is the right petitioners actually seek here. . . .

2

. . .

Neither *Lawrence* nor any other precedent in the privacy line of cases supports the right that petitioners assert here [either]. Unlike criminal laws banning contraceptives and sodomy, the marriage laws at issue here involve no government intrusion. They create no crime and impose no punishment. Same-sex couples remain free to live together, to engage in intimate conduct, and to raise their families as they see fit. No one is "condemned to live in loneliness" by the laws challenged in these cases—no one. At the same time, the laws in no way interfere with the "right to be let alone."

. . .

In sum, the privacy cases provide no support for the majority's position, because petitioners do not seek privacy. Quite the opposite, they seek public recognition of their relationships, along with corresponding government benefits. . . .

3

. . . It is revealing that the majority's position requires it to effectively overrule *Glucksberg*, the leading modern case setting the bounds of substantive due process. At least this part of the majority opinion has the virtue of candor. Nobody could rightly accuse the majority of taking a careful approach.

Ultimately, only one precedent offers any support for the majority's methodology: *Lochner v. New York* . . .

To be fair, the majority does not suggest that its individual autonomy right is entirely unconstrained. The constraints it sets are precisely those that accord with its own "reasoned judgment," informed by its "new insight" into the "nature of injustice," which was invisible to all who came before but has become clear "as we learn [the] meaning" of liberty. The truth is that today's decision rests on nothing more than the majority's own conviction that same-sex couples should be allowed to marry because they want to, and that "it would disparage their choices and diminish their personhood to deny them this right." Whatever force that belief may have as a matter of moral philosophy, it has no more basis in the Constitution than did the naked policy preferences adopted in *Lochner*. . . .

. . .

One immediate question invited by the majority's position is whether States may retain the definition of marriage as a union of two people. . . . Indeed, from the standpoint of history and tradition, a leap from opposite-sex marriage to same-sex marriage is much greater than one from a two-person union to plural unions, which have deep roots in some cultures around the world. If the majority is willing to take the big leap, it is hard to see how it can say no to the shorter one.

It is striking how much of the majority's reasoning would apply with equal force to the claim of a fundamental right to plural marriage. . . .

. . . When asked about a plural marital union at oral argument, petitioners asserted that a State "doesn't have such an institution.". . . But that is exactly the point: the States at issue here do not have an institution of same-sex marriage, either.

4

. . .

. . . The elevation of the fullest individual self-realization over the constraints that society has expressed in law may or may not be attractive moral philosophy. But a Justice's commission does not confer any special moral, philosophical, or social insight sufficient to justify imposing those perceptions on fellow citizens under the pretense of "due process." There is indeed a process due the people on issues of this sort—the democratic process. Respecting that understanding requires the Court to be guided by law, not any particular school of social thought. . . .

The majority's understanding of due process lays out a tantalizing vision of the future for Members of this Court: If an unvarying social institution enduring over all of recorded history cannot inhibit judicial policymaking, what can? But this approach is dangerous for the rule of law. . . .

III

. . . The majority does not seriously engage with [the Equal Protection Clause] claim. Its discussion is, quite frankly, difficult to follow. . . . Absent . . . is anything resembling our usual framework for deciding equal protection cases. . . .

. . . In any event, the marriage laws at issue here do not violate the Equal Protection Clause, because distinguishing between opposite-sex and same-sex couples is rationally related to the States' "legitimate state interest" in "preserving the traditional institution of marriage." *Lawrence*, 539 U. S., at 585 (O'Connor, J., concurring in judgment).

It is important to note with precision which laws petitioners have challenged. Although they discuss some of the ancillary legal benefits that accompany marriage, such as hospital visitation rights and recognition of spousal status on official documents, petitioners' lawsuits target the laws defining marriage generally rather than those allocating benefits specifically. The equal protection analysis might be different, in my view, if we were confronted with a more focused challenge to the denial of certain tangible benefits. Of course, those more selective claims will not arise now that the Court has taken the drastic step of requiring every State to license and recognize marriages between same-sex couples.

IV

. . .

Nowhere is the majority's extravagant conception of judicial supremacy more evident than in its description—and dismissal—of the public debate regarding same-sex marriage. . . .

Those who founded our country would not recognize the majority's conception of the judicial role. They after all risked their lives and fortunes for the precious right to govern themselves. They would never have imagined yielding that right on a question of social policy to unaccountable and unelected judges. . . .

The Court's accumulation of power does not occur in a vacuum. It comes at the expense of the people. And they know it. . . .

. . .

. . . There will be consequences to shutting down the political process on an issue of such profound public significance. Closing debate tends to close minds. People denied a voice are less likely to accept the ruling of a court on an issue that does not seem to be the sort of thing courts usually decide. As a thoughtful commentator observed about another issue, "The political process was moving . . ., not swiftly enough for advocates of quick, complete change, but majoritarian institutions were listening and acting. Heavy-handed judicial intervention was difficult to justify and appears to have provoked, not resolved, conflict." Ginsburg, Some Thoughts on Autonomy and Equality in Relation to Roe v. Wade, 63 N. C. L. Rev. 375, 385–386 (1985). . . . Indeed, however heartened the proponents of same-sex marriage might be on this day, it is worth acknowledging what they have lost, and lost forever: the opportunity to win the true acceptance that comes from persuading their fellow citizens of the justice of their cause. And they lose this just when the winds of change were freshening at their backs.

Federal courts . . . do not have the flexibility of legislatures to address concerns of parties not before the court or to anticipate problems that may arise from the exercise of a new right. Today's decision, for example, creates serious questions about religious liberty. . . .

Respect for sincere religious conviction has led voters and legislators in every State that has adopted same-sex marriage democratically to include accommodations for religious practice. The majority's decision imposing same-sex marriage cannot, of course, create any such accommodations. . . .

Hard questions arise when people of faith exercise religion in ways that may be seen to conflict with the new right to same-sex marriage—when, for example, a religious college provides married student housing only to opposite-sex married couples, or a religious adoption agency declines to place children with same-sex married couples. Indeed, the Solicitor General candidly acknowledged that the tax exemptions of some religious institutions would be in question if they opposed same-sex marriage. . . . There is little doubt that these and similar questions will soon be before this Court. Unfortunately, people of faith can take no comfort in the treatment they receive from the majority today.

Perhaps the most discouraging aspect of today's decision is the extent to which the majority feels compelled to sully those on the other side of the debate. . . . By the majority's account, Americans who did nothing more than follow the understanding of marriage that has existed for our entire history—in particular, the tens of millions of people who voted to reaffirm their States' enduring definition of marriage—have acted to "lock . . . out," "disparage," "disrespect and subordinate," and inflict "[d]ignitary wounds" upon their gay and lesbian neighbors. These apparent assaults on the character of fairminded people . . . are entirely gratuitous. It is one thing for the majority to conclude that the Constitution protects a right to same-sex marriage; it is something else to portray everyone who does not share the majority's "better informed understanding" as bigoted.

. . .

If you are among the many Americans—of whatever sexual orientation—who favor expanding same-sex marriage, by all means celebrate today's decision. Celebrate the achievement of a desired goal. Celebrate the opportunity for a new expression of commitment to a partner. Celebrate the availability of new benefits. But do not celebrate the Constitution. It had nothing to do with it.

I respectfully dissent.

Justice Scalia, with whom Justice Thomas joins, dissenting.

I join the Chief Justice's opinion in full. I write separately to call attention to this Court's threat to American democracy.

. . . [I]t is not of special importance to me what the law says about marriage. It is of overwhelming importance, however, who it is that rules me. Today's decree says that my Ruler, and the Ruler of 320 million Americans coast-to-coast, is a majority of the nine lawyers on the Supreme Court. The opinion in these cases is the furthest extension in fact—and the furthest extension one can even imagine—of the Court's claimed power to create "liberties" that the Constitution and its Amendments neglect to mention. . . .

I

. . .

. . . When the Fourteenth Amendment was ratified in 1868, every State limited marriage to one man and one woman, and no one doubted the constitutionality of doing so. That resolves these cases. . . . We have no basis for striking down a practice that is not expressly prohibited by the Fourteenth Amendment's text, and that bears the endorsement of a long tradition of open, widespread, and unchallenged use dating back to the Amendment's ratification. Since there is no doubt whatever that the People never decided to prohibit the limitation of marriage to opposite-sex couples, the public debate over same-sex marriage must be allowed to continue.

But the Court ends this debate, in an opinion lacking even a thin veneer of law. . . . [R]ather than focusing on *the People's* understanding of "liberty"—at the time of ratification or even today—the majority focuses on four "principles and traditions" that, *in the majority's view*, prohibit States from defining marriage as an institution consisting of one man and one woman.

This is a naked judicial claim to legislative—indeed, *super*-legislative—power; a claim fundamentally at odds with our system of government. . . . A system of government that makes the People subordinate to a committee of nine unelected lawyers does not deserve to be called a democracy.

. . . [T]o allow the policy question of same-sex marriage to be considered and resolved by a select, patrician, highly unrepresentative panel of nine is to violate a principle even more fundamental than no taxation without representation: no social transformation without representation.

II

But what really astounds is the hubris reflected in today's judicial Putsch. The five Justices who compose today's majority are entirely comfortable concluding that every State violated the Constitution for all of the 135 years between the Fourteenth Amendment's ratification and Massachusetts' permitting of same-sex marriages in 2003. They have discovered in the Fourteenth Amendment a "fundamental right" overlooked by every person alive at the time of ratification, and almost everyone else in the time since. . . . These Justices *know* that limiting marriage to one man and one woman is contrary to reason; they *know* that an institution as old as government itself, and accepted by every nation in history until 15 years ago, cannot possibly be supported by anything other than ignorance or bigotry. And they are willing to say that any citizen who does not agree with that, who adheres to what was, until 15 years ago, the unanimous judgment of all generations and all societies, stands against the Constitution.

The opinion is couched in a style that is as pretentious as its content is egotistic. . . . The world does not expect logic and precision in poetry or inspirational pop-philosophy; it demands them in the law. The stuff contained in today's opinion has to diminish this Court's reputation for clear thinking and sober analysis.

* * *

. . . With each decision of ours that takes from the People a question properly left to them—with each decision that is unabashedly based not on law, but on the "reasoned judgment" of a bare majority of this Court—we move one step closer to being reminded of our impotence.

Justice Thomas, with whom Justice Scalia joins, dissenting.

The Court's decision today is at odds not only with the Constitution, but with the principles upon which our Nation was built. Since well before 1787, liberty has been understood as freedom from government action, not entitlement to government benefits. The Framers created our Constitution to preserve that understanding of liberty. Yet the majority invokes our Constitution in the name of a "liberty" that the Framers would not have recognized, to the detriment of the liberty they sought to protect. . . . [I]t rejects the idea—captured in our Declaration of Independence—that human dignity is innate and suggests instead that it comes from the Government. This distortion of our Constitution not only ignores the text, it inverts the relationship between the individual and the state in our Republic. I cannot agree with it.

. . .

II

Even if the doctrine of substantive due process were somehow defensible— it is not—petitioners still would not have a claim. To invoke the protection of the Due Process Clause at all—whether under a theory of "substantive" or "procedural" due process—a party must first identify a deprivation of "life, liberty, or property." The majority claims these state laws deprive petitioners of "liberty," but the concept of "liberty" it conjures up bears no resemblance to any plausible meaning of that word as it is used in the Due Process Clauses.

. . .

Both of the Constitution's Due Process Clauses reach back to Magna Carta. . . .

. . .

The Framers . . . adopt[ed] provisions in early State Constitutions that replicated Magna Carta's language, but were modified to refer specifically to "life, liberty, or property." State decisions interpreting these provisions between the founding and the ratification of the Fourteenth Amendment almost uniformly construed the word "liberty" to refer only to freedom from physical restraint. . . .

In enacting the Fifth Amendment's Due Process Clause, the Framers similarly chose to employ the "life, liberty, or property" formulation. . . . When read in light of the history of that formulation, it is hard to see how the "liberty" protected by the Clause could be interpreted to include anything broader than freedom from physical restraint. That was the consistent usage of the time when "liberty" was paired with "life" and "property.". . . And that usage avoids rendering superfluous those protections for "life" and "property."

If the Fifth Amendment uses "liberty" in this narrow sense, then the Fourteenth Amendment likely does as well. . . . That the Court appears to have lost its way in more recent years does not justify deviating from the original meaning of the Clauses.

. . .

Even assuming that the "liberty" in those Clauses encompasses something more than freedom from physical restraint, it would not include the types of rights claimed by the majority. In the American legal tradition, liberty has long been understood as individual freedom from governmental action, not as a right to a particular governmental entitlement.

. . .

The founding-era idea of civil liberty as natural liberty constrained by human law necessarily involved only those freedoms that existed outside of government. . . .

. . .

Whether we define "liberty" as locomotion or freedom from governmental action more broadly, petitioners have in no way been deprived of it. Petitioners cannot claim, under the most plausible definition of "liberty," that they have been imprisoned or physically restrained by the States for participating in same-sex relationships. To the contrary, they have been able to cohabitate and raise their children in peace. They have been able to hold civil marriage ceremonies in States that recognize same-sex marriages and private religious ceremonies in all States. They have been able to travel freely around the country, making their homes where they please. Far from being incarcerated or physically restrained, petitioners have been left alone to order their lives as they see fit.

Nor, under the broader definition, can they claim that the States have restricted their ability to go about their daily lives as they would be able to absent governmental restrictions. Petitioners do not ask this Court to order the States to stop restricting their ability to enter same-sex relationships, to engage in intimate behavior, to make vows to their partners in public ceremonies, to engage in religious wedding ceremonies, to hold themselves out as married, or to raise children. The States have imposed no such restrictions.

Nor have the States prevented petitioners from approximating a number of incidents of marriage through private legal means, such as wills, trusts, and powers of attorney.

Instead, the States have refused to grant them governmental entitlements. Petitioners claim that as a matter of "liberty," they are entitled to access privileges and benefits that exist solely because of the government. They want, for example, to receive the State's imprimatur on their marriages—on state issued marriage licenses, death certificates, or other official forms. And they want to receive various monetary benefits, including reduced inheritance taxes upon the death of a spouse, compensation if a spouse dies as a result of a work-related injury, or loss of consortium damages in tort suits. But receiving governmental recognition and benefits has nothing to do with any understanding of "liberty" that the Framers would have recognized.

To the extent that the Framers would have recognized a natural right to marriage that fell within the broader definition of liberty, it would not have included a right to governmental recognition and benefits. . . . Petitioners misunderstand the institution of marriage when they say that it would "mean little" absent governmental recognition. . . .

Petitioners' misconception of liberty carries over into their discussion of our precedents identifying a right to marry, not one of which has expanded the concept of "liberty" beyond the concept of negative liberty. Those precedents all involved absolute prohibitions on private actions associated with marriage. Loving v. Virginia, . . . for example, involved a couple who was criminally prosecuted for marrying in the District of Columbia and cohabiting in Virginia, . . . In a similar vein, Zablocki v. Redhail . . . involved a man who was prohibited, on pain of criminal penalty, from "marry[ing] in Wisconsin or elsewhere" because of his outstanding child-support obligations. . . . And Turner v. Safley . . . involved state inmates who were prohibited from entering marriages without the permission of the superintendent of the prison, permission that could not be granted absent compelling reasons. . . . In *none* of those cases were individuals denied solely governmental recognition and benefits associated with marriage.

. . . As a philosophical matter, liberty is only freedom from governmental action, not an entitlement to governmental benefits. And as a constitutional matter, it is likely even narrower than that, encompassing only freedom from physical restraint and imprisonment. . . .

III

The majority's inversion of the original meaning of liberty will likely cause collateral damage to other aspects of our constitutional order that protect liberty.

A

The majority apparently disregards the political process as a protection for liberty. . . . As a general matter, when the States act through their representative governments or by popular vote, the liberty of their residents is fully vindicated. . . .

. . . The definition of marriage has been the subject of heated debate in the States. Legislatures have repeatedly taken up the matter on behalf of the People, and 35 States have put the question to the People themselves. In 32 of those 35 States, the People have opted to retain the traditional definition of marriage. . . , That petitioners disagree with the result of that process does not make it any less legitimate. Their civil liberty has been vindicated.

B

Aside from undermining the political processes that protect our liberty, the majority's decision threatens the religious liberty our Nation has long sought to protect.

. . .

Numerous *amici*—even some not supporting the States—have cautioned the Court that its decision here will "have unavoidable and wide-ranging implications for religious liberty.". . . In our society, marriage is not simply a governmental institution; it is a religious institution as well. . . . Today's decision might change the former, but it cannot change the latter. It appears all but inevitable that the two will come into conflict, particularly as individuals and churches are confronted with demands to participate in and endorse civil marriages between same-sex couples.

The majority appears unmoved by that inevitability. . . .

. . . Had the majority allowed the definition of marriage to be left to the political process—as the Constitution requires—the People could have considered the religious liberty implications of deviating from the traditional definition as part of their deliberative process. Instead, the majority's decision short-circuits that process, with potentially ruinous consequences for religious liberty.

IV

Perhaps recognizing that these cases do not actually involve liberty as it has been understood, the majority goes to great lengths to assert that its decision will advance the "dignity" of same-sex couples. The flaw in that reasoning, of course, is that the Constitution contains no "dignity" Clause, and even if it did, the government would be incapable of bestowing dignity.

Human dignity has long been understood in this country to be innate. . . .

The corollary . . . is that human dignity cannot be taken away by the government. Slaves did not lose their dignity (any more than they lost their humanity) because the government allowed them to be enslaved. Those held in internment camps did not lose their dignity because the government confined them. And those denied governmental benefits certainly do not lose their dignity because the government denies them those benefits. The government cannot bestow dignity, and it cannot take it away.

The majority's . . . rejection of laws preserving the traditional definition of marriage can have no effect on the dignity of the people who voted for them [either]. Its invalidation of those laws can have no effect on the dignity of the people who continue to adhere to the traditional definition of marriage. And its disdain for the understandings of liberty and dignity upon which this Nation was founded can have no effect on the dignity of Americans who continue to believe in them.

. . .

Justice Alito, with whom Justice Scalia and Justice Thomas join, dissenting.

. . .

I

. . .

To prevent five unelected Justices from imposing their personal vision of liberty upon the American people, the Court has held that "liberty" under the Due Process Clause should be understood to protect only those rights that are " 'deeply rooted in this Nation's history and tradition.' " Washington v. Glucksberg. . . . And it is beyond dispute that the right to same-sex marriage is not among those rights. See United States v. Windsor, . . . (Alito, J., dissenting). . . . Indeed:

> "In this country, no State permitted same-sex marriage until the Massachusetts Supreme Judicial Court held in 2003 that limiting marriage to opposite-sex couples violated the State Constitution. See Goodridge v. Department of Public Health, 440 Mass. 309, 798 N. E. 2d 941. Nor is the right to same-sex marriage deeply rooted in the traditions of other nations. No country allowed same-sex couples to marry until the Netherlands did so in 2000.

> "What [those arguing in favor of a constitutional right to same sex marriage] seek, therefore, is not the protection of a deeply rooted right but the recognition of a very new right, and they seek this innovation not from a legislative body elected by the people, but from unelected judges. Faced with such a request, judges have cause for both caution and humility." Id.. . . .

For today's majority, it does not matter that the right to same-sex marriage lacks deep roots or even that it is contrary to long-established tradition. The Justices in the majority claim the authority to confer constitutional protection upon that right simply because they believe that it is fundamental.

II

Attempting to circumvent the problem presented by the newness of the right found in these cases, the majority claims that the issue is the right to equal treatment. Noting that marriage is a fundamental right, the majority argues that a State has no valid reason for denying that right to same-sex couples. This reasoning is dependent upon a particular understanding of the purpose of civil marriage. . . . [T]he Court['s] . . . argument is that the fundamental purpose of marriage is to promote the well-being of those who choose to marry. . . . This understanding of the States' reasons for recognizing marriage enables the majority to argue that same-sex marriage serves the States' objectives in the same way as opposite-sex marriage.

This understanding of marriage . . . is shared by many people today, but it is not the traditional one. For millennia, marriage was inextricably linked to the one thing that only an opposite-sex couple can do: procreate.

. . . [Respondents'] basic argument is that States formalize and promote marriage, unlike other fulfilling human relationships, in order to encourage potentially procreative conduct to take place within a lasting unit that has long been thought to provide the best atmosphere for raising children. They thus argue that there are reasonable secular grounds for restricting marriage to opposite-sex couples.

. . .

. . . States that do not want to recognize same-sex marriage have not yet given up on the traditional understanding. They worry that by officially abandoning the older understanding, they may contribute to marriage's further decay. It is far beyond the outer reaches of this Court's authority to say that a State may not adhere to the understanding of marriage that has long prevailed, not just in this country and others with similar cultural roots, but also in a great variety of countries and cultures all around the globe.

. . .

III

Today's decision usurps the constitutional right of the people to decide whether to keep or alter the traditional understanding of marriage. The decision will also have other important consequences.

It will be used to vilify Americans who are unwilling to assent to the new orthodoxy. . . .

. . . I assume that those who cling to old beliefs will be able to whisper their thoughts in the recesses of their homes, but if they repeat those views in public, they will risk being labeled as bigots and treated as such by governments, employers, and schools.

. . . If the issue of same-sex marriage had been left to the people of the States, it is likely that some States would recognize same-sex marriage and others would not. It is also possible that some States would tie recognition to protection for conscience rights. The majority today makes that impossible. By imposing its own views on the entire country, the majority facilitates the marginalization of the many Americans who have traditional ideas. . . .

. . .

Today's decision shows that decades of attempts to restrain this Court's abuse of its authority have failed. A lesson that some will take from today's decision is that preaching about the proper method of interpreting the Constitution or the virtues of judicial self-restraint and humility cannot compete with the temptation to achieve what is viewed as a noble end by any practicable means. I do not doubt that my colleagues in the majority sincerely see in the Constitution a vision of liberty that happens to coincide with their own. But this sincerity is cause for concern, not comfort. What it evidences is the deep and perhaps irremediable corruption of our legal culture's conception of constitutional interpretation.

. . .

C. PERSONAL AUTONOMY

Page 600. Add after Gonzales v. Carhart:

Whole Woman's Health v. Hellerstedt
579 U.S. ____, 136 S.Ct. 2292, ____ L.Ed.2d ____ (2016).

Justice Breyer delivered the opinion of the Court.

In Planned Parenthood of Southeastern Pa. v. Casey, 505 U. S. 833, 878 (1992), a plurality of the Court concluded that there "exists" an "undue burden" on a woman's right to decide to have an abortion, and consequently a provision of law is constitutionally invalid, if the "*purpose or effect*" of the provision "*is to place a substantial obstacle* in the path of a woman seeking an abortion before the fetus attains viability." (Emphasis added.) The plurality added that "[u]nnecessary health regulations that have the purpose or effect of presenting a substantial obstacleto a woman seeking an abortion impose an undue burden on the right." *Ibid.*

We must here decide whether two provisions of Texas' House Bill 2 violate the Federal Constitution as interpreted in *Casey*. The first provision, which we shall call the "*admitting-privileges requirement,*" says that

> "[a] physician performing or inducing an abortion . . . must, on the date the abortion is performed or induced, have active admitting privileges at a hospital that . . . is located not further than 30 miles from the location at which the abortion is performed or induced." Tex. Health & Safety Code Ann. § 171.0031(a) (West Cum. Supp. 2015).

This provision amended Texas law that had previously required an abortion facility to maintain a written protocol "for managing medical emergencies and the transfer of patients requiring further emergency care to a hospital." 38 Tex. Reg. 6546 (2013).

The second provision, which we shall call the "*surgical center requirement,*" says that

> "the minimum standards for an abortion facility must be equivalent to the minimum standards adopted under [the Texas Health and Safety Code section] for ambulatory surgical centers." Tex. Health & Safety Code Ann. § 245.010(a).

We conclude that neither of these provisions offers medical benefits sufficient to justify the burdens upon access that each imposes. Each places a substantial obstacle in the path of women seeking a previability abortion, each constitutes an undue burden on abortion access, *Casey, supra*, at 878 (plurality opinion), and each violates the Federal Constitution. Amdt. 14, § 1.

I

In July 2013, the Texas Legislature enacted House Bill 2 (H. B. 2 or Act). In September (before the new law took effect), a group of Texas abortion providers [sued] seeking facial invalidation of the law's admitting-privileges provision. In late October, the District Court granted the injunction. . . . But three days later, the Fifth Circuit vacated the injunction, thereby permitting the provision to take effect. . . .

The Fifth Circuit subsequently upheld the provision. . . . [Its] opinion . . . explained that the plaintiffs had not provided sufficient evidence "that abortion practitioners will likely be unable to comply with the privileges requirement.". . . The court said that all "of the major Texas cities, including Austin, Corpus Christi, Dallas, El Paso, Houston, and San Antonio," would "continue to have multiple clinics where many physicians will have or obtain hospital admitting privileges.". . . The . . . plaintiffs did not file a petition for certiorari in this Court.

[O]ne week after the Fifth Circuit's decision, petitioners, a group of abortion providers (many of whom were plaintiffs in the previous lawsuit), filed the present lawsuit in Federal District Court. They sought an injunction preventing enforcement of the admitting-privileges provision as applied to physicians at two abortion facilities, one operated by Whole Woman's Health in McAllen and the other operated by Nova Health Systems in El Paso. They also sought an injunction prohibiting enforcement of the surgical-center provision anywhere in Texas. . . .

[After trial, the District Court made extensive findings concluding that, before H.B. 2 was enacted, there were more than 40 licensed abortion facilities in Texas; that almost half of those disappeared in the period leading up to and in the wake of enforcement of the admitting-privileges requirement; that if the surgical-center provision were allowed to take effect, the number would be reduced to 7 or 8, which would not be able to meet the demand of the entire state; that the geographical distribution of the remaining facilities would leave 2 million women of reproductive age more than 50 miles from an abortion provider, 1.3 million more than 100 miles away, 900,000 more than 150 miles distant, and 750,000 more than 200 miles from an abortion provider. Other findings included that the "two requirements erect a particularly high barrier for poor, rural, or disadvantaged women"; that before the Act "abortion in Texas was extremely safe with particularly low rates of serious complications and virtually no deaths occurring on account of the procedure"; that abortion was shown to be "much safer . . . than many common medical procedures not subject to such intense regulation and scrutiny[,]" such as colonoscopies, vasectomies, endometrial biopsies, and plastic surgery; that "risks are not appreciably lowered for patients who undergo abortions at ambulatory surgical centers as compared to nonsurgical-center facilities"; and that the "cost of coming into compliance" with the surgical-center requirement "for existing clinics is significant," "undisputedly approach[ing] 1 million dollars," and "most likely exceed[ing] 1.5 million dollars," with "[s]ome . . . clinics" unable to "comply due to physical size limitations of their sites."]

On the basis of these and other related findings, the District Court determined that the surgical-center requirement "imposes an undue burden on the right of women throughout Texas to seek a previability abortion," and that the "admitting-privileges requirement, . . . in conjunction with the ambulatory-surgical-center requirement, imposes an undue burden on the right of women in the Rio Grande Valley, El Paso, and West Texas to seek a previability abortion.". . . [T]he court enjoined the enforcement of the two provisions. . . .

[The Fifth Circuit stayed the injunction and again reversed, largely based on res judicata principles, but also based on the conclusion that the two requirements were rationally related to the legitimate state interest in protecting the health and welfare of women seeking abortions, and the conclusion that the plaintiffs had failed to show that either of the provisions "imposes an undue burden on a large fraction of women." The Court of Appeals also concluded that "[t]he District Court erred in finding that, if the surgical-center requirement takes effect, there will be too few abortion providers in Texas to meet the demand." In particular, the " 'record lacks any actual evidence regarding the current or future capacity of the eight clinics' "; and there is no "evidence in the record that" the providers that currently meet the surgical-center requirement "are operating at full capacity or that they cannot increase capacity."]

. . . The Court of Appeals upheld in part the District Court's more specific holding that the requirements are unconstitutional as applied to the McAllen facility and . . . a doctor at that facility . . . , but it reversed the District Court's holding that the surgical-center requirement is unconstitutional as applied to the facility in El Paso. In respect to this last claim, the Court of Appeals said that women in El Paso wishing to have an abortion could use abortion providers in nearby New Mexico.

II

[The Court first held "that res judicata neither bars petitioners' challenges to the admitting-privileges requirement nor prevents us from awarding facial relief." It said in part:]

. . . Petitioners' postenforcement as-applied challenge is not "the very same claim" as their preenforcement facial challenge. The Restatement of Judgments notes that development of new material facts can mean that a new case and an otherwise similar previous case do not present the same claim. . . .

. . . Factual developments may show that constitutional harm, which seemed too remote or speculative to afford relief at the time of an earlier suit, was in fact indisputable. In our view, such changed circumstances will give rise to a new constitutional claim. . . . Justice Alito's dissenting opinion is simply wrong that changed circumstances showing that a challenged law has an unconstitutional effect can never give rise to a new claim.

... We are concerned with H. B. 2's "effect ... on women seeking abortions." And that effect has changed dramatically since petitioners filed their first lawsuit. ...

When individuals claim that a particular statute will produce serious constitutionally relevant adverse consequences before they have occurred—and when the courts doubt their likely occurrence—the factual difference that those adverse consequences *have in fact occurred* can make all the difference. ... In sum, the Restatement, cases from the Courts of Appeals, our own precedent, and simple logic combine to convince us that res judicata does not bar this claim.

... [Moreover, n]othing prevents this Court from awarding facial relief as the appropriate remedy for petitioners' as-applied claims.

[Next, the Court held that claim preclusion principles did not prevent the challenge to the surgical-center provision either, as it was a "separate, distinct provision[ ] of H.B. 2" from the admitting-privileges provision.]

III

Undue Burden—Legal Standard

. . .

The Court of Appeals' articulation of the relevant standard is incorrect. [It] may be read to imply that a district court should not consider the existence or nonexistence of medical benefits when considering whether a regulation of abortion constitutes an undue burden. The rule announced in *Casey*, however, requires that courts consider the burdens a law imposes on abortion access together with the benefits those laws confer. ... And [it] is wrong to equate the judicial review applicable to the regulation of a constitutionally protected personal liberty with the less strict review applicable where, for example, economic legislation is at issue. ... *Casey* ... asks courts to consider whether any burden imposed on abortion access is "undue."

The statement that legislatures, and not courts, must resolve questions of medical uncertainty is also inconsistent with this Court's case law. Instead, the Court, when determining the constitutionality of laws regulating abortion procedures, has placed considerable weight upon evidence and argument presented in judicial proceedings. ...

Unlike in Gonzales [v. Carhart, 550 U. S. 124 (2007)], the relevant statute here does not set forth any legislative findings. ... For a district court to give significant weight to evidence in the judicial record in these circumstances is consistent with this Court's case law. As we shall describe, the District Court did so here. It did not simply substitute its own judgment for that of the legislature. It considered the evidence in the record—including expert evidence, presented in stipulations, depositions, and testimony. It then weighed the asserted benefits against the burdens. We hold that, in so doing, the District Court applied the correct legal standard.

IV

Undue Burden—Admitting-Privileges Requirement

. . . We conclude that there is adequate legal and factual support for the District Court's conclusion [that the admitting-privileges requirement imposed an "undue burden" on a woman's right to have an abortion.]

The purpose of the admitting-privileges requirement is to help ensure that women have easy access to a hospital should complications arise during an abortion procedure. . . . But the District Court found that it brought about no such health-related benefit. . . .

The evidence upon which the court based this conclusion included [peer-reviewed studies and expert testimony]. . . .

We have found nothing in Texas' record evidence that shows that, compared to prior law (which required a "working arrangement" with a doctor with admitting privileges), the new law advanced Texas' legitimate interest in protecting women's health.

We add that, when directly asked at oral argument whether Texas knew of a single instance in which the new requirement would have helped even one woman obtain better treatment, Texas admitted that there was no evidence in the record of such a case. See Tr. of Oral Arg. 47. . . .

At the same time, the record evidence indicates that the admitting-privileges requirement places a "substantial obstacle in the path of a woman's choice." *Casey*, 505 U. S., at 877 (plurality opinion). The District Court found, as of the time the admitting-privileges requirement began to be enforced, the number of facilities providing abortions dropped in half, from about 40 to about 20. . . . Eight abortion clinics closed in the months leading up to the requirement's effective date. . . . Eleven more closed on the day the admitting-privileges requirement took effect. . . .

Other evidence helps to explain why the new requirement led to the closure of clinics. We read that other evidence in light of a brief filed in this Court by the Society of Hospital Medicine[, which] describes the undisputed general fact that "hospitals often condition admitting privileges on reaching a certain number of admissions per year.". . . In a word, doctors would be unable to maintain admitting privileges or obtain those privileges for the future, because the fact that abortions are so safe meant that providers were unlikely to have any patients to admit.

. . . [And t]he admitting-privileges requirement does not serve any relevant credentialing function.

In our view, the record contains sufficient evidence that the admitting-privileges requirement led to the closure of half of Texas' clinics, or thereabouts. Those closures meant fewer doctors, longer waiting times, and increased crowding. Record evidence also supports the finding that after the admitting-privileges provision went into effect, the "number of women of reproductive age living in a county . . . more than 150 miles from a provider increased from approximately 86,000 to 400,000 . . . and the number of women living in a county more than 200 miles from a provider from approximately 10,000 to 290,000."... We recognize that increased driving distances do not always constitute an "undue burden."... But here, those increases are but one additional burden, which, when taken together with others that the closings brought about, and when viewed in light of the virtual absence of any health benefit, lead us to conclude that the record adequately supports the District Court's "undue burden" conclusion....

The dissent's only argument why these clinic closures, as well as the ones discussed in Part V, *infra*, may not have imposed an undue burden is this: Although "H. B. 2 caused the closure of *some* clinics" (emphasis added), other clinics may have closed for other reasons (so we should not "actually count" the burdens resulting from those closures against H. B. 2). But petitioners satisfied their burden to present evidence of causation by presenting direct testimony as well as plausible inferences to be drawn from the timing of the clinic closures.... The dissent's speculation that perhaps other evidence, not presented at trial or credited by the District Court, might have shown that some clinics closed for unrelated reasons does not provide sufficient ground to disturb the District Court's factual finding on that issue.

. . .

V

Undue Burden—Surgical-Center Requirement

[Justice Breyer first reviewed the "host of health and safety requirements" Texas had in place before the surgical-center requirement, as well as the many additional standards that would have to be met for abortion providers to comply with ambulatory surgical center requirements.]

There is considerable evidence in the record supporting the District Court's findings indicating that the statutory provision requiring all abortion facilities to meet all surgical-center standards does not benefit patients and is not necessary. The District Court found that "risks are not appreciably lowered for patients who undergo abortions at ambulatory surgical centers as compared to nonsurgical-center facilities."... The court added that women "will not obtain better care or experience more frequent positive outcomes at an ambulatory surgical center as compared to a previously licensed facility."... And these findings are well supported.

The record makes clear that the surgical-center requirement provides no benefit when complications arise in the context of an abortion produced through medication. That is because, in such a case, complications would almost always arise only after the patient has left the facility.... The record also contains evidence indicating that abortions taking place in an abortion facility are safe—indeed, safer than numerous procedures that take place outside hospitals and to which Texas does not apply its surgical-center requirements.... Nationwide, childbirth is 14 times more likely than abortion to result in death, ... but Texas law allows a midwife to oversee childbirth in the patient's own home. Colonoscopy, a procedure that typically takes place outside a hospital (or surgical center) setting, has a mortality rate 10 times higher than an abortion. . . . And Texas partly or wholly grandfathers (or waives in whole or in part the surgical-center requirement for) about two-thirds of the facilities to which the surgical-center standards apply. But it neither grandfathers nor provides waivers for any of the facilities that perform abortions. . . . These facts indicate that the surgical-center provision imposes "a requirement that simply is not based on differences" between abortion and other surgical procedures "that are reasonably related to" preserving women's health, the asserted "purpos[e] of the Act in which it is found.". . .

Moreover, many surgical-center requirements are inappropriate as applied to surgical abortions. . . . Further, since the few instances in which serious complications do arise following an abortion almost always require hospitalization, not treatment at a surgical center, . . . surgical-center standards will not help in those instances either.

The upshot is that this record evidence, along with the absence of any evidence to the contrary, provides ample support for the District Court's conclusion that "[m]any of the building standards mandated by the act and its implementing rules have such a tangential relationship to patient safety in the context of abortion as to be nearly arbitrary.". . . That conclusion, along with the supporting evidence, provides sufficient support for the more general conclusion that the surgical-center requirement "will not [provide] better care or . . . more frequent positive outcomes.". . . The record evidence thus supports the ultimate legal conclusion that the surgical-center requirement is not necessary.

At the same time, the record provides adequate evidentiary support for the District Court's conclusion that the surgical-center requirement places a substantial obstacle in the path of women seeking an abortion. . . .

   . . .

For one thing, the record contains charts and oral testimony . . . that, as a result of the surgical-center requirement, the number of abortions that the clinics would have to provide would rise from " '14,000 abortions annually' " to " '60,000 to 70,000' "—an increase by a factor of about five. . . .

For another thing, common sense suggests that, more often than not, a physical facility that satisfies a certain physical demand will not be able to meet five times that demand without expanding or otherwise incurring significant costs. . . . The dissent takes issue with this general, intuitive point by arguing that many places operate below capacity and that in any event, facilities could simply hire additional providers. We disagree that, according to common sense, medical facilities, well known for their wait times, operate below capacity as a general matter. And the fact that so many facilities were forced to close by the admitting-privileges requirement means that hiring more physicians would not be quite as simple as the dissent suggests. Courts are free to base their findings on commonsense inferences drawn from the evidence. And that is what the District Court did here.

   . . .

Texas suggests that the seven or eight remaining clinics could expand sufficiently to provide abortions for the 60,000 to 72,000 Texas women who sought them each year. Because petitioners had satisfied their burden, the obligation was on Texas, if it could, to present evidence rebutting that issue to the District Court. Texas admitted that it presented no such evidence. . . .

. . .

More fundamentally, in the face of no threat to women's health, Texas seeks to force women to travel long distances to get abortions in crammed-to-capacity superfacilities. Patients seeking these services are less likely to get the kind of individualized attention, serious conversation, and emotional support that doctors at less taxed facilities may have offered. Healthcare facilities and medical professionals are not fungible commodities. Surgical centers attempting to accommodate sudden, vastly increased demand, . . . may find that quality of care declines. Another commonsense inference that the District Court made is that these effects would be harmful to, not supportive of, women's health.

Finally, the District Court found that the costs that a currently licensed abortion facility would have to incur to meet the surgical-center requirements were considerable, ranging from $1 million per facility (for facilities with adequate space) to $3 million per facility (where additional land must be purchased). . . . This evidence supports the conclusion that more surgical centers will not soon fill the gap when licensed facilities are forced to close.

We agree with the District Court that the surgical-center requirement, like the admitting-privileges requirement, provides few, if any, health benefits for women, poses a substantial obstacle to women seeking abortions, and constitutes an "undue burden" on their constitutional right to do so.

VI

We consider three additional arguments that Texas makes and deem none persuasive.

First, Texas argues that facial invalidation of both challenged provisions is precluded by H. B. 2's severability clause. . . . Texas argues . . . that facial invalidation of parts of the statute is not an option; instead, it says, the severability clause mandates a more narrowly tailored judicial remedy. But the challenged provisions of H. B. 2 close most of the abortion facilities in Texas and place added stress on those facilities able to remain open. They vastly increase the obstacles confronting women seeking abortions in Texas without providing any benefit to women's health capable of withstanding any meaningful scrutiny. The provisions are unconstitutional on their face: Including a severability provision in the law does not change that conclusion.

. . . A severability clause is not grounds for a court to "devise a judicial remedy that . . . entail[s] quintessentially legislative work." Ayotte v. Planned Parenthood of Northern New Eng., 546 U. S. 320, 329 (2006). Such an approach would inflict enormous costs on both courts and litigants, who would be required to proceed in this manner whenever a single application of a law might be valid. We reject Texas' invitation to pave the way for legislatures to immunize their statutes from facial review.

Texas similarly argues that instead of finding the entire surgical-center provision unconstitutional, we should invalidate (as applied to abortion clinics) only those specific surgical-center regulations that unduly burden the provision of abortions, while leaving in place other surgical-center regulations. . . . As we have explained, Texas' attempt to broadly draft a requirement to sever "applications" does not require us to proceed in piecemeal fashion when we have found the statutory provisions at issue facially unconstitutional.

Nor is that approach to the regulations even required by H. B. 2 itself. The statute was meant to require abortion facilities to meet the integrated surgical-center standards—not some subset thereof. . . .

Second, Texas claims that the provisions at issue here do not impose a substantial obstacle because the women affected by those laws are not a "large fraction" of Texan women "of reproductive age," which Texas reads *Casey* to have required. . . . But *Casey* used the language "large fraction" to refer to "a large fraction of cases in which [the provision at issue] is *relevant*," a class narrower than "all women," "pregnant women," or even "the class of *women seeking abortions* identified by the State." 505 U. S., at 894–895 (opinion of the Court) (emphasis added). Here, as in *Casey*, the relevant denominator is "those [women] for whom [the provision] is an actual rather than an irrelevant restriction."

Third, Texas looks for support to Simopoulos v. Virginia, 462 U. S. 506 (1983), a case in which this Court upheld a surgical-center requirement as applied to second-trimester abortions. This case, however, . . . involves restrictions applicable to all abortions, not simply to those that take place during the second trimester. Most abortions in Texas occur in the first trimester, not the second. . . . More importantly, in *Casey* we discarded the trimester framework, and we now use "viability" as the relevant point at which a State may begin limiting women's access to abortion for reasons unrelated to maternal health. . . . Because the second trimester includes time that is both previability and postviability, *Simopoulos* cannot provide clear guidance. Further, the Court in *Simopoulos* found that the petitioner in that case, unlike petitioners here, had waived any argument that the regulation did not significantly help protect women's health. . . .

* * *

For these reasons the judgment of the Court of Appeals is reversed, and the case is remanded for further proceedings consistent with this opinion.

Justice Ginsburg, concurring.

. . . H. B. 2 inevitably will reduce the number of clinics and doctors allowed to provide abortion services. Texas argues that H. B. 2's restrictions are constitutional because they protect the health of women who experience complications from abortions. In truth, "complications from an abortion are both rare and rarely dangerous.". . . See Brief for American College of Obstetricians and Gynecologists et al. as *Amici Curiae* 6–10 (collecting studies and concluding "[a]bortion is one of the safest medical procedures performed in the United States"); Brief for Social Science Researchers as *Amici Curiae* 5–9 (compiling studies that show "[c]omplication rates from abortion are very low"). Many medical procedures, including childbirth, are far more dangerous to patients, yet are not subject to ambulatory-surgical-center or hospital admitting-privileges requirements. . . . Given those realities, it is beyond rational belief that H. B. 2 could genuinely protect the health of women, and certain that the law "would simply make it more difficult for them to obtain abortions.". . . When a State severely limits access to safe and legal procedures, women in desperate circumstances may resort to unlicensed rogue practitioners, *faute de mieux*, at great risk to their health and safety. . . . So long as this Court adheres to Roe v. Wade, 410 U. S. 113 (1973), and Planned Parenthood of Southeastern Pa. v. Casey, 505 U. S. 833 (1992), Targeted Regulation of Abortion Providers laws like H. B. 2 that "do little or nothing for health, but rather strew impediments to abortion," . . . cannot survive judicial inspection.

Justice Thomas, dissenting.

. . . [T]oday's decision perpetuates the Court's habit of applying different rules to different constitutional rights—especially the putative right to abortion.

. . . Ordinarily, plaintiffs cannot file suits to vindicate the constitutional rights of others. But the Court employs a different approach to rights that it favors. So in this case and many others, the Court has erroneously allowed doctors and clinics to vicariously vindicate the putative constitutional right of women seeking abortions.

This case also underscores the Court's increasingly common practice of invoking a given level of scrutiny—here, the abortion-specific undue burden standard—while applying a different standard of review entirely. . . . [T]he majority eviscerates important features of that test to return to a regime like the one that *Casey* repudiated.

. . .

. . . The central question under the Court's abortion precedents is whether there is an undue burden on a woman's access to abortion. . . . But the Court's permissive approach to third-party standing encourages litigation that deprives us of the information needed to resolve that issue. Our precedents encourage abortion providers to sue—and our cases then relieve them of any obligation to prove what burdens women actually face. . . .

. . .

I remain fundamentally opposed to the Court's abortion jurisprudence. . . . Even taking *Casey* as the baseline, however, the majority radically rewrites the undue-burden test in three ways. First, today's decision requires courts to "consider the burdens a law imposes on abortion access together with the benefits those laws confer." Second, today's opinion tells the courts that, when the law's justifications are medically uncertain, they need not defer to the legislature, and must instead assess medical justifications for abortion restrictions by scrutinizing the record themselves. Finally, even if a law imposes no "substantial obstacle" to women's access to abortions, the law now must have more than a "reasonabl[e] relat[ion] to . . . a legitimate state interest." These precepts are nowhere to be found in *Casey* or its successors, and transform the undue-burden test to something much more akin to strict scrutiny.

. . .

The majority's furtive reconfiguration of the standard of scrutiny applicable to abortion restrictions also points to a deeper problem. The undue-burden standard is just one variant of the Court's tiers-of-scrutiny approach to constitutional adjudication. And the label the Court affixes to its level of scrutiny in assessing whether the governmentcan restrict a given right—be it "rational basis," intermediate, strict, or something else—is increasingly a meaningless formalism. As the Court applies whatever standard it likes to any given case, nothing but empty words separates our constitutional decisions from judicial fiat.

. . .

The illegitimacy of using "made-up tests" to "displace longstanding national traditions as the primary determinant of what the Constitution means" has long been apparent. United States v. Virginia, 518 U. S. 515, 570 (1996) (Scalia, J., dissenting). . . .

But the problem now goes beyond that. If our recent cases illustrate anything, it is how easily the Court tinkers with levels of scrutiny to achieve its desired result. . . .

. . .

. . . The Court should abandon the pretense that anything other than policy preferences underlies its balancing of constitutional rights and interests in any given case.

. . .

Justice Alito, with whom The Chief Justice and Justice Thomas join, dissenting.

. . .

. . . The Court . . . , determined to strike down two provisions of a new Texas abortion statute in all of their applications, . . . simply disregards basic rules that apply in all other cases.

. . .

Under the rules that apply in regular cases, petitioners could not relitigate the exact same claim in a second suit. . . .

In this abortion case, however, that rule is disregarded. The Court awards a victory to petitioners on the very claim that they unsuccessfully pressed in the earlier case. . . .

Here is one more example: the Court's treatment of H. B. 2's "severability clause.". . . H. B. 2 contains what must surely be the most emphatic severability clause ever written. This clause says that every single word of the statute and every possible application of its provisions is severable. But despite this language, the Court holds that no part of the challenged provisions and no application of any part of them can be saved. . . .

The Court's patent refusal to apply well-established law in a neutral way is indefensible and will undermine public confidence in the Court as a fair and neutral arbiter.

[Justice Alito's lengthy analysis of the res judicata issue included the following:]

Section 19 of the second Restatement [of Judgments] sets out the general claim-preclusion rule that applies in a case like the one before us: "A valid and final personal judgment rendered in favor of the defendant bars another action by the plaintiff on the same claim.". . .

Both the claim asserted in petitioners' first suit and the claim now revived by the Court involve the same "nucleus of operative facts." Indeed, they involve the very same "operative facts," namely, the enactment of the admitting privileges requirement, which, according to the theory underlying petitioners' facial claims, would inevitably have the effect of causing abortion clinics to close. This is what petitioners needed to show—and what they attempted to show in their first facial attack: not that the admitting privileges requirement had *already* imposed a substantial burden on the right of Texas women to obtain abortions, but only that it *would have* that effect once clinics were able to assess whether they could practicably comply.

. . .

. . . What matters is that the "operative fact" in the prior case was the enactment of the admitting privileges requirement, and that is precisely the same operative fact underlying petitioners' facial attack in the case now before us.

. . .

. . . [T]he Court's main argument [is] that the second facial challenge is a different claim because of "changed circumstances." What the Court means by this is that petitioners now have better evidence than they did at the time of the first case with respect to the number of clinics that would have to close as a result of the admitting privileges requirement. This argument is contrary to a cardinal rule of res judicata, namely, that a plaintiff who loses in a first case cannot later bring the same case simply because it has now gathered better evidence. . . .

In an effort to get around this hornbook rule, the Court cites a potpourri of our decisions that have no bearing on the question at issue. Some . . . endorse the unremarkable proposition that a prior judgment does not preclude new claims based on acts occurring after the time of the first judgment. But petitioners' second facial challenge is not based on new acts postdating the first suit. Rather, it is based on the same underlying act, the enactment of H. B. 2, which allegedly posed an undue burden.

. . .

. . . As best I can tell, the Court's new rule must be something like this: If a plaintiff initially loses because it failed to provide adequate proof that a challenged law will have an unconstitutional effect and if subsequent developments tend to show that the law will in fact have those effects, the plaintiff may relitigate the same claim. Such a rule would be unprecedented, and I am unsure of its wisdom, but I am certain of this: There is no possible justification for such a rule unless the plaintiff, at the time of the first case, could not have reasonably shown what the effects of the law would be. And that is not the situation in this case.

. . .

Even if the Court thinks that petitioners' evidence in the first case was insufficient, the Court does not claim that petitioners, with reasonable effort, could not have gathered sufficient evidence to show with some degree of accuracy what the effects of the admitting privileges requirement would be. [I]n their first trial petitioners introduced a survey of 27 abortion clinics indicating that 15 would close because of the admitting privileges requirement. The Court does not identify what additional evidence petitioners needed but were unable to gather. There is simply no reason why petitioners should be allowed to relitigate their facial claim.

[As for "the application of principles of claim preclusion to a claim that petitioners did include in their second complaint, namely, their facial challenge to the requirement in H. B. 2 that abortion clinics comply with the rules that govern ambulatory surgical centers (ASCs)[,]" Justice Alito first invoked precedents supporting the idea that "the doctrine of claim preclusion not only bars the relitigation of previously litigated claims; it can also bar claims that are closely related to the claims unsuccessfully litigated in a prior case." He then insisted that "[p]etitioners challenge two provisions of one law, not just two provisions of a regulatory scheme[,]" and he continued in part:]

. . . The two claims here are very closely related. They are two parts of the same bill. They both impose new requirements on abortion clinics. They are justified by the State on the same ground, protection of the safety of women seeking abortions. They are both challenged as imposing the same kind of burden (impaired access to clinics) on the same kind of right (the right to abortion, as announced in Roe v. Wade, 410 U. S. 113 (1973), and *Casey*, 505 U. S. 833). And petitioners attack the two provisions as a package. According to petitioners, the two provisions were both enacted for the same illegitimate purpose—to close down Texas abortion clinics. . . . And . . . petitioners rely on the combined effect of the two requirements. Petitioners have made little effort to identify the clinics that closed as a result of each requirement but instead aggregate the two requirements' effects.

For these reasons, the two challenges "form a convenient trial unit." Restatement (Second) of Judgments § 24(2). . . .

. . .

. . . [P]etitioners' facial attack on the ASC requirements, like their facial attack on the admitting privileges rule, is precluded.

III

Even if res judicata did not bar either facial claim, a sweeping, statewide injunction against the enforcement of the admitting privileges and ASC requirements would still be unjustified. . . .

[W]hat matters for present purposes is not the effect of the H. B. 2 provisions on petitioners but the effect on their patients. Under our cases, petitioners must show that the admitting privileges and ASC requirements impose an "undue burden" on women seeking abortions. Gonzales v. Carhart, 550 U. S. 124, 146 (2007). And in order to obtain the sweeping relief they seek—facial invalidation of those provisions—they must show, at a minimum, that these provisions have an unconstitutional impact on at least a "large fraction" of Texas women of reproductive age. . . . Such a situation could result if the clinics able to comply with the new requirements either lacked the requisite overall capacity or were located too far away to serve a "large fraction" of the women in question.

Petitioners did not make that showing. Instead of offering direct evidence, they relied on two crude inferences. First, they pointed to the number of abortion clinics that closed after the enactment of H. B. 2, and asked that it be inferred that all these closures resulted from the two challenged provisions. . . . They made little effort to show why particular clinics closed. Second, they pointed to the number of abortions performed annually at ASCs before H. B. 2 took effect and, because this figure is well below the total number of abortions performed each year in the State, they asked that it be inferred that ASC-compliant clinics could not meet the demands of women in the State. . . . Petitioners failed to provide any evidence of the actual capacity of the facilities that would be available to perform abortions in compliance with the new law— even though they provided this type of evidence in their first case to the District Court at trial and then to this Court in their application for interim injunctive relief.

A

. . .

While there can be no doubt that H. B. 2 caused some clinics to cease operation, the absence of proof regarding the reasons for particular closures is a problem because some clinics have or may have closed for at least four reasons other than the two H. B. 2 requirements at issue here. These are [(1) the provision of H. B. 2 that regulates medication abortion, which was previously upheld and not relitigated in this case, which was followed by a decrease of nearly 7,000 such abortions in the first six months after it took effect; (2) a Texas law preventing family planning grants to providers that perform abortions, which may have caused some clinics to close for lack of funding; (3) a nationwide decline in abortion demand; and (4) physician retirements or other localized factors.]

At least nine Texas clinics may have ceased performing abortions (or reduced capacity) for one or more of the reasons having nothing to do with the provisions challenged here. . . .

Neither petitioners nor the District Court properly addressed these complexities in assessing causation—and for no good reason. . . .

Precise findings are important because the key issue here is not the number or percentage of clinics affected, but the effect of the closures on women seeking abortions, *i.e.*, on the capacity and geographic distribution of clinics used by those women. To the extent that clinics closed (or experienced a reduction in capacity) for any reason unrelated to the challenged provisions of H. B. 2, the corresponding burden on abortion access may not be factored into the access analysis. . . . Petitioners—who, as plaintiffs, bore the burden of proof—cannot simply point to temporal correlation and call it causation.

B

Even if the District Court had properly filtered out immaterial closures, its analysis would have been incomplete for a second reason. Petitioners offered scant evidence on the capacity of the clinics that are able to comply with the admitting privileges and ASC requirements, or on those clinics' geographic distribution. Reviewing the evidence in the record, it is far from clear that there has been a material impact on access to abortion.

. . .

. . . First, it is not unassailable "common sense" to hold that current utilization equals capacity. . . . Faced with increased demand, ASCs could potentially increase the number of abortions performed without prohibitively expensive changes. Among other things, they might hire more physicians who perform abortions, utilize their facilities more intensively or efficiently, or shift the mix of services provided. Second, what matters for present purposes is not the capacity of just those ASCs that performed abortions prior to the enactment of H. B. 2 but the capacity of those that would be available to perform abortions after the statute took effect. And since the enactment of H. B. 2, the number of ASCs performing abortions has increased by 50%—from six in 2012 to nine today.

The most serious problem with the Court's reasoning is that its conclusion is belied by petitioners' own submissions to this Court. . . .

. . .

. . . The important point is that petitioners put on evidence of actual clinic capacity in their earlier case, and there is no apparent reason why they could not have done the same here. Indeed, the Court asserts that, after the admitting privileges requirement took effect, clinics "were not able to accommodate increased demand," but petitioners' own evidence suggested that the requirement had *no* effect on capacity. . . . On this point, like the question of the reason for clinic closures, petitioners did not discharge their burden, and the District Court did not engage in the type of analysis that should have been conducted before enjoining an important state law.

So much for capacity. The other potential obstacle to abortion access is the distribution of facilities throughout the State. This might occur if the two challenged H. B. 2 requirements, by causing the closure of clinics in some rural areas, led to a situation in which a "large fraction" of women of reproductive age live too far away from any open clinic. Based on the Court's holding in . . . *Casey*, . . . it appears that the need to travel up to 150 miles is not an undue burden, and the evidence in this case shows that if the only clinics in the State were those that would have remained open if the judgment of the Fifth Circuit had not been enjoined, roughly 95% of the women of reproductive age in the State would live within 150 miles of an open facility (or lived outside that range before H. B. 2). Because the record does not show why particular facilities closed, the real figure may be even higher than 95%.

We should decline to hold that these statistics justify the facial invalidation of the H. B. 2 requirements. The possibility that the admitting privileges requirement *might* have caused a closure in Lubbock is no reason to issue a facial injunction exempting Houston clinics from that requirement. I do not dismiss the situation of those women who would no longer live within 150 miles of a clinic as a result of H. B. 2. But under current doctrine such localized problems can be addressed by narrow as-applied challenges.

IV

Even if the Court were right to hold that res judicata does not bar this suit and that H. B. 2 imposes an undue burden on abortion access—it is, in fact, wrong on both counts—it is still wrong to conclude that the admitting privileges and surgical center provisions must be enjoined in their entirety[, because of H. B. 2's] extraordinarily broad severability clause. . . .

A

Applying H. B. 2's severability clause to the admitting privileges requirement is easy. Simply put, the requirement must be upheld in every city in which its application does not pose an undue burden. It surely does not pose that burden anywhere in the eastern half of the State, where most Texans live and where virtually no woman of reproductive age lives more than 150 miles from an open clinic. . . . And petitioners would need to show that the requirement caused specific West Texas clinics to close . . . before they could be entitled to an injunction tailored to address those closures.

B

Applying severability to the surgical center requirement calls for the identification of the particular provisions of the ASC regulations that result in the imposition of an undue burden. These regulations are lengthy and detailed, and while compliance with some might be expensive, compliance with many others would not. And many serve important health and safety purposes. Thus, the surgical center requirements cannot be judged as a package. . . .

. . .

[H. B. 2's severability provision] indisputably requires that all surgical center regulations that are not themselves unconstitutional be left standing. . . .

. . .

. . . Federal courts have no authority to carpet-bomb state laws, knocking out provisions that are perfectly consistent with federal law, just because it would be too much bother to separate them from unconstitutional provisions.

In any event, it should not have been hard in this case for the District Court to separate any bad provisions from the good. Petitioners should have identified the particular provisions that would entail what they regard as an undue expense, and the District Court could have then concentrated its analysis on those provisions. In fact, petitioners *did* do this in their trial brief, . . . but they changed their position once the District Court awarded blanket relief. . . . I do not see how it "would inflict enormous costs on both courts and litigants" to single out the ASC regulations that this Court and petitioners have both targeted as the core of the challenge.

By forgoing severability, the Court strikes down numerous provisions that could not plausibly impose an undue burden. . . .

Any responsible application of the H. B. 2 severability provision would leave much of the law intact. At a minimum, both of the requirements challenged here should be held constitutional as applied to clinics in any Texas city that will have a surgical center providing abortions (*i.e.*, those areas in which there cannot possibly have been an undue burden on abortion access). Moreover, as even the District Court found, the surgical center requirement is clearly constitutional as to new abortion facilities and facilities already licensed as surgical centers. . . . And we should uphold every application of every surgical center regulation that does not pose an undue burden—at the very least, all of the regulations as to which petitioners have never made a specific complaint supported by specific evidence. . . .

. . .

When we decide cases on particularly controversial issues, we should take special care to apply settled procedural rules in a neutral manner. The Court has not done that here.

I therefore respectfully dissent.

Page 608. Add after Lawrence v. Texas:

Obergefell v. Hodges

576 U.S. ___, 135 S.Ct. 2584, 109 L.Ed.2d 609 (2015).

[The report of this case appears supra at page 87.]

CHAPTER 10

THE EQUAL PROTECTION CLAUSE AND THE REVIEW OF THE REASONABLENESS OF LEGISLATION

3. SUSPECT CLASSIFICATIONS

E. "BENIGN" DISCRIMINATION: AFFIRMATIVE ACTION, QUOTAS, PREFERENCES BASED ON GENDER OR RACE

2. CLASSIFICATIONS ADVANTAGING RACIAL MINORITIES

Page 782. Add after Easley v. Cromartie:

Alabama Legislative Black Caucus v. Alabama, 575 U.S. ___, 135 S.Ct. 1257 (2015). The report in this case appears, infra, at page 163.

Page 799. Add after Gratz v. Bollinger:

Fisher v. University of Texas at Austin, 570 U.S. ___, 133 S.Ct. 2411 (2013). A rejected white applicant contended that the undergraduate admissions process of the University of Texas at Austin (UT), which aimed to achieve a "critical mass" of racial minorities in the undergraduate population, denied her equal protection by impermissibly considering race in a manner that allegedly conflicted with *Grutter*, among other decisions. Reversing a grant of summary judgment by the Court of Appeals that—purporting to apply *Grutter*—had upheld the admissions program, the Supreme Court, with only Justice Ginsburg dissenting (and Justice Kagan not participating), held that the Court of Appeals "did not apply the correct standard of strict scrutiny" insofar as it "confined the strict scrutiny inquiry in too narrow a way by deferring to the University's good faith in its use of racial classifications and affirming the grant of summary judgment on that basis." Accordingly, the Court remanded the case "so that the admissions process can be considered and judged under a correct analysis.... Unlike *Grutter*, which was decided after trial, this case arises from cross-motions for summary judgment. In ... determining whether summary judgment in favor of the University would be appropriate, the Court of Appeals must assess whether the University has offered sufficient evidence that would prove that its admissions program is narrowly tailored to obtain the educational benefits of diversity. Whether this record—and not 'simple ... assurances of good intention,' *Croson* ... —is sufficient is a question for the Court of Appeals in the first instance."

The record as it stood showed that following a pre-*Grutter*, 1996 Court of Appeals decision that invalidated a former race-conscious admissions program, the "Texas State Legislature ... enacted ... the Top Ten Percent Law grant[ing] automatic admission to any public state college, including the University, to all students in the top 10% of their class at high schools in Texas that comply with certain standards." Together with a new race-neutral, but "holistic" UT admissions process, UT ended up in the year before *Grutter* with an "entering class [that] was 4.5% African-American and 16.9% Hispanic"— compared to an "entering freshman class [that] was 4.1% African-American and 14.5% Hispanic" in the pre-1996 era of race-conscious admissions. Disappointed, however, by a study of undergraduate classes of 5–24 students showing few with "significant enrollment by members of racial minorities[,]" and by " 'anecdotal' reports from students regarding their 'interaction in the classroom[,]' " UT decided in 2004—after *Grutter*—to again take race into account as "a meaningful factor" in admissions.

Justice Kennedy's majority opinion emphasized that although among the Justices there "is disagreement about whether *Grutter* was consistent with the principles of equal protection in approving th[e] compelling interest in diversity[,] ... the parties here do not ask the Court to revisit that aspect of *Grutter*'s holding." He then continued:

"Once the University has established that its goal of diversity is consistent with strict scrutiny, however, there must still be a further judicial determination that the admissions process meets strict scrutiny in its implementation. The University must prove that the means chosen by the University to attain diversity are narrowly tailored to that goal. On this point, the University receives no deference. *Grutter* made clear that it is for the courts, not for university administrators, to ensure that '[t]he means chosen to accomplish the [government's] asserted purpose must be specifically and narrowly framed to accomplish that purpose.' ... True, a court can take account of a university's experience and expertise in adopting or rejecting certain admissions processes. But, as the Court said in *Grutter*, it remains at all times the University's obligation to demonstrate, and the Judiciary's obligation to determine, that admissions processes 'ensure that each applicant is evaluated as an individual and not in a way that makes an applicant's race or ethnicity the defining feature of his or her application.' ...

"Narrow tailoring also requires that the reviewing court verify that it is 'necessary' for a university to use race to achieve the educational benefits of diversity. *Bakke*, ... This involves a careful judicial inquiry into whether a university could achieve sufficient diversity without using racial classifications. Although '[n]arrow tailoring does not require exhaustion of every *conceivable* race-neutral alternative,' strict scrutiny does require a court to examine with care, and not defer to, a university's 'serious, good faith consideration of workable race-neutral alternatives.' See *Grutter*, ... (emphasis added). Consideration by the university is of course *necessary*, but it is not sufficient to satisfy strict scrutiny: The reviewing court must ultimately be satisfied that no workable race-neutral alternatives would produce the educational benefits of diversity. . . . A plaintiff, of course, bears the burden of placing the validity of a university's adoption of an affirmative action plan in issue. But strict scrutiny imposes on the university the ultimate burden of demonstrating, before turning to racial classifications, that available, workable race-neutral alternatives do not suffice.

"Rather than perform this searching examination, however, the Court of Appeals held petitioner could challenge only 'whether [the University's] decision to reintroduce race as a factor in admissions was made in good faith.' . . . And in considering such a challenge, the court would 'presume the University acted in good faith' and place on petitioner the burden of rebutting that presumption. . . . The Court of Appeals held that to 'second-guess the merits' of this aspect of the University's decision was a task it was 'ill-equipped to perform' and that it would attempt only to 'ensure that [the University's] decision to adopt a race-conscious admissions policy followed from [a process of] good faith consideration.' . . . The Court of Appeals thus concluded that 'the narrow-tailoring inquiry—like the compelling-interest inquiry—is undertaken with a degree of deference to the Universit[y].' . . . Because 'the efforts of the University have been studied, serious, and of high purpose,' the Court of Appeals held that the use of race in the admissions program fell within 'a constitutionally protected zone of discretion.' . . .

"These expressions of the controlling standard are at odds with *Grutter*'s command that 'all racial classifications imposed by government "must be analyzed by a reviewing court under strict scrutiny." ' . . .

"*Grutter* did not hold that good faith would forgive an impermissible consideration of race. It must be remembered that 'the mere recitation of a "benign" or legitimate purpose for a racial classification is entitled to little or no weight.' *Croson*, ... Strict scrutiny does not permit a court to accept a school's assertion that its admissions process uses race in a permissible way without a court giving close analysis to the evidence of how the process works in practice.

"The higher education dynamic does not change the narrow tailoring analysis of strict scrutiny applicable in other contexts. . . ."

Justice Kennedy concluded the majority opinion with these remarks:

"Strict scrutiny must not be ' "strict in theory, but fatal in fact," ' *Adarand* . . . ; see also *Grutter*. . . . But the opposite is also true. Strict scrutiny must not be strict in theory but feeble in fact. In order for judicial review to be meaningful, a university must make a showing that its plan is narrowly tailored to achieve the only interest that this Court has approved in this context: the benefits of a student body diversity that 'encompasses a . . . broa[d] array of qualifications and characteristics of which racial or ethnic origin is but a single though important element.' *Bakke*, . . . (opinion of Powell, J.)."

Justice Scalia "join[ed] the Court's opinion in full[,]" but concurred as well to reiterate his view in *Grutter* that the Constitution forbids race discrimination in state-provided education, and to emphasize that "petitioner in this case did not ask us to overrule *Grutter*'s holding that a 'compelling interest' in the educational benefits of diversity can justify racial preferences in university admissions." Justice Thomas also concurred, but added that he "would overrule *Grutter* . . . and hold that a State's use of race in higher education admissions decisions is categorically prohibited by the Equal Protection Clause." He reiterated his dissenting position in *Grutter* "that the educational benefits flowing from student body diversity—assuming they exist—hardly qualify as a compelling state interest. . . . [J]ust as the alleged educational benefits of segregation were insufficient to justify racial discrimination [at the time of *Brown v. Board of Education*], the alleged educational benefits of diversity cannot justify racial discrimination today." He elaborated in part:

"[I]n our desegregation cases, we rejected arguments that are virtually identical to those advanced by the University today. The University asserts, for instance, that the diversity obtained through its discriminatory admissions program prepares its students to become leaders in a diverse society. . . . The segregationists likewise defended segregation on the ground that it provided more leadership opportunities for blacks. . . .

"The University also asserts that student body diversity improves interracial relations. . . . In this argument, too, the University repeats arguments once marshaled in support of segregation. . . . We flatly rejected this line of arguments in *McLaurin* v. *Oklahoma State Regents for Higher Ed.*, 339 U.S. 637 (1950), where we held that segregation would be unconstitutional even if white students never tolerated blacks. . . . It is, thus, entirely irrelevant whether the University's racial discrimination increases or decreases tolerance.

"Finally, while the University admits that racial discrimination in admissions is not ideal, it asserts that it is a temporary necessity because of the enduring race consciousness of our society. . . . Yet again, the University echoes the hollow justifications advanced by the segregationists. . . . The Fourteenth Amendment views racial bigotry as an evil to be stamped out, not as an excuse for perpetual racial tinkering by the State. . . ."

Justice Thomas went on to argue that "the lesson of history is clear enough: Racial discrimination is never benign. . . . The University's professed good intentions cannot excuse its outright racial discrimination any more than such intentions justified the now denounced arguments of slaveholders and segregationists." In addition, he asserted "that racial engineering does in fact have insidious consequences" in the form of injury not only to "white and Asian applicants who are denied admission because of their race[,]" but to "Blacks and Hispanics admitted to the University as a result of racial discrimination[, who] are, on average, far less prepared than their white and Asian classmates." Concerning the latter injury, he observed that the "University admits minorities who otherwise would have attended less selective colleges where they would have been more evenly matched. But, as a result of the mismatching, many blacks and Hispanics who likely would have excelled at less elite schools are placed in a position where underperformance is all but inevitable because they are less academically prepared than the white and Asian students with whom they must compete." He found "some evidence that students admitted as a result of racial discrimination are more likely to abandon their initial aspirations to become scientists and engineers than are students with similar qualifications who attend less selective schools[,]" and he suggested that "[t]hese students may well drift towards less competitive majors because the mismatch caused by racial discrimination in admissions makes it difficult for them to compete in more rigorous majors." Finally, he reiterated his view that "the University's discrimination . . . taints the accomplishment of all those who are admitted as a result" and "all those who are the same race as those [so] admitted. . . ." Thus, "[a]lthough cloaked in good intentions, the University's racial tinkering harms the very people it claims to be helping."

Justice Ginsburg's solo dissent urged that *Grutter*'s requirements had been satisfied. For her, it sufficed that "the University's admissions policy flexibly considers race only as a 'factor of a factor of a factor of a factor' in the calculus . . . ; followed a yearlong review through which the University reached the reasonable, good-faith judgment that supposedly race-neutral initiatives were insufficient to achieve, in appropriate measure, the educational benefits of student body diversity . . . ; and is subject to periodic review to ensure that the consideration of race remains necessary and proper to achieve the University's educational objectives[.]"

Fisher v. University of Texas at Austin (II), 579 U.S. ___, 136 S.Ct. ____ (2016). Following the Court's remand in *Fisher I*, the Court of Appeals again entered summary judgment in the University's favor, and this time the Supreme Court affirmed. Justice Kennedy again authored the majority opinion—in a 4–3 vote, however, with Justice Scalia having died, and Justice Kagan again recused.

Justice Kennedy noted that "up to 75 percent of the places in the freshman class are filled through the [Top Ten Percent] Plan[, though a]s a practical matter, this 75 percent cap, . . . now . . . fixed by statute, means that . . . a student actually needs to finish in the top seven or eight percent of his or her class . . . to be admitted in this category." The rest of the incoming class is "admitted based on a combination of their AI [Academic Index, a combination of SAT and high school academic performance] and PAI [Personal Achievement Index] scores." The PAI is "a numerical score based on a holistic review of an application." That review scores two required essays from 1–6, and separately involves another 1–6 score from a full-file evaluation (the "Personal Achievement Score" or PAS). The PAS involves a rereading of the essays, supplemental information like letters of recommendation, and an evaluation of "the applicant's potential contributions to the University's student body based on the applicant's leadership experience, extracurricular activities, awards/honors, community service, and other 'special circumstances.'" The "special circumstances" category includes "the socioeconomic status of the applicant's family, the socioeconomic status of the applicant's school, the applicant's family responsibilities, whether the applicant lives in a single-parent home, the applicant's SAT score in relation to the average SAT score at the applicant's school, the language spoken at the applicant's home, and, finally, the applicant's race." Justice Kennedy offered this characterization:

" . . . Race enters the admissions process, then, at one stage and one stage only—the calculation of the PAS.

"Therefore, although admissions officers can consider race as a positive feature of a minority student's application, there is no dispute that race is but a 'factor of a factor of a factor' in the holistic-review calculus. . . . Furthermore, consideration of race is contextual and does not operate as a mechanical plus factor for underrepresented minorities. . . . There is also no dispute, however, that race, when considered in conjunction with other aspects of an applicant's background, can alter an applicant's PAS score. Thus, race, in this indirect fashion, considered with all of the other factors that make up an applicant's AI and PAI scores, can make a difference to whether an application is accepted or rejected."

Reiterating the legal principles set forth in *Fisher I*, Justice Kennedy wrote that the Court had remanded the case "with instructions to evaluate the record under the correct standard and to determine whether the University had made 'a showing that its plan is narrowly tailored to achieve' the educational benefits that flow from diversity." The Court majority was now satisfied that the University in fact had "met its burden of showing that the admissions policy it used at the time it rejected petitioner's application was narrowly tailored." Justice Kennedy's reasoning included the following:

III

"The University's program is *sui generis* [in that] it combines holistic review with a percentage plan. This approach gave rise to an unusual consequence in this case: The component of the University's admissions policy that had the largest impact on petitioner's chances of admission was not the school's consideration of race under its holistic-review process but rather the Top Ten Percent Plan. Because petitioner did not graduate in the top 10 percent of her high school class, she was categorically ineligible for more than three-fourths of the slots in the incoming freshman class. It seems quite plausible, then, to think that petitioner would have had a better chance of being admitted to the University if the school used race-conscious holistic review to select its entire incoming class. . . .

"Despite the Top Ten Percent Plan's outsized effect on petitioner's chances of admission, she has not challenged it. For that reason, throughout this litigation, the Top Ten Percent Plan has been taken, somewhat artificially, as a given premise.

"[That] complicates this Court's review. In particular, it has led to a record that is almost devoid of information about the students who secured admission to the University through the Plan. The Court thus cannot know how students admitted solely based on their class rank differ in their contribution to diversity from students admitted through holistic review.

" . . . When petitioner's application was rejected, . . . the University's combined percentage-plan/holisticreview approach to admission had been in effect for just three years. While studies undertaken over the eight years since then may be of significant value in determining the constitutionality of the

University's current admissions policy, that evidence has little bearing on whether petitioner received equal treatment when her application was rejected in 2008. If the Court were to remand, therefore, further factfinding would be limited to a narrow 3 year sample, review of which might yield little insight.

"Furthermore, . . . the University lacks any authority to alter the role of the [legislatively mandated] Top Ten Percent Plan in its admissions process. . . . If the University had no reason to think that it could deviate from the Top Ten Percent Plan, it similarly had no reason to keep extensive data on the Plan or the students admitted under it—particularly in the years before *Fisher I* clarified the stringency of the strict-scrutiny burden for a school that employs race-conscious review.

"[A] remand would do nothing more than prolong a suit that has already persisted for eight years and cost the parties on both sides significant resources. Petitioner long since has graduated from another college, and the University's policy—and the data on which it first was based—may have evolved or changed in material ways.

" . . .

"[The University does have a] continuing obligation to satisfy the burden of strict scrutiny in light of changing circumstances. The University engages in periodic reassessment of the constitutionality, and efficacy, of its admissions program. . . . Going forward, that assessment must be undertaken in light of the experience the school has accumulated and the data it has gathered since the adoption of its admissions plan.

"As the University examines this data, it should remain mindful that diversity takes many forms. Formalistic racial classifications may sometimes fail to capture diversity in all of its dimensions and, when used in a divisive manner, could undermine the educational benefits the University values. Through regular evaluation of data and consideration of student experience, the University must tailor its approach in light of changing circumstances, ensuring that race plays no greater role than is necessary to meet its compelling interest. The University's examination of the data it has acquired in the years since petitioner's application, for these reasons, must proceed with full respect for the constraints imposed by the EqualProtection Clause. The type of data collected, and the manner in which it is considered, will have a significant bearing on how the University must shape its admissions policy to satisfy strict scrutiny in the years to come. Here, however, the Court is necessarily limited to the narrow question before it: whether, drawing all reasonable inferences in her favor, petitioner has shown by a preponderance of the evidence that she was denied equal treatment at the time her application was rejected.

IV

" . . . [P]etitioner makes four arguments. First, she argues that the University has not articulated its compelling interest with sufficient clarity. According to petitioner, the University must set forth more precisely the level of minority enrollment that would constitute a 'critical mass.' . . .

"[H]owever, the compelling interest that justifies consideration of race in college admissions is not an interest in enrolling a certain number of minority students. Rather, a university may institute a race-conscious admissions program as a means of obtaining 'the educational benefits that flow from student body diversity.' *Fisher I*, . . . ; see also *Grutter*. . . . As this Court has said, enrolling a diverse student body 'promotes cross-racial understanding, helps to break down racial stereotypes, and enables students to better understand persons of different races.' . . . Equally important, 'student body diversity promotes learning outcomes, and better prepares students for an increasingly diverse workforce and society.' . . .

"Increasing minority enrollment may be instrumental to these educational benefits, but it is not, as petitioner seems to suggest, a goal that can or should be reduced to pure numbers. Indeed, since the University is prohibited from seeking a particular number or quota of minority students, it cannot be faulted for failing to specify the particular level of minority enrollment at which it believes the educational benefits of diversity will be obtained.

"On the other hand, asserting an interest in the educational benefits of diversity writ large is insufficient. A university's goals cannot be elusory or amorphous—they must be sufficiently measurable to permit judicial scrutiny of the policies adopted to reach them.

"The record reveals that in first setting forth its current admissions policy, the University articulated concrete and precise goals[, . . .] identif[ying] the educational values it seeks to realize through its admissions process: the destruction of stereotypes, the ' "promot[ion of] cross-racial understanding," ' the preparation of a student body ' "for an increasingly diverse workforce and society, " ' and the ' "cultivat[ion of] a set of leaders with legitimacy in the eyes of the citizenry. " ' . . . [Also,] the University explains that it strives to provide an 'academic environment' that offers a 'robust exchange of ideas, exposure to differing cultures, preparation for the challenges of an increasingly diverse workforce, and acquisition of competencies required of future leaders.' . . . All of these objectives, as a general matter, mirror the 'compelling interest' this Court has approved in its prior cases.

"The University has provided in addition a 'reasoned, principled explanation' for its decision to pursue these goals. *Fisher I*, ... The University's 39-page proposal was written following a year-long study, which concluded that '[t]he use of race-neutral policies and programs ha[d] not been successful' in 'provid[ing] an educational setting that fosters cross-racial understanding, provid[ing] enlightened discussion and learning, [or] prepar[ing] students to function in an increasingly diverse workforce and society.' . . . Further support . . . can be found in the depositions and affidavits from various admissions officers. . . . Petitioner's contention that the University's goal was insufficiently concrete is rebutted by the record.

"Second, petitioner argues that the University has no need to consider race because it had already 'achieved critical mass' by 2003 using the Top Ten Percent Plan and race-neutral holistic review. . . . Petitioner is correct that a university bears a heavy burden in showing that it had not obtained the educational benefits of diversity before it turned to a race-conscious plan. The record reveals, however, that, at the time of petitioner's application, the University could not be faulted on this score. Before changing its policy the University conducted 'months of study and deliberation, including retreats, interviews, [and] review of data,' . . . and concluded that '[t]he use of race-neutral policies and programs ha[d] not been successful in achieving' sufficient racial diversity at the University. . . . At no stage in this litigation has petitioner challenged the University's good faith in conducting its studies, and the Court properly declines to consider the extrarecord materials the dissent relies upon, many of which are tangential to this case at best and none of which the University has had a full opportunity to respond to. . . .

"The record itself contains significant evidence, both statistical and anecdotal, in support of the University's position. [D]emographic data . . . show consistent stagnation in terms of the percentage of minority students enrolling at the University from 1996 to 2002. . . . Although demographics alone are by no means dispositive, they do have some value as a gauge of the University's ability to enroll students who can offer underrepresented perspectives.

"In addition . . . , the University put forward evidence that minority students admitted under the *Hopwood* [no consideration of race] regime experienced feelings of loneliness and isolation. . . .

"This anecdotal evidence is, in turn, bolstered by further, more nuanced quantitative data. . . . [O]nly 21 percent of undergraduate classes with five or more students in them had more than one African-American student enrolled. Twelve percent of these classes had no Hispanic students, as compared to 10 percent in 1996. . . . Though a college must continually reassess its need for race-conscious review, here that assessment appears to have been done with care, and a reasonable determination was made that the University had not yet attained its goals.

"Third, petitioner argues that considering race was not necessary because such consideration has had only a '"minimal impact" in advancing the [University's] compelling interest.' Again, the record does not support this assertion. In 2003, 11 percent of the Texas residents enrolled through holistic review were Hispanic and 3.5 percent were African-American. . . . In 2007, by contrast, 16.9 percent of the Texas holistic-review freshmen were Hispanic and 6.8 percent were African-American. . . . Those increases—of 54 percent and 94 percent, respectively—show that consideration of race has had a meaningful, if still limited, effect on the diversity of the University's freshman class.

"In any event, it is not a failure of narrow tailoring for the impact of racial consideration to be minor. The fact that race consciousness played a role in only a small portion of admissions decisions should be a hallmark of narrow tailoring, not evidence of unconstitutionality.

"Petitioner's final argument is that 'there are numerous other available race-neutral means of achieving' the University's compelling interest. . . . A review of the record reveals, however, that, at the time of petitioner's application, none of her proposed alternatives was a workable means for the

University to attain the benefits of diversity it sought. . . . [T]he University spent seven years attempting to achieve its compelling interest using race-neutral holistic review. None of these efforts succeeded, and petitioner fails to offer any meaningful way in which the University could have improved upon them at the time of her application.

"Petitioner also suggests altering the weight given to academic and socioeconomic factors in the University's admissions calculus. This proposal ignores the fact that the University tried, and failed, to increase diversity through enhanced consideration of socioeconomic and other factors. And it further ignores this Court's precedent making clear that the Equal Protection Clause does not force universities to choose between a diverse student body and a reputation for academic excellence. *Grutter*. . . .

"Petitioner's final suggestion is to uncap the Top Ten Percent Plan, and admit more—if not all—the University's students through a percentage plan. As an initial matter, petitioner overlooks the fact that the Top Ten Percent Plan, though facially neutral, cannot be understood apart from its basic purpose, which is to boost minority enrollment. . . . Consequently, petitioner cannot assert simply that increasing the University's reliance on a percentage plan would make its admissions policy more race neutral.

"Even if, as a matter of raw numbers, minority enrollment would increase under such a regime, petitioner would be hard-pressed to find convincing support for the proposition that college admissions would be improved if they were a function of class rank alone. . . .

" . . . [P]rivileging one characteristic above all others does not lead to a diverse student body. Indeed, to compel universities to admit students based on class rank alone is in deep tension with the goal of educational diversity as this Court's cases have defined it. See *Grutter*, ... At its center, the Top Ten Percent Plan is a blunt instrument that may well compromise the University's own definition of the diversity it seeks.

"In addition to these fundamental problems, an admissions policy that relies exclusively on class rank creates perverse incentives for applicants. Percentage plans 'encourage parents to keep their children in low-performing segregated schools, and discourage students from taking challenging classes that might lower their grade point averages.' *Gratz*, . . . (Ginsburg, J., dissenting).

" . . .

"In short, none of petitioner's suggested alternatives—nor other proposals considered or discussed in the course of this litigation—have been shown to be 'available' and 'workable' means through which the University could have met its educational goals, as it understood and defined them in 2008. . . . The University has thus met its burden of showing that the admissions policy it used at the time it rejected petitioner's application was narrowly tailored.

* * *

" . . . Considerable deference is owed to a university in defining those intangible characteristics, like student body diversity, that are central to its identity and educational mission. But still, it remains an enduring challenge to our Nation's education system to reconcile the pursuit of diversity with the constitutional promise of equal treatment and dignity.

"The University now has at its disposal valuable data about the manner in which different approaches to admissions may foster diversity or instead dilute it. The University must continue to use this data to scrutinize the fairness of its admissions program; to assess whether changing demographics have undermined the need for a race-conscious policy; and to identify the effects, both positive and negative, of the affirmative-action measures it deems necessary.

"The Court's affirmance of the University's admissions policy today does not necessarily mean the University may rely on that same policy without refinement. It is the University's ongoing obligation to engage in constant deliberation and continued reflection regarding its admissions policies."

Justice Alito dissented at length, joined by Chief Justice Roberts and Justice Thomas (who reiterated in a brief separate dissent that he "would overrule *Grutter*"). Justice Alito faulted the University for having failed to satisfy *Fisher I*'s "obligat[ion] (1) to identify the interests justifying its plan with enough specificity to permit a reviewing court to determine whether the requirements of strict scrutiny were met, and (2) to show that those requirements were in fact satisfied." His opinion states in pertinent part:

"To the extent that UT has ever moved beyond a plea for deference and identified the relevant interests in more specific terms, its efforts have been shifting, unpersuasive, and, at times, less than candid. When it adopted its race-based plan, UT said that the plan was needed to promote classroom diversity. . . . It pointed to a study showing that African-American, Hispanic, and Asian-American students were underrepresented in many classes. . . . But UT has never shown that its race-conscious plan actually ameliorates this situation. The University presents no evidence that its admissions officers, in administering the 'holistic' component of its plan, make any effort to determine whether an African-American, Hispanic, or Asian-American student is likely to enroll in classes in which minority students are underrepresented. And although UT's records should permit it to determine without much difficulty whether holistic admittees are any more likely than students admitted through the Top Ten Percent Law . . . to enroll in the classes lacking racial or ethnic diversity, UT either has not crunched those numbers or has not revealed what they show. Nor has UT explained why the underrepresentation of Asian-American students in many classes justifies its plan, which discriminates *against* those students.

"At times, UT has claimed that its plan is needed to achieve a 'critical mass' of African-American and Hispanic students, but it has never explained what this term means. . . .

"UT has also claimed at times that the race-based component of its plan is needed because the Top Ten Percent Plan admits *the wrong kind* of African-American and Hispanic students, namely, students from poor families who attend schools in which the student body is predominantly African-American or Hispanic. . . .

" . . .

"Although UT now disowns th[at] argument . . . , the Fifth Circuit majority . . . [accepted that] the Top Ten African-American and Hispanic admittees cannot match the holistic African-American and Hispanic admittees when it comes to 'records of personal achievement,' a 'variety of perspectives' and 'life experiences,' and 'unique skills.' . . .

"The Fifth Circuit reached this conclusion with little direct evidence regarding the characteristics of the Top Ten Percent and holistic admittees. Instead, the assumption behind the Fifth Circuit's reasoning is that most of the African-American and Hispanic students admitted under the race-neutral component of UT's plan were able to rank in the top decile of their high school classes only because they did not have to compete against white and Asian-American students. This insulting stereotype is not supported by the record. African-American and Hispanic students admitted under the Top Ten Percent Plan receive higher college grades than the African-American and Hispanic students admitted under the race-conscious program. . . .

" . . .

"[I]f the majority is determined to give UT yet another chance, we should reverse and send this case back to the District Court. What the majority has now done— awarding a victory to UT in an opinion that fails to address the important issues in the case—is simply wrong."

Justice Alito's recounting of the evolution of UT's admissions system emphasized that, post-*Grutter*, UT's reintroduction of a race-conscious component "did not analyze the backgrounds, life experiences, leadership qualities, awards, extracurricular activities, community service, personal attributes, or other characteristics of the minority students who were already being admitted to UT under the holistic, race-neutral process." He also emphasized that "[e]ven though UT's classroom study showed that more classes lacked Asian-American students than lacked Hispanic students, . . . UT deemed Asian-Americans *'overrepresented'* based on state demographics"; that "[a]lthough UT claims that race is but a 'factor of a factor of a factor of a factor,' . . . UT acknowledges that 'race is the only one of [its] holistic factors that appears on the cover of every application,' [and, in his view, c]onsideration of race therefore pervades every aspect of UT's admissions process"; and that "UT asserts that it has no idea which students were admitted as a result of its race-conscious system and which students would have been admitted under a race-neutral process[,] thus mak[ing] no effort to assess how the individual characteristics of students admitted as the result of racial preferences differ (or do not differ) from those of students who would have been admitted without them."

Elaborating his criticisms, Justice Alito wrote that "UT has failed to define its interest in using racial preferences with clarity[, with the] result [that] the narrow tailoring inquiry is impossible, and UT cannot satisfy strict scrutiny"; that UT's "intentionally imprecise interest" in obtaining a "critical mass" of underrepresented minority students needed to obtain the full educational benefits of diversity was "designed to insulate UT's program from meaningful judicial review"; and that "without knowing in reasonably specific terms what critical mass is or how it can be measured, a reviewing court cannot conduct the requisite 'careful judicial inquiry' into whether the use of race was ' "necessary." ' *Fisher I*, ..." He continued:

"To be sure, I agree with the majority that our precedents do not require UT to pinpoint 'an interest in enrolling a certain number of minority students.' But in order for us to assess whether UT's program is narrowly tailored, the University must identify *some sort of concrete interest*. . . .

"The majority acknowledges that 'asserting an interest in the educational benefits of diversity writ large is insufficient,' and that '[a] university's goals cannot be elusory or amorphous—they must be sufficiently measurable to permit judicial scrutiny of the policies adopted to reach them.' According to the majority, however, UT has articulated the following 'concrete and precise goals': 'the destruction of stereotypes, the promot[ion of] cross-racial understanding, the preparation of a student body for an increasingly diverse workforce and society, and the cultivat[ion of] a set of leaders with legitimacy in the eyes of the citizenry.'

"These are laudable goals, but they are not concrete or precise, and they offer no limiting principle for the use of racial preferences. For instance, how will a court ever be able to determine whether stereotypes have been adequately destroyed? Or whether cross-racial understanding has been adequately achieved? If a university can justify racial discrimination simply by having a few employees opine that racial preferences are necessary to accomplish these nebulous goals, . . . then the narrow tailoring inquiry is meaningless. Courts will be required to defer to the judgment of university administrators, and affirmative-action policies will be completely insulated from judicial review.

" . . .

"A court cannot ensure that an admissions process is narrowly tailored if it cannot pin down the goals that the process is designed to achieve. . . .

"Although UT's primary argument is that it need not point to any interest more specific than 'the educational benefits of diversity,' . . . it has—at various points in this litigation—identified four more specific goals: demographic parity, classroom diversity, intraracial diversity, and avoiding racial isolation. Neither UT nor the majority has demonstrated that any of these four goals provides a sufficient basis for satisfying strict scrutiny. And UT's arguments to the contrary depend on a series of invidious assumptions.

" . . .

"To the extent that UT is pursuing parity with Texas demographics, that is nothing more than 'outright racial balancing,' which this Court has time and again held 'patently unconstitutional.' *Fisher I*, . . .); see *Grutter*, ...

"The record here demonstrates the pitfalls inherent in racial balancing. Although UT claims an interest in the educational benefits of diversity, it appears to have paid little attention to anything other than the number of minority students on its campus and in its classrooms. . . .

"The majority, for its part, claims that '[a]lthough demographics alone are by no means dispositive, they do have some value as a gauge of the University's ability to enroll students who can offer underrepresented perspectives.' But even if UT merely 'view[s] the demographic disparity as cause for concern,' Brief for United States as *Amicus Curiae* 29, and is seeking only to reduce—rather than eliminate—the disparity, that undefined goal cannot be properly subjected to strict scrutiny. In that case, there is simply no way for a court to know what specific demographic interest UT is pursuing, why a race-neutral alternative could not achieve that interest, and when that demographic goal would be satisfied. If a demographic discrepancy can serve as 'a gauge' that justifies the use of racial discrimination, then racial discrimination can be justified on that basis until demographic parity is reached. There is no logical stopping point short of patently unconstitutional racial balancing. Demographic disparities thus cannot be used to satisfy strict scrutiny here. . . .

"The other major explanation UT offered . . . was its desire to promote classroom diversity. . . . UT relied on a study of select classes containing five or more students. [T]he study indicated that 52% of these classes had no African-Americans, 16% had no Asian-Americans, and 12% had no Hispanics. . . . The study further suggested that only 21% of these classes had two or more African-Americans, 67% had two or more Asian-Americans, and 70% had two or more Hispanics. . . . Based on this study, UT concluded that it had a 'compelling educational interest' in employing racial preferences to ensure that it did not 'have large numbers of classes in which there are no students—or only a single student—of a given underrepresented race or ethnicity.'

"UT now equivocates, disclaiming any discrete interest in classroom diversity. . . . But UT has failed to identify the level of classroom diversity it deems sufficient, again making it impossible to apply strict scrutiny. . . .

"Putting aside UT's effective abandonment of its interest in classroom diversity, the evidence cited in support of that interest is woefully insufficient to show that UT's race-conscious plan was necessary to achieve the educational benefits of a diverse student body. As far as the record shows, UT failed to even scratch the surface of the available data before reflexively resorting to racial preferences. For instance, because UT knows which students were admitted through the Top Ten Percent Plan and which were not, as well as which students enrolled in which classes, it would seem relatively easy to determine whether Top Ten Percent students were more or less likely than holistic admittees to enroll in the types of classes where diversity was lacking. But UT never bothered to figure this out. . . . [UT] has not demonstrated that its race-conscious policy would promote classroom diversity any better than race-neutral options, such as expanding the Top Ten Percent Plan or using race-neutral holistic admissions.

"Moreover, . . . UT's own study . . . demonstrated that classroom diversity was more lacking for students classified as Asian-American than for those classified as Hispanic. . . . But the UT plan discriminates *against* Asian-American students. UT is apparently unconcerned that Asian-Americans 'may be made to feel isolated or may be seen as . . . "spokesperson[s]" of their race or ethnicity.' . . . And unless the University is engaged in unconstitutional racial balancing based on Texas demographics (where Hispanics outnumber Asian-Americans), . . . it seemingly views the classroom contributions of Asian-American students as less valuable than those of Hispanic students. . . .

"While both the majority and the Fifth Circuit rely on UT's classroom study, . . . they completely ignore its finding that Hispanics are better represented than Asian-Americans in UT classrooms. In fact, they act almost as if Asian-American students do not exist. . . .

"   . . .

"Perhaps the majority finds discrimination against Asian-American students benign, since Asian-Americans are "*overrepresented*" at UT. . . . But . . . [b]y accepting the classroom study as proof that UT satisfied strict scrutiny, the majority 'move[s] us from "separate but equal" to "unequal but benign."' *Metro Broadcasting*, . . . (Kennedy, J., dissenting).

"In addition to demonstrating that UT discriminates against Asian-American students, the classroom study also exhibits UT's use of a few crude, overly simplistic racial and ethnic categories. . . .

"For example, students labeled 'Asian American,' . . . seemingly include 'individuals of Chinese, Japanese, Korean, Vietnamese, Cambodian, Hmong, Indian and other backgrounds comprising roughly 60% of the world's population,' . . . . It would be ludicrous to suggest that all of these students have similar backgrounds and similar ideas and experiences to share. So why has UT lumped them together and concluded that it is appropriate to discriminate against Asian-American students because they are 'overrepresented' in the UT student body? UT has no good answer. And UT makes no effort to ensure that it has a critical mass of, say, 'Filipino Americans' or 'Cambodian Americans.' . . . As long as there are a sufficient number of 'Asian Americans,' UT is apparently satisfied.

"UT's failure to provide any definition of the various racial and ethnic groups is also revealing. . . . UT evidently labels each student as falling into only a single racial or ethnic group, . . . without explaining how individuals with ancestors from different groups are to be characterized. As racial and ethnic prejudice recedes, more and more students will have parents (or grandparents) who fall into more than one of UT's five groups. . . . UT's crude classification system is ill suited for the more integrated country that we are rapidly becoming. . . .

"Finally, it seems clear that the lack of classroom diversity is attributable in good part to factors other than the representation of the favored groups in the UT student population. UT offers . . . courses in subjects that are likely to have special appeal to members of the minority groups given preferential treatment under its challenged plan, and this of course diminishes the number of other courses in which these students can enroll. . . . Having designed an undergraduate program that virtually ensures a lack of classroom diversity, UT is poorly positioned to argue that this very result provides a justification for racial and ethnic discrimination, which the Constitution rarely allows.

"UT's purported interest in intraracial diversity . . . also falls short. At bottom, this argument relies on the unsupported assumption that there is something deficient or at least radically different about the African-American and Hispanic students admitted through the Top Ten Percent Plan.

" . . .

"Ultimately, UT's intraracial diversity rationale relies on the baseless assumption that there is something wrong with African-American and Hispanic students admitted through the Top Ten Percent Plan, because they are 'from the lower-performing, racially identifiable schools.' [Tr. of Oral Arg.] (explaining that 'the basis' for UT's conclusion that it was 'not getting a variety of perspectives among African-Americans or Hispanics' was the fact that the Top Ten Percent Plan admits underprivileged minorities from highly segregated schools). . . . UT's assumptions appear to be based on the pernicious stereotype that the African-Americans and Hispanics admitted through the Top Ten Percent Plan only got in because they did not have to compete against very many whites and Asian-Americans. . . .

"In addition to relying on stereotypes, UT's argument that it needs racial preferences to admit privileged minorities turns the concept of affirmative action on its head. When affirmative action programs were first adopted, it was for the purpose of helping the disadvantaged. . . . Now we are told that a program that tends to admit poor and disadvantaged minority students is inadequate because it does not work to the advantage of those who are more fortunate. This is affirmative action gone wild.

"It is also far from clear that UT's assumptions about the socioeconomic status of minorities admitted through the Top Ten Percent Plan are even remotely accurate. . . . As . . . statistics make plain, the minorities that UT characterizes as 'coming from depressed socioeconomic backgrounds,' . . . generally come from households with education levels exceeding the norm in Texas.

"Or consider income levels. . . . The household income levels for Top Ten Percent African-American and Hispanic admittees were on par [with the median annual household income in Texas.] . . . UT is asserting that it needs affirmative action to ensure that its minority students disproportionally come from families that are wealthier and better educated than the average Texas family.

"In addition[,] . . . UT argues that it needs race-conscious admissions to enroll academically superior minority students with higher SAT scores. Regrettably, the majority seems to embrace this argument as well. . . .

"This argument fails for a number of reasons. First, it is simply not true that Top Ten Percent minority admittees are academically inferior to holistic admittees. . . . Indeed, the statistics in the record reveal that, for each year between 2003 and 2007, African-American in-state freshmen who were admitted under the Top Ten Percent Law earned a higher mean grade point average than those admitted outside of the Top Ten Percent Law. . . . The same is true for Hispanic students. . . .

    " . . .

"Finally, UT's shifting positions on intraracial diversity, and the fact that intraracial diversity was not emphasized in the [Admissions] Proposal, suggest that it was not 'the actual purpose underlying the discriminatory classification.' *Mississippi Univ. for Women v. Hogan*, 458 U. S. 718, 730 (1982). Instead, it appears to be a *post hoc* rationalization.

"UT also alleges—and the majority embraces—an interest in avoiding 'feelings of loneliness and isolation' among minority students. In support of this argument, they cite only demographic data and anecdotal statements by UT officials that some students (we are not told how many) feel 'isolated.' This vague interest cannot possibly satisfy strict scrutiny.

    " . . .

" . . . UT never explains why the Hispanic students—but not the Asian-American students—are isolated and lonely enough to receive an admissions boost, notwithstanding the fact that there are more Hispanics than Asian-Americans in the student population. . . .

"Ultimately, UT has failed to articulate its interest in preventing racial isolation with any clarity, and it has provided no clear indication of how it will know when such isolation no longer exists. Like UT's purported interests in demographic parity, classroom diversity, and intraracial diversity, its interest in avoiding racial isolation cannot justify the use of racial preferences.

"Even assuming UT is correct that, under *Grutter*, it need only cite a generic interest in the educational benefits of diversity, its plan still fails strict scrutiny because it is not narrowly tailored. . . . [T]here is no evidence that race-blind, holistic review would not achieve UT's goals at least 'about as well' as UT's race-based policy. In addition, UT could have adopted other approaches to further its goals, such as intensifying its outreach efforts, uncapping the Top Ten Percent Law, or placing greater weight on socioeconomic factors.

" . . . [T]he majority devotes only a single, conclusory sentence to the most obvious race-neutral alternative: race-blind, holistic review that considers the applicant's unique characteristics and personal circumstances. . . . Because UT has failed to provide any evidence whatsoever that race-conscious holistic review will achieve its diversity objectives more effectively than race-blind holistic review, it cannot satisfy the heavy burden imposed by the strict scrutiny standard.

"The fact that UT's racial preferences are unnecessary to achieve its stated goals is further demonstrated by their minimal effect on UT's diversity. . . .

[R]ace [probably] was determinative for only 15 African-American students and 18 Hispanic students in 2008 (representing 0.2% and 0.3%, respectively, of the total enrolled first-time freshmen from Texas high schools). . . .

" . . . Where, as here, racial preferences have only a slight impact on minority enrollment, a race-neutral alternative likely could have reached the same result. . . . And in this case, a race-neutral alternative could accomplish UT's objectives without gratuitously branding the covers of tens of thousands of applications with a bare racial stamp and 'tell[ing] each student he or she is to be defined by race.'

" . . .

"[S]omehow, the majority concludes that *petitioner* must lose as a result of UT's failure to provide evidence justifying its decision to employ racial discrimination. Tellingly, the Court frames its analysis as if petitioner bears the burden of proof here. But . . . [t]o the extent the record is inadequate, the responsibility lies with UT. . . .

" . . . [T]he majority cites three reasons for breaking from the normal strict scrutiny standard. None . . . is convincing.

"First, the Court states that, while 'th[e] evidentiary gap perhaps could be filled by a remand to the district court for further factfinding' in 'an ordinary case,' that will not work here because '[w]hen petitioner's application was rejected, . . . the University's combined percentage-plan/holistic-review approach to admission had been in effect for just three years,' so 'further factfinding' 'might yield little insight.' This reasoning is dangerously incorrect. The Equal Protection Clause does not provide a 3-year grace period for racial discrimination. Under strict scrutiny, UT was required to identify evidence that race-based admissions were necessary to achieve a compelling interest *before* it put them in place—not three or more years after. . . .

"Second, in an effort to excuse UT's lack of evidence, the Court argues that because 'the University lacks any authority to alter the role of the Top Ten Percent Plan,' 'it similarly had no reason to keep extensive data on the Plan or the students admitted under it—particularly in the years before *Fisher I* clarified the stringency of the strict-scrutiny burden for a school that employs race-conscious review.' But UT has long been aware that it bears the burden of justifying its racial discrimination under strict scrutiny. . . . In light of this burden, UT had *every* reason to keep data on the students admitted through the Top Ten Percent Plan. . . . Its failure to do so demonstrates that UT unthinkingly employed a race-based process without examining whether the use of race was actually necessary. . . .

" . . .

"Third, the majority notes that this litigation has persisted for many years, that petitioner has already graduated from another college, that UT's policy may have changed over time, and that this case may offer little prospective guidance. At most, these considerations counsel in favor of dismissing this case as improvidently granted. . . . None of these considerations has any bearing whatsoever on the merits of this suit. The majority cannot side with UT simply because it is tired of this case."

Page 813. Add the following after Parents Involved in Community Schools v. Seattle School Dist. No. 1:

NOTE ON CHALLENGES TO LAWS THAT SEEK TO REPEAL RACE-BASED AFFIRMATIVE ACTION PROGRAMS

In Schuette v. Coalition to Defend Affirmative Action Integration and Immigration Rights By Any Means Necessary (BAMN), 572 U.S. ___, 134 S.Ct. 1623, 188 L.Ed.2d 613 (2014), the Court rejected—by a 6–2 vote but without a majority opinion—an equal protection challenge brought against a voter-enacted Michigan state constitutional amendment that prohibited the use of race-based preferences in state university admissions. For a fuller treatment of this ruling, and predecessor cases on which the Court drew in resolving *Schuette*, see Chapter 12, Section 2(C)(4), beginning at page 1052.

G. WHAT OTHER CLASSIFICATIONS WILL PROVOKE HEIGHTENED SCRUTINY?

2.   CLASSIFICATIONS DISADVANTAGING THE RETARDED, HOMOSEXUALS, THE ELDERLY, THE POOR, ETC.

Page 843. Add after Lawrence v. Texas:

United States v. Windsor
570 U.S. ___, 133 S.Ct. 2675, 186 L.Ed.2d 808 (2013).

Justice Kennedy delivered the opinion of the Court.

Two women then resident in New York were married in a lawful ceremony in Ontario, Canada, in 2007. Edith Windsor and Thea Spyer returned to their home in New York City. When Spyer died in 2009, she left her entire estate to Windsor. Windsor sought to claim the estate tax exemption for surviving spouses. She was barred from doing so, however, by a federal law, the Defense of Marriage Act, which excludes a same-sex partner from the definition of "spouse" as that term is used in federal statutes. Windsor paid the taxes but filed suit to challenge the constitutionality of this provision. The United States District Court and the Court of Appeals ruled that this portion of the statute is unconstitutional and ordered the United States to pay Windsor a refund. This Court . . . now affirms the judgment in Windsor's favor.

I

In 1996, as some States were beginning to consider the concept of same-sex marriage, . . . and before any State had acted to permit it, Congress enacted the Defense of Marriage Act (DOMA). . . . DOMA contains two operative sections: Section 2, which has not been challenged here, allows States to refuse to recognize same-sex marriages performed under the laws of other States. See 28 U.S.C. § 1738C.

Section 3 is at issue here. It amends the Dictionary Act in Title 1, § 7, of the United States Code to provide a federal definition of "marriage" and "spouse." Section 3 of DOMA provides as follows:

"In determining the meaning of any Act of Congress, or of any ruling, regulation, or interpretation of the various administrative bureaus and agencies of the United States, the word 'marriage' means only a legal union between one man and one woman as husband and wife, and the word 'spouse' refers only to a person of the opposite sex who is a husband or a wife." 1 U.S.C. § 7.

The definitional provision does not by its terms forbid States from enacting laws permitting same-sex marriages or civil unions or providing state benefits to residents in that status. The enactment's comprehensive definition of marriage for purposes of all federal statutes and other regulations or directives covered by its terms, however, does control over 1,000 federal laws in which marital or spousal status is addressed as a matter of federal law. . . .

. . . Windsor and Spyer registered as domestic partners when New York City gave that right to same-sex couples in 1993. Concerned about Spyer's health, the couple made the 2007 trip to Canada for their marriage, but they continued to reside in New York City. The State of New York deems their Ontario marriage to be a valid one. . . .

. . . Because DOMA denies federal recognition to same-sex spouses, Windsor did not qualify for the marital exemption from the federal estate tax, which excludes from taxation "any interest in property which passes or has passed from the decedent to his surviving spouse." 26 U.S.C. § 2056(a). Windsor paid $363,053 in estate taxes and sought a refund. The Internal Revenue Service denied the refund, concluding that, under DOMA, Windsor was not a "surviving spouse." Windsor['s] . . . refund suit . . . contended that DOMA violates the guarantee of equal protection, as applied to the Federal Government through the Fifth Amendment.

While the tax refund suit was pending, the Attorney General of the United States notified the Speaker of the House of Representatives, pursuant to 28 U.S.C. § 530D, that the Department of Justice would no longer defend the constitutionality of DOMA's § 3. Noting that "the Department has previously defended DOMA against . . . challenges involving legally married same-sex couples," . . . the Attorney General informed Congress that "the President has concluded that given a number of factors, including a documented history of discrimination, classifications based on sexual orientation should be subject to a heightened standard of scrutiny.". . . The Department of Justice has submitted many § 530D letters over the years refusing to defend laws it deems unconstitutional, when, for instance, a federal court has rejected the Government's defense of a statute and has issued a judgment against it. This case is unusual, however, because the § 530D letter was not preceded by an adverse judgment. The letter instead reflected the Executive's own conclusion, relying on a definition still being debated and considered in the courts, that heightened equal protection scrutiny should apply to laws that classify on the basis of sexual orientation.

Although "the President . . . instructed the Department not to defend the statute in *Windsor*," he also decided "that Section 3 will continue to be enforced by the Executive Branch" and that the United States had an "interest in providing Congress a full and fair opportunity to participate in the litigation of those cases.". . . The stated rationale for this dual-track procedure (determination of unconstitutionality coupled with ongoing enforcement) was to "recogniz[e] the judiciary as the final arbiter of the constitutional claims raised.". . .

[The Bipartisan Legal Advisory Group (BLAG) of the House of Representatives was permitted to intervene as an interested party to defend § 3's constitutionality. The District Court invalidated § 3, and on appeals by "[b]oth the Justice Department and BLAG[,]" the Court of Appeals affirmed.] It applied heightened scrutiny to classifications based on sexual orientation, as both the Department and Windsor had urged. The United States has not complied with the judgment. Windsor has not received her refund, and the Executive Branch continues to enforce § 3 of DOMA.

 . . .

II

[Although the Government agreed with Windsor that § 3 is unconstitutional, and despite the fact that the District Court had ordered a refund, the majority ruled that the appeal by the United States still presented a justiciable controversy under Article III of the Constitution, given "Windsor's ongoing claim for funds that the United States refuses to pay." (The Court did note that "[i]t would be a different case if the Executive had taken the further step of paying Windsor the refund to which she was entitled under the District Court's ruling"). The majority acknowledged the serious concern that the "Executive's agreement with Windsor's legal argument raises the risk" of a lack of adversarial presentation—a concern it considered "prudential" and not constitutional. It found more persuasive, however, at least two "countervailing" prudential factors. First, "BLAG's sharp adversarial presentation of the issues satisfies the prudential concerns that otherwise might counsel against hearing an appeal from a decision with which the principal parties agree." Second, were the appeals to be dismissed, the lack of "precedential guidance . . . in cases involving the whole of DOMA's sweep involving over 1,000 federal statutes and a myriad of federal regulations" would result in "immense" judicial resource costs and litigation expenses "for all persons adversely affected." These "unusual and urgent circumstances" rendered it proper for the Court to rule on the appeal by the United States, and "the Court need not decide whether BLAG would have standing to challenge the District Court's ruling and its affirmance in the Court of Appeals on BLAG's own authority."

[The majority did perceive difficulties were it to become a "common practice in ordinary cases" for the Executive—in agreement with the challenger—to ask the Court to rule against the constitutionality of an Act of Congress, but it also declared that "if the Executive's agreement with a plaintiff that a law is unconstitutional is enough to preclude judicial review, then the Supreme Court's primary role in determining the constitutionality of a law that has inflicted real injury on a plaintiff who has brought a justiciable legal claim would become only secondary to the President's." And "[s]imilarly, with respect to the legislative power, when Congress has passed a statute and a President has signed it, it poses grave challenges to the separation of powers for the Executive at a particular moment to be able to nullify Congress' enactment solely on its own initiative and without any determination from the Court." These considerations were thought to "support the Court's decision to proceed to the merits."]

III

. . .

. . . [Over time,] New York recognized same-sex marriages performed elsewhere; and then it later amended its own marriage laws to permit same sex marriage. New York, in common with, as of this writing, 11 other States and the District of Columbia, decided that same-sex couples should have the right to marry and so live with pride in themselves and their union and in a status of equality with all other married persons. . . .

Against this background of lawful same-sex marriage in some States, the design, purpose, and effect of DOMA should be considered as the beginning point in deciding whether it is valid under the Constitution. By history and tradition the definition and regulation of marriage . . . has been treated as being within the authority and realm of the separate States. Yet it is further established that Congress, in enacting discrete statutes, can make determinations that bear on marital rights and privileges. . . .

. . .

Though . . . discrete examples establish the constitutionality of limited federal laws that regulate the meaning of marriage in order to further federal policy, DOMA has a far greater reach; for it enacts a directive applicable to over 1,000 federal statutes and the whole realm of federal regulations. And its operation is directed to a class of persons that the laws of New York, and of 11 other States, have sought to protect. . . .

In order to assess the validity of that intervention it is necessary to discuss the extent of the state power and authority over marriage as a matter of history and tradition. State laws defining and regulating marriage, of course, must respect the constitutional rights of persons, see, *e.g., Loving* v. *Virginia*, 388 U.S. 1 (1967); but, subject to those guarantees, "regulation of domestic relations" is "an area that has long been regarded as a virtually exclusive province of the States." *Sosna* v. *Iowa*, 419 U.S. 393, 404 (1975).

The recognition of civil marriages is central to state domestic relations law applicable to its residents and citizens. . . .

Consistent with this allocation of authority, the Federal Government, through our history, has deferred to state law policy decisions with respect to domestic relations. . . .

. . . Marriage laws vary in some respects from State to State. . . . But these rules are in every event consistent within each State.

. . . DOMA rejects the long established precept that the incidents, benefits, and obligations of marriage are uniform for all married couples within each State, though they may vary, subject to constitutional guarantees, from one State to the next. Despite these considerations, it is unnecessary to decide whether this federal intrusion on state power is a violation of the Constitution because it disrupts the federal balance. The State's power in defining the marital relation is of central relevance in this case quite apart from principles of federalism. Here the State's decision to give this class of persons the right to marry conferred upon them a dignity and status of immense import. When the State used its historic and essential authority to define the marital relation in this way, its role and its power in making the decision enhanced the recognition, dignity, and protection of the class in their own community. DOMA, because of its reach and extent, departs from this history and tradition of reliance on state law to define marriage. " '[D]iscriminations of an unusual character especially suggest careful consideration to determine whether they are obnoxious to the constitutional provision.' " *Romer* v. *Evans*, 517 U.S. 620, 633 (1996). . . .

The Federal Government uses this state-defined class for the opposite purpose—to impose restrictions and disabilities. That result requires this Court now to address whether the resulting injury and indignity is a deprivation of an essential part of the liberty protected by the Fifth Amendment. What the State of New York treats as alike the federal law deems unlike by a law designed to injure the same class the State seeks to protect.

The States' interest in defining and regulating the marital relation, subject to constitutional guarantees, stems from the understanding that marriage is more than a routine classification for purposes of certain statutory benefits. Private, consensual sexual intimacy between two adult persons of the same sex may not be punished by the State, and it can form "but one element in a personal bond that is more enduring." *Lawrence* v. *Texas*, 539 U.S. 558, 567 (2003). By its recognition of the validity of same-sex marriages performed in other jurisdictions and then by authorizing same-sex unions and same-sex marriages, New York sought to give further protection and dignity to that bond. For same-sex couples who wished to be married, the State acted to give their lawful conduct a lawful status. This status is a far-reaching legal acknowledgment of the intimate relationship between two people, a relationship deemed by the State worthy of dignity in the community equal with all other marriages. It reflects both the community's considered perspective on the historical roots of the institution of marriage and its evolving understanding of the meaning of equality.

IV

DOMA seeks to injure the very class New York seeks to protect. By doing so it violates basic due process and equal protection principles applicable to the Federal Government. . . . The Constitution's guarantee of equality "must at the very least mean that a bare congressional desire to harm a politically unpopular group cannot" justify disparate treatment of that group. *Department of Agriculture* v. *Moreno*, 413 U.S. 528, 534–535 (1973). . . . DOMA's unusual deviation from the usual tradition of recognizing and accepting state definitions of marriage here operates to deprive same-sex couples of the benefits and responsibilities that come with the federal recognition of their marriages. This is strong evidence of a law having the purpose and effect of disapproval of that class. The avowed purpose and practical effect of the law here in question are to impose a disadvantage, a separate status, and so a stigma upon all who enter into same-sex marriages made lawful by the unquestioned authority of the States.

The history of DOMA's enactment and its own text demonstrate that interference with the equal dignity of same-sex marriages, a dignity conferred by the States in the exercise of their sovereign power, was more than an incidental effect of the federal statute. It was its essence. The House Report announced its conclusion that "it is both appropriate and necessary for Congress to do what it can to defend the institution of traditional heterosexual marriage. . . . H. R. 3396 is appropriately entitled the 'Defense of Marriage Act.' The effort to redefine 'marriage' to extend to homosexual couples is a truly radical proposal that would fundamentally alter the institution of marriage." H. R. Rep. No. 104–664, pp. 12–13 (1996). The House concluded that DOMA expresses "both moral disapproval of homosexuality, and a moral conviction that heterosexuality better comports with traditional (especially Judeo-Christian) morality.". . . The stated purpose of the law was to promote an "interest in protecting the traditional moral teachings reflected in heterosexual-only marriage laws." *Ibid.* Were there any doubt of this far-reaching purpose, the title of the Act confirms it: The Defense of Marriage.

. . . The Act's demonstrated purpose is to ensure that if any State decides to recognize same-sex marriages, those unions will be treated as second-class marriages for purposes of federal law. This raises a most serious question under the Constitution's Fifth Amendment.

. . . DOMA writes inequality into the entire United States Code. . . . Among the over 1,000 statutes and numerous federal regulations that DOMA controls are laws pertaining to Social Security, housing, taxes, criminal sanctions, copyright, and veterans' benefits.

DOMA's principal effect is to identify a subset of state sanctioned marriages and make them unequal. The principal purpose is to impose inequality, not for other reasons like governmental efficiency. Responsibilities, as well as rights, enhance the dignity and integrity of the person. And DOMA contrives to deprive some couples married under the laws of their State, but not other couples, of both rights and responsibilities. By creating two contradictory marriage regimes within the same State, DOMA forces same-sex couples to live as married for the purpose of state law but unmarried for the purpose of federal law, thus diminishing the stability and predictability of basic personal relations the State has found it proper to acknowledge and protect. By this dynamic DOMA undermines both the public and private significance of state-sanctioned same-sex marriages; for it tells those couples, and all the world, that their otherwise valid marriages are unworthy of federal recognition. This places same-sex couples in an unstable position of being in a second-tier marriage.

The differentiation demeans the couple, whose moral and sexual choices the Constitution protects, see *Lawrence*, 539 U.S. 558, and whose relationship the State has sought to dignify. And it humiliates tens of thousands of children now being raised by same-sex couples. The law in question makes it even more difficult for the children to understand the integrity and closeness of their own family and its concord with other families in their community and in their daily lives.

Under DOMA, same-sex married couples have their lives burdened, by reason of government decree, in visible and public ways. By its great reach, DOMA touches many aspects of married and family life, from the mundane to the profound. It prevents same-sex married couples from obtaining government healthcare benefits they would otherwise receive. . . . It deprives them of the Bankruptcy Code's special protections for domestic-support obligations. . . . It forces them to follow a complicated procedure to file their state and federal taxes jointly. . . . It prohibits them from being buried together in veterans' cemeteries. . . .

. . .

What has been explained to this point should more than suffice to establish that the principal purpose and the necessary effect of this law are to demean those persons who are in a lawful same-sex marriage. This requires the Court to hold, as it now does, that DOMA is unconstitutional as a deprivation of the liberty of the person protected by the Fifth Amendment of the Constitution.

. . . While the Fifth Amendment itself withdraws from Government the power to degrade or demean in the way this law does, the equal protection guarantee of the Fourteenth Amendment makes that Fifth Amendment right all the more specific and all the better understood and preserved.

. . . DOMA instructs all federal officials, and indeed all persons with whom same-sex couples interact, including their own children, that their marriage is less worthy than the marriages of others. The federal statute is invalid, for no legitimate purpose overcomes the purpose and effect to disparage and to injure those whom the State, by its marriage laws, sought to protect in personhood and dignity. By seeking to displace this protection and treating those persons as living in marriages less respected than others, the federal statute is in violation of the Fifth Amendment. This opinion and its holding are confined to those lawful marriages.

. . .

Chief Justice Roberts, dissenting.

I agree with Justice Scalia that this Court lacks jurisdiction to review the decisions of the courts below. On the merits of the constitutional dispute the Court decides to decide, I also agree with Justice Scalia that Congress acted constitutionally in passing the Defense of Marriage Act. . . . Interests in uniformity and stability amply justified Congress's decision to retain the definition of marriage that, at that point, had been adopted by every State in our Nation, and every nation in the world.

The majority sees a more sinister motive. . . . At least without some more convincing evidence that the Act's principal purpose was to codify malice, and that it furthered *no* legitimate government interests, I would not tar the political branches with the brush of bigotry.

But while I disagree with the result to which the majority's analysis leads it in this case, I think it more important to point out that its analysis leads no further. The Court does not have before it, and the logic of its opinion does not decide, the distinct question whether the States, in the exercise of their "historic and essential authority to define the marital relation" may continue to utilize the traditional definition of marriage.

The majority goes out of its way to make this explicit in the penultimate sentence of its opinion. . . . The dominant theme of the majority opinion is that the Federal Government's intrusion into an area "central to state domestic relations law applicable to its residents and citizens" is sufficiently "unusual" to set off alarm bells. I think the majority goes off course, . . . but it is undeniable that its judgment is based on federalism.

. . . [W]hile "[t]he State's power in defining the marital relation is of central relevance" to the majority's decision to strike down DOMA here, that power will come into play on the other side of the board in future cases about the constitutionality of state marriage definitions. So too will the concerns for state diversity and sovereignty that weigh against DOMA's constitutionality in this case.

. . .

Justice Scalia, with whom Justice Thomas joins, and with whom the Chief Justice joins as to Part I, dissenting.

. . . We have no power to decide this case. And even if we did, we have no power under the Constitution to invalidate this democratically adopted legislation. . . .

I

[Because "Windsor won below, and so *cured* her injury, and the President was glad to see it[,]" the Court lacked power to decide the merits of this case. Doing so "is an assertion of judicial supremacy over the people's Representatives in Congress and the Executive [that] envisions a Supreme Court . . . at the apex of government, empowered to decide all constitutional questions, always and everywhere 'primary' in its role." In fact, "[a]s Justice Brandeis put it, we cannot 'pass upon the constitutionality of legislation in a friendly, non-adversary, proceeding'; absent a ' "real, earnest and vital controversy between individuals," ' we have neither any work to do nor any power to do it. *Ashwander* v. *TVA*, 297 U.S. 288, 346 (1936) (concurring opinion) . . . " Justice Scalia insisted that "[i]n the more than two centuries that this Court has existed as an institution, we have never suggested that we have the power to decide a question when every party agrees with both its nominal opponent *and the court below* on that question's answer." The Article III (not prudential) "question is whether there is any controversy (which requires *contradiction*) between the United States and Ms. Windsor. There is not."

[Nor did Justice Alito's contention that the Court had power to decide the merits based on the standing of BLAG to pursue the appeals suffice. Accepting BLAG's standing "would create a system in which Congress can hale the Executive before the courts not only to vindicate its own institutional powers to act, but to correct a perceived inadequacy in the execution of its laws." Rather than resolve such disputes through the courts, "[i]f majorities in both Houses of Congress care enough about the matter, they have available innumerable ways to compel executive action without a lawsuit—from refusing to confirm Presidential appointees to the elimination of funding." Direct confrontation of the President by Congress is the preferable and designed mechanism under our constitutional system in these circumstances.]

II

. . . We should vacate the decision below and remand . . . with instructions to dismiss the appeal. Given that the majority has volunteered its view of the merits, however, I proceed to discuss that as well.

A

[After complaining about "how rootless and shifting" the majority's justifications are—first "fooling many readers . . . into thinking that this is a federalism opinion" only to "disclaim[ ] reliance upon principles of federalism" and then shifting to "perplexing" references to equal protection—Justice Scalia continued:]

[I]f this is meant to be an equal-protection opinion, it is a confusing one. The opinion does not resolve and indeed does not even mention what had been the central question in this litigation: whether, under the Equal Protection Clause, laws restricting marriage to a man and a woman are reviewed for more than mere rationality. . . . In accord with my previously expressed skepticism about the Court's "tiers of scrutiny" approach, I would review this classification only for its rationality. . . . As nearly as I can tell, the Court agrees with that; its opinion does not apply strict scrutiny, and its central propositions are taken from rational-basis cases like *Moreno*. But the Court certainly does not *apply* anything that resembles that deferential framework. . . .

. . . [T]he opinion does not argue that same-sex marriage is "deeply rooted in this Nation's history and tradition," *Washington* v. *Glucksberg*, 521 U.S. 702, 720–721 (1997), a claim that would of course be quite absurd. So would the further suggestion (also necessary, under our substantive-due-process precedents) that a world in which DOMA exists is one bereft of " 'ordered liberty.' " *Id.*, at 721. . . .

. . . The sum of all the Court's nonspecific hand-waving is that this law is invalid (maybe on equal-protection grounds, maybe on substantive-due process grounds, and perhaps with some amorphous federalism component playing a role) because it is motivated by a " 'bare . . . desire to harm' " couples in same-sex marriages. It is this proposition with which I will therefore engage.

B

. . . [T]he Constitution neither requires nor forbids our society to approve of same-sex marriage, much as it neither requires nor forbids us to approve of no-fault divorce, polygamy, or the consumption of alcohol.

However, even setting aside traditional moral disapproval of same-sex marriage (or indeed same-sex sex), there are many perfectly valid—indeed, downright boring—justifying rationales for this legislation. Their existence ought to be the end of this case. For they give the lie to the Court's conclusion that only those with hateful hearts could have voted "aye" on this Act. And more importantly, they serve to make the contents of the legislators' hearts quite irrelevant: "It is a familiar principle of constitutional law that this Court will not strike down an otherwise constitutional statute on the basis of an alleged illicit legislative motive." *United States* v. *O'Brien*, 391 U.S. 367, 383 (1968). Or at least it *was* a familiar principle. By holding to the contrary, the majority has declared open season on any law that (in the opinion of the law's opponents and any panel of like-minded federal judges) can be characterized as mean-spirited.

The majority concludes that the only motive for this Act was the "bare . . . desire to harm a politically unpopular group." Bear in mind that the object of this condemnation is . . . our respected coordinate branches, the Congress and Presidency of the United States. Laying such a charge against them should require the most extraordinary evidence. . . . The majority [instead] . . . affirmatively conceal[s] . . . the arguments that exist in justification. . . .

. . . DOMA avoids difficult choice-of-law issues that will now arise absent a uniform federal definition of marriage. . . . Imagine a pair of women who marry in Albany and then move to Alabama, which does not "recognize as valid any marriage of parties of the same sex." Ala. Code § 30–1–19(e) (2011). When the couple files their next federal tax return, may it be a joint one? Which State's law controls, for federal-law purposes: their State of celebration (which recognizes the marriage) or their State of domicile (which does not)? . . . DOMA avoided . . . uncertainty by specifying which marriages would be recognized for federal purposes. That is a classic purpose for a definitional provision.

Further, DOMA preserves the intended effects of prior legislation against then-unforeseen changes in circumstance. . . . DOMA's definitional section was enacted to ensure that state-level experimentation did not automatically alter the basic operation of federal law, unless and until Congress made the further judgment to do so on its own. That is not animus—just stabilizing prudence. . . .

The Court mentions none of this. Instead, it accuses the Congress that enacted this law and the President who signed it of . . . act[ing] with *malice*— with *the "purpose"* "to disparage and to injure" same-sex couples. It says that the motivation for DOMA was to "demean"; to "impose inequality"; to "impose . . . a stigma"; to deny people "equal dignity"; to brand gay people as "unworthy"; and to "*humiliat*[*e*]" their children (emphasis added).

I am sure these accusations are quite untrue. . . . [T]o defend traditional marriage is not to condemn, demean, or humiliate those who would prefer other arrangements, any more than to defend the Constitution of the United States is to condemn, demean, or humiliate other constitutions. To hurl such accusations so casually demeans *this institution*. . . . [The] Act . . . did no more than codify an aspect of marriage that had been unquestioned in our society for most of its existence—indeed, had been unquestioned in virtually all societies for virtually all of human history. It is one thing for a society to elect change; it is another for a court of law to impose change by adjudging those who oppose it . . . enemies of the human race.

* * *

. . . It takes real cheek for today's majority to assure us, as it is going out the door, that a constitutional requirement to give formal recognition to same-sex marriage is not at issue here—when what has preceded that assurance is a lecture on how superior the majority's moral judgment in favor of same-sex marriage is to the Congress's hateful moral judgment against it. . . .

I do not mean to suggest disagreement with the Chief Justice's view that lower federal courts and state courts can distinguish today's case when the issue before them is state denial of marital status to same-sex couples—or even that this Court could *theoretically* do so. . . .

In my opinion, however, the view that *this* Court will take of state prohibition of same-sex marriage is indicated beyond mistaking by today's opinion. . . . In sum, that Court which finds it so horrific that Congress irrationally and hatefully robbed same-sex couples of the "personhood and dignity" which state legislatures conferred upon them, will of a certitude be similarly appalled by state legislatures' irrational and hateful failure to acknowledge that "personhood and dignity" in the first place. . . .

By formally declaring anyone opposed to same-sex marriage an enemy of human decency, the majority arms well every challenger to a state law restricting marriage to its traditional definition. . . .

. . . Since DOMA's passage, citizens on all sides of the question have seen victories and they have seen defeats. There have been plebiscites, legislation, persuasion, and loud voices—in other words, democracy. . . .

. . . We might have covered ourselves with honor today, by promising all sides of this debate that it was theirs to settle and that we would respect their resolution. We might have let the People decide.

But that the majority will not do. . . .

Justice Alito, with whom Justice Thomas joins as to Parts II and III, dissenting.

. . . I would . . . hold that Congress did not violate Windsor's constitutional rights by enacting § 3. . . .

I

. . . The United States does not ask us to overturn the judgment of the court below or to alter that judgment in any way. Quite to the contrary, the United States argues emphatically in favor of the correctness of that judgment.

We have never before reviewed a decision at the sole behest of a party that took such a position, and to do so would be to render an advisory opinion, in violation of Article III's dictates. For the reasons given in Justice Scalia's dissent, I do not find the Court's arguments to the contrary to be persuasive.

[But BLAG has standing to petition for review, because "in the narrow category of cases in which a court strikes down an Act of Congress and the Executive declines to defend the Act, Congress both has standing to defend the undefended statute and is a proper party to do so."]

II

. . .

Same-sex marriage presents a highly emotional and important question of public policy—but not a difficult question of constitutional law. The Constitution does not guarantee the right to enter into a same-sex marriage. Indeed, no provision of the Constitution speaks to the issue.

. . .

It is beyond dispute that the right to same-sex marriage is not deeply rooted in this Nation's history and tradition. . . .

What Windsor and the United States seek, therefore, is not the protection of a deeply rooted right but the recognition of a very new right, and they seek this innovation not from a legislative body elected by the people, but from unelected judges. Faced with such a request, judges have cause for both caution and humility.

. . .

. . . [I]f same sex marriage becomes widely accepted[, t]he long-term consequences . . . are not now known and are unlikely to be ascertainable for some time to come There are those who think that allowing same-sex marriage will seriously undermine the institution of marriage. . . . Others think that recognition of same-sex marriage will fortify a now-shaky institution. . . .

. . . [I]f the Constitution contained a provision guaranteeing the right to marry a person of the same sex, it would be our duty to enforce that right. But the Constitution simply does not speak to the issue of same-sex marriage. In our system of government, ultimate sovereignty rests with the people, and the people have the right to control their own destiny. Any change on a question so fundamental should be made by the people through their elected officials.

III

Perhaps because they cannot show that same-sex marriage is a fundamental right under our Constitution, Windsor and the United States couch their arguments in equal protection terms. . . .

. . . But that framework is ill suited for use in evaluating the constitutionality of laws based on the traditional understanding of marriage, which fundamentally turn on what marriage is.

. . .

By asking the Court to strike down DOMA as not satisfying some form of heightened scrutiny, Windsor and the United States are really seeking to have the Court resolve a debate between two competing views of marriage.

The first and older view, which I will call the "traditional" or "conjugal" view, sees marriage as an intrinsically opposite-sex institution. . . . While modern cultural changes have weakened the link between marriage and procreation in the popular mind, there is no doubt that, throughout human history and across many cultures, marriage has been viewed as an exclusively opposite-sex institution and as one inextricably linked to procreation and biological kinship.

The other, newer view is what I will call the "consent based" vision of marriage, a vision that primarily defines marriage as the solemnization of mutual commitment—marked by strong emotional attachment and sexual attraction—between two persons. . . . Proponents of same-sex marriage argue that because gender differentiation is not relevant to this vision, the exclusion of same-sex couples from the institution of marriage is rank discrimination.

The Constitution does not codify either of these views of marriage. . . . The silence of the Constitution on this question should be enough to end the matter as far as the judiciary is concerned. . . . Because our constitutional order assigns the resolution of questions of this nature to the people, I would not presume to enshrine either vision of marriage in our constitutional jurisprudence.

. . . [B]oth Congress and the States are entitled to enact laws recognizing either of the two understandings of marriage. . . .

. . .

To the extent that the Court takes the position that the question of same-sex marriage should be resolved primarily at the state level, I wholeheartedly agree. I hope that the Court will ultimately permit the people of each State to decide this question for themselves. Unless the Court is willing to allow this to occur, the whiffs of federalism in the today's opinion of the Court will soon be scattered to the wind.

In any event, § 3 of DOMA, in my view, does not encroach on the prerogatives of the States. . . . Section 3 does not prevent any State from recognizing same-sex marriage or from extending to same-sex couples any right, privilege, benefit, or obligation stemming from state law. All that § 3 does is to define a class of persons to whom federal law extends certain special benefits and upon whom federal law imposes certain special burdens. . . .

Obergefell v. Hodges
576 U.S. ___, 135 S.Ct. 2584, 192 L.Ed.2d 609 (2015).

[The report of this case appears supra at page 87.]

4. PROTECTION OF PERSONAL LIBERTIES

B. VOTING AND ELECTIONS

2. LEGISLATIVE DISTRICTING

Page 855. Add after Brown v. Thomson:

Evenwel v. Abbott, 578 U.S. ___, 136 S.Ct. 1120 (2016). Texas voters challenged a redistricting map for the Texas Senate, which was drawn, as virtually all legislative district maps are, based on the total population of its districts. As Justice Ginsburg's majority opinion described it, the "map's maximum total-population deviation is 8.04%, safely within the presumptively permissible 10% range. But measured by a voter-population baseline—eligible voters or registered voters—the map's maximum population deviation exceeds 40%." The plaintiffs "contend[ed] that basing apportionment on total population dilutes their votes in relation to voters in other Senate districts, in violation of the one-person, one-vote principle of the Equal Protection Clause[.]" They "insist[ed] that the Equal Protection Clause requires jurisdictions to draw state and local legislative districts with equal voter-eligible populations, thus protecting 'voter equality,' *i.e.,* 'the right of eligible voters to an equal vote.'" The Court responded this way:

" . . . [W]e reject appellants' attempt to locate a voter-equality mandate in the Equal Protection Clause. As history, precedent, and practice demonstrate, it is plainly permissible for jurisdictions to measure equalization by the total population of state and local legislative districts."

As to constitutional history, Justice Ginsburg cited the views of the Framers of the original Constitution, and of the Fourteenth Amendment, to the effect that the House of Representatives must be apportioned in accordance with the number of inhabitants, not with the number of voters, leaving it "beyond doubt that the principle of representational equality figured prominently in the decision to count people, whether or not they qualify as voters." And the Court rejected the plaintiffs' attempt to distinguish apportionment in Congress from apportionment of state and local legislatures: "[T]he constitutional scheme for congressional apportionment rests in part on the same representational concerns that exist regarding state and local legislative districting. The Framers' answer to the apportionment question in the congressional context therefore undermines appellants' contention that districts must be based on voter population."

With respect to plaintiffs' argument that language from the Court's past decisions demonstrated "that the Court had in mind, and constantly meant, that States should equalize the voter-eligible population of districts[,]" Justice Ginsburg replied:

"For every sentence appellants quote from the Court's opinions, one could respond with a line casting the one-person, one-vote guarantee in terms of equality of representation, not voter equality. . . . And the Court has suggested, repeatedly, that districting based on total population serves *both* the State's interest in preventing vote dilution *and* its interest in ensuring equality of representation. . . .

"Moreover, from *Reynolds* on, the Court has consistently looked to total-population figures when evaluating whether districting maps violate the Equal Protection Clause by deviating impermissibly from perfect population equality. . . . Appellants point to no instance in which the Court has determined the permissibility of deviation based on eligible- or registered-voter data. It would hardly make sense for the Court to have mandated voter equality *sub silentio* and then used a total-population baseline to evaluate compliance with that rule. More likely, we think, the Court has always assumed the permissibility of drawing districts to equalize total population."

Finally, "settled practice confirms [that a]dopting voter-eligible apportionment as constitutional command would upset a well-functioning approach to districting that all 50 States and countless local jurisdictions have followed for decades, even centuries." Further:

"As the Framers of the Constitution and the Fourteenth Amendment comprehended, representatives serve all residents, not just those eligible or registered to vote. Nonvoters have an important stake in many policy debates— children, their parents, even their grandparents, for example, have a stake in a strong public-education system—and in receiving constituent services, such as help navigating public-benefits bureaucracies. By ensuring that each representative is subject to requests and suggestions from the same number of constituents, total-population apportionment promotes equitable and effective representation."

Justice Ginsburg concluded the majority opinion with this:

"Because history, precedent, and practice suffice to reveal the infirmity of appellants' claims, we need not and do not resolve whether, as Texas now argues, States may draw districts to equalize voter-eligible population rather than total population."

Justice Thomas concurred only in the judgment:

"I write separately because this Court has never provided a sound basis for the one-person, one-vote principle. For 50 years, the Court has struggled to define what right that principle protects. Many of our precedents suggest that it protects the right of eligible voters to cast votes that receive equal weight. Despite that frequent explanation, our precedents often conclude that the Equal Protection Clause is satisfied when all individuals within a district— voters or not—have an equal share of representation. The majority today concedes that our cases have not produced a clear answer on this point.

"[T]he majority has failed to provide a sound basis for the one-person, one-vote principle because no such basis exists. The Constitution does not prescribe any one basis for apportionment within States. It instead leaves States significant leeway in apportioning their own districts to equalize total population, to equalize eligible voters, or to promote any other principle consistent with a republican form of government. The majority should recognize the futility of choosing only one of these options. The Constitution leaves the choice to the people alone—not to this Court."

The "fundamental" problem, wrote Justice Thomas, is that

"[t]here is simply no way to make a principled choice between interpreting one person, one vote as protecting eligible voters or as protecting total inhabitants within a State. That is because, though those theories are noble, the Constitution does not make either of them the exclusive means of apportionment for state and local representatives. In guaranteeing to the States a 'Republican Form of Government,' Art. IV, §4, the Constitution did not resolve whether the ultimate basis of representation is the right of citizens to cast an equal ballot or the right of all inhabitants to have equal representation. The Constitution instead reserves these matters to the people. The majority's attempt today to divine a single ' "theory of the Constitution" '—apportionment based on representation . . . —rests on a flawed reading of history and wrongly picks one side of a debate that the Framers did not resolve in the Constitution."

" . . .

"So far as the Constitution is concerned, there is no single 'correct' way to design a republican government. Any republic will have to reconcile giving power to the people with diminishing the influence of special interests. The wisdom of the Framers was that they recognized this dilemma and left it to the people to resolve. In trying to impose its own theory of democracy, the Court is hopelessly adrift amid political theory and interest-group politics with no guiding legal principles.

" . . .

"I agree with the majority's ultimate disposition of this case. As far as the original understanding of the Constitution is concerned, a State has wide latitude in selecting its population base for apportionment. . . . It can use total population, eligible voters, or any other nondiscriminatory voter base. . . . And States with a bicameral legislature can have some mixture of these theories, such as one population base for its lower house and another for its upper chamber.

" . . . [T]he choice is best left for the people of the States to decide for themselves how they should apportion their legislature."

Justice Alito also concurred only in the judgment, joined for the most part by Justice Thomas. His agreement with the Court was succinct:

"Both practical considerations and precedent support the conclusion that the use of total population is consistent with the one-person, one-vote rule. The decennial census required by the Constitution tallies total population. Art. I,

§2, cl. 3; Amdt. 14, §2. These statistics are more reliable and less subject to manipulation and dispute than statistics concerning eligible voters. Since *Reynolds*, States have almost uniformly used total population in attempting to create legislative districts that are equal in size. And with one notable exception, *Burns v. Richardson*, 384 U. S. 73 (1966), this Court's post-*Reynolds* cases have likewise looked to total population. Moreover, much of the time, creating districts that are equal in total population also results in the creation of districts that are at least roughly equal in eligible voters. I therefore agree that States are permitted to use total population in redistricting plans."

His disagreement with the Court was directed at the suggestion "that the use of total population is supported by the Constitution's formula for allocating seats in the House of Representatives among the States." After reviewing the constitutional history from a different perspective than the majority's, Justice Alito concluded:

"In light of the history of Article I, § 2, of the original Constitution and §2 of the Fourteenth Amendment, it is clear that the apportionment of seats in the House of Representatives was based in substantial part on the distribution of political power among the States and not merely on some theory regarding the proper nature of representation. It is impossible to draw any clear constitutional command from this complex history."

Page 876. Add after Easley v. Cromartie:

Alabama Legislative Black Caucus v. Alabama, 575 U.S. ___, 135 S.Ct. 1257 (2015). The Caucus and the Alabama Democratic Conference challenged Alabama's 2012 redistricting of its State House of Representatives and State Senate, claiming that new district boundaries constituted impermissible racial gerrymanders. In addition to seeking "to achieve numerous traditional districting objectives, such as compactness, not splitting counties or precincts, minimizing change, and protecting incumbents[,]" Alabama "placed yet greater importance on achieving two other goals" in its redistricting plan—(1) "creating a set of districts in which no district would deviate from the theoretical, precisely equal ideal by more than 1%—*i.e.*, a more rigorous deviation standard than our precedents have found necessary under the Constitution. See *Brown* v. *Thomson*, 462 U.S. 835, 842 (1983) (5% deviation from ideal generally permissible)[;]" and (2) ensuring compliance with the non-retrogression criterion of § 5 of the VRA, which Alabama believed required it "to maintain roughly the same black population percentage in existing majority-minority districts." As Justice Breyer's majority opinion for five Justices explained the problem:

"Compliance with these two goals posed particular difficulties with respect to many of the State's 35 majority-minority districts (8 in the Senate, 27 in the House). That is because many of these districts were (compared with the average district) underpopulated. In order for Senate District 26, for example, to meet the State's no-more-than 1% population-deviation objective, the State would have to add about 16,000 individuals to the district. And, prior to redistricting, 72.75% of District 26's population was black. Accordingly,

Alabama's plan added 15,785 new individuals, and only 36 of those newly added individuals were white.

"This suit . . . focuses in large part upon Alabama's efforts to achieve these two goals. The Caucus and the Conference basically claim that the State, in adding so many new minority voters to majority-minority districts (and to others), went too far. They allege the State created a constitutionally forbidden 'racial gerrymander'—a gerrymander that (*e.g.*, when the State adds more minority voters than needed for a minority group to elect a candidate of its choice) might, among other things, harm the very minority voters that Acts such as the Voting Rights Act sought to help."

On appeal, the Court vacated the judgment of a three-judge district court rejecting the racial gerrymandering claim, and remanded the case for further proceedings, because the Court concluded that the district court had not applied the correct legal standards and thus may have reached the wrong conclusion. First, because the District Court erroneously and "repeatedly referred to the racial gerrymandering claims as claims that race improperly motivated the drawing of boundary lines of the State *considered as a whole*[,]" whereas "a claim of racial gerrymandering [is] a claim that race was improperly used in the drawing of the boundaries of one or more *specific electoral districts*"; and because the Court's generous "review of the record indicates that the plaintiffs did not claim only that the legislature had racially gerrymandered the State 'as' an undifferentiated 'whole[,' but] their evidence and their arguments embody the claim that individual majority-minority districts were racially gerrymandered[;]" the district court needed to reconsider those specific districts, which it had not done, taking into account, among other considerations, "statewide *evidence*" that might be presented in order to prove racial gerrymandering in a particular district.

Second, unlike the district court, which held that the Conference lacked standing to challenge individual districts as well as the statewide redistricting plan as a whole, the majority found it "highly likely that a 'statewide' organization with members in 'almost every county,' the purpose of which is to help 'blacks and other minorities and poor people,' will have members in each majority-minority district[.]" As a consequence, "elementary principles of procedural fairness required that the District Court . . . give the Conference an opportunity to provide evidence of member residence" in the challenged districts.

Third, contrary to the district court's alternative holding "that the claims of racial gerrymandering must fail because '[r]ace was not the predominant motivating factor' in the creation of any of the challenged districts"—a conclusion based in large part on Alabama's equal population goal playing such a prominent role in its redistricting plan—the "equal population goal is not one factor among others to be weighed against the use of race to determine whether race 'predominates.' Rather, it is part of the redistricting background, taken as a given, when determining whether race, or other factors, predominate in a legislator's determination as to *how* equal population objectives will be met." Accordingly, the Court "agree[d] with the United States that the requirement that districts have approximately equal populations is a background rule against which redistricting takes place. . . . It is not a factor to be treated like other nonracial factors when a court determines whether race predominated over other, 'traditional' factors in the drawing of district boundaries." This important clarification led the Court to conclude that "with respect to District 26 and likely others as well, had the District Court treated equal population goals as background factors, it might have concluded that race was the predominant boundary-drawing consideration. Thus, on remand, the District Court should reconsider its 'no predominance' conclusions with respect to Senate District 26 and others to which our analysis is applicable."

Finally, the Court also held that the district court holding that the racial gerrymandering claim failed in any event, because the districting acts would satisfy strict scrutiny, "rests upon a misperception of the law. Section 5 . . . does not require a covered jurisdiction to maintain a particular numerical minority percentage. It requires the jurisdiction to maintain a minority's ability to elect a preferred candidate of choice." The majority's rejection of the district court's approach is captured in this paragraph:

"[T]he District Court . . . said that a plan is 'narrowly tailored . . . when the race-based action taken was *reasonably necessary*' to achieve a compelling interest. . . . And it held that preventing retrogression is a compelling interest. . . . While we do not here decide whether, given *Shelby County* v. *Holder*, 570 U.S. ___ (2013), continued compliance with § 5 remains a compelling interest, we conclude that the District Court and the legislature asked the wrong question with respect to narrow tailoring. They asked: 'How can we maintain present minority percentages in majority-minority districts?' But given § 5's language, its purpose, the Justice Department Guidelines, and the relevant precedent, they should have asked: 'To what extent must we preserve existing minority percentages in order to maintain the minority's present ability to elect the candidate of its choice?' Asking the wrong question may well have led to the wrong answer. Hence, we cannot accept the District Court's 'compelling interest/narrow tailoring' conclusion."

Justice Scalia dissented, joined by Chief Justice Roberts and Justices Thomas and Alito. He objected to the Court acting "as standby counsel for sympathetic litigants," when the challengers failed to show that they had standing, and failed to allege impermissible racial gerrymandering of specific districts, instead making only statewide claims, which "the Court rightly concludes that our racial gerrymandering jurisprudence does not allow. . . ." It may be "understandable, if not excusable, that the Court balks at denying merits review simply because appellants pursued a flawed litigation strategy. But allowing appellants a second bite at the apple invites lower courts similarly to depart from the premise that ours is an adversarial system whenever they deem the stakes sufficiently high." The majority thus was not justified in "repackaging the claims for a second round of litigation."[a]

---

[a] Justice Thomas filed a separate dissent as well, criticizing the Court's racial gerrymandering jurisprudence generally, including its attention to the Voting Rights Act. He said that Alabama's "redistricting effort was indeed tainted, but it was tainted by our voting

Harris v. Arizona Independent Redistricting Commission, 578 U.S. ___, 136 S.Ct. 1301 (2016). A group of Arizona voters challenged a redistricting plan for the State's legislature crafted by the Commission following the 2010 census, at a time when Arizona was subject to the Voting Rights Act. Their "basic claim [was] that deviations in their apportionment plan from absolute equality of population reflect[ed] the Commission's political efforts to help the Democratic Party." Writing for a unanimous Court, Justice Breyer rejected that "claim because, as the district court concluded, the deviations predominantly reflected Commission efforts to achieve compliance with the federal Voting Rights Act, not to secure political advantage for one party." The total population deviation in the final map was 8.8%, somewhat larger than the initial map that "had a maximum population deviation from absolute equality of districts of 4.07%." The change reflected efforts "to adjust the plan's initial boundaries in order to enhance minority voting strength" and secure preclearance from the Justice Department, which was forthcoming. In the course of his opinion, Justice Breyer wrote:

"[I]n a case like this one, those attacking a state-approved plan must show that it is more probable than not that a deviation of less than 10% reflects the predominance of illegitimate reapportionment factors rather than the 'legitimate considerations' to which we have referred in *Reynolds* and later cases. Given the inherent difficulty of measuring and comparing factors that may legitimately account for small deviations from strict mathematical equality, we believe that attacks on deviations under 10% will succeed only rarely, in unusual cases. And we are not surprised that the appellants have failed to meet their burden here.

" . . .

" . . . [T]he District Court majority found that 'the population deviations were primarily a result of good-faith efforts to comply with the Voting Rights Act . . . even though partisanship played some role.' . . . This conclusion was well supported in the record. And as a result, appellants have not shown that it is more probable than not that illegitimate considerations were the predominant motivation behind the plan's deviations from mathematically equal district populations—deviations that were under 10%. Consequently, they have failed to show that the Commission's plan violates the Equal Protection Clause as interpreted in *Reynolds* and subsequent cases.

" . . .

---

rights jurisprudence and the uses to which the Voting Rights Act has been put. Long ago, the DOJ and special-interest groups like the ACLU hijacked the Act, and they have been using it ever since to achieve their vision of maximized black electoral strength, often at the expense of the voters they purport to help. States covered by § 5 have been whipsawed, first required to create 'safe' majority-black districts, then told not to 'diminis[h]' the ability to elect, and now told they have been too rigid in preventing any 'diminishing' of the ability to elect.

"Worse, the majority's solution to the appellants' gerrymandering claims requires States to analyze race even *more* exhaustively, not less, by accounting for black voter registration and turnout statistics. The majority's command to analyze black voting patterns enroute to adopting the 'correct' racial quota does nothing to ease the conflict between our color-blind Constitution and the 'consciously segregated districting system' the Court has required in the name of equality."

" . . . Even assuming, without deciding, that partisanship is an illegitimate redistricting factor, appellants have not carried their burden."

CHAPTER 11

DEFINING THE SCOPE OF "LIBERTY" AND "PROPERTY" PROTECTED BY THE DUE PROCESS CLAUSE—THE PROCEDURAL DUE PROCESS CASES

1. WHEN DOES DUE PROCESS MANDATE CONSTITUTIONAL PROCEDURES?

A. WHAT "PROPERTY" AND "LIBERTY" IS PROTECTED?

Page 998. Add the following before Subsection B:

Kerry v. Din, 576 U.S. ___, 135 S.Ct. 2128 (2015). Din is a citizen and resident of the United States, whose husband is a citizen and resident of Afghanistan and a former civil servant in the Taliban regime. Din successfully petitioned to have her husband classified as her "immediate relative," a status under the Immigration and Nationality Act (INA) that allowed her to sponsor him via a special visa-application process for aliens for entry into the United States. When he applied for the visa, however, he was interviewed, and his application was denied, by the U.S. Embassy in Islamabad, Pakistan, pursuant to INA § 1182(a)(3)(B), which makes an otherwise admissible person inadmissible if he or she has engaged in a "terrorist activity," defined broadly to include "providing material support to a terrorist organization and serving as a terrorist organization's representative. § 1182(a)(3)(B)(i),(iii)–(vi)." After her husband was informed by a consular officer that "he was inadmissible under § 1182(a)(3)(B) but [was] provided no further explanation[,]" Din sued on his behalf, claiming "that the Government denied her due process of law when, without adequate explanation of the reason for the visa denial, it deprived her of her constitutional right to live in the United States with her spouse." (As an "unadmitted and nonresident alien, he[r husband] has no right of entry into the United States, and no cause of action to press in furtherance of his claim for admission.")

With no majority opinion, the Court rejected Din's due process claim. The plurality opinion of Justice Scalia, joined by Chief Justice Roberts and Justice Thomas, concluded that no process was due, because "[t]here is no such constitutional right" to live in the United States with one's spouse. He argued that the historical understanding of "liberty" in the Fifth Amendment derived from Magna Carta and was limited to freedom from imprisonment, confinement, or forcible detention. He argued further that *"even if* one accepts the textually unsupportable doctrine of implied fundamental rights, Din's arguments would fail." He elaborated as follows:

"... [B]efore conferring constitutional status upon a previously unrecognized 'liberty,' we have required 'a careful description of the asserted fundamental liberty interest,' as well as a demonstration that the interest is 'objectively, deeply rooted in this Nation's history and tradition, and implicit in the concept of ordered liberty, such that neither liberty nor justice would exist if [it was] sacrificed.' ...

"Din describes the denial of [the] visa application as implicating, alternately, a 'liberty interest in her marriage,' ..., a 'right of association with one's spouse,' ... 'a liberty interest in being reunited with certain blood relatives,' ... and 'the liberty interest of a U. S. citizen under the Due Process Clause to be free from arbitrary restrictions on his right to live with his spouse,' .... To be sure, this Court has at times indulged a propensity for grandiloquence when reviewing the sweep of implied rights, describing them so broadly that they would include not only the interests Din asserts but many others as well. ... But this Court is not bound by dicta, especially dicta that have been repudiated by the holdings of our subsequent cases. And the actual holdings of the cases Din relies upon hardly establish the capacious right she now asserts.

"Unlike the States in Loving v. Virginia, 388 U. S. 1 (1967), Zablocki v. Redhail, 434 U. S. 374 (1978), and Turner v. Safley, 482 U. S. 78 (1987), the Federal Government here has not attempted to forbid a marriage. ...

" ...

"Nothing in the cases Din cites establishes a free-floating and categorical liberty interest in marriage (or any other formulation Din offers) sufficient to trigger constitutional protection whenever a regulation in any way touches upon an aspect of the marital relationship. ... Even if we might 'imply' a liberty interest in marriage generally speaking, that must give way when there is a tradition denying the specific application of that general interest. ...

"Here, a long practice of regulating spousal immigration precludes Din's claim that the denial of [the] visa application has deprived her of a fundamental liberty interest. Although immigration was effectively unregulated prior to 1875, as soon as Congress began legislating in this area it enacted a complicated web of regulations that erected serious impediments to a person's ability to bring a spouse into the United States. ...

" ...

" ... Only by diluting the meaning of a fundamental liberty interest and jettisoning our established jurisprudence could we conclude that the denial of [the] visa application implicates any of Din's fundamental liberty interests."

As for Justice Breyer's dissenting arguments, Justice Scalia wrote this:

"Justice Breyer suggests that procedural due process rights attach to liberty interests that either are (1) created by nonconstitutional law, such as a statute, or (2) 'sufficiently important' so as to 'flow "implicit[ly]" from the design, object, and nature of the Due Process Clause.'

"The first point is unobjectionable, at least given this Court's case law. . . . But it is unhelpful to Din, who does not argue that a statute confers on her a liberty interest protected by the Due Process Clause. . . . The legal benefits afforded to marriages and the preferential treatment accorded to visa applicants with citizen relatives are insufficient to confer on Din a right that can be deprived only pursuant to procedural due process.

"Justice Breyer's second point—that procedural due process rights attach even to some nonfundamental liberty interests that have not been created by statute—is much more troubling. . . . [H]e argues that the term 'liberty' in the Due Process Clause includes implied rights that, although not so fundamental as to deserve substantive-due-process protection, are important enough to deserve procedural-due-process protection. In other words, there are two categories of implied rights protected by the Due Process Clause: really fundamental rights, which cannot be taken away at all absent a compelling state interest; and not-so-fundamental rights, which can be taken away so long as procedural due process is observed.

"The dissent fails to cite a single case supporting its novel theory of implied nonfundamental rights. . . .

" . . .

" . . . Justice Breyer proposes . . . a dangerous doctrine. . . . Even shallow-rooted liberties would, thanks to this new procedural-rights-only notion of quasi-fundamental rights, qualify for judicially imposed procedural requirements. Moreover, Justice Breyer gives no basis for distinguishing the fundamental rights recognized in the cases he depends on from the nonfundamental right he believes they give rise to in the present case.

"Neither Din's right to live with her spouse nor her right to live within this country is implicated here. . . . The Government has not refused to recognize Din's marriage . . . , and Din remains free to live with her husband anywhere in the world that both individuals are permitted to reside. And the Government has not expelled Din from the country."

Justice Kennedy, joined by Justice Alito, concurred in the judgment, "[b]ut rather than deciding, as the plurality does, whether Din has a protected liberty interest, my view is that, even assuming she does, the notice she received regarding her husband's visa denial satisfied due process." Indeed, "[t]oday's disposition should not be interpreted as deciding whether a citizen has a protected liberty interest in the visa application of her alien spouse." Given the national security context, he relied on the analysis in Kleindienst v. Mandel, 408 U.S. 753 (1972), and concluded "that the Government satisfied any obligation it might have had to provide Din with a facially legitimate and bona fide reason for its action when it provided notice that her husband was denied admission to the country under § 1182(a)(3)(B)."

Justice Breyer's dissent was joined by Justices Ginsburg, Sotomayor, and Kagan. He wrote in pertinent part:

"The liberty interest that Ms. Din seeks to protect consists of her freedom to live together with her husband in the United States. She seeks procedural, not substantive, protection for this freedom. . . .

"Our cases make clear that the Due Process Clause entitles her to such procedural rights as long as (1) she seeks protection for a liberty interest sufficiently important for procedural protection to flow 'implicit[ly]' from the design, object, and nature of the Due Process Clause, or (2) nonconstitutional law (a statute, for example) creates 'an expectation' that a person will not be deprived of that kind of liberty without fair procedures. . . .

"The liberty for which Ms. Din seeks protection easily satisfies both standards. As this Court has long recognized, the institution of marriage, which encompasses the right of spouses to live together and to raise a family, is central to human life, requires and enjoys community support, and plays a central role in most individuals' 'orderly pursuit of happiness,'. . . . Similarly, the Court has long recognized that a citizen's right to live within this country, being fundamental, enjoys basic procedural due process protection. See Ng Fung Ho v. White, 259 U.S. 276, 284–285 (1922). . . .

"At the same time, the law, including visa law, surrounds marriage with a host of legal protections to the point that it creates a strong expectation that government will not deprive married individuals of their freedom to live together without strong reasons and (in individual cases) without fair procedure. . . . Justice Scalia's response—that nonconstitutional law creates an 'expectation' that merits procedural protection under the Due Process Clause only if there is an unequivocal statutory right—is sorely mistaken. . . .

"Justice Scalia's more general response—claiming that I have created a new category of constitutional rights—misses the mark. I break no new ground here. Rather, this Court has already recognized that the Due Process Clause guarantees that the government will not, without fair procedure, deprive individuals of a host of rights, freedoms, and liberties that are no more important, and for which the state has created no greater expectation of continued benefit, than the liberty interest at issue here. . . . See, e.g., Wolff v. McDonnell, 418 U. S. 539, 556–557 (1974) (prisoner's right to maintain 'goodtime' credits shortening term of imprisonment; procedurally protected liberty interest based on nonconstitutional law); Paul v. Davis, 424 U. S. 693, 701 (1976) (right to certain aspects of reputation; procedurally protected liberty interest arising under the Constitution); Goss v. Lopez, 419 U. S. 565, 574–575 (1975) (student's right not to be suspended from school class; procedurally protected liberty interest arising under the Constitution); Vitek v. Jones, 445 U. S. 480, 491–495 (1980) (prisoner's right against involuntary commitment; procedurally protected liberty interest arising under the Constitution); Washington v. Harper, 494 U. S. 210, 221–222 (1990) (mentally ill prisoner's right not to take psychotropic drugs; procedurally protected liberty interest arising under the Constitution); see generally Goldberg [v. Kelly, 397 U. S. 254, 262–3 (1970)] (right to welfare benefits; procedurally protected property interest based on nonconstitutional law). How could a Constitution that protects individuals against the arbitrary deprivation of so diverse a set of interests not also offer some form of procedural protection to a citizen threatened with governmental deprivation of her freedom to live together with her spouse in America? . . .

II

A

"The more difficult question is the nature of the procedural protection required by the Constitution. . . .

"[H]ere, the Government makes individualized visa determinations through the application of a legal rule to particular facts. Individualized adjudication normally calls for the ordinary application of Due Process Clause procedures. . . . And those procedures normally include notice of an adverse action, an opportunity to present relevant proofs and arguments, before a neutral decisionmaker, and reasoned decisionmaking. See Hamdi v. Rumsfeld, 542 U. S. 507, 533 (2004) (plurality opinion). . . . These procedural protections help to guarantee that government will not make a decision directly affecting an individual arbitrarily but will do so through the reasoned application of a rule of law. It is that rule of law, stretching back at least 800 years to Magna Carta, which in major part the Due Process Clause seeks to protect. . . .

"Here, we need . . . consider only the minimum procedure that Ms. Din has requested—namely, a statement of reasons, some kind of explanation, as to why the State Department denied her husband a visa.

" . . .

" . . . [A] statement of reasons, even one provided after a visa denial, serves much the same function as a 'notice' of a proposed action. It allows Ms. Din, who suffered a 'serious loss,' a fair 'opportunity to meet' 'the case' that has produced separation from her husband. . . . Properly apprised of the grounds for the Government's action, Ms. Din can then take appropriate action—whether this amounts to an appeal, internal agency review, or (as is likely here) an opportunity to submit additional evidence and obtain reconsideration. . . .

" . . . [I]n the absence of some highly unusual circumstance (not shown to be present here . . .), the Constitution requires the Government to provide an adequate reason why it refused to grant Ms. Din's husband a visa. That reason, in my view, could be either the factual basis for the Government's decision or a sufficiently specific statutory subsection that conveys effectively the same information."

Justice Breyer found inadequate the State Department's statement that the denial was under "8 U. S. C. § 1182 (a)(3)(B)—the terrorism and national security bars to admissibility":

"For one thing, . . . § 1182(a)(3)(B), sets forth, not one reason, but dozens. It is a complex provision with 10 different subsections, many of which cross-reference other provisions of law. . . . Taken together the subsections, directly or through cross-reference, cover a vast waterfront of human activity potentially benefitting, sometimes in major ways, sometimes hardly at all, sometimes directly, sometimes indirectly, sometimes a few people, sometimes many, sometimes those with strong links, sometimes those with hardly a link, to a loosely or strongly connected group of individuals, which, through many different kinds of actions, might fall within the broad statutorily defined term 'terrorist.' . . .

"For another thing, the State Department's reason did not set forth any factual basis for the Government's decision. . . .

"The generality of the statutory provision cited and the lack of factual support mean that here, the reason given is analogous to telling a criminal defendant only that he is accused of 'breaking the law'; telling a property owner only that he cannot build because environmental rules forbid it; or telling a driver only that police pulled him over because he violated traffic laws. As such, the reason given cannot serve its procedural purpose. It does not permit Ms. Din to assess the correctness of the State Department's conclusion; it does not permit her to determine what kinds of facts she might provide in response; and it does not permit her to learn whether, or what kind of, defenses might be available. In short, any 'reason' that Ms. Din received is not constitutionally adequate."

Finally, in response to Justice Kennedy's opinion, Justice Breyer said in part:

" . . . [T]he presence of [national] security considerations does not suspend the Constitution. Hamdi, 542 U. S., at 527–537 (plurality opinion). Rather, it requires us to take security needs into account when determining, for example, what 'process' is 'due.' Ibid.

"Yet how can we take proper account of security considerations without knowing what they are, without knowing how and why they require modification of traditional due process requirements, and without knowing whether other, less restrictive alternatives are available? How exactly would it harm important security interests to give Ms. Din a better explanation? Is there no way to give Ms. Din such an explanation while also maintaining appropriate secrecy? I believe we need answers to these questions before we can accept as constitutional a major departure from the procedural requirements that the Due Process Clause ordinarily demands."

CHAPTER 12

APPLICATION OF THE POST CIVIL WAR AMENDMENTS TO PRIVATE CONDUCT: CONGRESSIONAL POWER TO ENFORCE THE AMENDMENTS

2. APPLICATION OF THE CONSTITUTION TO PRIVATE CONDUCT

C. GOVERNMENT FINANCING, REGULATION AND AUTHORIZATION OF PRIVATE CONDUCT

4. GOVERNMENT APPROVAL OF PRIVATE ACTIVITY

Page 1058. Add the following before Section 3:

Schuette v. Coalition to Defend Affirmative Action Integration and Immigration Rights By Any Means Necessary (BAMN), 572 U.S. ___, 134 S.Ct. 1623, 188 L.Ed.2d 613 (2014). After the Court's rulings in *Gratz v. Bollinger*, 539 U.S. 244 (2003), and *Grutter v. Bollinger*, 539 U.S. 306, 343 (2003), holding, respectively, that the University of Michigan undergraduate admissions policy's use of race violated the Equal Protection Clause but that the University of Michigan Law School's more limited use of race did not, Michigan voters passed Proposal 2, now Article I, § 26 of the State Constitution, which prohibits race-based preferences altogether in state university admissions. Plaintiffs challenged Proposal 2 as violating the principles elaborated in *Washington v. Seattle School Dist. No. 1* and the cases on which the *Seattle* Court relied. The U.S Court of Appeals for the Sixth Circuit, both in a three-judge panel and then en banc, embraced the plaintiffs' argument and struck down Proposal 2. By a 6–2 vote—Justice Kagan did not participate—the Court reversed. Justice Kennedy, announcing the judgment of the Court and writing an opinion for himself, Chief Justice Roberts and Justice Alito, canvassed the *Seattle* line of cases, going back to *Reitman v. Mulkey*. According to Justice Kennedy: "*Seattle* is best understood as a case in which the state action in question (the bar on busing enacted by the State's voters) had the serious risk, if not purpose, of causing specific injuries on account of race, just as had been the case in *Mulkey* and *Hunter*. Although there had been no judicial finding of *de jure* segregation with respect to Seattle's school district, it appears as though school segregation in the district in the 1940's and 1950's may have been the partial result of school board policies that 'permitted white students to transfer out of black schools while restricting the transfer of black students into white schools.' *Parents Involved in Community Schools* v. *Seattle School Dist. No. 1*, 551 U.S. 701, 807–808 (2007) (Breyer, J., dissenting)." In other words, according to Justice Kennedy, "[t]he *Seattle* Court, accepting the validity of the school board's busing remedy as a predicate to its analysis of the constitutional question, found that the State's disapproval of the school board's busing remedy was an aggravation of the very racial injury in which the State itself was complicit."

Justice Kennedy's opinion recognized that the analysis seemingly employed in *Seattle* might be thought to support the plaintiffs' challenge, but that what might be thought of as *Seattle*'s larger framework should not be employed here: "The broad language used in *Seattle* . . . went well beyond the analysis needed to resolve the case. The Court there seized upon the statement in Justice Harlan's concurrence in *Hunter* that the procedural change in that case had 'the clear purpose of making it more difficult for certain racial and religious minorities to achieve legislation that is in their interest.' . . . That language, taken in the context of the facts in *Hunter*, is best read simply to describe the necessity for finding an equal protection violation where specific injuries from hostile discrimination were at issue. The *Seattle* Court, however, used the language from the *Hunter* concurrence to establish a new and far-reaching rationale. *Seattle* stated that where a government policy 'inures primarily to the benefit of the minority' and minorities . . . consider the policy to be 'in their interest,' then any state action that 'place[s] effective decisionmaking authority over' that policy 'at a different level of government' must be reviewed under strict scrutiny. . . . In essence, according to the broad reading of *Seattle*, any state action with a 'racial focus' that makes it 'more difficult for certain racial minorities than for other groups' to 'achieve legislation that is in their interest' is subject to strict scrutiny. . . . It is this reading of *Seattle* that the Court of Appeals found to be controlling here. And that reading must be rejected."

He went on to explain: "The broad rationale that the Court of Appeals adopted goes beyond the necessary holding and the meaning of the precedents said to support it; and in the instant case neither the formulation of the general rule just set forth nor the precedents cited to authenticate it suffice to invalidate Proposal 2. The expansive reading of *Seattle* has no principled limitation and raises serious questions of compatibility with the Court's settled equal protection jurisprudence. To the extent *Seattle* is read to require the Court to determine and declare which political policies serve the 'interest' of a group defined in racial terms, that rationale was unnecessary to the decision in *Seattle*. . . ; it has no support in precedent; and it raises serious constitutional concerns. That expansive language does not provide a proper guide for decisions and should not be deemed authoritative or controlling. The rule that the Court of Appeals elaborated and respondents seek to establish here would contradict central equal protection principles."

"In cautioning against 'impermissible racial stereotypes,' this Court has rejected the assumption that 'members of the same racial group—regardless of their age, education, economic status, or the community in which they live—think alike, share the same political interests, and will prefer the same candidates at the polls.' *Shaw* v. *Reno*, 509 U.S. 630, 647 (1993); see also *Metro Broadcasting, Inc.* v. *FCC*, 497 U.S. 547, 636 (1990) (Kennedy, J., dissenting) (rejecting the 'demeaning notion that members of . . . defined racial groups ascribe to certain "minority views" that must be different from those of other citizens'). It cannot be entertained as a serious proposition that all individuals of the same race think alike. Yet that proposition would be a necessary beginning point were the *Seattle* formulation to control, as the Court of Appeals held it did in this case. And if it were deemed necessary to probe how some races define their own interest in political matters, still another beginning point would be to define individuals according to race. But in a society in which those lines are becoming more blurred, the attempt to define race-based categories also raises serious questions of its own. Government action that classifies individuals on the basis of race is inherently suspect and carries the danger of perpetuating the very racial divisions the polity seeks to transcend. . . . Were courts to embark upon this venture not only would it be undertaken with no clear legal standards or accepted sources to guide judicial decision but also it would result in, or at least impose a high risk of, inquiries and categories dependent upon demeaning stereotypes, classifications of questionable constitutionality on their own terms."

Justice Scalia, joined by Justice Thomas, wrote an opinion concurring in the judgment and arguing that Justice Kennedy's (re)characterization of Seattle was factually and analytically unconvincing, but that *Hunter* and *Seattle* should be overruled. Justice Breyer wrote an opinion concurring in the judgment in which he argued that the kind of overt "restructuring" of the political process at issue in *Hunter* and *Seattle* was not implicated here, and in which he observed that the present case does not deal with the elimination of "race-conscious admissions programs designed to remedy past exclusionary racial discrimination or the direct effects of that discrimination." Justice Sotomayor, joined by Justice Ginsburg, dissented, arguing that the Court of Appeals correctly applied *Seattle*. Her dissent also took issue with the Court's general approach to dealing with cases involving racial discrimination: "My colleagues are of the view that we should leave race out of the picture entirely and let the voters sort it out. . . . We have seen this reasoning before. See *Parents Involved*, 551 U.S., at 748 ('The way to stop discrimination on the basis of race is to stop discriminating on the basis of race'). It is a sentiment out of touch with reality, one not required by our Constitution, and one that has properly been rejected as [inadequate] to resolve cases of this nature." She went on: "In my colleagues' view, examining the racial impact of legislation only perpetuates racial discrimination. This refusal to accept the stark reality that race matters is regrettable. The way to stop discrimination on the basis of race is to speak openly and candidly on the subject of race, and to apply the Constitution with eyes open to the unfortunate effects of centuries of racial discrimination. As members of the judiciary tasked with intervening to carry out the guarantee of equal protection, we ought not sit back and wish away, rather than confront, the racial inequality that exists in our society. It is this view that works harm, by perpetuating the facile notion that what makes race matter is acknowledging the simple truth that race *does* matter."

This dissent prompted Chief Justice Roberts to write a separate concurring opinion in which he observed: "[I]t is not 'out of touch with reality' to conclude that racial preferences may themselves have the debilitating effect of reinforcing precisely that doubt, and—if so—that the preferences do more harm than good. To disagree with the dissent's views on the costs and benefits of racial preferences is not to 'wish away, rather than confront' racial inequality. People can disagree in good faith on this issue, but it similarly does more harm than good to question the openness and candor of those on either side of the debate."

6. THE SCOPE OF CONGRESSIONAL POWER TO REDEFINE THE AMENDMENTS

A. "REMEDIAL" POWER

Page 1084. Add the following before Subsection B:

Shelby County v. Holder

570 U.S. ___, 133 S.Ct. 2612, 186 L.Ed.2d 651 (2013).

Chief Justice Roberts delivered the opinion of the Court.

The Voting Rights Act of 1965 employed extraordinary measures to address an extraordinary problem. Section 5 of the Act required States to obtain federal permission before enacting any law related to voting—a drastic departure from basic principles of federalism. And § 4 of the Act applied that requirement only to some States—an equally dramatic departure from the principle that all States enjoy equal sovereignty. This was strong medicine, but Congress determined it was needed to address entrenched racial discrimination in voting, "an insidious and pervasive evil which had been perpetuated in certain parts of our country through unremitting and ingenious defiance of the Constitution." *South Carolina v. Katzenbach*, 383 U.S. 301, 309 (1966). As we explained in upholding the law, "exceptional conditions can justify legislative measures not otherwise appropriate." *Id.*, at 334. Reflecting the unprecedented nature of these measures, they were scheduled to expire after five years. See Voting Rights Act of 1965, § 4(a), 79 Stat. 438.

Nearly 50 years later, they are still in effect; indeed, they have been made more stringent, and are now scheduled to last until 2031. There is no denying, however, that the conditions that originally justified these measures no longer characterize voting in the covered jurisdictions. By 2009, "the racial gap in voter registration and turnout [was] lower in the States originally covered by § 5 than it [was] nationwide." *Northwest Austin Municipal Util. Dist. No. One v. Holder*, 557 U.S. 193, 203–204 (2009). Since that time, Census Bureau data indicate that African-American voter turnout has come to exceed white voter turnout in five of the six States originally covered by § 5, with a gap in the sixth State of less than one half of one percent. . . .

At the same time, voting discrimination still exists; no one doubts that. The question is whether the Act's extraordinary measures, including its disparate treatment of the States, continue to satisfy constitutional requirements. As we put it a short time ago, "the Act imposes current burdens and must be justified by current needs." *Northwest Austin*, 557 U.S., at 203.

I

A

The Fifteenth Amendment was ratified in 1870, in the wake of the Civil War. It provides that "[t]he right of citizens of the United States to vote shall not be denied or abridged by the United States or by any State on account of race, color, or previous condition of servitude," and it gives Congress the "power to enforce this article by appropriate legislation."

"The first century of congressional enforcement of the Amendment, however, can only be regarded as a failure." *Id.*, at 197. In the 1890s, Alabama, Georgia, Louisiana, Mississippi, North Carolina, South Carolina, and Virginia began to enact literacy tests for voter registration and to employ other methods designed to prevent African-Americans from voting. *Katzenbach*, 383 U.S., at 310. Congress passed statutes outlawing some of these practices and facilitating litigation against them, but litigation remained slow and expensive, and the States came up with new ways to discriminate as soon as existing ones were struck down. Voter registration of African-Americans barely improved. *Id.*, at 313–314.

Inspired to action by the civil rights movement, Congress responded in 1965 with the Voting Rights Act. Section 2 was enacted to forbid, in all 50 States, any "standard, practice, or procedure . . . imposed or applied . . . to deny or abridge the right of any citizen of the United States to vote on account of race or color." 79 Stat. 437. The current version forbids any "standard, practice, or procedure" that "results in a denial or abridgement of the right of any citizen of the United States to vote on account of race or color." 42 U.S.C. § 1973(a). Both the Federal Government and individuals have sued to enforce § 2, . . . and injunctive relief is available in appropriate cases to block voting laws from going into effect, see 42 U.S.C. § 1973j(d). Section 2 is permanent, applies nationwide, and is not at issue in this case.

Other sections targeted only some parts of the country. At the time of the Act's passage, these "covered" jurisdictions were those States or political subdivisions that had maintained a test or device as a prerequisite to voting as of November 1, 1964, and had less than 50 percent voter registration or turnout in the 1964 Presidential election. § 4(b), 79 Stat. 438. Such tests or devices included literacy and knowledge tests, good moral character requirements, the need for vouchers from registered voters, and the like. § 4(c), *id.*, at 438–439. A covered jurisdiction could "bail out" of coverage if it had not used a test or device in the preceding five years "for the purpose or with the effect of denying or abridging the right to vote on account of race or color." § 4(a), *id.*, at 438. In

1965, the covered States included Alabama, Georgia, Louisiana, Mississippi, South Carolina, and Virginia. The additional covered subdivisions included 39 counties in North Carolina and one in Arizona. . . .

In those jurisdictions, § 4 of the Act banned all such tests or devices. § 4(a), 79 Stat. 438. Section 5 provided that no change in voting procedures could take effect until it was approved by federal authorities in Washington, D.C.—either the Attorney General or a court of three judges. *Id.*, at 439. A jurisdiction could obtain such "preclearance" only by proving that the change had neither "the purpose [nor] the effect of denying or abridging the right to vote on account of race or color." *Ibid.*

Sections 4 and 5 were intended to be temporary; they were set to expire after five years. See § 4(a), *id.*, at 438; *Northwest Austin, supra*, at 199. In *South Carolina v. Katzenbach*, we upheld the 1965 Act against constitutional challenge, explaining that it was justified to address "voting discrimination where it persists on a pervasive scale." 383 U.S., at 308. In 1970, Congress reauthorized the Act for another five years, and extended the coverage formula in § 4(b) to jurisdictions that had a voting test and less than 50 percent voter registration or turnout as of 1968. Voting Rights Act Amendments of 1970, §§ 3–4, 84 Stat. 315. That swept in several counties in California, New Hampshire, and New York. . . . Congress also extended the ban in § 4(a) on tests and devices nationwide. § 6, 84 Stat. 315.

In 1975, Congress reauthorized the Act for seven more years, and extended its coverage to jurisdictions that had a voting test and less than 50 percent voter registration or turnout as of 1972. Voting Rights Act Amendments of 1975, §§ 101, 202, 89 Stat. 400, 401. Congress also amended the definition of "test or device" to include the practice of providing English-only voting materials in places where over five percent of voting-age citizens spoke a single language other than English. § 203, *id.*, at 401–402. As a result of these amendments, the States of Alaska, Arizona, and Texas, as well as several counties in California, Florida, Michigan, New York, North Carolina, and South Dakota, became covered jurisdictions. . . . Congress correspondingly amended sections 2 and 5 to forbid voting discrimination on the basis of membership in a language minority group, in addition to discrimination on the basis of race or color. §§ 203, 206, 89 Stat. 401, 402. Finally, Congress made the nationwide ban on tests and devices permanent. § 102, id., at 400.

In 1982, Congress reauthorized the Act for 25 years, but did not alter its coverage formula. See Voting Rights Act Amendments, 96 Stat. 131. Congress did, however, amend the bailout provisions, allowing political subdivisions of covered jurisdictions to bail out. Among other prerequisites for bailout, jurisdictions and their subdivisions must not have used a forbidden test or device, failed to receive preclearance, or lost a § 2 suit, in the ten years prior to seeking bailout. § 2, *id.*, at 131–133.

We upheld each of these reauthorizations against constitutional challenge. See *Georgia v. United States*, 411 U.S. 526 (1973); *City of Rome v. United States*, 446 U.S. 156 (1980); *Lopez v. Monterey County*, 525 U.S. 266 (1999).

In 2006, Congress again reauthorized the Voting Rights Act for 25 years, again without change to its coverage formula. Fannie Lou Hamer, Rosa Parks, and Coretta Scott King Voting Rights Act Reauthorization and Amendments Act, 120 Stat. 577. Congress also amended § 5 to prohibit more conduct than before. § 5, *id.*, at 580–581. . . . Section 5 now forbids voting changes with "any discriminatory purpose" as well as voting changes that diminish the ability of citizens, on account of race, color, or language minority status, "to elect their preferred candidates of choice." 42 U.S.C. §§ 1973c(b)-(d).

Shortly after this reauthorization, a Texas utility district brought suit, seeking to bail out from the Act's coverage and, in the alternative, challenging the Act's constitutionality. See *Northwest Austin*, 557 U.S., at 200–201. A three-judge District Court explained that only a State or political subdivision was eligible to seek bailout under the statute, and concluded that the utility district was not a political subdivision, a term that encompassed only "counties, parishes, and voter-registering subunits." *Northwest Austin Municipal Util. Dist. No. One v. Mukasey*, 573 F.Supp.2d 221, 232 (D.D.C.2008). The District Court also rejected the constitutional challenge. *Id.*, at 283.

We reversed. We explained that " 'normally the Court will not decide a constitutional question if there is some other ground upon which to dispose of the case.' " *Northwest Austin, supra*, at 205 (quoting *Escambia County v. McMillan*, 466 U.S. 48, 51(1984) (per curiam)). Concluding that "underlying constitutional concerns," among other things, "compel[led] a broader reading of the bailout provision," we construed the statute to allow the utility district to seek bailout. *Northwest Austin*, 557 U.S., at 207. In doing so we expressed serious doubts about the Act's continued constitutionality.

We explained that § 5 "imposes substantial federalism costs" and "differentiates between the States, despite our historic tradition that all the States enjoy equal sovereignty." *Id.*, at 202, 203. We also noted that "[t]hings have changed in the South. Voter turnout and registration rates now approach parity. Blatantly discriminatory evasions of federal decrees are rare. And minority candidates hold office at unprecedented levels." *Id.*, at 202. Finally, we questioned whether the problems that § 5 meant to address were still "concentrated in the jurisdictions singled out for preclearance." *Id.*, at 203.

Eight Members of the Court subscribed to these views, and the remaining Member would have held the Act unconstitutional. Ultimately, however, the Court's construction of the bailout provision left the constitutional issues for another day.

B

Shelby County is located in Alabama, a covered jurisdiction. It has not sought bailout, as the Attorney General has recently objected to voting changes proposed from within the county. . . . Instead, in 2010, the county sued the Attorney General in Federal District Court in Washington, D.C., seeking a declaratory judgment that sections 4(b) and 5 of the Voting Rights Act are facially unconstitutional, as well as a permanent injunction against their enforcement. The District Court ruled against the county and upheld the

Act. . . . The court found that the evidence before Congress in 2006 was sufficient to justify reauthorizing § 5 and continuing the § 4(b) coverage formula.

The Court of Appeals for the D.C. Circuit affirmed. In assessing § 5, the D.C. Circuit considered six primary categories of evidence: Attorney General objections to voting changes, Attorney General requests for more information regarding voting changes, successful § 2 suits in covered jurisdictions, the dispatching of federal observers to monitor elections in covered jurisdictions, § 5 preclearance suits involving covered jurisdictions, and the deterrent effect of § 5. See 679 F. 3d 848, 862–63 (2012). After extensive analysis of the record, the court accepted Congress's conclusion that § 2 litigation remained inadequate in the covered jurisdictions to protect the rights of minority voters, and that § 5 was therefore still necessary.

Turning to § 4, the D.C. Circuit noted that the evidence for singling out the covered jurisdictions was "less robust" and that the issue presented "a close question." *Id.* at 879. But the court looked to data comparing the number of successful § 2 suits in the different parts of the country. Coupling that evidence with the deterrent effect of § 5, the court concluded that the statute continued "to single out the jurisdictions in which discrimination is concentrated," and thus held that the coverage formula passed constitutional muster. *Id.*, at 883.

Judge Williams dissented. He found "no positive correlation between inclusion in § 4(b)'s coverage formula and low black registration or turnout." *Id.*, at 891. Rather, to the extent there was any correlation, it actually went the other way: "condemnation under § 4(b) is a marker of higher black registration and turnout." *Ibid.* (emphasis added). Judge Williams also found that "[c]overed jurisdictions have *far more* black officeholders as a proportion of the black population than do uncovered ones." *Id.*, at 892. As to the evidence of successful § 2 suits, Judge Williams disaggregated the reported cases by State, and concluded that "[t]he five worst uncovered jurisdictions . . . have worse records than eight of the covered jurisdictions." *Id.*, at 897. He also noted that two covered jurisdictions—Arizona and Alaska—had not had any successful reported § 2 suit brought against them during the entire 24 years covered by the data. *Ibid.* Judge Williams would have held the coverage formula of § 4(b) "irrational" and unconstitutional. *Id.*, at 885.

We granted certiorari. 568 U.S. ___ (2012).

II

In *Northwest Austin*, we stated that "the Act imposes current burdens and must be justified by current needs." 557 U.S., at 203. And we concluded that "a departure from the fundamental principle of equal sovereignty requires a showing that a statute's disparate geographic coverage is sufficiently related to the problem that it targets." *Ibid.* These basic principles guide our review of the question before us.

A

The Constitution and laws of the United States are "the supreme Law of the Land." U.S. Const., Art. VI, cl. 2. State legislation may not contravene federal law. The Federal Government does not, however, have a general right to review and veto state enactments before they go into effect. A proposal to grant such authority to "negative" state laws was considered at the Constitutional Convention, but rejected in favor of allowing state laws to take effect, subject to later challenge under the Supremacy Clause. See 1 Records of the Federal Convention of 1787, pp. 21, 164–168 (M. Farrand ed. 1911); 2 id., at 27–29, 390–392.

Outside the strictures of the Supremacy Clause, States retain broad autonomy in structuring their governments and pursuing legislative objectives. Indeed, the Constitution provides that all powers not specifically granted to the Federal Government are reserved to the States or citizens. Amdt. 10. This "allocation of powers in our federal system preserves the integrity, dignity, and residual sovereignty of the States." *Bond v. United States*, 564 U.S. ___, ___ (2011). But the federal balance "is not just an end in itself: Rather, federalism secures to citizens the liberties that derive from the diffusion of sovereign power." *Ibid.*

More specifically, " 'the Framers of the Constitution intended the States to keep for themselves, as provided in the Tenth Amendment, the power to regulate elections.' " *Gregory v. Ashcroft*, 501 U.S. 452, 461–462 (1991) (quoting *Sugarman v. Dougall*, 413 U.S. 634, 647 (1973). Of course, the Federal Government retains significant control over federal elections. For instance, the Constitution authorizes Congress to establish the time and manner for electing Senators and Representatives. Art. I, § 4, cl. 1. . . . But States have "broad powers to determine the conditions under which the right of suffrage may be exercised." *Carrington v. Rash*, 380 U.S. 89, 91(1965). . . . And "[e]ach State has the power to prescribe the qualifications of its officers and the manner in which they shall be chosen." *Boyd v. Nebraska ex rel. Thayer*, 143 U.S. 135 (1892). Drawing lines for congressional districts is likewise "primarily the duty and responsibility of the State." *Perry v. Perez*, 565 U.S. ___, ___ (2012) (per curiam).

Not only do States retain sovereignty under the Constitution, there is also a "fundamental principle of *equal* sovereignty" among the States. *Northwest Austin, supra*, at 203 (citing *United States v. Louisiana*, 363 U.S. 1, 16 (1960); *Lessee of Pollard v. Hagan*, 3 How. 212, 223(1845); and *Texas v. White*, 7 Wall. 700, 725–726 (1869); emphasis added). Over a hundred years ago, this Court explained that our Nation "was and is a union of States, equal in power, dignity and authority." *Coyle v. Smith*, 221 U.S. 559, 567 (1911). Indeed, "the constitutional equality of the States is essential to the harmonious operation of the scheme upon which the Republic was organized." *Id.*, at 580. *Coyle* concerned the admission of new States, and *Katzenbach* rejected the notion that the principle operated as a *bar* on differential treatment outside that context. 383 U.S., at 328–329. At the same time, as we made clear in *Northwest Austin*, the fundamental principle of equal sovereignty remains highly pertinent in assessing subsequent disparate treatment of States. 557 U.S., at 203.

The Voting Rights Act sharply departs from these basic principles. It suspends "all changes to state election law—however innocuous—until they have been precleared by federal authorities in Washington, D.C." *Id.*, at 202. States must beseech the Federal Government for permission to implement laws that they would otherwise have the right to enact and execute on their own, subject of course to any injunction in a § 2 action. The Attorney General has 60 days to object to a preclearance request, longer if he requests more information. If a State seeks preclearance from a three-judge court, the process can take years.

And despite the tradition of equal sovereignty, the Act applies to only nine States (and several additional counties). While one State waits months or years and expends funds to implement a validly enacted law, its neighbor can typically put the same law into effect immediately, through the normal legislative process. Even if a noncovered jurisdiction is sued, there are important differences between those proceedings and preclearance proceedings; the preclearance proceeding "not only switches the burden of proof to the supplicant jurisdiction, but also applies substantive standards quite different from those governing the rest of the nation." 679 F.3d, at 884 (Williams, J., dissenting) (case below).

All this explains why, when we first upheld the Act in 1966, we described it as "stringent" and "potent." *Katzenbach*, 383 U.S., at 308. We recognized that it "may have been an uncommon exercise of congressional power," but concluded that "legislative measures not otherwise appropriate" could be justified by "exceptional conditions." *Id.*, at 334. We have since noted that the Act "authorizes federal intrusion into sensitive areas of state and local policymaking," *Lopez*, 525 U.S., at 282, and represents an "extraordinary departure from the traditional course of relations between the States and the Federal Government," *Presley v. Etowah County Comm'n*, 502 U.S. 491, 500–501 (1992). As we reiterated in *Northwest Austin*, the Act constitutes "extraordinary legislation otherwise unfamiliar to our federal system." 557 U.S., at 211.

B

In 1966, we found these departures from the basic features of our system of government justified. The "blight of racial discrimination in voting" had "infected the electoral process in parts of our country for nearly a century." *Katzenbach*, 383 U.S., at 308. Several States had enacted a variety of requirements and tests "specifically designed to prevent" African-Americans from voting. *Id.*, at 310. Case-by-case litigation had proved inadequate to prevent such racial discrimination in voting, in part because States "merely switched to discriminatory devices not covered by the federal decrees," "enacted difficult new tests," or simply "defied and evaded court orders." *Id.*, at 314. Shortly before enactment of the Voting Rights Act, only 19.4 percent of African-Americans of voting age were registered to vote in Alabama, only 31.8 percent in Louisiana, and only 6.4 percent in Mississippi. *Id.*, at 313. Those figures were roughly 50 percentage points or more below the figures for whites. *Ibid.*

In short, we concluded that "[u]nder the compulsion of these unique circumstances, Congress responded in a permissibly decisive manner." *Id.*, at 334, 335. We also noted then and have emphasized since that this extraordinary legislation was intended to be temporary, set to expire after five years. *Id.*, at 333; *Northwest Austin, supra*, at 199.

At the time, the coverage formula—the means of linking the exercise of the unprecedented authority with the problem that warranted it—made sense. We found that "Congress chose to limit its attention to the geographic areas where immediate action seemed necessary." *Katzenbach*, 383 U.S., at 328. The areas where Congress found "evidence of actual voting discrimination" shared two characteristics: "the use of tests and devices for voter registration, and a voting rate in the 1964 presidential election at least 12 points below the national average." *Id.*, at 330. We explained that "[t]ests and devices are relevant to voting discrimination because of their long history as a tool for perpetrating the evil; a low voting rate is pertinent for the obvious reason that widespread disenfranchisement must inevitably affect the number of actual voters." *Ibid.* We therefore concluded that "the coverage formula [was] rational in both practice and theory." *Ibid.* It accurately reflected those jurisdictions uniquely characterized by voting discrimination "on a pervasive scale," linking coverage to the devices used to effectuate discrimination and to the resulting disenfranchisement. *Id.*, at 308. The formula ensured that the "stringent remedies [were] aimed at areas where voting discrimination ha[d] been most flagrant." *Id.*, at 315.

C

Nearly 50 years later, things have changed dramatically. Shelby County contends that the preclearance requirement, even without regard to its disparate coverage, is now unconstitutional. Its arguments have a good deal of force. In the covered jurisdictions, "[v]oter turnout and registration rates now approach parity. Blatantly discriminatory evasions of federal decrees are rare. And minority candidates hold office at unprecedented levels." *Northwest Austin*, 557 U.S., at 202. The tests and devices that blocked access to the ballot have been forbidden nationwide for over 40 years. See § 6, 84 Stat. 315; § 102, 89 Stat. 400.

Those conclusions are not ours alone. Congress said the same when it reauthorized the Act in 2006, writing that "[s]ignificant progress has been made in eliminating first generation barriers experienced by minority voters, including increased numbers of registered minority voters, minority voter turnout, and minority representation in Congress, State legislatures, and local elected offices." § 2(b)(1), 120 Stat. 577. The House Report elaborated that "the number of African-Americans who are registered and who turn out to cast ballots has increased significantly over the last 40 years, particularly since 1982," and noted that "[i]n some circumstances, minorities register to vote and cast ballots at levels that surpass those of white voters." H.R.Rep. 109–478, at 12 (2006), 2006 U.S.C.C.A.N. 618, 627. That Report also explained that there have been "significant increases in the number of African-Americans serving in elected offices"; more specifically, there has been approximately a 1,000 percent increase since 1965 in the number of African-American elected officials in the six States originally covered by the Voting Rights Act. *Id.*, at 18.

The following chart, compiled from the Senate and House Reports, compares voter registration numbers from 1965 to those from 2004 in the six originally covered States. These are the numbers that were before Congress when it reauthorized the Act in 2006:

	1965			2004		
	White	Black	Gap	White	Black	Gap
Alabama	69.2	19.3	49.9	73.8	72.9	0.9
Georgia	62.[6]	27.4	35.2	63.5	64.2	-0.7
Louisiana	80.5	31.6	48.9	75.1	71.1	4.0
Mississippi	69.9	6.7	63.2	72.3	76.1	-3.8
South Carolina	75.7	37.3	38.4	74.4	71.1	3.3
Virginia	61.1	38.3	22.8	68.2	57.4	10.8

See S.Rep. No. 109–295, p. 11 (2006); H.R.Rep. No. 109–478, at 12. The 2004 figures come from the Census Bureau. Census Bureau data from the most recent election indicate that African-American voter turnout exceeded white voter turnout in five of the six States originally covered by § 5, with a gap in the sixth State of less than one half of one percent. . . . The preclearance statistics are also illuminating. In the first decade after enactment of § 5, the Attorney General objected to 14.2 percent of proposed voting changes. H. R Rep. No. 109–478, at 22. In the last decade before reenactment, the Attorney General objected to a mere 0.16 percent. S.Rep. No. 109–295, at 13.

There is no doubt that these improvements are in large part *because of* the Voting Rights Act. The Act has proved immensely successful at redressing racial discrimination and integrating the voting process. See § 2(b)(1), 120 Stat. 577. During the "Freedom Summer" of 1964, in Philadelphia, Mississippi, three men were murdered while working in the area to register African-American voters. See *United States v. Price*, 383 U.S. 787, 790 (1966). On "Bloody Sunday" in 1965, in Selma, Alabama, police beat and used tear gas against hundreds marching in support of African-American enfranchisement. . . . Today both of those towns are governed by African-American mayors. Problems remain in these States and others, but there is no denying that, due to the Voting Rights Act, our Nation has made great strides.

Yet the Act has not eased the restrictions in § 5 or narrowed the scope of the coverage formula in § 4(b) along the way. Those extraordinary and unprecedented features were reauthorized—as if nothing had changed. In fact, the Act's unusual remedies have grown even stronger. . . .

We have also previously highlighted the concern that "the preclearance requirements in one State [might] be unconstitutional in another." *Northwest Austin*, 557 U.S., at 203; see *Georgia v. Ashcroft*, 539 U.S., at 491(Kennedy, J., concurring) ("considerations of race that would doom a redistricting plan under the Fourteenth Amendment or § 2 [of the Voting Rights Act] seem to be what save it under § 5"). Nothing has happened since to alleviate this troubling concern about the current application of § 5.

Respondents do not deny that there have been improvements on the ground, but argue that much of this can be attributed to the deterrent effect of § 5, which dissuades covered jurisdictions from engaging in discrimination that they would resume should § 5 be struck down. Under this theory, however, § 5 would be effectively immune from scrutiny; no matter how "clean" the record of covered jurisdictions, the argument could always be made that it was deterrence that accounted for the good behavior.

The provisions of § 5 apply only to those jurisdictions singled out by § 4. We now consider whether that coverage formula is constitutional in light of current conditions.

III

A

When upholding the constitutionality of the coverage formula in 1966, we concluded that it was "rational in both practice and theory." *Katzenbach*, 383 U.S., at 330. The formula looked to cause (discriminatory tests) and effect (low voter registration and turnout), and tailored the remedy (preclearance) to those jurisdictions exhibiting both.

By 2009, however, we concluded that the "coverage formula raise[d] serious constitutional questions." *Northwest Austin*, 557 U.S., at 204. As we explained, a statute's "current burdens" must be justified by "current needs," and any "disparate geographic coverage" must be "sufficiently related to the problem that it targets." *Id.*, at 203. The coverage formula met that test in 1965, but no longer does so.

Coverage today is based on decades-old data and eradicated practices. The formula captures States by reference to literacy tests and low voter registration and turnout in the 1960s and early 1970s. But such tests have been banned nationwide for over 40 years. § 6, 84 Stat. 315; § 102, 89 Stat. 400. And voter registration and turnout numbers in the covered States have risen dramatically in the years since. H.R.Rep. No. 109–478, at 12. Racial disparity in those numbers was compelling evidence justifying the preclearance remedy and the coverage formula. . . . There is no longer such a disparity.

In 1965, the States could be divided into two groups: those with a recent history of voting tests and low voter registration and turnout, and those without those characteristics. Congress based its coverage formula on that distinction. Today the Nation is no longer divided along those lines, yet the Voting Rights Act continues to treat it as if it were.

B

The Government's defense of the formula is limited. First, the Government contends that the formula is "reverse-engineered": Congress identified the jurisdictions to be covered and *then* came up with criteria to describe them.

Brief for Federal Respondent 48–49. Under that reasoning, there need not be any logical relationship between the criteria in the formula and the reason for coverage; all that is necessary is that the formula happen to capture the jurisdictions Congress wanted to single out.

The Government suggests that *Katzenbach* sanctioned such an approach, but the analysis in *Katzenbach* was quite different. *Katzenbach* reasoned that the coverage formula was rational because the "formula . . . was relevant to the problem": "Tests and devices are relevant to voting discrimination because of their long history as a tool for perpetrating the evil; a low voting rate is pertinent for the obvious reason that widespread disenfranchisement must inevitably affect the number of actual voters." 383 U.S., at 329.

Here, by contrast, the Government's reverse-engineering argument does not even attempt to demonstrate the continued relevance of the formula to the problem it targets. And in the context of a decision as significant as this one—subjecting a disfavored subset of States to "extraordinary legislation otherwise unfamiliar to our federal system," *Northwest Austin, supra,* at 211—that failure to establish even relevance is fatal.

The Government falls back to the argument that because the formula was relevant in 1965, its continued use is permissible so long as any discrimination remains in the States Congress identified back then—regardless of how that discrimination compares to discrimination in States unburdened by coverage. Brief for Federal Respondent 49–50. This argument does not look to "current political conditions," *Northwest Austin, supra,* at 203, but instead relies on a comparison between the States in 1965. That comparison reflected the different histories of the North and South. It was in the South that slavery was upheld by law until uprooted by the Civil War, that the reign of Jim Crow denied African-Americans the most basic freedoms, and that state and local governments worked tirelessly to disenfranchise citizens on the basis of race. The Court invoked that history—rightly so—in sustaining the disparate coverage of the Voting Rights Act in 1966. See *Katzenbach, supra,* at 308 ("The constitutional propriety of the Voting Rights Act of 1965 must be judged with reference to the historical experience which it reflects.").

But history did not end in 1965. By the time the Act was reauthorized in 2006, there had been 40 more years of it. In assessing the "current need[ ]" for a preclearance system that treats States differently from one another today, that history cannot be ignored. During that time, largely because of the Voting Rights Act, voting tests were abolished, disparities in voter registration and turnout due to race were erased, and African-Americans attained political office in record numbers. And yet the coverage formula that Congress reauthorized in 2006 ignores these developments, keeping the focus on decades-old data relevant to decades-old problems, rather than current data reflecting current needs.

The Fifteenth Amendment commands that the right to vote shall not be denied or abridged on account of race or color, and it gives Congress the power to enforce that command. The Amendment is not designed to punish for the past; its purpose is to ensure a better future. See *Rice v. Cayetano,* 528 U.S.

495, 512 (2000) ("Consistent with the design of the Constitution, the [Fifteenth] Amendment is cast in fundamental terms, terms transcending the particular controversy which was the immediate impetus for its enactment."). To serve that purpose, Congress—if it is to divide the States—must identify those jurisdictions to be singled out on a basis that makes sense in light of current conditions. It cannot rely simply on the past. We made that clear in *Northwest Austin*, and we make it clear again today.

C

In defending the coverage formula, the Government, the intervenors, and the dissent also rely heavily on data from the record that they claim justify disparate coverage. Congress compiled thousands of pages of evidence before reauthorizing the Voting Rights Act. The court below and the parties have debated what that record shows—they have gone back and forth about whether to compare covered to noncovered jurisdictions as blocks, how to disaggregate the data State by State, how to weigh § 2 cases as evidence of ongoing discrimination, and whether to consider evidence not before Congress, among other issues. . . . Regardless of how to look at the record, however, no one can fairly say that it shows anything approaching the "pervasive," "flagrant," "widespread," and "rampant" discrimination that faced Congress in 1965, and that clearly distinguished the covered jurisdictions from the rest of the Nation at that time. *Katzenbach*, *supra*, at 308, 315, 331; *Northwest Austin*, 557 U.S., at 201.

But a more fundamental problem remains: Congress did not use the record it compiled to shape a coverage formula grounded in current conditions. It instead reenacted a formula based on 40-year-old facts having no logical relation to the present day. The dissent relies on "second-generation barriers," which are not impediments to the casting of ballots, but rather electoral arrangements that affect the weight of minority votes. That does not cure the problem. Viewing the preclearance requirements as targeting such efforts simply highlights the irrationality of continued reliance on the § 4 coverage formula, which is based on voting tests and access to the ballot, not vote dilution. We cannot pretend that we are reviewing an updated statute, or try our hand at updating the statute ourselves, based on the new record compiled by Congress. Contrary to the dissent's contention, . . . we are not ignoring the record; we are simply recognizing that it played no role in shaping the statutory formula before us today.

The dissent also turns to the record to argue that, in light of voting discrimination in Shelby County, the county cannot complain about the provisions that subject it to preclearance. . . . But that is like saying that a driver pulled over pursuant to a policy of stopping all redheads cannot complain about that policy, if it turns out his license has expired. Shelby County's claim is that the coverage formula here is unconstitutional in all its applications, because of how it selects the jurisdictions subjected to preclearance. The county was selected based on that formula, and may challenge it in court.

D

The dissent proceeds from a flawed premise. It quotes the famous sentence from McCulloch v. Maryland, 4 Wheat. 316 (1819), with the following emphasis: "Let the end be legitimate, let it be within the scope of the constitution, and *all means which are appropriate, which are plainly adapted to that end*, which are not prohibited, but consist with the letter and spirit of the constitution, are constitutional.". . . But this case is about a part of the sentence that the dissent does not emphasize—the part that asks whether a legislative means is "consist[ent] with the letter and spirit of the constitution." The dissent states that "[i]t cannot tenably be maintained" that this is an issue with regard to the Voting Rights Act, . . . but four years ago, in an opinion joined by two of today's dissenters, the Court expressly stated that "[t]he Act's preclearance requirement and its coverage formula raise serious constitutional questions." *Northwest Austin, supra*, at 204. The dissent does not explain how those "serious constitutional questions" became untenable in four short years.

The dissent treats the Act as if it were just like any other piece of legislation, but this Court has made clear from the beginning that the Voting Rights Act is far from ordinary. At the risk of repetition, *Katzenbach* indicated that the Act was "uncommon" and "not otherwise appropriate," but was justified by "exceptional" and "unique" conditions. 383 U.S., at 334, 335. Multiple decisions since have reaffirmed the Act's "extraordinary" nature. See, *e.g., Northwest Austin, supra*, at 211. Yet the dissent goes so far as to suggest instead that the preclearance requirement and disparate treatment of the States should be upheld into the future "unless there [is] no or almost no evidence of unconstitutional action by States.". . .

In other ways as well, the dissent analyzes the question presented as if our decision in *Northwest Austin* never happened. For example, the dissent refuses to consider the principle of equal sovereignty, despite *Northwest Austin*'s emphasis on its significance. *Northwest Austin* also emphasized the "dramatic" progress since 1965, 557 U.S., at 201, but the dissent describes current levels of discrimination as "flagrant," "widespread," and "pervasive," . . . Despite the fact that *Northwest Austin* requires an Act's "disparate geographic coverage" to be "sufficiently related" to its targeted problems, 557 U.S., at 203, the dissent maintains that an Act's limited coverage actually eases Congress's burdens, and suggests that a fortuitous relationship should suffice. Although *Northwest Austin* stated definitively that "current burdens" must be justified by "current needs," *ibid.*, the dissent argues that the coverage formula can be justified by history, and that the required showing can be weaker on reenactment than when the law was first passed.

There is no valid reason to insulate the coverage formula from review merely because it was previously enacted 40 years ago. If Congress had started from scratch in 2006, it plainly could not have enacted the present coverage formula. It would have been irrational for Congress to distinguish between States in such a fundamental way based on 40-year-old data, when today's statistics tell an entirely different story. And it would have been irrational to base coverage on the use of voting tests 40 years ago, when such tests have been illegal since that time. But that is exactly what Congress has done.

* * *

Striking down an Act of Congress "is the gravest and most delicate duty that this Court is called on to perform." *Blodgett v. Holden*, 275 U.S. 142, 148 (Holmes, J., concurring). We do not do so lightly. That is why, in 2009, we took care to avoid ruling on the constitutionality of the Voting Rights Act when asked to do so, and instead resolved the case then before us on statutory grounds. But in issuing that decision, we expressed our broader concerns about the constitutionality of the Act. Congress could have updated the coverage formula at that time, but did not do so. Its failure to act leaves us today with no choice but to declare § 4(b) unconstitutional. The formula in that section can no longer be used as a basis for subjecting jurisdictions to preclearance.

Our decision in no way affects the permanent, nationwide ban on racial discrimination in voting found in § 2. We issue no holding on § 5 itself, only on the coverage formula. Congress may draft another formula based on current conditions. Such a formula is an initial prerequisite to a determination that exceptional conditions still exist justifying such an "extraordinary departure from the traditional course of relations between the States and the Federal Government." *Presley*, 502 U.S., at 500–501. Our country has changed, and while any racial discrimination in voting is too much, Congress must ensure that the legislation it passes to remedy that problem speaks to current conditions.

The judgment of the Court of Appeals is reversed.

It is so ordered.

Justice Thomas, concurring.

I join the Court's opinion in full but write separately to explain that I would find § 5 of the Voting Rights Act unconstitutional as well. The Court's opinion sets forth the reasons.

. . .

Justice Ginsburg, with whom Justice Breyer, Justice Sotomayor, and Justice Kagan join, dissenting.

In the Court's view, the very success of § 5 of the Voting Rights Act demands its dormancy. Congress was of another mind. Recognizing that large progress has been made, Congress determined, based on a voluminous record, that the scourge of discrimination was not yet extirpated. The question this case presents is who decides whether, as currently operative, § 5 remains justifiable, this Court, or a Congress charged with the obligation to enforce the post-Civil War Amendments "by appropriate legislation." With overwhelming support in both Houses, Congress concluded that, for two prime reasons, § 5 should continue in force, unabated. First, continuance would facilitate completion of the impressive gains thus far made; and second, continuance would guard against backsliding. Those assessments were well within

Congress' province to make and should elicit this Court's unstinting approbation.

I

. . . [Although no one doubts that voting discrimination still exists,] the Court today terminates the remedy that proved to be best suited to block that discrimination. The Voting Rights Act of 1965 (VRA) has worked to combat voting discrimination where other remedies had been tried and failed. Particularly effective is the VRA's requirement of federal preclearance for all changes to voting laws in the regions of the country with the most aggravated records of rank discrimination against minority voting rights.

A century after the Fourteenth and Fifteenth Amendments guaranteed citizens the right to vote free of discrimination on the basis of race, the "blight of racial discrimination in voting" continued to "infec[t] the electoral process in parts of our country." *South Carolina v. Katzenbach*, 383 U.S. 301 (1966). Early attempts to cope with this vile infection resembled battling the Hydra. Whenever one form of voting discrimination was identified and prohibited, others sprang up in its place. This Court repeatedly encountered the remarkable "variety and persistence" of laws disenfranchising minority citizens. *Id.*, at 311. To take just one example, the Court, in 1927, held unconstitutional a Texas law barring black voters from participating in primary elections, *Nixon v. Herndon*, 273 U.S. 536, 541; in 1944, the Court struck down a "reenacted" and slightly altered version of the same law, *Smith v. Allwright*, 321 U.S. 649, 658; and in 1953, the Court once again confronted an attempt by Texas to "circumven[t]" the Fifteenth Amendment by adopting yet another variant of the all-white primary, *Terry v. Adams*, 345 U.S. 461, 469.

During this era, the Court recognized that discrimination against minority voters was a quintessentially political problem requiring a political solution. As Justice Holmes explained: If "the great mass of the white population intends to keep the blacks from voting," "relief from [that] great political wrong, if done, as alleged, by the people of a State and the State itself, must be given by them or by the legislative and political department of the government of the United States." *Giles v. Harris*, 189 U.S. 475, 488 (1903).

Congress learned from experience that laws targeting particular electoral practices or enabling case-by-case litigation were inadequate to the task. . . . Patently, a new approach was needed.

Answering that need, the Voting Rights Act became one of the most consequential, efficacious, and amply justified exercises of federal legislative power in our Nation's history. Requiring federal preclearance of changes in voting laws in the covered jurisdictions—those States and localities where opposition to the Constitution's commands were most virulent—the VRA provided a fit solution for minority voters as well as for States. Under the preclearance regime established by § 5 of the VRA, covered jurisdictions must submit proposed changes in voting laws or procedures to the Department of Justice (DOJ), which has 60 days to respond to the changes. 79 Stat. 439, codified at 42 U.S.C. § 1973c(a). A change will be approved unless DOJ finds it has "the purpose [or] . . . the effect of denying or abridging the right to vote on account of race or color." *Ibid.* In the alternative, the covered jurisdiction may seek approval by a three-judge District Court in the District of Columbia.

. . .

Although the VRA wrought dramatic changes in the realization of minority voting rights, the Act, to date, surely has not eliminated all vestiges of discrimination against the exercise of the franchise by minority citizens. Jurisdictions covered by the preclearance requirement continued to submit, in large numbers, proposed changes to voting laws that the Attorney General declined to approve, auguring that barriers to minority voting would quickly resurface were the preclearance remedy eliminated. *City of Rome v. United States*, 446 U.S. 156, 181 (1980). Congress also found that as "registration and voting of minority citizens increas[ed], other measures may be resorted to which would dilute increasing minority voting strength." *Ibid.* (quoting H.R.Rep. No. 94–196, p. 10 (1975)). See also *Shaw v. Reno*, 509 U.S. 630, 640 (1993) ("[I]t soon became apparent that guaranteeing equal access to the polls would not suffice to root out other racially discriminatory voting practices" such as voting dilution). Efforts to reduce the impact of minority votes, in contrast to direct attempts to block access to the ballot, are aptly described as "second-generation barriers" to minority voting.

Second-generation barriers come in various forms. One of the blockages is racial gerrymandering, the redrawing of legislative districts in an "effort to segregate the races for purposes of voting." *Id.*, at 642. Another is adoption of a system of at-large voting in lieu of district-by-district voting in a city with a sizable black minority. By switching to at-large voting, the overall majority could control the election of each city council member, effectively eliminating the potency of the minority's votes. . . . A similar effect could be achieved if the city engaged in discriminatory annexation by incorporating majority-white areas into city limits, thereby decreasing the effect of VRA-occasioned increases in black voting. Whatever the device employed, this Court has long recognized that vote dilution, when adopted with a discriminatory purpose, cuts down the right to vote as certainly as denial of access to the ballot. . . .

In response to evidence of these substituted barriers, Congress reauthorized the VRA for five years in 1970, for seven years in 1975, and for 25 years in 1982. . . . Each time, this Court upheld the reauthorization as a valid exercise of congressional power. . . . As the 1982 reauthorization approached its 2007 expiration date, Congress again considered whether the VRA's preclearance mechanism remained an appropriate response to the problem of voting discrimination in covered jurisdictions.

Congress did not take this task lightly. Quite the opposite. The 109th Congress that took responsibility for the renewal started early and conscientiously. In October 2005, the House began extensive hearings, which continued into November and resumed in March 2006. S.Rep. No. 109–295, p. 2 (2006). In April 2006, the Senate followed suit, with hearings of its own. *Ibid.* In May 2006, the bills that became the VRA's reauthorization were introduced in both Houses. *Ibid.* The House held further hearings of considerable length, as did the Senate, which continued to hold hearings into June and July. H.R. Rep. 109–478, at 5; S. Rep. 109–295, at 3–4. In mid-July, the House considered and rejected four amendments, then passed the reauthorization by a vote of 390 yeas to 33 nays. 152 Cong. Rec. H5207 (July 13, 2006). . . . The bill was read and debated in the Senate, where it passed by a vote of 98 to 0. 152 Cong. Rec. S8012 (July 20, 2006). President Bush signed it a week later, on July 27, 2006, recognizing the need for "further work . . . in the fight against injustice," and calling the reauthorization "an example of our continued commitment to a united America where every person is valued and treated with dignity and respect." 152 Cong. Rec. S8781 (Aug. 3, 2006).

In the long course of the legislative process, Congress "amassed a sizable record." *Northwest Austin Municipal Util. Dist. No. One v. Holder*, 557 U.S. 193, 205 (2009). See also 679 F.3d 848, 865–873 (C.A.D.C.2012) (describing the "extensive record" supporting Congress' determination that "serious and widespread intentional discrimination persisted in covered jurisdictions"). The House and Senate Judiciary Committees held 21 hearings, heard from scores of witnesses, received a number of investigative reports and other written documentation of continuing discrimination in covered jurisdictions. In all, the legislative record Congress compiled filled more than 15,000 pages. H.R. Rep. 109–478, at 5, 11–12; S. Rep. 109–295, at 2–4, 15. The compilation presents countless "examples of flagrant racial discrimination" since the last reauthorization; Congress also brought to light systematic evidence that "intentional racial discrimination in voting remains so serious and widespread in covered jurisdictions that section 5 preclearance is still needed." 679 F.3d, at 866.

After considering the full legislative record, Congress made the following findings: The VRA has directly caused significant progress in eliminating first-generation barriers to ballot access, leading to a marked increase in minority voter registration and turnout and the number of minority elected officials. 2006 Reauthorization § 2(b)(1). But despite this progress, "second generation barriers constructed to prevent minority voters from fully participating in the electoral process" continued to exist, as well as racially polarized voting in the covered jurisdictions, which increased the political vulnerability of racial and language minorities in those jurisdictions. §§ 2(b)(2)-(3), 120 Stat. 577. Extensive "[e]vidence of continued discrimination," Congress concluded, "clearly show[ed] the continued need for Federal oversight" in covered jurisdictions. §§ 2(b)(4)-(5), *id.*, at 577–578. The overall record demonstrated to the federal lawmakers that, "without the continuation of the Voting Rights Act of 1965 protections, racial and language minority citizens will be deprived of the opportunity to exercise their right to vote, or will have their votes diluted, undermining the significant gains made by minorities in the last 40 years." § 2(b)(9), *id.*, at 578.

Based on these findings, Congress reauthorized preclearance for another 25 years, while also undertaking to reconsider the extension after 15 years to ensure that the provision was still necessary and effective. 42 U.S.C.

§ 1973b(a)(7), (8) (2006 ed., Supp. V). The question before the Court is whether Congress had the authority under the Constitution to act as it did.

II

In answering this question, the Court does not write on a clean slate. It is well established that Congress' judgment regarding exercise of its power to enforce the Fourteenth and Fifteenth Amendments warrants substantial deference. The VRA addresses the combination of race discrimination and the right to vote, which is "preservative of all rights." *Yick Wo v. Hopkins*, 118 U.S. 356, 370 (1886). When confronting the most constitutionally invidious form of discrimination, and the most fundamental right in our democratic system, Congress' power to act is at its height.

The basis for this deference is firmly rooted in both constitutional text and precedent. The Fifteenth Amendment, which targets precisely and only racial discrimination in voting rights, states that, in this domain, "Congress shall have power to enforce this article by appropriate legislation." In choosing this language, the Amendment's framers invoked Chief Justice Marshall's formulation of the scope of Congress' powers under the Necessary and Proper Clause:

> "Let the end be legitimate, let it be within the scope of the constitution, and *all means which are appropriate, which are plainly adapted to that end*, which are not prohibited, but consist with the letter and spirit of the constitution, are constitutional." *McCulloch v. Maryland*, 4 Wheat. 316, 421(1819) (emphasis added).

It cannot tenably be maintained that the VRA, an Act of Congress adopted to shield the right to vote from racial discrimination, is inconsistent with the letter or spirit of the Fifteenth Amendment, or any provision of the Constitution read in light of the Civil War Amendments. Nowhere in today's opinion, or in *Northwest Austin*, is there clear recognition of the transformative effect the Fifteenth Amendment aimed to achieve. Notably, "the Founders' first successful amendment told Congress that it could 'make no law' over a certain domain"; in contrast, the Civil War Amendments used "language [that] authorized transformative new federal statutes to uproot all vestiges of unfreedom and inequality" and provided "sweeping enforcement powers . . . to enact 'appropriate' legislation targeting state abuses." A. Amar, America's Constitution: A Biography 361, 363, 399 (2005). See also McConnell, Institutions and Interpretation: A Critique of City of Boerne v. Flores, 111 Harv. L.Rev. 153, 182 (1997) (quoting Civil War-era framer that "the remedy for the violation of the fourteenth and fifteenth amendments was expressly not left to the courts. The remedy was legislative.").

The stated purpose of the Civil War Amendments was to arm Congress with the power and authority to protect all persons within the Nation from violations of their rights by the States. In exercising that power, then, Congress may use "all means which are appropriate, which are plainly adapted" to the constitutional ends declared by these Amendments. *McCulloch*, 4 Wheat., at 421. So when Congress acts to enforce the right to vote free from racial discrimination, we ask not whether Congress has chosen the means most wise, but whether Congress has rationally selected means appropriate to a legitimate end. "It is not for us to review the congressional resolution of [the need for its chosen remedy]. It is enough that we be able to perceive a basis upon which the Congress might resolve the conflict as it did." *Katzenbach v. Morgan*, 384 U.S. 641, 653 (1966).

Until today, in considering the constitutionality of the VRA, the Court has accorded Congress the full measure of respect its judgments in this domain should garner. *South Carolina v. Katzenbach* supplies the standard of review: "As against the reserved powers of the States, Congress may use any rational means to effectuate the constitutional prohibition of racial discrimination in voting." 383 U.S., at 324. Faced with subsequent reauthorizations of the VRA, the Court has reaffirmed this standard. *E.g.*, *City of Rome*, 446 U.S., at 178. Today's Court does not purport to alter settled precedent establishing that the dispositive question is whether Congress has employed "rational means."

For three reasons, legislation *re*authorizing an existing statute is especially likely to satisfy the minimal requirements of the rational-basis test. First, when reauthorization is at issue, Congress has already assembled a legislative record justifying the initial legislation. Congress is entitled to consider that preexisting record as well as the record before it at the time of the vote on reauthorization. This is especially true where, as here, the Court has repeatedly affirmed the statute's constitutionality and Congress has adhered to the very model the Court has upheld. See id., at 174 ("The appellants are asking us to do nothing less than overrule our decision in *South Carolina v. Katzenbach* . . . , in which we upheld the constitutionality of the Act."); *Lopez v. Monterey County*, 525 U.S. 266, 283 (1999) (similar).

Second, the very fact that reauthorization is necessary arises because Congress has built a temporal limitation into the Act. It has pledged to review, after a span of years (first 15, then 25) and in light of contemporary evidence, the continued need for the VRA. Cf. *Grutter v. Bollinger*, 539 U.S. 306, 343 (2003) (anticipating, but not guaranteeing, that, in 25 years, "the use of racial preferences [in higher education] will no longer be necessary").

Third, a reviewing court should expect the record supporting reauthorization to be less stark than the record originally made. Demand for a record of violations equivalent to the one earlier made would expose Congress to a catch-22. If the statute was working, there would be less evidence of discrimination, so opponents might argue that Congress should not be allowed to renew the statute. In contrast, if the statute was not working, there would be plenty of evidence of discrimination, but scant reason to renew a failed regulatory regime. . . .

This is not to suggest that congressional power in this area is limitless. It is this Court's responsibility to ensure that Congress has used appropriate means. The question meet for judicial review is whether the chosen means are "adapted to carry out the objects the amendments have in view." *Ex parte Virginia*, 100 U.S. 339, 346 (1880). The Court's role, then, is not to substitute its judgment for that of Congress, but to determine whether the legislative record sufficed to show that "Congress could rationally have determined that [its chosen] provisions were appropriate methods." *City of Rome*, 446 U.S., at 176–177.

In summary, the Constitution vests broad power in Congress to protect the right to vote, and in particular to combat racial discrimination in voting. This Court has repeatedly reaffirmed Congress' prerogative to use any rational means in exercise of its power in this area. And both precedent and logic dictate that the rational-means test should be easier to satisfy, and the burden on the statute's challenger should be higher, when what is at issue is the reauthorization of a remedy that the Court has previously affirmed, and that Congress found, from contemporary evidence, to be working to advance the legislature's legitimate objective.

III

The 2006 reauthorization of the Voting Rights Act fully satisfies the standard stated in *McCulloch* . . . : Congress may choose any means "appropriate" and "plainly adapted to" a legitimate constitutional end. . . .

A

. . .

True, conditions in the South have impressively improved since passage of the Voting Rights Act. Congress noted this improvement and found that the VRA was the driving force behind it. 2006 Reauthorization § 2(b)(1). But Congress also found that voting discrimination had evolved into subtler second-generation barriers, and that eliminating preclearance would risk loss of the gains that had been made. §§ 2(b)(2), (9). Concerns of this order, the Court previously found, gave Congress adequate cause to reauthorize the VRA. *City of Rome*, 446 U.S., at 180–182 (congressional reauthorization of the preclearance requirement was justified based on "the number and nature of objections interposed by the Attorney General" since the prior reauthorization; extension was "necessary to preserve the limited and fragile achievements of the Act and to promote further amelioration of voting discrimination"). Facing such evidence then, the Court expressly rejected the argument that disparities in voter turnout and number of elected officials were the only metrics capable of justifying reauthorization of the VRA. *Ibid.*

B

I turn next to the evidence on which Congress based its decision to reauthorize the coverage formula in § 4(b). Because Congress did not alter the coverage formula, the same jurisdictions previously subject to preclearance continue to be covered by this remedy. . . .

There is no question . . . that the covered jurisdictions have a unique history of problems with racial discrimination in voting. . . .

Of particular importance, even after 40 years and thousands of discriminatory changes blocked by preclearance, conditions in the covered jurisdictions demonstrated that the formula was still justified by "current needs." *Northwest Austin*, 557 U.S., at 203.

Congress learned of these conditions through a report, known as the Katz study, that looked at § 2 suits between 1982 and 2004. . . .

Although covered jurisdictions account for less than 25 percent of the country's population, the Katz study revealed that they accounted for 56 percent of successful § 2 litigation since 1982. . . . Controlling for population, there were nearly four times as many successful § 2 cases in covered jurisdictions as there were in noncovered jurisdictions. . . . The Katz study further found that § 2 lawsuits are more likely to succeed when they are filed in covered jurisdictions than in noncovered jurisdictions. . . . From these findings—ignored by the Court—Congress reasonably concluded that the coverage formula continues to identify the jurisdictions of greatest concern.

The evidence before Congress, furthermore, indicated that voting in the covered jurisdictions was more racially polarized than elsewhere in the country. H.R.Rep. No. 109–478, at 34–35. While racially polarized voting alone does not signal a constitutional violation, it is a factor that increases the vulnerability of racial minorities to discriminatory changes in voting law. The reason is twofold. First, racial polarization means that racial minorities are at risk of being systematically outvoted and having their interests underrepresented in legislatures. Second, "when political preferences fall along racial lines, the natural inclinations of incumbents and ruling parties to entrench themselves have predictable racial effects. Under circumstances of severe racial polarization, efforts to gain political advantage translate into race-specific disadvantages." Ansolabehere, Persily, & Stewart, Regional Differences in Racial Polarization in the 2012 Presidential Election: Implications for the Constitutionality of Section 5 of the Voting Rights Act, 126 Harv. L.Rev. Forum 205, 209 (2013).

In other words, a governing political coalition has an incentive to prevent changes in the existing balance of voting power. When voting is racially polarized, efforts by the ruling party to pursue that incentive "will inevitably discriminate against a racial group." *Ibid.* Just as buildings in California have a greater need to be earthquake-proofed, places where there is greater racial polarization in voting have a greater need for prophylactic measures to prevent purposeful race discrimination. This point was understood by Congress and is well recognized in the academic literature. See 2006 Reauthorization § 2(b)(3), 120 Stat. 577 ("The continued evidence of racially polarized voting in each of the jurisdictions covered by the [preclearance requirement] demonstrates that racial and language minorities remain politically vulnerable"); H.R.Rep. No. 109–478, at 35 (2006), 2006 U.S.C.C.A.N. 618. . . .

. . .

IV

Congress approached the 2006 reauthorization of the VRA with great care and seriousness. The same cannot be said of the Court's opinion today. The Court makes no genuine attempt to engage with the massive legislative record that Congress assembled. Instead, it relies on increases in voter registration and turnout as if that were the whole story. . . . Without even identifying a standard of review, the Court dismissively brushes off arguments based on "data from the record," and declines to enter the "debat[e about] what [the] record shows.". . . One would expect more from an opinion striking at the heart of the Nation's signal piece of civil-rights legislation.

I note the most disturbing lapses. First, by what right, given its usual restraint, does the Court even address Shelby County's facial challenge to the VRA? Second, the Court veers away from controlling precedent regarding the "equal sovereignty" doctrine without even acknowledging that it is doing so. Third, hardly showing the respect ordinarily paid when Congress acts to implement the Civil War Amendments, and as just stressed, the Court does not even deign to grapple with the legislative record.

A

Shelby County launched a purely facial challenge to the VRA's 2006 reauthorization. "A facial challenge to a legislative Act," the Court has other times said, "is, of course, the most difficult challenge to mount successfully, since the challenger must establish that no set of circumstances exists under which the Act would be valid." *United States v. Salerno*, 481 U.S. 739, 745 (1987).

. . . "Embedded in the traditional rules governing constitutional adjudication is the principle that a person to whom a statute may constitutionally be applied will not be heard to challenge that statute on the ground that it may conceivably be applied unconstitutionally to others, in other situations not before the Court." *Broadrick* [*v. Oklahoma*], 413 U.S., at 610 [1973]. Yet the Court's opinion in this case contains not a word explaining why Congress lacks the power to subject to preclearance the particular plaintiff that initiated this lawsuit—Shelby County, Alabama. The reason for the Court's silence is apparent, for as applied to Shelby County, the VRA's preclearance requirement is hardly contestable.

Alabama is home to Selma, site of the "Bloody Sunday" beatings of civil-rights demonstrators that served as the catalyst for the VRA's enactment. Following those events, Martin Luther King, Jr., led a march from Selma to Montgomery, Alabama's capital, where he called for passage of the VRA. If the Act passed, he foresaw, progress could be made even in Alabama, but there had to be a steadfast national commitment to see the task through to completion. In King's words, "the arc of the moral universe is long, but it bends toward justice." G. May, Bending Toward Justice: The Voting Rights Act and the Transformation of American Democracy 144 (2013).

History has proved King right. Although circumstances in Alabama have changed, serious concerns remain. Between 1982 and 2005, Alabama had one of the highest rates of successful § 2 suits, second only to its VRA-covered neighbor Mississippi. 679 F.3d, at 897 (Williams, J., dissenting). In other words, even while subject to the restraining effect of § 5, Alabama was found to have "deni[ed] or abridge[d]" voting rights "on account of race or color" more frequently than nearly all other States in the Union. 42 U.S.C. § 1973(a). This fact prompted the dissenting judge below to concede that "a more narrowly

APPLICATION OF THE POST CIVIL WAR AMENDMENTS TO PRIVATE
CONDUCT: CONGRESSIONAL POWER TO ENFORCE THE AMENDMENTS   CHAPTER 12

200

tailored coverage formula" capturing Alabama and a handful of other
jurisdictions with an established track record of racial discrimination in voting
"might be defensible." 679 F.3d, at 897 (opinion of Williams, J.). That is an
understatement. Alabama's sorry history of § 2 violations alone provides
sufficient justification for Congress' determination in 2006 that the State
should remain subject to § 5's preclearance requirement.

   . . .

[R]ecent episodes forcefully demonstrate that § 5's preclearance
requirement is constitutional as applied to Alabama and its political
subdivisions. And under our case law, that conclusion should suffice to resolve
this case. See *United States v. Raines*, 362 U.S. 17, 24–25 (1960) ("[I]f the
complaint here called for an application of the statute clearly constitutional
under the Fifteenth Amendment, that should have been an end to the question
of constitutionality."). See also *Nevada Dept. of Human Resources v. Hibbs*, 538
U.S. 721, 743 (2003) (Scalia, J., dissenting) (where, as here, a state or local
government raises a facial challenge to a federal statute on the ground that it
exceeds Congress' enforcement powers under the Civil War Amendments, the
challenge fails if the opposing party is able to show that the statute "could
constitutionally be applied to some jurisdictions").

   . . .

B

The Court stops any application of § 5 by holding that § 4(b)'s coverage
formula is unconstitutional. It pins this result, in large measure, to "the
fundamental principle of equal sovereignty." In *Katzenbach*, however, the Court
held, in no uncertain terms, that the principle *"applies only to the terms upon
which States are admitted to the Union*, and not to the remedies for local evils
which have subsequently appeared." 383 U.S., at 328–329 (emphasis added).

   . . . [T]he Court clouds [this] once clear understanding by citing dictum
from *Northwest Austin* to convey that the principle of equal sovereignty
"remains highly pertinent in assessing subsequent disparate treatment of
States.". . . If the Court is suggesting that dictum in *Northwest Austin* silently
overruled *Katzenbach*'s limitation of the equal sovereignty doctrine to "the
admission of new States," the suggestion is untenable. *Northwest Austin* cited
Katzenbach's holding in the course of *declining to decide* whether the VRA was
constitutional or even what standard of review applied to the question. 557
U.S., at 203–204. In today's decision, the Court ratchets up what was pure
dictum in *Northwest Austin*, attributing breadth to the equal sovereignty
principle in flat contradiction of *Katzenbach*. The Court does so with nary an
explanation of why it finds *Katzenbach* wrong, let alone any discussion of
whether *stare decisis* nonetheless counsels adherence to *Katzenbach*'s ruling on
the limited "significance" of the equal sovereignty principle.

Today's unprecedented extension of the equal sovereignty principle outside
its proper domain—the admission of new States—is capable of much mischief.
Federal statutes that treat States disparately are hardly novelties. See, e.g., 28
U.S.C. § 3704 (no State may operate or permit a sports-related gambling

scheme, unless that State conducted such a scheme "at any time during the period beginning January 1, 1976, and ending August 31, 1990"); 26 U.S.C. § 142(*l*) (EPA required to locate green building project in a State meeting specified population criteria); 42 U.S.C. § 3796bb (at least 50 percent of rural drug enforcement assistance funding must be allocated to States with "a population density of fifty-two or fewer persons per square mile or a State in which the largest county has fewer than one hundred and fifty thousand people, based on the decennial census of 1990 through fiscal year 1997"); §§ 13925, 13971 (similar population criteria for funding to combat rural domestic violence); § 10136 (specifying rules applicable to Nevada's Yucca Mountain nuclear waste site, and providing that "[n]o State, other than the State of Nevada, may receive financial assistance under this subsection after December 22, 1987"). Do such provisions remain safe given the Court's expansion of equal sovereignty's sway?

Of gravest concern, Congress relied on our pathmarking *Katzenbach* decision in each reauthorization of the VRA. It had every reason to believe that the Act's limited geographical scope would weigh in favor of, not against, the Act's constitutionality. See, *e.g.*, *United States v. Morrison*, 529 U.S. 598, 626–627 (2000) (confining preclearance regime to States with a record of discrimination bolstered the VRA's constitutionality). Congress could hardly have foreseen that the VRA's limited geographic reach would render the Act constitutionally suspect. . . .

In the Court's conception, it appears, defenders of the VRA could not prevail upon showing what the record overwhelmingly bears out, *i.e.*, that there is a need for continuing the preclearance regime in covered States. In addition, the defenders would have to disprove the existence of a comparable need elsewhere. See Tr. of Oral Arg. 61–62 (suggesting that proof of egregious episodes of racial discrimination in covered jurisdictions would not suffice to carry the day for the VRA, unless such episodes are shown to be absent elsewhere). I am aware of no precedent for imposing such a double burden on defenders of legislation.

C

The Court has time and again declined to upset legislation of this genre unless there was no or almost no evidence of unconstitutional action by States. See, *e.g.*, *City of Boerne v. Flores*, 521 U.S. 507, 530 (1997) (legislative record "mention[ed] no episodes [of the kind the legislation aimed to check] occurring in the past 40 years"). No such claim can be made about the congressional record for the 2006 VRA reauthorization. Given a record replete with examples of denial or abridgment of a paramount federal right, the Court should have left the matter where it belongs: in Congress' bailiwick.

Instead, the Court strikes § 4(b)'s coverage provision because, in its view, the provision is not based on "current conditions.". . . It discounts, however, that one such condition was the preclearance remedy in place in the covered jurisdictions, a remedy Congress designed both to catch discrimination before it causes harm, and to guard against return to old ways. 2006 Reauthorization § 2(b)(3), (9). Volumes of evidence supported Congress' determination that the

202

APPLICATION OF THE POST CIVIL WAR AMENDMENTS TO PRIVATE
CONDUCT: CONGRESSIONAL POWER TO ENFORCE THE AMENDMENTS   CHAPTER 12

prospect of retrogression was real. Throwing out preclearance when it has worked and is continuing to work to stop discriminatory changes is like throwing away your umbrella in a rainstorm because you are not getting wet.

. . .

* * *

For the reasons stated, I would affirm the judgment of the Court of Appeals.

PART 4

CONSTITUTIONAL PROTECTION OF EXPRESSION AND CONSCIENCE

CHAPTER 14

RESTRICTIONS ON TIME, PLACE, OR MANNER OF EXPRESSION

1. THE TRADITIONAL PUBLIC FORUM: SPEECH ACTIVITIES IN STREETS AND PARKS

Page 1341. Replace Hill v. Colorado with the following:

McCullen v. Coakley

573 U.S. ___, 134 S.Ct. 2518, 189 L.Ed.2d 502 (2014).

Chief Justice Roberts delivered the opinion of the Court.

A Massachusetts statute makes it a crime to knowingly stand on a "public way or sidewalk" within 35 feet of an entrance or driveway to any place, other than a hospital, where abortions are performed.... Petitioners ... approach and talk to women outside such facilities, attempting to dissuade them from having abortions. The statute prevents petitioners from doing so near the facilities' entrances. The question presented is whether the statute violates the First Amendment.

I

A

[In 2000, Massachusetts passed a law] designed to address clashes between abortion opponents and advocates of abortion rights that were occurring outside clinics where abortions were performed. The Act established a defined area with an 18-foot radius around the entrances and driveways of such facilities. § 120E½(b). Anyone could enter that area, but once within it, no one (other than certain exempt individuals) could knowingly approach within six feet of another person—unless that person consented—"for the purpose of passing a leaflet or handbill to, displaying a sign to, or engaging in oral protest, education, or counseling with such other person.".... A separate provision subjected to criminal punishment anyone who "knowingly obstructs, detains, hinders, impedes or blocks another person's entry to or exit from a reproductive health care facility." § 120E½(e).

The statute was modeled on a similar Colorado law that this Court had upheld in *Hill v. Colorado*, 530 U.S. 703 (2000)....

By 2007, some Massachusetts legislators and law enforcement officials had come to regard the 2000 statute as inadequate. At legislative hearings, multiple witnesses recounted apparent violations of the law. [Among others, reports that prospective patients occasionally retreated from the clinics rather than try to make their way to the clinic entrances or parking lots, and that the six-foot no-approach zone was difficult to enforce, led the legislature to amend the statute,] replacing the six-foot no-approach zones (within the 18-foot area) with a 35-foot fixed buffer zone from which individuals are categorically excluded. The statute now provides:

> "No person shall knowingly enter or remain on a public way or sidewalk adjacent to a reproductive health care facility within a radius of 35 feet of any portion of an entrance, exit or driveway of a reproductive healthcare facility or within the area within a rectangle created by extending the outside boundaries of any entrance, exit or driveway of a reproductive health care facility in straight lines to the point where such lines intersect the sideline of the street in front of such entrance, exit or driveway." Mass. Gen. Laws, ch. 266, § 120E½(b) (West 2012).

A "reproductive health care facility," . . . is defined as "a place, other than within or upon the grounds of a hospital, where abortions are offered or performed." § 120E½(a).

The 35-foot buffer zone applies only "during a facility's business hours," and the area must be "clearly marked and posted." § 120E½(c). In practice, facilities typically mark the zones with painted arcs and posted signs on adjacent sidewalks and streets. A first violation . . . is punishable by a fine of up to $500, up to three months in prison, or both, while a subsequent offense is punishable by a fine of between $500 and $5,000, up to two and a half years in prison, or both. § 120E½(d).

The Act exempts four classes of individuals: (1) "persons entering or leaving such facility"; (2) "employees or agents of such facility acting within the scope of their employment"; (3) "law enforcement, ambulance, firefighting, construction, utilities, public works and other municipal agents acting within the scope of their employment"; and (4) "persons using the public sidewalk or street right-of-way adjacent to such facility solely for the purpose of reaching a destination other than such facility." § 120E½(b)(1)–(4). The legislature also retained the separate provision from the 2000 version that proscribes the knowing obstruction of access to a facility. § 120E½(e).

B

Some of the individuals who stand outside Massachusetts abortion clinics are fairly described as protestors, who express their moral or religious opposition to abortion through signs and chants or, in some cases, more aggressive methods such as face-to-face confrontation. Petitioners take a different tack. They attempt to engage women approaching the clinics in what they call "sidewalk counseling," which involves offering information about alternatives to abortion and help pursuing those options. McCullen and the other petitioners consider it essential to maintain a caring demeanor, a calm tone of voice, and direct eye contact during these exchanges. Such interactions, petitioners believe, are a much more effective means of dissuading women from having abortions than confrontational methods such as shouting or brandishing signs, which in petitioners' view tend only to antagonize their intended audience. In unrefuted testimony, petitioners say they have collectively persuaded hundreds of women to forgo abortions.

The buffer zones have displaced petitioners from their previous positions outside the clinics. . . . [In Boston, the "upshot is that petitioners are effectively excluded from a 56-foot-wide expanse of the public sidewalk in front of the [Planned Parenthood] clinic." In Worcester and Springfield, because the clinics are "well back from the public street and sidewalks[,]" they "must now stand either some distance down the sidewalk from the private walkway and driveway or across the street."]

Petitioners at all three clinics claim that the buffer zones have considerably hampered their counseling efforts. Although they have managed to conduct some counseling and to distribute some literature outside the buffer zones—particularly at the Boston clinic—they say they have had many fewer conversations and distributed many fewer leaflets since the zones went into effect. . . .

The second statutory exemption allows clinic employees and agents acting within the scope of their employment to enter the buffer zones. Relying on this exemption, the Boston clinic uses "escorts" to greet women as they approach the clinic, accompanying them through the zones to the clinic entrance. Petitioners claim that the escorts sometimes thwart petitioners' attempts to communicate with patients by blocking petitioners from handing literature to patients, telling patients not to "pay any attention" or "listen to" petitioners, and disparaging petitioners as "crazy." . . .

C

[P]etitioners sued . . . to enjoin enforcement of the Act, alleging that it violates the First and Fourteenth Amendments, both on its face and as applied to them. [The District Court rejected their challenges and the First Circuit affirmed.]

II

By its very terms, the Massachusetts Act regulates access to "public way[s]" and "sidewalk[s]." . . . Such areas occupy a "special position in terms of First Amendment protection" because of their historic role as sites for discussion and debate. *United States* v. *Grace*, 461 U.S. 171, 180 (1983). . . .

It is no accident that public streets and sidewalks have developed as venues for the exchange of ideas. Even today, they remain one of the few places where a speaker can be confident that he is not simply preaching to the choir. With respect to other means of communication, an individual confronted with an uncomfortable message can always turn the page, change the channel, or leave the Web site. Not so on public streets and sidewalks. There, a listener often encounters speech he might otherwise tune out. In light of the First Amendment's purpose "to preserve an uninhibited marketplace of ideas in which truth will ultimately prevail," . . . this aspect of traditional public fora is a virtue, not a vice.

. . .

. . . [T]he guiding First Amendment principle that the "government has no power to restrict expression because of its message, its ideas, its subject matter, or its content" applies with full force in a traditional public forum. *Police Dept. of Chicago* v. *Mosley*, 408 U.S. 92, 95 (1972). As a general rule, in such a forum the government may not "selectively . . . shield the public from some kinds of speech on the ground that they are more offensive than others." *Erznoznik* v. *Jacksonville*, 422 U.S. 205, 209 (1975).

We have, however, afforded the government somewhat wider leeway to regulate features of speech unrelated to its content. "[E]ven in a public forum the government may impose reasonable restrictions on the time, place, or manner of protected speech, provided the restrictions 'are justified without reference to the content of the regulated speech, that they are narrowly tailored to serve a significant governmental interest, and that they leave open ample alternative channels for communication of the information.'" *Ward* [v. *Rock Against Racism*, 491 U.S. 781 (1989),] at 791. . . .

. . .

III

Petitioners contend that the Act is not content neutral for two independent reasons: First, they argue that it discriminates against abortion-related speech because it establishes buffer zones only at clinics that perform abortions. Second, petitioners contend that the Act, by exempting clinic employees and agents, favors one viewpoint about abortion over the other. If either of these arguments is correct, then the Act must satisfy strict scrutiny—that is, it must be the least restrictive means of achieving a compelling state interest. . . . Respondents do not argue that the Act can survive this exacting standard.

. . .

A

. . . [P]etitioners argue [that] "virtually all speech affected by the Act is speech concerning abortion," thus rendering the Act content based. . . .

We disagree. To begin, the Act does not draw content based distinctions on its face. Contrast *Boos* v. *Barry*, 485 U.S. 312, 315 (1988) (ordinance prohibiting the display within 500 feet of a foreign embassy of any sign that tends to bring the foreign government into " 'public odium' " or " 'public disrepute' "); *Carey* v. *Brown*, 447 U.S. 455, 465 (1980) (statute prohibiting all residential picketing except "peaceful labor picketing"). The Act would be content based if it required "enforcement authorities" to "examine the content of the message that is conveyed to determine whether" a violation has occurred. . . . But it does not. Whether petitioners violate the Act "depends" not "on what they say," *Humanitarian Law Project*, . . . but simply on where they say it. Indeed, petitioners can violate the Act merely by standing in a buffer zone, without displaying a sign or uttering a word.

It is true, of course, that by limiting the buffer zones to abortion clinics, the Act has the "inevitable effect" of restricting abortion-related speech more than speech on other subjects. Brief for Petitioners 24 (quoting *United States* v. *O'Brien*, 391 U.S. 367, 384 (1968)). But a facially neutral law does not become content based simply because it may disproportionately affect speech on certain topics. On the contrary, "[a] regulation that serves purposes unrelated to the content of expression is deemed neutral, even if it has an incidental effect on some speakers or messages but not others." *Ward*,.... The question in such a case is whether the law is " 'justified without reference to the content of the regulated speech.' "...

The Massachusetts Act is. Its stated purpose is to "increase forthwith public safety at reproductive health care facilities." 2007 Mass. Acts p. 660. Respondents have articulated similar purposes before this Court—namely, "public safety, patient access to healthcare, and the unobstructed use of public sidewalks and roadways."...

We have previously deemed the foregoing concerns to be content neutral.... Obstructed access and congested sidewalks are problems no matter what caused them. A group of individuals can obstruct clinic access and clog sidewalks just as much when they loiter as when they protest abortion or counsel patients.

To be clear, the Act would not be content neutral if it were concerned with undesirable effects that arise from "the direct impact of speech on its audience" or "[l]isteners' reactions to speech."... If, for example, the speech outside Massachusetts abortion clinics caused offense or made listeners uncomfortable, such offense or discomfort would not give the Commonwealth a content-neutral justification to restrict the speech. All of the problems identified by the Commonwealth here, however, arise irrespective of any listener's reactions. Whether or not a single person reacts to abortion protestors' chants or petitioners' counseling, large crowds outside abortion clinics can still compromise public safety, impede access, and obstruct sidewalks.

Petitioners do not really dispute that the Commonwealth's interests in ensuring safety and preventing obstruction are, as a general matter, content neutral. But petitioners note that these interests "apply outside every building in the State that hosts any activity that might occasion protest or comment," not just abortion clinics.... By choosing to pursue these interests only at abortion clinics, petitioners argue, the Massachusetts Legislature evinced a purpose to "single[ ] out for regulation speech about one particular topic: abortion."...

We cannot infer such a purpose from the Act's limited scope.... The Massachusetts Legislature amended the Act in 2007 in response to a problem that was, in its experience, limited to abortion clinics. There was a record of crowding, obstruction, and even violence outside such clinics. There were apparently no similar recurring problems associated with other kinds of healthcare facilities, let alone with "every building in the State that hosts any activity that might occasion protest or comment."... In light of the limited nature of the problem, it was reasonable for the Massachusetts Legislature to enact a limited solution. When selecting among various options for combating a particular problem, legislatures should be encouraged to choose the one that restricts less speech, not more.

Justice Scalia objects that the statute does restrict more speech than necessary, because "only one [Massachusetts abortion clinic] is known to have been beset by the problems that the statute supposedly addresses." But there are no grounds for inferring content based discrimination here simply because the legislature acted with respect to abortion facilities generally rather than proceeding on a facility-by-facility basis. On these facts, the poor fit noted by Justice Scalia goes to the question of narrow tailoring, which we consider below.

B

Petitioners also argue that the Act is content based because [of . . .] the exemption allow[ing] clinic employees and agents—including the volunteers who "escort" patients arriving at the Boston clinic—to speak inside the buffer zones.

It is of course true that "an exemption from an otherwise permissible regulation of speech may represent a governmental 'attempt to give one side of a debatable public question an advantage in expressing its views to the people.'" *City of Ladue* v. *Gilleo*, 512 U.S. 43, 51 (1994). . . . At least on the record before us, however, the statutory exemption for clinic employees and agents acting within the scope of their employment does not appear to be such an attempt.

. . . [T]he exemption cannot be regarded as simply a carve-out for the clinic escorts; it also covers employees such as the maintenance worker shoveling a snowy sidewalk or the security guard patrolling a clinic entrance. . . .

Given the need for an exemption for clinic employees, the "scope of their employment" qualification simply ensures that the exemption is limited to its purpose of allowing the employees to do their jobs. . . . There is no suggestion in the record that any of the clinics authorize their employees to speak about abortion in the buffer zones. The "scope of their employment" limitation thus seems designed to protect against exactly the sort of conduct that petitioners and Justice Scalia fear.

Petitioners did testify in this litigation about instances in which escorts at the Boston clinic had expressed views about abortion to the women they were accompanying, thwarted petitioners' attempts to speak and hand literature to the women, and disparaged petitioners in various ways. . . . It is unclear from petitioners' testimony whether these alleged incidents occurred within the buffer zones. There is no viewpoint discrimination problem if the incidents occurred outside the zones because petitioners are equally free to say whatever they would like in that area.

Even assuming the incidents occurred inside the zones, the record does not suggest that they involved speech within the scope of the escorts' employment. If the speech was beyond the scope of their employment, then each of the alleged incidents would violate the Act's express terms. Petitioners' complaint would then be that the police were failing to *enforce* the Act equally against clinic escorts. . . . While such allegations might state a claim of official viewpoint discrimination, that would not go to the validity of the Act. In any event, petitioners nowhere allege selective enforcement.

It would be a very different question if it turned out that a clinic authorized escorts to speak about abortion inside the buffer zones. See Alito, J., (concurring in judgment). In that case, the escorts would not seem to be violating the Act because the speech would be within the scope of their employment. The Act's exemption for clinic employees would then facilitate speech on only one side of the abortion debate—a clear form of viewpoint discrimination that would support an as-applied challenge to the buffer zone at that clinic. But the record before us contains insufficient evidence to show that the exemption operates in this way at any of the clinics, perhaps because the clinics do not want to doom the Act by allowing their employees to speak about abortion within the buffer zones.[4]

We thus conclude that the Act is neither content nor viewpoint based and therefore need not be analyzed under strict scrutiny.

IV

Even though the Act is content neutral, it still must be "narrowly tailored to serve a significant governmental interest.". . . By demanding a close fit between ends and means, the tailoring requirement prevents the government from too readily "sacrific[ing] speech for efficiency.". . .

For a content-neutral time, place, or manner regulation to be narrowly tailored, it must not "burden substantially more speech than is necessary to further the government's legitimate interests." *Ward,*. . . .

As noted, respondents claim that the Act promotes "public safety, patient access to healthcare, and the unobstructed use of public sidewalks and roadways.". . . Petitioners do not dispute the significance of these interests. . . . The buffer zones clearly serve these interests.

At the same time, the buffer zones impose serious burdens on petitioners' speech. At each of the three Planned Parenthood clinics where petitioners attempt to counsel patients, the zones carve out a significant portion of the adjacent public sidewalks, pushing petitioners well back from the clinics' entrances and driveways. The zones thereby compromise petitioners' ability to initiate the close, personal conversations that they view as essential to "sidewalk counseling."

---

[4] Of course we do not hold that "[s]peech restrictions favoring one viewpoint over another are not content based unless it can be shown that the favored viewpoint has actually been expressed." We instead apply an uncontroversial principle of constitutional adjudication: that a plaintiff generally cannot prevail on an *as-applied* challenge without showing that the law has in fact been (or is sufficiently likely to be) unconstitutionally *applied* to him. Specifically, when someone challenges a law as viewpoint discriminatory but it is not clear from the face of the law which speakers will be allowed to speak, he must show that he was prevented from speaking while someone espousing another viewpoint was permitted to do so. . . .

. . . Given these limitations, McCullen is often reduced to raising her voice at patients from outside the zone—a mode of communication sharply at odds with the compassionate message she wishes to convey. . . .

These burdens on petitioners' speech have clearly taken their toll, [drastically reducing the number of women they previously had persuaded not to terminate their pregnancies].

The buffer zones have also made it substantially more difficult for petitioners to distribute literature to arriving patients. . . . In short, the Act operates to deprive petitioners of their two primary methods of communicating with patients.

[W]hile the First Amendment does not guarantee a speaker the right to any particular form of expression, some forms—such as normal conversation and leafletting on a public sidewalk—have historically been more closely associated with the transmission of ideas than others.

In the context of petition campaigns, we have observed that "one-on-one communication" is "the most effective, fundamental, and perhaps economical avenue of political discourse." *Meyer* v. *Grant*, 486 U.S. 414, 424 (1988). See also *Schenck*, *supra*, at 377 (invalidating a "floating" buffer zone around people entering an abortion clinic partly on the ground that it prevented protestors "from communicating a message from a normal conversational distance or handing leaflets to people entering or leaving the clinics who are walking on the public sidewalks"). . . . When the government makes it more difficult to engage in these modes of communication, it imposes an especially significant First Amendment burden.

Respondents also emphasize that the Act does not prevent petitioners from engaging in various forms of "protest"—such as chanting slogans and displaying signs—outside the buffer zones. . . . That misses the point. Petitioners are not protestors. They seek not merely to express their opposition to abortion, but to inform women of various alternatives and to provide help in pursuing them. Petitioners believe that they can accomplish this objective only through personal, caring, consensual conversations. And for good reason: It is easier to ignore a strained voice or a waving hand than a direct greeting or an outstretched arm. While the record indicates that petitioners have been able to have a number of quiet conversations outside the buffer zones, respondents have not refuted petitioners' testimony that the conversations have been far less frequent and far less successful since the buffer zones were instituted. It is thus no answer to say that petitioners can still be "seen and heard" by women within the buffer zones. . . . If all that the women can see and hear are vociferous opponents of abortion, then the buffer zones have effectively stifled petitioners' message.

. . .

B

1

The buffer zones burden substantially more speech than necessary to achieve the Commonwealth's asserted interests. . . . [T]he Act is truly exceptional: Respondents and their *amici* identify no other State with a law that creates fixed buffer zones around abortion clinics.[6] That . . . raise[s] concern that the Commonwealth has too readily forgone options that could serve its interests just as well, without substantially burdening the kind of speech in which petitioners wish to engage.

That is the case here. The Commonwealth's interests include ensuring public safety outside abortion clinics, preventing harassment and intimidation of patients and clinic staff, and combating deliberate obstruction of clinic entrances. The Act itself contains a separate provision, subsection (e)—unchallenged by petitioners—that prohibits much of this conduct. That provision subjects to criminal punishment "[a]ny person who knowingly obstructs, detains, hinders, impedes or blocks another person's entry to or exit from a reproductive health care facility.". . . If Massachusetts determines that broader prohibitions along the same lines are necessary, it could enact legislation similar to the federal Freedom of Access to Clinic Entrances Act of 1994 (FACE Act), 18 U.S.C. § 248(a)(1), which subjects to both criminal and civil penalties anyone who "by force or threat of force or by physical obstruction, intentionally injures, intimidates or interferes with or attempts to injure, intimidate or interfere with any person because that person is or has been, or in order to intimidate such person or any other person or any class of persons from, obtaining or providing reproductive health services." Some dozen other States have done so. . . . If the Commonwealth is particularly concerned about harassment, it could also consider an ordinance such as the one adopted in New York City that not only prohibits obstructing access to a clinic, but also makes it a crime "to follow and harass another person within 15 feet of the premises of a reproductive health care facility.". . .[8]

The Commonwealth points to a substantial public safety risk created when protestors obstruct driveways leading to the clinics. . . . That is, however, an example of its failure to look to less intrusive means of addressing its concerns. Any such obstruction can readily be addressed through existing local ordinances. . . .

All of the foregoing measures are, of course, in addition to available generic criminal statutes forbidding assault, breach of the peace, trespass, vandalism, and the like.

In addition, subsection (e) of the Act, the FACE Act, and the New York City anti-harassment ordinance are all enforceable not only through criminal prosecutions but also through public and private civil actions for injunctions

---

[6] *Amici* do identify five localities with laws similar to the Act here. . . .

[8] We do not "give [our] approval" to this or any of the other alternatives we discuss. We merely suggest that a law like the New York City ordinance could in principle constitute a permissible alternative. . . .

and other equitable relief. . . . We have previously noted the First Amendment virtues of targeted injunctions as alternatives to broad, prophylactic measures. Such an injunction "regulates the activities, and perhaps the speech, of a group," but only "because of the group's past *actions* in the context of a specific dispute between real parties." *Madsen*,. . . . Moreover, given the equitable nature of injunctive relief, courts can tailor a remedy to ensure that it restricts no more speech than necessary. See, *e.g., id.,* at 770; *Schenck*, 519 U.S., at 380–381. In short, injunctive relief focuses on the precise individuals and the precise conduct causing a particular problem. The Act, by contrast, categorically excludes nonexempt individuals from the buffer zones, unnecessarily sweeping in innocent individuals and their speech.

The Commonwealth also asserts an interest in preventing congestion in front of abortion clinics. According to respondents, even when individuals do not deliberately obstruct access to clinics, they can inadvertently do so simply by gathering in large numbers. But the Commonwealth could address that problem through more targeted means. Some localities, for example, have ordinances that require crowds blocking a clinic entrance to disperse when ordered to do so by the police, and that forbid the individuals to reassemble within a certain distance of the clinic for a certain period. . . .

And to the extent the Commonwealth argues that even these types of laws are ineffective, it has another problem. The portions of the record that respondents cite to support the anticongestion interest pertain mainly to one place at one time: the Boston Planned Parenthood clinic on Saturday mornings. . . . Respondents point us to no evidence that individuals regularly gather at other clinics, or at other times in Boston, in sufficiently large groups to obstruct access. For a problem shown to arise only once a week in one city at one clinic, creating 35-foot buffer zones at every clinic across the Commonwealth is hardly a narrowly tailored solution.

. . .

2

Respondents have but one reply: "We have tried other approaches, but they do not work." . . .

Although respondents claim that Massachusetts "tried other laws already on the books," they identify not a single prosecution brought under those laws within at least the last 17 years. And while they also claim that the Commonwealth "tried injunctions," . . . the last injunctions they cite date to the 1990s. . . . In short, the Commonwealth has not shown that it seriously undertook to address the problem with less intrusive tools readily available to it. Nor has it shown that it considered different methods that other jurisdictions have found effective.

Respondents contend that the alternatives we have discussed suffer from two defects: First, given the "widespread" nature of the problem, it is simply not "practicable" to rely on individual prosecutions and injunctions. . . . But far from being "widespread," the problem appears from the record to be limited principally to the Boston clinic on Saturday mornings. Moreover, by their own account, the police appear perfectly capable of singling out lawbreakers. The legislative testimony preceding the 2007 Act revealed substantial police and video monitoring at the clinics, especially when large gatherings were anticipated. Captain Evans testified that his officers are so familiar with the scene outside the Boston clinic that they "know all the players down there.". . . And Attorney General Coakley relied on video surveillance to show legislators conduct she thought was "clearly against the law.". . . If Commonwealth officials can compile an extensive record of obstruction and harassment to support their preferred legislation, we do not see why they cannot do the same to support injunctions and prosecutions against those who might deliberately flout the law.

The second supposed defect in the alternatives we have identified is that laws like subsection (e) of the Act and the federal FACE Act require a showing of intentional or deliberate obstruction, intimidation, or harassment, which is often difficult to prove. . . .

. . . To meet the requirement of narrow tailoring, the government must demonstrate that alternative measures that burden substantially less speech would fail to achieve the government's interests, not simply that the chosen route is easier. A painted line on the sidewalk is easy to enforce, but the prime objective of the First Amendment is not efficiency. In any case, we do not think that showing intentional obstruction is nearly so difficult in this context as respondents suggest. To determine whether a protestor intends to block access to a clinic, a police officer need only order him to move. If he refuses, then there is no question that his continued conduct is knowing or intentional.

For similar reasons, respondents' reliance on our decision in *Burson v. Freeman* is misplaced. There, we upheld a state statute that established 100-foot buffer zones outside polling places on election day within which no one could display or distribute campaign materials or solicit votes. 504 U.S., at 193–194. We approved the buffer zones as a valid prophylactic measure, noting that existing"[i]ntimidation and interference laws fall short of serving a State's compelling interests because they 'deal with only the most blatant and specific attempts' to impede elections.". . . Such laws were insufficient because "[v]oter intimidation and election fraud are . . . difficult to detect.". . . Obstruction of abortion clinics and harassment of patients, by contrast, are anything but subtle.

We also noted in *Burson* that under state law, "law enforcement officers generally are barred from the vicinity of the polls to avoid any appearance of coercion in the electoral process," with the result that "many acts of interference would go undetected.". . . Not so here. Again, the police maintain a significant presence outside Massachusetts abortion clinics. The buffer zones in *Burson* were justified because less restrictive measures were inadequate. Respondents have not shown that to be the case here.

. . .

Justice Scalia, with whom Justice Kennedy and Justice Thomas join, concurring in the judgment.

Today's opinion carries forward this Court's practice of giving abortion-rights advocates a pass when it comes to suppressing the free-speech rights of their opponents. There is an entirely separate, abridged edition of the First Amendment applicable to speech against abortion. See, *e.g.*, *Hill* v. *Colorado*, 530 U.S. 703 (2000); *Madsen* v. *Women's Health Center, Inc.*, 512 U.S. 753 (1994).

. . .

I.   The Court's Content-Neutrality Discussion Is Unnecessary

. . . Inasmuch as Part IV holds that the Act is unconstitutional because it does not survive the lesser level of scrutiny associated with content-neutral "time, place, and manner" regulations, there is no principled reason for the majority to decide whether the statute is subject to strict scrutiny.

. . .

II.   The Statute Is Content Based and Fails Strict Scrutiny

. . .

A.   Application to Abortion Clinics Only

. . .

. . . It blinks reality to say, as the majority does, that a blanket prohibition on the use of streets and sidewalks where speech on only one politically controversial topic is likely to occur—and where that speech can most effectively be communicated—is not content based. Would the Court exempt from strict scrutiny a law banning access to the streets and sidewalks surrounding the site of the Republican National Convention? Or those used annually to commemorate the 1965 Selma-to-Montgomery civil rights marches? Or those outside the Internal Revenue Service? Surely not.

The majority says, correctly enough, that a facially neutral speech restriction escapes strict scrutiny, even when it "may disproportionately affect speech on certain topics," so long as it is "justified without reference to the content of the regulated speech." But the cases in which the Court has previously found that standard satisfied—in particular, *Renton* v. *Playtime Theatres, Inc.*, 475 U.S. 41 (1986), and *Ward* v. *Rock Against Racism*, 491 U.S. 781 (1989), both of which the majority cites—are a far cry from what confronts us here.

. . .

. . . The majority points only to the statute's stated purpose of increasing " 'public safety' " at abortion clinics and to the additional aims articulated by respondents before this Court—namely, protecting " 'patient access to healthcare . . . and the unobstructed use of public sidewalks and roadways.' " Really? Does a statute become "justified without reference to the content of the regulated speech" simply because the statute itself and those defending it in court *say* that it is? Every objective indication shows that the provision's primary purpose is to restrict speech that opposes abortion.

I begin . . . with the fact that the Act burdens only the public spaces outside abortion clinics. . . . [A]lthough the statute applies to all abortion clinics in Massachusetts, only one is known to have been beset by the problems that the statute supposedly addresses. The Court uses this striking fact . . . as a basis for concluding that the law is insufficiently "tailored" to safety and access concerns (Part IV) rather than as a basis for concluding that it is not *directed* to those concerns at all, but to the suppression of antiabortion speech. That is rather like invoking the eight missed human targets of a shooter who has killed one victim to prove, not that he is guilty of attempted mass murder, but that *he has bad aim.*

. . . Showing that a law that suppresses speech on a specific subject is so far reaching that it applies even when the asserted non-speech-related problems are not present is persuasive evidence that the law is content based. . . .

The structure of the Act also indicates that it rests on content-based concerns. The goals of "public safety, patient access to healthcare, and the unobstructed use of public sidewalks and roadways," . . . are already achieved by an earlier-enacted subsection of the statute, which provides criminal penalties for "[a]ny person who knowingly obstructs, detains, hinders, impedes or blocks another person's entry to or exit from a reproductive health care facility." § 120E½(e). As the majority recognizes, that provision is easy to enforce. Thus, the speech-free zones carved out by subsection (b) add nothing to safety and access; what they achieve, and what they were obviously designed to achieve, is the suppression of speech opposing abortion.

Further contradicting the Court's fanciful defense of the Act is the fact that subsection (b) was enacted as a more easily enforceable substitute for a prior provision. That provision did not exclude people entirely from the restricted areas around abortion clinics; rather, it forbade people in those areas to approach within six feet of another person *without that person's consent* "for the purpose of passing a leaflet or handbill to, displaying a sign to, or engaging in oral protest, education or counseling with such other person." § 120E½(b). . . . As the majority acknowledges, that provision was "modeled on a . . . Colorado law that this Court had upheld in *Hill*." And in that case, the Court recognized that the statute in question was directed at the suppression of unwelcome speech, vindicating what *Hill* called "[t]he unwilling listener's interest in avoiding unwanted communication.". . . The Court held that interest to be content neutral. . . .

The provision at issue here was indisputably meant to serve the same interest in protecting citizens' supposed right to avoid speech that they would rather not hear. For that reason, we granted a second question for review in this case . . . : whether *Hill* should be cut back or cast aside. . . . The majority avoids that question by declaring the Act content neutral on other (entirely unpersuasive) grounds. In concluding that the statute is content based and therefore subject to strict scrutiny, I necessarily conclude that *Hill* should be overruled. . . . Protecting people from speech they do not want to hear is not a function that the First Amendment allows the government to undertake in the public streets and sidewalks.

. . . It . . . should be argued in the next case, that by stating that "the Act would not be content neutral if it were concerned with undesirable effects that arise from . . . '[l]isteners' reactions to speech,' " . . . and then holding the Act unconstitutional for being insufficiently tailored to safety and access concerns, the Court itself has *sub silentio* (and perhaps inadvertently) overruled *Hill*. The unavoidable implication of that holding is that protection against unwelcome speech cannot justify restrictions on the use of public streets and sidewalks.

B.   Exemption for Abortion-Clinic Employees or Agents

. . .

It goes without saying that "[g]ranting waivers to favored speakers (or . . . denying them to disfavored speakers) would of course be unconstitutional." *Thomas* v. *Chicago Park Dist.*, 534 U.S. 316, 325 (2002). . . .

Is there any serious doubt that *abortion-clinic employees or agents* "acting within the scope of their employment" near clinic entrances may—indeed, often will—speak in favor of abortion . . . ? Or speak in opposition to the message of abortion opponents—saying, for example, that "this is a safe facility" to rebut the statement that it is not? . . . The Court's contrary assumption is simply incredible. And the majority makes no attempt to establish the further necessary proposition that abortion-clinic employees and agents do not engage in nonspeech activities directed to the suppression of antiabortion speech by hampering the efforts of counselors to speak to prospective clients. Are we to believe that a clinic employee sent out to "escort" prospective clients into the building would not seek to prevent a counselor like Eleanor McCullen from communicating with them? . . .

. . . Whatever other activity is permitted, so long as the statute permits speech favorable to abortion rights while excluding antiabortion speech, it discriminates on the basis of viewpoint.

The Court takes the peculiar view that, so long as the clinics have not specifically authorized their employees to speak in favor of abortion (or, presumably, to impede antiabortion speech), there is no viewpoint discrimination. . . . [I]t is implausible that clinics would bar escorts from engaging in the sort of activity mentioned above. Moreover, a statute that forbids one side but not the other to convey its message does not become viewpoint neutral simply because the favored side chooses voluntarily to abstain from activity that the statute permits.

There is not a shadow of a doubt that the assigned or foreseeable conduct of a clinic employee or agent can include both speaking in favor of abortion rights and countering the speech of people like petitioners. See Alito, J., concurring in judgment. Indeed, as the majority acknowledges, the trial record includes testimony that escorts at the Boston clinic "expressed views about abortion to the women they were accompanying, thwarted petitioners' attempts to speak and hand literature to the women, and disparaged petitioners in various ways, "including by calling them " 'crazy.' " What a surprise! The Web site for the Planned Parenthood League of Massachusetts (which operates the three abortion facilities where petitioners attempt to counsel women), urges readers to "Become a Clinic Escort Volunteer" in order to "provide a safe space for patients by escorting them through protestors to the health center.". . . The dangers that the Web site attributes to "protestors" are related entirely to speech, not to safety or access. "Protestors," it reports, "hold signs, try to speak to patients entering the building, and distribute literature that can be misleading.". . . The "safe space" provided by escorts is protection from that speech.

. . . [T]he majority's opinion contends that . . . [s]peech restrictions favoring one viewpoint over another are not content based unless it can be shown that the favored viewpoint has actually been expressed. A city ordinance closing a park adjoining the Republican National Convention to all speakers except those whose remarks have been approved by the Republican National Committee is thus not subject to strict scrutiny unless it can be shown that someone has given committee-endorsed remarks. For this Court to suggest such a test is astonishing.

. . . Having determined that the Act is content based and does not withstand strict scrutiny, I need not pursue the inquiry conducted in Part IV of the Court's opinion—whether the statute is " 'narrowly tailored to serve a significant governmental interest.' ". . . [I]f I did, I suspect I would agree with the majority that the legislation is not narrowly tailored to advance the interests asserted by respondents. But I prefer not to take part in the assembling of an apparent but specious unanimity. . . .

. . .

The obvious purpose of the challenged [provision] is to "protect" prospective clients of abortion clinics from having to hear abortion-opposing speech on public streets and sidewalks. The provision is thus unconstitutional root and branch and cannot be saved, as the majority suggests, by limiting its application to the single facility that has experienced the safety and access problems to which it is quite obviously not addressed. I concur only in the judgment that the statute is unconstitutional under the First Amendment.

Justice Alito, concurring in the judgment.

. . . [T]he Massachusetts law discriminates on the basis of viewpoint. . . .

. . . [D]uring business hours, individuals who wish to counsel against abortion or to criticize the particular clinic may not do so within the buffer zone. If they engage in such conduct, they commit a crime. See § 120E½(d). By contrast, employees and agents of the clinic may enter the zone and engage in any conduct that falls within the scope of their employment. A clinic may direct or authorize an employee or agent, while within the zone, to express favorable views about abortion or the clinic, and if the employee exercises that authority, the employee's conduct is perfectly lawful. In short, petitioners and other critics of a clinic are silenced, while the clinic may authorize its employees to express speech in support of the clinic and its work.

. . .

It is clear on the face of the Massachusetts law that it discriminates based on viewpoint. Speech in favor of the clinic and its work by employees and agents is permitted; speech criticizing the clinic and its work is a crime. This is blatant viewpoint discrimination.

. . .

. . . I do not think that it is possible to reach a judgment about the intent of the Massachusetts Legislature without taking into account the fact that the law that the legislature enacted blatantly discriminates based on viewpoint. In light of this feature, as well as the overbreadth that the Court identifies, it cannot be said, based on the present record, that the law would be content neutral even if the exemption for clinic employees and agents were excised. However, if the law were truly content neutral, I would agree with the Court that the law would still be unconstitutional on the ground that it burdens more speech than is necessary to serve the Commonwealth's asserted interests.

3.   SPEECH ON PRIVATE PREMISES

Page 1379. Add at end of subsection 3:

Reed v. Town of Gilbert, 576 U.S. ___, 135 S.Ct. 2218 (2015). Though dividing on the proper analytical approach, the Court unanimously found the Town's comprehensive code governing the display of outdoor signs invalid under the First Amendment. The Sign Code prohibited the display of outdoor signs anywhere within the Town without a permit, but it exempted 23 categories of signs, three of which the majority found "particularly relevant" to this case. "Ideological Signs" were treated "most favorably, allowing them to be up to 20 square feet in area and to be placed in all 'zoning districts' without time limits." "Political Signs"—meaning any "temporary sign designed to influence the outcome of an election called by a public body"—were treated "less favorably": the Code allowed "the placement of political signs up to 16 square feet on residential property and up to 32 square feet on nonresidential property, undeveloped municipal property, and 'rights-of-way[,]'" but they could only "be displayed up to 60 days before a primary election and up to 15 days following a general election." Treated "even less favorably than political signs" were "'Temporary Directional Signs Relating to a Qualifying Event,' loosely defined as signs directing the public to a meeting of a nonprofit group." Temporary directional signs could "be no larger than six square feet"; could "be placed on private property or on a public right-of-way, [though] no more than four [could] be placed on a single property at any time"; and they could "be displayed no more than 12 hours before the 'qualifying event' and no more than 1 hour afterward."

In this case, a church that held its services at a variety of different Town locations "began placing 15 to 20 temporary signs around the Town, frequently in the public right-of-way abutting the street[,]" to inform the public of "the time and location of [an] upcoming service." Typically, "Church members would post the signs early in the day on Saturday and then remove them around midday on Sunday[,]" but "the Town's Sign Code compliance manager . . . twice cited the Church for violating the Code" by exceeding the permissible time limits and later "promised to punish any future violations." The Church sought an injunction and lost in the lower federal courts, but the Supreme Court reversed.

Justice Thomas's majority opinion held these Code provisions to be "content-based regulations of speech that cannot survive strict scrutiny." He wrote in part:

"Government regulation of speech is content based if a law applies to particular speech because of the topic discussed or the idea or message expressed. . . . This commonsense meaning of the phrase 'content based' requires a court to consider whether a regulation of speech 'on its face' draws distinctions based on the message a speaker conveys. . . . Some facial distinctions based on a message are obvious, defining regulated speech by particular subject matter, and others are more subtle, defining regulated speech by its function or purpose. Both are distinctions drawn based on the message a speaker conveys, and, therefore, are subject to strict scrutiny.

"Our precedents have also recognized a separate and additional category of laws that, though facially content neutral, will be considered content-based regulations of speech: laws that cannot be ' "justified without reference to the content of the regulated speech,' " or that were adopted by the government 'because of disagreement with the message [the speech] conveys,' Ward v. Rock Against Racism, 491 U. S. 781, 791 (1989). Those laws, like those that are content based on their face, must also satisfy strict scrutiny."

He found the "Town's Sign Code . . . content based on its face." Its "restrictions . . . depend entirely on the communicative content of the sign. If a sign informs its reader of the time and place a book club will discuss John Locke's Two Treatises of Government, that sign will be treated differently from a sign expressing the view that one should vote for one of Locke's followers in an upcoming election, and both signs will be treated differently from a sign expressing an ideological view rooted in Locke's theory of government. More to the point, the Church's signs inviting people to attend its worship services are treated differently from signs conveying other types of ideas. On its face, the Sign Code is a content-based regulation of speech. We thus have no need to consider the government's justifications or purposes for enacting the Code to determine whether it is subject to strict scrutiny."

Justice Thomas rejected the argument of the United States "that a sign regulation is content neutral—even if it expressly draws distinctions based on the sign's communicative content—if those distinctions can be ' "justified without reference to the content of the regulated speech[,]" ' because it "skips the crucial first step [of] determining whether the law is content neutral on its face. A law that is content based on its face is subject to strict scrutiny regardless of the government's benign motive, content-neutral justification, or lack of 'animus toward the ideas contained' in the regulated speech. Cincinnati v. Discovery Network, Inc., 507 U. S. 410, 429 (1993). . . . [A]n innocuous justification cannot transform a facially content-based law into one that is content neutral."

He reasoned that "[i]nnocent motives do not eliminate the danger of censorship presented by a facially content-based statute, as future government officials may one day wield such statutes to suppress disfavored speech." Indeed, in this case, "one could easily imagine a Sign Code compliance manager who disliked the Church's substantive teachings deploying the Sign Code to make it more difficult for the Church to inform the public of the location of its services."

As for the argument that a sign regulation should not be considered content-based if its provisions are neutral as to particular ideas or viewpoints within each category regulated, Justice Thomas responded as follows:

"This analysis conflates two distinct but related limitations that the First Amendment places on government regulation of speech. Government discrimination among viewpoints . . . is a 'more blatant' and 'egregious form of content discrimination.' Rosenberger v. Rector and Visitors of Univ. of Va., 515 U. S. 819, 829 (1995). But it is well established that '[t]he First Amendment's hostility to content-based regulation extends not only to restrictions on particular viewpoints, but also to prohibition of public discussion of an entire topic.' Consolidated Edison Co. of N. Y. v. Public Serv. Comm'n of N. Y., 447 U. S. 530, 537 (1980)."

Finally, the majority rejected, "on both factual and legal grounds[,]" the attempt to characterize the Code's distinctions "as turning on ' "the content-neutral elements of who is speaking through the sign and whether and when an event is occurring." ':

"[The] Code's distinctions are not speaker based. The restrictions for political, ideological, and temporary event signs apply equally no matter who sponsors them. If a local business, for example, sought to put up signs advertising the Church's meetings, those signs would be subject to the same limitations as such signs placed by the Church. And if [Pastor] Reed had decided to display signs in support of a particular candidate, he could have made those signs far larger—and kept them up for far longer—than signs inviting people to attend his church services. If the Code's distinctions were truly speaker based, both types of signs would receive the same treatment.

"In any case, the fact that a distinction is speaker based does not, as the Court of Appeals seemed to believe, automatically render the distinction content neutral. Because '[s]peech restrictions based on the identity of the speaker are all too often simply a means to control content,' Citizens United v. Federal Election Comm'n, 558 U. S. 310, 340 (2010), we have insisted that 'laws favoring some speakers over others demand strict scrutiny when the legislature's speaker preference reflects a content preference,'. . . . Thus, a law limiting the content of newspapers, but only newspapers, could not evade strict scrutiny simply because it could be characterized as speaker based. Likewise, a content-based law that restricted the political speech of all corporations would not become content neutral just because it singled out corporations as a class of speakers. See Citizens United, supra, at 340–341. Characterizing a distinction as speaker based is only the beginning—not the end—of the inquiry."

Nor did "the fact that a distinction is event based . . . render it content neutral. . . . Here, the Code singles out signs bearing a particular message: the time and location of a specific event. This type of ordinance may seem like a perfectly rational way to regulate signs, but a clear and firm rule governing content neutrality is an essential means of protecting the freedom of speech, even if laws that might seem 'entirely reasonable' will sometimes be 'struck down because of their content-based nature.' City of Ladue v. Gilleo, 512 U. S. 43, 60 (1994) (O'Connor, J., concurring)."

The Town could not carry its strict scrutiny "burden to demonstrate that the Code's differentiation between temporary directional signs and other types of signs, such as political signs and ideological signs, furthers a compelling governmental interest and is narrowly tailored to that end." "Assuming for the sake of argument that" the Town's two proffered interests—"preserving the Town's aesthetic appeal and traffic safety"—"are compelling governmental interests, the Code's distinctions fail as hopelessly underinclusive." As to the former, "temporary directional signs are 'no greater an eyesore,' Discovery Network, 507 U. S., at 425, than ideological or political ones. . . . The Town cannot claim that placing strict limits on temporary directional signs is necessary to beautify the Town while at the same time allowing unlimited numbers of other types of signs that create the same problem." As to the latter, the "Town similarly has not shown that limiting temporary directional signs is necessary to eliminate threats to traffic safety, but that limiting other types of signs is not."

At the conclusion of the majority opinion, Justice Thomas asserted that "[o]ur decision today will not prevent governments from enacting effective sign laws." He cited "ample content-neutral options available to resolve problems with safety and aesthetics[,]" such as regulations addressing "many aspects of signs that have nothing to do with a sign's message: size, building materials, lighting, moving parts, and portability." Further, "on public property, the Town may go a long way toward entirely forbidding the posting of signs, so long as it does so in an evenhanded, content-neutral manner." Finally, a "sign ordinance narrowly tailored to the challenges of protecting the safety of pedestrians, drivers, and passengers—such as warning signs marking hazards on private property, signs directing traffic, or street numbers associated with private houses—well might survive strict scrutiny."

Justice Alito, joined by Justices Kennedy and Sotomayor, emphasized two points in his concurring opinion. First, "[l]imiting speech based on its 'topic' or 'subject' favors those who do not want to disturb the status quo. Such regulations may interfere with democratic self-government and the search for truth." Second, he offered "some rules that would not be content based[,]" including those regulating size of signs; "the locations in which signs may be placed"; "distinguishing between lighted and unlighted signs"; "distinguishing between signs with fixed messages and electronic signs with messages that change"; distinguishing "between the placement of signs on private and public property"; "distinguishing between the placement of signs on commercial and residential property"; "distinguishing between on-premises and off-premises signs"; "restricting the total number of signs allowed per mile of roadway"; and "time restrictions on signs advertising a one-time event." In addition, "government entities ... [,] consistent with the principles that allow governmental speech[,] ... may put up all manner of signs to promote safety, as well as directional signs and signs pointing out historic sites and scenic spots."

Justice Kagan, joined by Justices Ginsburg and Breyer, concurred only in the judgment, fearing that the "consequence" of the Court's invocation of strict scrutiny in this context—"unless courts water down strict scrutiny to something unrecognizable—is that our communities will find themselves in an unenviable bind: They will have to either repeal the exemptions that allow for helpful signs on streets and sidewalks, or else lift their sign restrictions altogether and resign themselves to the resulting clutter." She argued that "the subject-matter exemptions included in many sign ordinances do not implicate" the "two important and related reasons for subjecting content-based speech regulations to the most exacting standard of review[,]" namely " 'to preserve an uninhibited marketplace of ideas in which truth will ultimately prevail' " and "to ensure that the government has not regulated speech 'based on hostility—or favoritism—towards the underlying message expressed.' " She elaborated:

"We apply strict scrutiny to facially content-based regulations of speech ... when there is any 'realistic possibility that official suppression of ideas is afoot.' ... That is always the case when the regulation facially differentiates on the basis of viewpoint.... It is also the case (except in nonpublic or limited public forums) when a law restricts 'discussion of an entire topic' in public debate.... Subject-matter regulation ... may have the intent or effect of favoring some ideas over others. When that is realistically possible—when the restriction 'raises the specter that the Government may effectively drive certain ideas or viewpoints from the marketplace'—we insist that the law pass the most demanding constitutional test....

"But when that is not realistically possible, we may do well to relax our guard so that 'entirely reasonable' laws imperiled by strict scrutiny can survive. This point is by no means new.... We can administer our content-regulation doctrine with a dose of common sense, so as to leave standing laws that in no way implicate its intended function.

"And indeed we have done just that: Our cases have been far less rigid than the majority admits in applying strict scrutiny to facially content-based laws—including in cases just like this one.... In Members of City Council of Los Angeles v. Taxpayers for Vincent, 466 U. S. 789 (1984), the Court declined to apply strict scrutiny to a municipal ordinance that exempted address numbers and markers commemorating 'historical, cultural, or artistic event[s]' from a generally applicable limit on sidewalk signs. Id., at 792, n. 1 (listing exemptions); see id., at 804–810 (upholding ordinance under intermediate scrutiny). After all, we explained, the law's enactment and enforcement revealed 'not even a hint of bias or censorship.' Id., at 804; see also Renton v. Playtime Theatres, Inc., 475 U. S. 41, 48 (1986).... And another decision involving a similar law provides an alternative model. In City of Ladue v.

Gilleo, 512 U. S. 43 (1994), the Court assumed arguendo that a sign ordinance's exceptions for address signs, safety signs, and for-sale signs in residential areas did not trigger strict scrutiny. See id., at 46–47, and n. 6 (listing exemptions); id., at 53 (noting this assumption). We did not need to, and so did not, decide the level-of-scrutiny question because the law's breadth made it unconstitutional under any standard.

"The majority could easily have taken *Ladue*'s tack here. The Town of Gilbert's defense of its sign ordinance—most notably, the law's distinctions between directional signs and others—does not pass strict scrutiny, or intermediate scrutiny, or even the laugh test. The Town, for example, provides no reason at all for prohibiting more than four directional signs on a property while placing no limits on the number of other types of signs. . . . Similarly, the Town offers no coherent justification for restricting the size of directional signs to 6 square feet while allowing other signs to reach 20 square feet. . . . The best the Town could come up with at oral argument was that directional signs 'need to be smaller because they need to guide travelers along a route. . . . Why exactly a smaller sign better helps travelers get to where they are going is left a mystery. The absence of any sensible basis for these and other distinctions dooms the Town's ordinance under even the intermediate scrutiny that the Court typically applies to 'time, place, or manner' speech regulations. Accordingly, there is no need to decide in this case whether strict scrutiny applies to every sign ordinance in every town across this country containing a subject-matter exemption.

"I suspect this Court and others will regret the majority's insistence today on answering that question in the affirmative. . . . (This Court may soon find itself a veritable Supreme Board of Sign Review.) . . . Because I see no reason why such an easy case calls for us to cast a constitutional pall on reasonable regulations quite unlike the law before us, I concur only in the judgment."

In addition to joining Justice Kagan's opinion, Justice Breyer filed a separate opinion concurring in the judgment. In his view, "the category 'content discrimination' is better considered in many contexts, including here, as a rule of thumb, rather than as an automatic 'strict scrutiny' trigger, leading to almost certain legal condemnation." He urged that "content discrimination, while helping courts to identify unconstitutional suppression of expression, cannot and should not always trigger strict scrutiny." He reasoned in part as follows:

" . . . [V]irtually all government activities involve speech, many of which involve the regulation of speech. Regulatory programs almost always require content discrimination. And to hold that such content discrimination triggers strict scrutiny is to write a recipe for judicial management of ordinary government regulatory activity.

"Consider a few examples of speech regulated by government that inevitably involve content discrimination, but where a strong presumption against constitutionality has no place. Consider governmental regulation of securities, e.g., 15 U. S. C. § 78l (requirements for content that must be included in a registration statement); of energy conservation labeling-practices, e.g., 42 U. S. C. § 6294 (requirements for content that must be included on labels of certain consumer electronics); of prescription drugs, e.g., 21 U. S. C. § 353(b)(4)(A) (requiring a prescription drug label to bear the symbol 'Rx only'); of doctor-patient confidentiality, e.g., 38 U. S. C. § 7332 (requiring confidentiality of certain medical records, but allowing a physician to disclose that the patient has HIV to the patient's spouse or sexual partner); of income tax statements, e.g., 26 U. S. C. § 6039F (requiring taxpayers to furnish information about foreign gifts received if the aggregate amount exceeds $10,000); of commercial airplane briefings, e.g., 14 CFR § 136.7 (2015) (requiring pilots to ensure that each passenger has been briefed on flight procedures, such as seat belt fastening); of signs at petting zoos, e.g., N. Y. Gen. Bus. Law Ann. § 399–ff(3) (West Cum. Supp. 2015) (requiring petting zoos to post a sign at every exit ' "strongly recommend[ing] that persons wash their hands upon exiting the petting zoo area" '); and so on.

"Nor can the majority avoid the application of strict scrutiny to all sorts of justifiable governmental regulations by relying on this Court's many subcategories and exceptions to the rule. . . .

"I recognize that the Court could escape the problem by watering down the force of the presumption against constitutionality that 'strict scrutiny' normally carries with it. But, in my view, doing so will weaken the First Amendment's protection in instances where 'strict scrutiny' should apply in full force.

"The better approach is to generally treat content discrimination as a strong reason weighing against the constitutionality of a rule where a traditional public forum, or where viewpoint discrimination, is threatened, but elsewhere treat it as a rule of thumb, finding it a helpful, but not determinative legal tool, in an appropriate case, to determine the strength of a justification. I would use content discrimination as a supplement to a more basic analysis, which, tracking most of our First Amendment cases, asks whether the regulation at issue works harm to First Amendment interests that is disproportionate in light of the relevant regulatory objectives. Answering this question requires examining the seriousness of the harm to speech, the importance of the countervailing objectives, the extent to which the law will achieve those objectives, and whether there are other, less restrictive ways of doing so. . . . Admittedly, this approach does not have the simplicity of a mechanical use of categories. But it does permit the government to regulate speech in numerous instances where the voters have authorized the government to regulate and where courts should hesitate to substitute judicial judgment for that of administrators.

"Here, regulation of signage along the roadside, for purposes of safety and beautification is at issue. There is no traditional public forum nor do I find any general effort to censor a particular viewpoint. Consequently, the specific regulation at issue does not warrant 'strict scrutiny.' Nonetheless, for the reasons that Justice Kagan sets forth, I believe that the Town of Gilbert's regulatory rules violate the First Amendment. I consequently concur in the Court's judgment only."

5. GOVERNMENT SUBSIDIES TO SPEECH

Page 1421. Replace Pleasant Grove City v. Summum with the following:

Walker v. Texas Division, Sons of Confederate Veterans

576 U.S. ___, 135 S.Ct. 2239, 192 L.Ed.2d 274 (2015).

Justice Breyer delivered the opinion of the Court.

Texas offers automobile owners a choice between ordinary and specialty license plates. Those who want the State to issue a particular specialty plate may propose a plate design, comprising a slogan, a graphic, or (most commonly) both. If the Texas Department of Motor Vehicles Board approves the design, the State will make it available for display on vehicles registered in Texas.

In this case, the Texas Division of the Sons of Confederate Veterans proposed a specialty license plate design featuring a Confederate battle flag. The Board rejected the proposal. We must decide whether that rejection violated the Constitution's free speech guarantees. See Amdts. 1, 14. We conclude that it did not.

I

A

Texas law requires all motor vehicles operating on the State's roads to display valid license plates.... And Texas makes available several kinds of plates. Drivers may choose to display the State's general-issue license plates.... In the alternative, drivers may choose from an assortment of specialty license plates[, which have on them] the word "Texas," a license plate number, and one of a selection of designs prepared by the State.... Finally, Texas law provides for personalized plates (also known as vanity plates)[, allowing] a vehicle owner [to] request a particular alphanumeric pattern for use as a plate number....

Here we are concerned only with ... specialty license plates, not with the personalization program. Texas offers vehicle owners a variety of specialty plates, generally for an annual fee.... And Texas selects the designs for specialty plates through three distinct processes.

First, the state legislature may specifically call for the development of a specialty license plate.... The legislature has enacted statutes authorizing, for example, plates that say "Keep Texas Beautiful" and "Mothers Against Drunk Driving," plates that "honor" the Texas citrus industry, and plates that feature an image of the World Trade Center towers and the words "Fight Terrorism."

Second, the Board may approve a specialty plate design proposal that a state-designated private vendor has created at the request of an individual or organization.... Among the plates created through the private-vendor process are plates promoting the "Keller Indians" and plates with the slogan "Get it Sold with RE/MAX."

Third, the Board "may create new specialty license plates on its own initiative or on receipt of an application from a" nonprofit entity seeking to sponsor a specialty plate. . . . A nonprofit must include in its application "a draft design of the specialty license plate.". . . And Texas law vests in the Board authority to approve or to disapprove an application. . . . The relevant statute says that the Board "may refuse to create a new specialty license plate" for a number of reasons, for example "if the design might be offensive to any member of the public . . . or for any other reason established by rule.". . . Specialty plates that the Board has sanctioned through this process include plates featuring the words "The Gator Nation," together with the Florida Gators logo, and plates featuring the logo of Rotary International and the words "SERVICE ABOVE SELF."

B

In 2009, the Sons of Confederate Veterans, Texas Division (a nonprofit entity), applied to sponsor a specialty license plate through this last-mentioned process. . . . At the bottom of the proposed plate were the words "SONS OF CONFEDERATE VETERANS." At the side was the organization's logo, a square Confederate battleflag framed by the words "Sons of Confederate Veterans 1896." A faint Confederate battle flag appeared in the background on the lower portion of the plate. [I]n the middle of the plate was the license plate number, and at the top was the State's name and silhouette. The Board's predecessor denied this application.

In 2010, SCV renewed its application. . . . The Board invited public comment. . . . After considering the responses, including a number of letters sent by elected officials who opposed the proposal, the Board voted unanimously against issuing the plate. The Board explained that it had found "it necessary to deny th[e] plate design application, specifically the confederate flag portion of the design, because public comments ha[d] shown that many members of the general public find the design offensive, and because such comments are reasonable.". . . The Board added "that a significant portion of the public associate the confederate flag with organizations advocating expressions of hate directed toward people or groups that is demeaning to those people or groups."

In 2012, SCV [sued,] . . . argu[ing] that the Board's decision violated the Free Speech Clause of the First Amendment, and it sought an injunction requiring the Board to approve the proposed plate design. The District Court entered judgment for the Board. A divided panel of the . . . Fifth Circuit reversed. . . .

We . . . reverse.

II

When government speaks, it is not barred by the Free Speech Clause from determining the content of what it says. Pleasant Grove City v. Summum, 555 U. S. 460, 467–468 (2009). That freedom in part reflects the fact that it is the democratic electoral process that first and foremost provides a check on government speech. See Board of Regents of Univ. of Wis. System v.

Southworth, 529 U. S. 217, 235 (2000). Thus, government statements (and government actions and programs that take the form of speech) do not normally trigger the First Amendment rules designed to protect the marketplace of ideas. See Johanns v. Livestock Marketing Assn., 544 U. S. 550, 559 (2005). Instead, the Free Speech Clause helps produce informed opinions among members of the public, who are then able to influence the choices of a government that, through words and deeds, will reflect its electoral mandate. . . .

Were the Free Speech Clause interpreted otherwise, government would not work. How could a city government create a successful recycling program if officials, when writing householders asking them to recycle cans and bottles, had to include in the letter a long plea from the local trash disposal enterprise demanding the contrary? How could a state government effectively develop programs designed to encourage and provide vaccinations, if officials also had to voice the perspective of those who oppose this type of immunization? "[I]t is not easy to imagine how government could function if it lacked th[e] freedom" to select the messages it wishes to convey. *Summum*, supra, at 468.

. . .

That is not to say that a government's ability to express itself is without restriction. Constitutional and statutory provisions outside of the Free Speech Clause may limit government speech. *Summum*, supra, at 468. And the Free Speech Clause itself may constrain the government's speech if, for example, the government seeks to compel private persons to convey the government's speech. But, as a general matter, when the government speaks it is entitled to promote a program, to espouse a policy, or to take a position. In doing so, it represents its citizens and it carries out its duties on their behalf.

III

In our view, specialty license plates issued pursuant to Texas's statutory scheme convey government speech. Our reasoning rests primarily on our analysis in *Summum*, a recent case that presented a similar problem. We conclude here, as we did there, that our precedents regarding government speech (and not our precedents regarding forums for private speech) provide the appropriate framework through which to approach the case. . . .

A

In *Summum*, we considered a religious organization's request to erect in a 2.5-acre city park a monument setting forth the organization's religious tenets. . . . In the park were 15 other permanent displays. . . . At least 11 of these—including a wishing well, a September 11 monument, a historic granary, the city's first fire station, and a Ten Commandments monument—had been donated to the city by private entities. . . . The religious organization argued that the Free Speech Clause required the city to display the organization's proposed monument because, by accepting a broad range of permanent exhibitions at the park, the city had created a forum for private speech in the form of monuments. . . .

This Court rejected the organization's argument. We held that the city had not "provid[ed] a forum for private speech" with respect to monuments. . . . Rather, the city, even when "accepting a privately donated monument and placing it on city property," had "engage[d] in expressive conduct.". . . The speech at issue, this Court decided, was "best viewed as a form of government speech" and "therefore [was] not subject to scrutiny under the Free Speech Clause.". . .

We based our conclusion on several factors. First, history shows that "[g]overnments have long used monuments to speak to the public.". . . Thus, we observed that "[w]hen a government entity arranges for the construction of a monument, it does so because it wishes to convey some thought or instill some feeling in those who see the structure.". . .

Second, we noted that it "is not common for property owners to open up their property for the installation of permanent monuments that convey a message with which they do not wish to be associated.". . . As a result, "persons who observe donated monuments routinely—and reasonably—interpret them as conveying some message on the property owner's behalf.". . . And "observers" of such monuments, as a consequence, ordinarily "appreciate the identity of the speaker.". . .

Third, we found relevant the fact that the city maintained control over the selection of monuments. We thought it "fair to say that throughout our Nation's history, the general government practice with respect to donated monuments has been one of selective receptivity.". . . And we observed that the city government in *Summum* " 'effectively controlled' the messages sent by the monuments in the [p]ark by exercising 'final approval authority' over their selection.". . .

In light of these and a few other relevant considerations, the Court concluded that the expression at issue was government speech. . . . And, in reaching that conclusion, the Court rejected the premise that the involvement of private parties in designing the monuments was sufficient to prevent the government from controlling which monuments it placed in its own public park. . . .

B

Our analysis in *Summum* leads us to the conclusion that here, too, government speech is at issue. First, the history of license plates shows that, insofar as license plates have conveyed more than state names and vehicle identification numbers, they long have communicated messages from the States. . . . In 1917, Arizona became the first State to display a graphic on its plates[. . . —]a depiction of the head of a Hereford steer. . . .

In 1928, Idaho became the first State to include a slogan on its plates. Th[at] plate proclaimed "Idaho Potatoes". . . .

Texas, too, has selected various messages to communicate through its license plate designs. By 1919, Texas had begun to display the Lone Star emblem on its plates. . . . In 1936, the State's general-issue plates featured the first slogan on Texas license plates: the word "Centennial.". . . In 1968, Texas plates promoted a San Antonio event by including the phrase "Hemisfair 68.". . . In 1977, Texas replaced the Lone Star with a small silhouette of the State. . . . And in 1995, Texas plates celebrated "150 Years of Statehood.". . . Additionally, the Texas Legislature has specifically authorized specialty plate designs stating, among other things, "Read to Succeed," "Houston Livestock Show and Rodeo," "Texans Conquer Cancer," and "Girl Scouts.". . . This kind of state speech has appeared on Texas plates for decades.

Second, Texas license plate designs "are often closely identified in the public mind with the [State]." *Summum*, supra, at 472. Each Texas license plate is a government article serving the governmental purposes of vehicle registration and identification. The governmental nature of the plates is clear from their faces: The State places the name "TEXAS" in large letters at the top of every plate. Moreover, the State requires Texas vehicle owners to display license plates, and every Texas license plate is issued by the State. . . . Texas also owns the designs on its license plates, including the designs that Texas adopts on the basis of proposals made by private individuals and organizations. . . . And Texas dictates the manner in which drivers may dispose of unused plates. . . .

Texas license plates are, essentially, government IDs. And issuers of ID "typically do not permit" the placement on their IDs of "message[s] with which they do not wish to be associated." *Summum*, 555 U. S., at 471. Consequently, "persons who observe" designs on IDs "routinely—and reasonably—interpret them as conveying some message on the [issuer's] behalf.". . .

Indeed, a person who displays a message on a Texas license plate likely intends to convey to the public that the State has endorsed that message. If not, the individual could simply display the message in question in larger letters on a bumper sticker right next to the plate. But the individual prefers a license plate design to the purely private speech expressed through bumper stickers. That may well be because Texas's license plate designs convey government agreement with the message displayed.

Third, Texas maintains direct control over the messages conveyed on its specialty plates. Texas law provides that the State "has sole control over the design, typeface, color, and alphanumeric pattern for all license plates.". . . The Board must approve every specialty plate design proposal before the design can appear on a Texas plate. . . . And the Board and its predecessor have actively exercised this authority. Texas asserts, and SCV concedes, that the State has rejected at least a dozen proposed designs. . . . Accordingly, like the city government in *Summum*, Texas "has 'effectively controlled' the messages [conveyed] by exercising 'final approval authority' over their selection." 555 U. S., at 473 (quoting *Johanns*, 544 U. S., at 560–561).

This final approval authority allows Texas to choose how to present itself and its constituency. Thus, Texas offers plates celebrating the many educational institutions attended by its citizens. . . . But it need not issue plates deriding schooling. Texas offers plates that pay tribute to the Texas citrus industry. . . . But it need not issue plates praising Florida's oranges as far better. And Texas offers plates that say "Fight Terrorism.". . . But it need not issue plates promoting al Qaeda.

These considerations, taken together, convince us that the specialty plates here in question are similar enough to the monuments in *Summum* to call for the same result. That is not to say that every element of our discussion in *Summum* is relevant here. For instance, in *Summum* we emphasized that monuments were "permanent" and we observed that "public parks can accommodate only a limited number of permanent monuments." 555 U. S., at 464, 470, 478. We believed that the speech at issue was government speech rather than private speech in part because we found it "hard to imagine how a public park could be opened up for the installation of permanent monuments by every person or group wishing to engage in that form of expression." Id., at 479. Here, a State could theoretically offer a much larger number of license plate designs, and those designs need not be available for time immemorial.

But those characteristics of the speech at issue in *Summum* were particularly important because the government speech at issue occurred in public parks, which are traditional public forums for "the delivery of speeches and the holding of marches and demonstrations" by private citizens. Id., at 478. By contrast, license plates are not traditional public forums for private speech.

And other features of the designs on Texas's specialty license plates indicate that the message conveyed by those designs is conveyed on behalf of the government. Texas, through its Board, selects each design featured on the State's specialty license plates. Texas presents these designs on government-mandated, government-controlled, and government-issued IDs that have traditionally been used as a medium for government speech. And it places the designs directly below the large letters identifying "TEXAS" as the issuer of the IDs. "The [designs] that are accepted, therefore, are meant to convey and have the effect of conveying a government message, and they thus constitute government speech." Id., at 472.

C

SCV believes that Texas's specialty license plate designs are not government speech, at least with respect to the designs (comprising slogans and graphics) that were initially proposed by private parties. According to SCV, the State . . . provides a forum for private speech by making license plates available to display the private parties' designs. We cannot agree.

. . . [F]orum analysis is misplaced here. Because the State is speaking on its own behalf, the First Amendment strictures that attend the various types of government-established forums do not apply.

The parties agree that Texas's specialty license plates are not a "traditional public forum," such as a street or a park. . . . "The Court has rejected the view that traditional public forum status extends beyond its historic confines." Arkansas Ed. Television Comm'n v. Forbes, 523 U. S. 666, 678 (1998). And state-issued specialty license plates lie far beyond those confines.

It is equally clear that Texas's specialty plates are neither a " 'designated public forum,' " which exists where "government property that has not traditionally been regarded as a public forum is intentionally opened up for that purpose," *Summum*, supra, at 469, nor a "limited public forum," which exists where a government has "reserv[ed a forum] for certain groups or for the discussion of certain topics," Rosenberger v. Rector and Visitors of Univ. of Va., 515 U. S. 819, 829 (1995). . . .

Texas's policies and the nature of its license plates indicate that the State did not intend its specialty license plates to serve as either a designated public forum or a limited public forum. First, the State exercises final authority over each specialty license plate design. This authority militates against a determination that Texas has created a public forum. . . . Second, Texas takes ownership of each specialty plate design, making it particularly untenable that the State intended specialty plates to serve as a forum for public discourse. Finally, Texas license plates have traditionally been used for government speech, are primarily used as a form of government ID, and bear the State's name. These features of Texas license plates indicate that Texas explicitly associates itself with the speech on its plates.

For similar reasons, we conclude that Texas's specialty license plates are not a "nonpublic for[um]," which exists "[w]here the government is acting as a proprietor, managing its internal operations." International Soc. for Krishna Consciousness, Inc. v. Lee, 505 U. S. 672, 678–679 (1992). With respect to specialty license plate designs, Texas is not simply managing government property, but instead is engaging in expressive conduct. As we have described, we reach this conclusion based on the historical context, observers' reasonable interpretation of the messages conveyed by Texas specialty plates, and the effective control that the State exerts over the design selection process. Texas's specialty license plate designs "are meant to convey and have the effect of conveying a government message." *Summum*, 555 U. S., at 472. They "constitute government speech." Ibid.

The fact that private parties take part in the design and propagation of a message does not extinguish the governmental nature of the message or transform the government's role into that of a mere forum-provider. . . . In this case, as in *Summum*, the "government entity may exercise [its] freedom to express its views" even "when it receives assistance from private sources for the purpose of delivering a government-controlled message." Id., at 468. And in this case, as in *Summum*, forum analysis is inapposite. See id., at 480.

Of course, Texas allows many more license plate designs than the city in *Summum* allowed monuments. But our holding in *Summum* was not dependent on the precise number of monuments found within the park. . . . Further, there may well be many more messages that Texas wishes to convey through its license plates than there were messages that the city in *Summum* wished to convey through its monuments. Texas's desire to communicate numerous messages does not mean that the messages conveyed are not Texas's own.

Additionally, the fact that Texas vehicle owners pay annual fees in order to display specialty license plates does not imply that the plate designs are merely a forum for private speech. . . . [T]he existence of government profit alone is insufficient to trigger forum analysis. . . . [W]e think it sufficiently clear that Texas is speaking through its specialty license plate designs, such that the existence of annual fees does not convince us that the specialty plates are a nonpublic forum.

. . .

IV

Our determination that Texas's specialty license plate designs are government speech does not mean that the designs do not also implicate the free speech rights of private persons. We have acknowledged that drivers who display a State's selected license plate designs convey the messages communicated through those designs. See Wooley v. Maynard, 430 U. S. 705, 717, n. 15, 715 (1977) (observing that a vehicle "is readily associated with its operator" and that drivers displaying license plates "use their private property as a 'mobile billboard' for the State's ideological message"). And we have recognized that the First Amendment stringently limits a State's authority to compel a private party to express a view with which the private party disagrees. See id., at 715; Hurley v. Irish-American Gay, Lesbian and Bisexual Group of Boston, Inc., 515 U. S. 557, 573 (1995); West Virginia Bd. of Ed. v. Barnette, 319 U. S. 624, 642 (1943). But here, compelled private speech is not at issue. And just as Texas cannot require SCV to convey "the State's ideological message," Wooley, supra, at 715, SCV cannot force Texas to include a Confederate battle flag on its specialty license plates.

. . .

Justice Alito, with whom the Chief Justice, Justice Scalia, and Justice Kennedy join, dissenting.

The Court's decision passes off private speech as government speech and, in doing so, establishes a precedent that threatens private speech that government finds displeasing. Under our First Amendment cases, the distinction between government speech and private speech is critical. The First Amendment "does not regulate government speech," and therefore when government speaks, it is free "to select the views that it wants to express." Pleasant Grove City v. Summum, 555 U. S. 460, 467–468 (2009). By contrast, "[i]n the realm of private speech or expression, government regulation may not favor one speaker over another." Rosenberger v. Rector and Visitors of Univ. of Va., 515 U. S. 819, 828 (1995).

Unfortunately, the Court's decision categorizes private speech as government speech and thus strips it of all First Amendment protection. The Court holds that all the privately created messages on the many specialty plates issued by the State of Texas convey a government message rather than the message of the motorist displaying the plate. Can this possibly be correct?

Here is a test. Suppose you sat by the side of a Texas highway and studied the license plates on the vehicles passing by. You would see, in addition to the standard Texas plates, an impressive array of specialty plates. (There are now more than 350 varieties.) You would likely observe plates that honor numerous colleges and universities. You might see plates bearing the name of a high school, a fraternity or sorority, the Masons, the Knights of Columbus, the Daughters of the American Revolution, a realty company, a favorite soft drink, a favorite burger restaurant, and a favorite NASCAR driver.

As you sat there watching these plates speed by, would you really think that the sentiments reflected in these specialty plates are the views of the State of Texas and not those of the owners of the cars? If a car with a plate that says "Rather Be Golfing" passed by at 8:30 am on a Monday morning, would you think: "This is the official policy of the State—better to golf than to work?" If you did your viewing at the start of the college football season and you saw Texas plates with the names of the University of Texas's out-of-state competitors in upcoming games—Notre Dame, Oklahoma State, the University of Oklahoma, Kansas State, Iowa State—would you assume that the State of Texas was officially (and perhaps treasonously) rooting for the Longhorns' opponents? . . .

The Court says that all of these messages are government speech. . . .

This capacious understanding of government speech takes a large and painful bite out of the First Amendment. . . . While all license plates unquestionably contain some government speech (e.g., the name of the State and the numbers and/or letters identifying the vehicle), the State of Texas has converted the remaining space on its specialty plates into little mobile billboards on which motorists can display their own messages. And what Texas did here was to reject one of the messages that members of a private group wanted to post on some of these little billboards because the State thought that many of its citizens would find the message offensive. That is blatant viewpoint discrimination.

If the State can do this with its little mobile billboards, could it do the same with big, stationary billboards? . . .

What if a state college or university did the same thing with a similar billboard or a campus bulletin board or dorm list serve? What if it allowed private messages that are consistent with prevailing views on campus but banned those that disturbed some students or faculty? Can there be any doubt that these examples of viewpoint discrimination would violate the First Amendment? I hope not, but the future uses of today's precedent remain to be seen.

I

A

Specialty plates like those involved in this case are a recent development. . . .

. . .

It was not until 1989 that anything that might be considered a message was featured regularly on Texas plates. The words "The Lone Star State" were added "as a means of bringing favorable recognition to Texas.". . .

Finally, in the late 1990's, license plates containing a small variety of messages, selected by the State, became available for the first time. . . .

Once the idea of specialty plates took hold, the number of varieties quickly multiplied, and today, we are told, Texas motorists can choose from more than 350 messages, including many designs proposed by nonprofit groups or by individuals and for-profit businesses through the State's third-party vendor. . . .

Drivers can select plates advertising organizations and causes like 4–H, the Boy Scouts, the American Legion, Be a Blood Donor, the Girl Scouts, Insure Texas Kids, Mothers Against Drunk Driving, Marine Mammal Recovery, Save Texas Ocelots, Share the Road, Texas Reads, Texas Realtors . . . , the Texas State Rifle Association . . . , the Texas Trophy Hunters Association, the World Wildlife Fund, the YMCA, and Young Lawyers.

There are plates for fraternities and sororities and for in-state schools, both public . . . and private. . . . An even larger number of schools from out-of-state are honored. . . .

There are political slogans, like "Come and Take It" and "Don't Tread on Me," and plates promoting the citrus industry and the "Cotton Boll." Commercial businesses can have specialty plates, too. There are plates advertising Remax . . . , Dr. Pepper . . . , and Mighty Fine Burgers.

B

[The Board's statement rejecting the SCV application based on the offensiveness of the Confederate flag portion of the design also] saw "a compelling public interest in protecting a conspicuous mechanism for identification, such as a license plate, from degrading into a possible public safety issue.". . . And it thought that the public interest required rejection of the plate design because the controversy surrounding the plate was so great that "the design could distract or disturb some drivers to the point of being unreasonably dangerous."

At the same meeting, the Board approved a Buffalo Soldiers plate design by a 5-to-3 vote. Proceeds from fees paid by motorists who select that plate benefit the Buffalo Soldier National Museum in Houston, which is "dedicated primarily to preserving the legacy and honor of the African American soldier.". . . The original Buffalo Soldiers fought with distinction in the Indian Wars, but the "Buffalo Soldiers" plate was opposed by some Native Americans. One leader commented that he felt " 'the same way about the Buffalo Soldiers' " as African-Americans felt about the Confederate flag. . . .

II

A

Relying almost entirely on one precedent—Pleasant Grove City v. Summum, 555 U. S. 460—the Court holds that messages that private groups succeed in placing on Texas license plates are government messages. The Court badly misunderstands *Summum*.

. . . [When w]e held that the monuments represented government speech[,] we identified several important factors that led to this conclusion.

First, governments have long used monuments as a means of expressing a government message. . . .

Second, there is no history of landowners allowing their property to be used by third parties as the site of large permanent monuments that do not express messages that the landowners wish to convey. . . . We were not presented in *Summum* with any examples of public parks that had been thrown open for private groups or individuals to put up whatever monuments they desired.

Third, spatial limitations played a prominent part in our analysis. . . . Because only a limited number of monuments can be built in any given space, governments do not allow their parks to be cluttered with monuments that do not serve a government purpose, a point well understood by those who visit parks and view the monuments they contain.

These characteristics, which rendered public monuments government speech in *Summum*, are not present in Texas's specialty plate program.

B

1

I begin with history. As we said in *Summum*, governments have used monuments since time immemorial to express important government messages, and there is no history of governments giving equal space to those wishing to express dissenting views. . . . Governments have always used public monuments to express a government message, and members of the public understand this.

The history of messages on license plates is quite different. After the beginning of motor vehicle registration in 1917, more than 70 years passed before the proliferation of specialty plates in Texas. It was not until the 1990's that motorists were allowed to choose from among 10 messages. . . .

Up to this point, the words on the Texas plates can be considered government speech. The messages were created by the State, and they plausibly promoted state programs. But when, at some point within the last 20 years or so, the State began to allow private entities to secure plates conveying their own messages, Texas crossed the line.

. . .

. . . [P]lates that are essentially commissioned by private entities (at a cost that exceeds $8,000) and that express a message chosen by those entities are very different—and quite new. Unlike in *Summum*, history here does not suggest that the messages at issue are government speech.

2

The Texas specialty plate program also does not exhibit the "selective receptivity" present in *Summum*. To the contrary, Texas's program is not selective by design. The Board's chairman, who is charged with approving designs, explained that the program's purpose is "to encourage private plates" in order to "generate additional revenue for the state.". . . . And most of the time, the Board "base[s] [its] decisions on rules that primarily deal with reflectivity and readability.". . .

. . .

. . . Texas does not take care to approve only those proposed plates that convey messages that the State supports. Instead, it proclaims that it is open to all private messages—except those, like the SCV plate, that would offend some who viewed them.

The Court believes that messages on privately created plates are government speech because motorists want a seal of state approval for their messages and therefore prefer plates over bumper stickers. This is dangerous reasoning. There is a big difference between government speech (that is, speech by the government in furtherance of its programs) and governmental blessing (or condemnation) of private speech. Many private speakers in a forum would welcome a sign of government approval. But in the realm of private speech, government regulation may not favor one viewpoint over another. *Rosenberger, supra*, at 828.

3

A final factor that was important in *Summum* was space. A park can accommodate only so many permanent monuments. Often large and made of stone, monuments can last for centuries and are difficult to move. License plates, on the other hand, are small, light, mobile, and designed to last for only a relatively brief time. The only absolute limit on the number of specialty plates that a State could issue is the number of registered vehicles. The variety of available plates is limitless, too. Today Texas offers more than 350 varieties. In 10 years, might it be 3,500?

In sum, the Texas specialty plate program has none of the factors that were critical in *Summum*, and the Texas program exhibits a very important characteristic that was missing in that case: Individuals who want to display a Texas specialty plate, instead of the standard plate, must pay an increased annual registration fee. . . . How many groups or individuals would clamor to pay $8,000 (the cost of the deposit required to create a new plate) in order to broadcast the government's message as opposed to their own? . . . The fees Texas collects pay for much more than merely the administration of the program.

States have not adopted specialty license plate programs like Texas's because they are now bursting with things they want to say on their license plates. Those programs were adopted because they bring in money. . . .

Texas has space available on millions of little mobile billboards. And Texas, in effect, sells that space to those who wish to use it to express a personal message—provided only that the message does not express a viewpoint that the State finds unacceptable. That is not government speech; it is the regulation of private speech.

III

What Texas has done by selling space on its license plates is to create what we have called a limited public forum. It has allowed state property (i.e., motor vehicle license plates) to be used by private speakers according to rules that the State prescribes. . . . Under the First Amendment, however, those rules cannot discriminate on the basis of viewpoint. . . . But that is exactly what Texas did here. . . .

The Confederate battle flag is a controversial symbol. To the Texas Sons of Confederate Veterans, it is said to evoke the memory of their ancestors and other soldiers who fought for the South in the Civil War. . . . To others, it symbolizes slavery, segregation, and hatred. Whatever it means to motorists who display that symbol and to those who see it, the flag expresses a viewpoint. The Board rejected the plate design because it concluded that many Texans would find the flag symbol offensive. That was pure viewpoint discrimination.

. . .

The Board's decision cannot be saved by its suggestion that the plate, if allowed, "could distract or disturb some drivers to the point of being unreasonably dangerous.". . . This rationale cannot withstand strict scrutiny. Other States allow specialty plates with the Confederate Battle Flag, and Texas has not pointed to evidence that these plates have led to incidents of road rage or accidents. Texas does not ban bumper stickers bearing the image of the Confederate battle flag. Nor does it ban any of the many other bumper stickers that convey political messages and other messages that are capable of exciting the ire of those who loathe the ideas they express. . . .

. . .

Page 1433. Add at end of section:

Agency for International Development v. Alliance for Open Society, 570 U.S. ___, 133 S.Ct. 2321 (2013). Congress passed the United States Leadership Against HIV/AIDS, Tuberculosis, and Malaria Act of 2003, in part to combat the spread of HIV/AIDS around the world. To assist in its comprehensive global strategy, Congress funded nongovernmental organizations on two conditions: none of the funding "may be used to promote or advocate the legalization or practice of prostitution or sex trafficking[,]" 22 U.S.C. § 7631(e), and no funds may be used by an organization "that does not have a policy explicitly opposing prostitution and sex trafficking[,]" § 7631(f). In a challenge to the latter condition, known as the Policy Requirement, brought by a group of domestic organizations that receive substantial private funding as well as billions in federal funding under the Leadership Act, the Court ruled that by conditioning federal funding on "the affirmation of a belief that by its nature cannot be confined within the scope of the Government program[,]" the Policy Requirement violated the First Amendment.

Chief Justice Roberts's majority opinion first noted that "[w]ere it enacted as a direct regulation of speech, the Policy Requirement would plainly violate the First Amendment. The question is whether the Government may nonetheless impose that requirement as a condition on the receipt of federal funds." Answering that question in the negative, the Chief Justice wrote in pertinent part:

" . . . In some cases, a funding condition can result in an unconstitutional burden on First Amendment rights. . . .

"The dissent thinks that can only be true when the condition is not relevant to the objectives of the program (although it has its doubts about that), or when the condition is actually coercive, in the sense of an offer that cannot be refused. Our precedents, however, are not so limited. In the present context, the relevant distinction that has emerged from our cases is between conditions that define the limits of the government spending program—those that specify the activities Congress wants to subsidize—and conditions that seek to leverage funding to regulate speech outside the contours of the program itself. The line is hardly clear, in part because the definition of a particular program can always be manipulated to subsume the challenged condition. We have held, however, that 'Congress cannot recast a condition on funding as a mere definition of its program in every case, lest the First Amendment be reduced to a simple semantic exercise.' Legal Services Corporation v. Velazquez, 531 U.S. 533, 547 (2001)."

Although "the distinction . . . between conditions that define the federal program and those that reach outside it . . . is not always self-evident[,] . . . [h]ere we are confident that the Policy Requirement falls on the unconstitutional side of the line." The first, unchallenged condition "itself ensures that federal funds will not be used for the prohibited purposes." Thus:

"The Policy Requirement must be doing something more—and it is. The dissent views the Requirement as simply a selection criterion by which the Government identifies organizations 'who believe in its ideas to carry them to fruition.' . . . [But] its effects go beyond selection. The Policy Requirement is an ongoing condition on recipients' speech and activities, a ground for terminating a grant after selection is complete. . . . In any event, as the Government acknowledges, it is not simply seeking organizations that oppose prostitution. . . . Rather, it explains, 'Congress has expressed its purpose "to eradicate" prostitution and sex trafficking, . . . and it wants recipients *to adopt* a similar stance.' Brief for Petitioners 32 (emphasis added). This case is not about the Government's ability to enlist the assistance of those with whom it already agrees. It is about compelling a grant recipient to adopt a particular belief as a condition of funding.

"By demanding that funding recipients adopt—as their own—the Government's view on an issue of public concern, the condition by its very nature affects 'protected conduct outside the scope of the federally funded program.' *Rust*, . . . A recipient cannot avow the belief dictated by the Policy Requirement when spending Leadership Act funds, and then turn around and assert a contrary belief, or claim neutrality, when participating in activities on its own time and dime. By requiring recipients to profess a specific belief, the Policy Requirement goes beyond defining the limits of the federally funded program to defining the recipient. . . ."

Finally, "the Government contends that 'if organizations awarded federal funds to implement Leadership Act programs could at the same time promote or affirmatively condone prostitution or sex trafficking, whether using public *or private* funds, it would undermine the government's program and confuse its message opposing prostitution and sex trafficking.' Brief for Petitioners 37 (emphasis added). But the Policy Requirement goes beyond preventing recipients from using private funds in a way that would undermine the federal program. It requires them to pledge allegiance to the Government's policy of eradicating prostitution. As to that, we cannot improve upon what Justice Jackson wrote for the Court 70 years ago: 'If there is any fixed star in our constitutional constellation, it is that no official, high or petty, can prescribe what shall be orthodox in politics, nationalism, religion, or other matters of opinion or force citizens to confess by word or act their faith therein.' [*West Virginia State Board of Education v.*] *Barnette*, 319 U.S., at 642."

The dissent by Justice Scalia, joined by Justice Thomas, viewed the Policy Requirement as "nothing more than a means of selecting suitable agents to implement the Government's chosen strategy to eradicate HIV/AIDS"—which would be "perfectly permissible." Moreover, he questioned what the Court's "constitutional line between conditions that operate *inside* a spending program and those that control speech *outside* of it . . . has to do with the First Amendment." He found the situation here "vastly different" than that in *Rust*: "Elimination of prostitution *is* an objective of the HIV/AIDS program, and *any* promotion of prostitution—whether made inside or outside the program—*does* harm the program." Furthermore, "the most obvious manner in which the admission to a program of an ideological opponent can frustrate the purpose of the program is by freeing up the opponent's funds for use in its ideological opposition. . . . Money is fungible. The economic reality is that when NGOs can conduct their AIDS work on the Government's dime, they can expend greater resources on policies that undercut the Leadership Act. The Government need not establish by record evidence that this will happen. To make it a valid consideration in determining participation in federal programs, it suffices that this is a real and obvious risk."

Nor did he think "the unconstitutional conditions doctrine" was of any help: "There is no case of ours in which a condition that is relevant to a statute's valid purpose and that is not in itself unconstitutional (*e.g.,* a religious-affiliation condition that violates the Establishment Clause) has been held to violate the doctrine. Moreover, . . . the contention that the condition here 'coerces' respondents' speech is on its face implausible." In "the circumstances of this case, 'compell[ing] *as a condition* of federal funding the affirmation of a belief,' *ante,* (emphasis mine), is no compulsion at all. It is the reasonable price of admission to a limited government-spending program that each organization remains free to accept or reject."

CHAPTER 15

PROTECTION OF PENUMBRAL FIRST AMENDMENT RIGHTS

2. COMPELLED AFFIRMATION OF BELIEF

Page 1452. Add at end of section 2:

Agency for International Development v. Alliance for Open Society, 570 U.S. ___, 133 S.Ct. 2321 (2013).

[The report of this case appears supra, page 239.]

3. FREEDOM OF ASSOCIATION

D. COMPULSORY MEMBERSHIP AND FUNDING FOR ASSOCIATION SPEECH

Page 1471. Add the following before United States v. United Foods, Inc.:

Harris v. Quinn, 573 U.S. ___, 134 S.Ct. 2618 (2014). Under the Illinois Home Services Program, Medicaid recipients are permitted to make use of "personal assistants" (PAs), who provide homecare services. Under Illinois law, the homecare recipients (designated "customers") control most aspects of the employment relationship, including the hiring, firing, training, supervising, and disciplining of PAs; they also define a PA's duties by proposing a "Service Plan." Other than compensating PAs, the State's involvement in employment matters is minimal. Its employer status was created by executive order, and later codified by the legislature, solely to permit PAs to join a labor union and engage in collective bargaining under Illinois' Public Labor Relations Act (PLRA). Pursuant to this scheme, Service Employees International Union Healthcare Illinois & Indiana (SEIU–HII) was designated as the exclusive union representative for Rehabilitation Program employees. The union entered into collective-bargaining agreements with the State that contained an agency-fee provision requiring all bargaining unit members who do not wish to join the union to pay the union a fee for the cost tied to the collective-bargaining process. A group of Rehabilitation Program PAs brought a class action against SEIU–HII and other respondents claiming that the PLRA violated the First Amendment insofar as it authorized the agency-fee provision. The lower courts rejected the claim, concluding that the PAs were state employees within the meaning of *Abood* v. *Detroit Bd. of Ed.*, 431 U.S. 209 (1977), and thus could be required to pay fees related to the cost of the collective-bargaining process. The Supreme Court reversed, 5–4.

Justice Alito's opinion for the Court, joined by Chief Justice Roberts and Justices Scalia, Kennedy and Thomas, traced the path by which the Court reached its result in *Abood*, starting with *Railway Employees* v. *Hanson*, 351 U.S. 225 (1956). The Court noted that "[t]he First Amendment analysis in *Hanson* was thin, and the Court's resulting First Amendment holding was narrow. As the Court later noted, 'all that was held in *Hanson* was that [the federal statute at issue there] was constitutional in its *bare authorization* of union-shop contracts requiring workers to give "financial support" to unions legally authorized to act as their collective bargaining agents.' "

The Court continued:

"Five years later, [in *Machinists* v. *Street*, 367 U.S. 740, 750 (1961)], the Court considered another case in which workers objected to a union shop. Employees of the Southern Railway System raised a First Amendment challenge, contending that a substantial part of the money that they were required to pay to the union was used to support political candidates and causes with which they disagreed. A Georgia court enjoined the enforcement of the union-shop provision and entered judgment for the dissenting employees in the amount of the payments that they had been forced to make to the union. The Georgia Supreme Court affirmed.

"Reviewing the State Supreme Court's decision, this Court recognized that the case presented constitutional questions 'of the utmost gravity,' but the Court found it unnecessary to reach those questions. Instead, the Court construed the [same federal law] 'as not vesting the unions with unlimited power to spend exacted money.' . . . Specifically, the Court held, the Act 'is to be construed to deny the unions, over an employee's objection, the power to use his exacted funds to support political causes which he opposes.' . . .

" . . .

"This brings us to *Abood*, which, unlike *Hanson* and *Street*, involved a public-sector collective-bargaining agreement. The Detroit Federation of Teachers served 'as the exclusive representative of teachers employed by the Detroit Board of Education.' . . . The collective-bargaining agreement between the union and the board contained an agency-shop clause requiring every teacher to 'pay the Union a service charge equal to the regular dues required of Union members.' . . . A putative class of teachers sued to invalidate this clause. Asserting that 'they opposed collective bargaining in the public sector,' the plaintiffs argued that 'a substantial part' of their dues would be used to fund union 'activities and programs which are economic, political, professional, scientific and religious in nature of which Plaintiffs do not approve, and in which they will have no voice.' . . .

"This Court treated the First Amendment issue as largely settled by *Hanson* and *Street*. . . .

" . . .

"The *Abood* Court's analysis is questionable on several grounds. Some of these were noted or apparent at or before the time of the decision, but several have become more evident and troubling in the years since then.

"The *Abood* Court seriously erred in treating *Hanson* and *Street* as having all but decided the constitutionality of compulsory payments to a public-sector union. As we have explained, *Street* was not a constitutional decision at all, and *Hanson* disposed of the critical question in a single, unsupported sentence that its author essentially abandoned a few years later. Surely a First Amendment issue of this importance deserved better treatment.

"The *Abood* Court fundamentally misunderstood the holding in *Hanson*, which was really quite narrow. As the Court made clear in *Street*, 'all that was held in *Hanson* was that [the Act in question] was constitutional *in its bare authorization* of union-shop contracts requiring workers to give financial support to unions legally authorized to act as their collective bargaining agents.' . . . In *Abood*, on the other hand, the State of Michigan did more than simply *authorize* the imposition of an agency fee. A state instrumentality, the Detroit Board of Education, actually *imposed* that fee. This presented a very different question.

"*Abood* failed to appreciate the difference between the core union speech involuntarily subsidized by dissenting public-sector employees and the core union speech involuntarily funded by their counterparts in the private sector. In the public sector, core issues such as wages, pensions, and benefits are important political issues, but that is generally not so in the private sector. In the years since *Abood*, as state and local expenditures on employee wages and benefits have mushroomed, the importance of the difference between bargaining in the public and private sectors has been driven home.

"*Abood* failed to appreciate the conceptual difficulty of distinguishing in public-sector cases between union expenditures that are made for collective-bargaining purposes and those that are made to achieve political ends. In the private sector, the line is easier to see. Collective bargaining concerns the union's dealings with the employer; political advocacy and lobbying are directed at the government. But in the public sector, both collective bargaining and political advocacy and lobbying are directed at the government.

"*Abood* does not seem to have anticipated the magnitude of the practical administrative problems that would result in attempting to classify public-sector union expenditures as either 'chargeable' (in *Abood*'s terms, expenditures for 'collective-bargaining, contract administration, and grievance-adjustment purposes,') or nonchargeable (*i.e.*, expenditures for political or ideological purposes). . . .

"*Abood* likewise did not foresee the practical problems that would face objecting nonmembers. . . .

"Finally, a critical pillar of the *Abood* Court's analysis rests on an unsupported empirical assumption, namely, that the principle of exclusive representation in the public sector is dependent on a union or agency shop. . . . . [T]his assumption is unwarranted. . . .

"Despite all this, the State of Illinois now asks us to approve a very substantial expansion of *Abood*'s reach. *Abood* involved full-fledged public employees, but in this case, the status of the personal assistants is much different. The Illinois Legislature has taken pains to specify that personal assistants are public employees for one purpose only: collective bargaining. For all other purposes, Illinois regards the personal assistants as private sector employees. . . .

" . . .

"Because of *Abood*'s questionable foundations, and because the personal assistants are quite different from full-fledged public employees, we refuse to extend *Abood* to the new situation now before us.[29] *Abood* itself has clear boundaries; it applies to public employees. Extending those boundaries to encompass partial-public employees, quasi-public employees, or simply private employees would invite problems. Consider a continuum, ranging, on the one hand, from full-fledged state employees to, on the other hand, individuals who follow a common calling and benefit from advocacy or lobbying conducted by a group to which they do not belong and pay no dues. A State may not force every person who benefits from this group's efforts to make payments to the group. . . . But what if regulation of this group is increased? What if the Federal Government or a State begins to provide or increases subsidies in this area? At what point, short of the point at which the individuals in question become full-fledged state employees, should *Abood* apply?

" . . .

"Because *Abood* is not controlling, we must analyze the constitutionality of the payments compelled by Illinois law under generally applicable First Amendment standards. As we explained in *Knox,* '[t]he government may not prohibit the dissemination of ideas that it disfavors, nor compel the endorsement of ideas that it approves.' . . . And 'compelled funding of the speech of other private speakers or groups' presents the same dangers as compelled speech. . . . As a result, we explained in *Knox* that an agency-fee provision imposes a 'significant impingement on First Amendment rights,' and this cannot be tolerated unless it passes 'exacting First Amendment scrutiny.' . . .

" . . .

"For present purposes, . . . no fine parsing of levels of First Amendment scrutiny is needed because the agency fee provision here cannot satisfy even the test used in *Knox*. Specifically, this provision does not serve a 'compelling state interes[t] . . . that cannot be achieved through means significantly less restrictive of associational freedoms.' . . . Respondents contend that the agency-fee provision in this case furthers several important interests, but none is sufficient."

Justice Kagan filed a dissenting opinion, in which Justices Ginsburg, Breyer and Sotomayor joined.

---

[29] It is therefore unnecessary for us to reach petitioners' argument that *Abood* should be overruled, and the dissent's extended discussion of *stare decisis* is beside the point. . . .

4. APPLICATION OF THE FIRST AMENDMENT TO GOVERNMENT REGULATION OF ELECTIONS

B. POLITICAL FUNDRAISING AND EXPENDITURES

Page 1507. Add the following before Citizens United v. Federal Election Commission:

Aggregate Contribution Limits

McCutcheon v. Federal Election Commission, 572 U.S. ___, 134 S.Ct. 1434, 188 L.Ed.2d 468 (2014). The Federal Election Campaign Act of 1971 (FECA), as amended by the Bipartisan Campaign Finance Reform Act of 2002 (BCRA), enacts two types of limits on campaign contributions. So-called base limits regulate how much money a donor may contribute to any particular candidate or political committee. For example, in the 2013–14 election cycle, federal law created a limit of $2,600 per election for donations to any single candidate and a limit of $32,400 for donations to a national party committee. So-called aggregate limits restrict how much money a donor may give to all candidates combined and (separately) to all committees combined. For the 2013–14 year, the limit on donations to all federal candidates combined was $48,600, and the limit on donations to all committees was $74,600. Plaintiff was an individual who in 2011–2012 donated to 16 different federal candidates and who wanted to contribute to an additional 12 candidates but was prevented from doing so by the aggregate candidate contribution limits in place for that cycle. (He also wished to donate more to political committees than he was permitted that year.) Along with the Republican National Committee (which wished to receive more contributions), he filed suit to challenge the aggregate contribution limits. By a 5–4 vote, the Court sustained the challenge. Chief Justice Roberts announced the judgment of the Court and wrote an opinion in which Justices Scalia, Kennedy and Alito joined. The Chief Justice began his analysis with a summary of the standards of review employed in, and the issues decided by, *Buckley*: "*Buckley* presented this Court with its first opportunity to evaluate the constitutionality of the original contribution and expenditure limits set forth in FECA. FECA imposed a $1,000 per election base limit on contributions from an individual to a federal candidate. It also imposed a $25,000 per year aggregate limit on all contributions from an individual to candidates or political committees. On the expenditures side, FECA imposed limits on both independent expenditures and candidates' overall campaign expenditures."

"*Buckley* recognized that 'contribution and expenditure limitations operate in an area of the most fundamental First Amendment activities.' . . . But it distinguished expenditure limits from contribution limits based on the degree to which each encroaches upon protected First Amendment interests. Expenditure limits, the Court explained, 'necessarily reduce[ ] the quantity of expression by restricting the number of issues discussed, the depth of their exploration, and the size of the audience reached.' . . . The Court thus subjected expenditure limits to 'the exacting scrutiny applicable to limitations on core

First Amendment rights of political expression.' . . . Under exacting scrutiny, the Government may regulate protected speech only if such regulation promotes a compelling interest and is the least restrictive means to further the articulated interest.

"By contrast, the Court concluded that contribution limits impose a lesser restraint on political speech because they 'permit[ ] the symbolic expression of support evidenced by a contribution but do[ ] not in any way infringe the contributor's freedom to discuss candidates and issues.' . . . As a result, the Court focused on the effect of the contribution limits on the freedom of political association and applied a lesser but still 'rigorous standard of review.' . . . Under that standard, '[e]ven a "significant interference" with protected rights of political association may be sustained if the State demonstrates a sufficiently important interest and employs means closely drawn to avoid unnecessary abridgement of associational freedoms.' . . .

"The primary purpose of FECA was to limit *quid pro quo* corruption and its appearance; that purpose satisfied the requirement of a 'sufficiently important' governmental interest. . . . As for the 'closely drawn' component, *Buckley* concluded that the $1,000 base limit 'focuses precisely on the problem of large campaign contributions . . . while leaving persons free to engage in independent political expression, to associate actively through volunteering their services, and to assist to a limited but nonetheless substantial extent in supporting candidates and committees with financial resources.' . . . The Court therefore upheld the $1,000 base limit under the 'closely drawn' test. . . .

      " . . .

"Finally, in one paragraph of its 139-page opinion, the Court turned to the $25,000 aggregate limit under FECA. As a preliminary matter, it noted that the constitutionality of the aggregate limit 'ha[d] not been separately addressed at length by the parties.' . . . Then, in three sentences, the Court disposed of any constitutional objections to the aggregate limit that the challengers might have had. . . .

"The parties and amici spend significant energy debating whether the line that *Buckley* drew between contributions and expenditures should remain the law. Notwithstanding the robust debate, we see no need in this case to revisit *Buckley*'s distinction between contributions and expenditures and the corollary distinction in the applicable standards of review. *Buckley* held that the Government's interest in preventing *quid pro quo* corruption or its appearance was 'sufficiently important,' . . . ; we have elsewhere stated that the same interest may properly be labeled 'compelling,' . . . so that the interest would satisfy even strict scrutiny. Moreover, regardless whether we apply strict scrutiny or *Buckley*'s 'closely drawn' test, we must assess the fit between the stated governmental objective and the means selected to achieve that objective. Or to put it another way, if a law that restricts political speech does not 'avoid unnecessary abridgement' of First Amendment rights, . . . it cannot survive 'rigorous' review.

"Because we find a substantial mismatch between the Government's stated objective and the means selected to achieve it, the aggregate limits fail even under the 'closely drawn' test. We therefore need not parse the differences between the two standards in this case.

"*Buckley* treated the constitutionality of the $25,000 aggregate limit as contingent upon that limit's ability to prevent circumvention of the $1,000 base limit, describing the aggregate limit as 'no more than a corollary' base limit. . . . The Court determined that circumvention could occur when an individual legally contributes 'massive amounts of money to a particular candidate through the use of unearmarked contributions' to entities that are themselves likely to contribute to the candidate. . . . For that reason, the Court upheld the $25,000 aggregate limit.

"Although *Buckley* provides some guidance, we think that its ultimate conclusion about the constitutionality of the aggregate limit in place under FECA does not control here. *Buckley* spent a total of three sentences analyzing that limit; in fact, the opinion pointed out that the constitutionality of the aggregate limit 'ha[d] not been separately addressed at length by the parties.' . . . We are now asked to address appellants' direct challenge to the aggregate limits in place under BCRA. BCRA is a different statutory regime, and the aggregate limits it imposes operate against a distinct legal backdrop.

"Most notably, statutory safeguards against circumvention have been considerably strengthened since *Buckley* was decided, through both statutory additions and the introduction of a comprehensive regulatory scheme. With more targeted anticircumvention measures in place today, the indiscriminate aggregate limits under BCRA appear particularly heavy-handed.

" . . .

"*Buckley* acknowledged that aggregate limits at least diminish an individual's right of political association. As the Court explained, the 'overall $25,000 ceiling does impose an ultimate restriction upon the number of candidates and committees with which an individual may associate himself by means of financial support.' . . . But the Court characterized that restriction as a 'quite modest restraint upon protected political activity.' . . . We cannot agree with that characterization. An aggregate limit on *how many* candidates and committees an individual may support through contributions is not a 'modest restraint' at all. The Government may no more restrict how many candidates or causes a donor may support than it may tell a newspaper how many candidates it may endorse.

"To put it in the simplest terms, the aggregate limits prohibit an individual from fully contributing to the primary and general election campaigns of ten or more candidates, even if all contributions fall within the base limits Congress views as adequate to protect against corruption. The individual may give up to $5,200 each to nine candidates, but the aggregate limits constitute an outright ban on further contributions to any other candidate (beyond the additional $1,800 that may be spent before reaching the $48,600 aggregate limit). At that point, the limits deny the individual all ability to exercise his expressive and associational rights by contributing to someone who will advocate for his policy preferences. A donor must limit the number of candidates he supports, and may have to choose which of several policy concerns he will advance—clear First Amendment harms that the dissent never acknowledges.

"It is no answer to say that the individual can simply contribute less money to more people. To require one person to contribute at lower levels than others because he wants to support more candidates or causes is to impose a special burden on broader participation in the democratic process. And as we have recently admonished, the Government may not penalize an individual for 'robustly exercis[ing]' his First Amendment rights. . . .

" . . .

"With the significant First Amendment costs for individual citizens in mind, we turn to the governmental interests asserted in this case. This Court has identified only one legitimate governmental interest for restricting campaign finances: preventing corruption or the appearance of corruption. We have consistently rejected attempts to suppress campaign speech based on other legislative objectives. No matter how desirable it may seem, it is not an acceptable governmental objective to 'level the playing field,' or to 'level electoral opportunities,' or to 'equaliz[e] the financial resources of candidates.' The First Amendment prohibits such legislative attempts to 'fine-tun[e]' the electoral process, no matter how well intentioned. . . .

"As we framed the relevant principle in *Buckley*, 'the concept that government may restrict the speech of some elements of our society in order to enhance the relative voice of others is wholly foreign to the First Amendment.' . . . The dissent's suggestion that *Buckley* supports the opposite proposition simply ignores what *Buckley* actually said on the matter.

"Moreover, while preventing corruption or its appearance is a legitimate objective, Congress may target only a specific type of corruption—'*quid pro quo*' corruption. As *Buckley* explained, Congress may permissibly seek to rein in 'large contributions [that] are given to secure a political *quid pro quo* from current and potential office holders.' . . . In addition to 'actual *quid pro quo* arrangements,' Congress may permissibly limit 'the appearance of corruption stemming from public awareness of the opportunities for abuse inherent in a regime of large individual financial contributions' to particular candidates. . . .

"Spending large sums of money in connection with elections, but not in connection with an effort to control the exercise of an officeholder's official duties, does not give rise to such *quid pro quo* corruption. Nor does the possibility that an individual who spends large sums may garner 'influence over or access to' elected officials or political parties. And because the Government's interest in preventing the appearance of corruption is equally confined to the appearance of *quid pro quo* corruption, the Government may not seek to limit the appearance of mere influence or access.

"The dissent advocates a broader conception of corruption, and would apply the label to any individual contributions above limits deemed necessary to protect 'collective speech.' . . . Thus, under the dissent's view, it is perfectly fine to contribute $5,200 to nine candidates but somehow corrupt to give the same amount to a tenth.

" . . .

" 'When the Government restricts speech, the Government bears the burden of proving the constitutionality of its actions.' . . . Here, the Government seeks to carry that burden by arguing that the aggregate limits further the permissible objective of preventing *quid pro quo* corruption.

"The difficulty is that once the aggregate limits kick in, they ban all contributions of *any* amount. But Congress's selection of a $5,200 base limit indicates its belief that contributions of that amount or less do not create a cognizable risk of corruption. If there is no corruption concern in giving nine candidates up to $5,200 each, it is difficult to understand how a tenth candidate can be regarded as corruptible if given $1,801, and all others corruptible if given a dime. And if there is no risk that additional candidates will be corrupted by donations of up to $5,200, then the Government must defend the aggregate limits by demonstrating that they prevent circumvention of the base limits.

"The problem is that they do not serve that function in any meaningful way. In light of the various statutes and regulations currently in effect, *Buckley*'s fear that an individual might 'contribute massive amounts of money to a particular candidate through the use of unearmarked contributions' to entities likely to support the candidate, . . . , is far too speculative. And— importantly—we 'have never accepted mere conjecture as adequate to carry a First Amendment burden.' " . . .

Justice Thomas concurred, reiterating his view that *Buckley* should be overruled and that contribution and expenditure limitations should be subjected to strict scrutiny, under which the provision at issue would not survive.

Justice Breyer, joined by Justices Ginsburg, Sotomayor and Kagan, dissented. He argued as follows: "The plurality's conclusion rests upon three separate but related claims. Each is fatally flawed. First, the plurality says that given the base limits on contributions to candidates and political committees, aggregate limits do not further any independent governmental objective worthy of protection. And that is because, given the base limits, '[s]pending large sums of money in connection with elections' does not 'give rise to . . . corruption.' . . . In making this argument, the plurality relies heavily upon a narrow definition of 'corruption' that excludes efforts to obtain 'influence over or access to elected officials or political parties.' . . .

"Second, the plurality assesses the instrumental objective of the aggregate limits, namely, safeguarding the base limits. It finds that they 'do not serve that function in any meaningful way.' . . . That is because, even without the aggregate limits, the possibilities for circumventing the base limits are 'implausible' and 'divorced from reality.' . . .

"Third, the plurality says the aggregate limits are not a 'reasonable" policy tool. . . . Rather, they are 'poorly tailored to the Government's interest in preventing circumvention of the base limits.' . . . The plurality imagines several alternative regulations that it says might just as effectively thwart circumvention. Accordingly, it finds, the aggregate caps are out of 'proportion to the [anticorruption] interest served.' . . .

"The plurality's first claim—that large aggregate contributions do not 'give rise' to 'corruption'—is plausible only because the plurality defines 'corruption' too narrowly. . . .

"   . . .

"[As to the plurality's second claim, the] plurality is wrong. Here, as in *Buckley*, in the absence of limits on aggregate political contributions, donors can and likely will find ways to channel millions of dollars to parties and to individual candidates, producing precisely the kind of 'corruption' or 'appearance of corruption' that previously led the Court to hold aggregate limits constitutional. . . . Those opportunities for circumvention will also produce the type of corruption that concerns the plurality today. The methods for using today's opinion to evade the law's individual contribution limits are complex, but they are well known, or will become well known, to party fundraisers.

"   . . .

"[Finally, the] plurality concludes that even if circumvention were a threat, the aggregate limits are 'poorly tailored' to address it. . . . The First Amendment requires 'a fit that is . . . reasonable,' . . . and there is no such 'fit' here because there are several alternative ways Congress could prevent evasion of the base limits. . . . For instance, the plurality posits, Congress (or the FEC) could 'tighten . . . transfer rules' . . . ; it could require 'contributions above the current aggregate limits to be deposited into segregated, nontransferable accounts and spent only by their recipients' . . . ; it could define 'how many candidates a PAC must support in order to ensure that a substantial portion of a donor's contribution is not rerouted to a certain candidate' . . . ; or it could prohibit 'donors who have contributed the current maximum sums from further contributing to political committees that have indicated they will support candidates to whom the donor has already contributed.' . . . The plurality, however, does not show, or try to show, that these hypothetical alternatives could effectively replace aggregate contribution limits.". . .

Page 1557. Add the following after Randall v. Sorrell:

Williams-Yulee v. Florida Bar, 575 U.S. ___, 135 S.Ct. 1656, 191 L.Ed.2d 570 (2015). Florida adopted in its Code of Judicial Conduct Canon 7C (1), which states that judicial candidates "shall not personally solicit campaign funds, . . . but may establish committees of responsible persons" to raise money for election campaigns. The Florida Bar disciplined a candidate for judicial office for violating a Florida Bar Rule that required adherence to Canon 7C (1) after she posted online and mailed a solicitation for contributions to her campaign. By a 5–4 vote, the Court affirmed a Florida Supreme Court ruling upholding the imposition of sanctions against her. Four Justices (Chief Justice

Roberts writing for himself and Justices Breyer, Sotomayor and Kagan) found strict scrutiny applicable because the Florida rule was content-based, but then found that Florida's rule was narrowly tailored to the compelling interest in preserving public confidence in the integrity of the judiciary. Justice Ginsburg agreed that strict scrutiny was satisfied, but wrote separately to make clear she would not have necessarily applied strict scrutiny in this setting. Those five Justices found no fatal underinclusiveness in Canon 7C (1), even though a candidate could solicit via a campaign committee, and could also thank (and therefore know the identity of) donors, because the State "has reasonably concluded that solicitation by the candidate personally creates a categorically different and more severe risk of undermining public confidence. . . ."

The majority sought to distinguish Republican Party of Minnesota v. White, 536 U.S. 765 (2002), which struck down a Minnesota ethics rule that prohibited candidates for elective judicial office from "announc[ing] [their] views on disputed legal or political issues," despite Minnesota's assertion that it needed to regulate candidate speech to ensure that the public believes that judges are sufficiently open-minded about important matters that might come before them. In *Williams-Yulee*, Justice Scalia wrote a dissent joined by Justice Thomas, and Justices Kennedy and Alito each wrote a separate dissent.

5. SPEECH AND ASSOCIATION RIGHTS OF GOVERNMENT EMPLOYEES

Page 1570. Add the following before Borough of Duryea v. Guarnieri:

Lane v. Franks, 573 U.S. ___, 134 S.Ct. 2369 (2014). Lane, who served as the Director of a Community Intensive Training for Youth (CITY) program at an Alabama Community College, conducted an audit of the program's expenses in which he discovered that Schmitz, an Alabama legislator on CITY's payroll, had not been reporting for work. When federal authorities indicted Schmitz on mail fraud charges concerning CITY, a program receiving federal funds, Lane was subpoenaed and testified about what he found in the audit. Lane was then fired by the head of the Community College, and filed suit claiming his termination was in retaliation for his having given testimony and violated the First Amendment. The Court unanimously reversed a lower court holding that Lane's testimony was not entitled to First Amendment protection. Applying the *Garcetti* framework, Justice Sotomayor's opinion first found that "[t]ruthful testimony under oath by a public employee outside the scope of his ordinary job duties is speech as a citizen for First Amendment purposes. That is so even when the testimony relates to his public employment or concerns information learned during that employment." The Court went on:

"Sworn testimony in judicial proceedings is a quintessential example of speech as a citizen for a simple reason: Anyone who testifies in court bears an obligation, to the court and society at large, to tell the truth. . . .

"In holding that Lane did not speak as a citizen when he testified, the [lower court] read *Garcetti* far too broadly. It reasoned that, because Lane learned of the subject matter of his testimony in the course of his employment with CITY, *Garcetti* requires that his testimony be treated as the speech of an employee rather than that of a citizen. It does not.

"The sworn testimony in this case is far removed from the speech at issue in *Garcetti*—an internal memorandum prepared by a deputy district attorney for his supervisors recommending dismissal of a particular prosecution. The *Garcetti* Court held that such speech was made pursuant to the employee's 'official responsibilities' because '[w]hen [the employee] went to work and performed the tasks he was paid to perform, [he] acted as a government employee. The fact that his duties sometimes required him to speak or write does not mean that his supervisors were prohibited from evaluating his performance.' . . .

"But *Garcetti* said nothing about speech that simply relates to public employment or concerns information learned in the course of public employment. The *Garcetti* Court made explicit that its holding did not turn on the fact that the memo at issue 'concerned the subject matter of [the prosecutor's] employment,' because '[t]he First Amendment protects some expressions related to the speaker's job.' . . . In other words, the mere fact that a citizen's speech concerns information acquired by virtue of his public employment does not transform that speech into employee—rather than citizen—speech. The critical question under *Garcetti* is whether the speech at issue is itself ordinarily within the scope of an employee's duties, not whether it merely concerns those duties."

The Court then turned to whether Lane's speech was on a matter of public concern, and quickly found that it was: "Speech involves matters of public concern 'when it can be fairly considered as relating to any matter of political, social, or other concern to the community, or when it 'is a subject of legitimate news interest; that is, a subject of general interest and of value and concern to the public.' . . . The inquiry turns on the 'content, form, and context' of the speech. . . . The content of Lane's testimony—corruption in a public program and misuse of state funds—obviously involves a matter of significant public concern."

Finally, the Court turned to the government's side of the balance and found no interest that could justify holding Lane's speech against him: "Here, the employer's side of the *Pickering* scale is entirely empty: Respondents do not assert, and cannot demonstrate, any government interest that tips the balance in their favor. There is no evidence, for example, that Lane's testimony at Schmitz' trials was false or erroneous or that Lane unnecessarily disclosed any sensitive, confidential, or privileged information while testifying. In these circumstances, we conclude that Lane's speech is entitled to protection under the First Amendment."

Although joining Justice Sotomayor's opinion, Justice Thomas, joined by Justices Scalia and Alito, wrote a concurring opinion to underscore that the Court had no occasion to decide whether public employee testimony undertaken in the course of ordinary job responsibilities would be speech "as a citizen."

Page 1570. Add the following after Lane v. Franks:

Heffernan v. City of Patterson, 577 U.S. ___, 136 S.Ct. 1412 (2016). Heffernan was a police officer working in the Office of the Police Chief of Patterson, New Jersey. Both the Chief of Police and Heffernan's supervisor were appointed by the incumbent Mayor of Patterson, Jose Torres. Torres was running for reelection against Lawrence Spagnola, one of Heffernan's good friends. The rest of the relevant facts are as follows:

"During the campaign, Heffernan's mother, who was bedridden, asked Heffernan to drive downtown and pick up a large Spagnola sign. She wanted to replace a smaller Spagnola sign, which had been stolen from her front yard. Heffernan went to a Spagnola distribution point and picked up the sign. While there, he spoke for a time to Spagnola's campaign manager and staff. Other members of the police force saw him, sign in hand, talking to campaign workers. Word quickly spread throughout the force.

"The next day, Heffernan's supervisors demoted Heffernan from detective to patrol officer and assigned him to a 'walking post.' In this way they punished Heffernan for what they thought was his 'overt involvement' in Spagnola's campaign. In fact, Heffernan was not involved in the campaign but had picked up the sign simply to help his mother. Heffernan's supervisors had made a factual mistake."

After Heffernan filed suit under 42 U.S.C. § 1983 to vindicate his rights under the First Amendment, the lower federal courts rejected his claim, reasoning, in the words of the Court of Appeals for the Third Circuit, that "a free-speech retaliation claim is actionable under § 1983 only where the adverse action at issue was prompted by an employee's *actual*, rather than *perceived*, exercise of constitutional rights."

The Supreme Court reversed and remanded by a 6–2 vote, with Justice Breyer writing for the Court:

"With a few exceptions, the Constitution prohibits a government employer from discharging or demoting an employee because the employee supports a particular political candidate. . . . In order to answer the question presented, we assume that the exceptions do not apply here. . . . We [also] assume that the activities that Heffernan's supervisors *thought* he had engaged in are of a kind that they cannot constitutionally prohibit or punish, . . . but [that] the supervisors were mistaken about the facts. Heffernan had not engaged in those protected activities. Does Heffernan's constitutional case consequently fail?

"We conclude that . . . the government's reason for demoting Heffernan is what counts here. When an employer demotes an employee out of a desire to prevent the employee from engaging in political activity that the First Amendment protects, the employee is entitled to challenge that unlawful action under the First Amendment and 42 U.S.C. §1983—even if, as here, the employer makes a factual mistake about the employee's behavior.

"We note that a rule of law finding liability in these circumstances tracks the language of the First Amendment more closely than would a contrary rule. Unlike, say, the Fourth Amendment, which begins by speaking of the 'right of the people to be secure in their persons, houses, papers, and effects . . . ,' the First Amendment begins by focusing upon the activity of the Government. It says that 'Congress shall make no law . . . abridging the freedom of speech.' The Government acted upon a constitutionally harmful policy whether Heffernan did or did not in fact engage in political activity. That which stands for a 'law' of 'Congress,' namely, the police department's reason for taking action, 'abridge[s] the freedom of speech' of employees aware of the policy. And Heffernan was directly harmed, namely, demoted, through application of that policy.

"We also consider relevant the constitutional implications of a rule that imposes liability. The constitutional harm at issue in the ordinary case consists in large part of discouraging employees—both the employee discharged (or demoted) and his or her colleagues—from engaging in protected activities. The discharge of one tells the others that they engage in protected activity at their peril. . . . Hence, we do not require plaintiffs in political affiliation cases to 'prove that they, or other employees, have been coerced into changing, either actually or ostensibly, their political allegiance.' . . . The employer's factual mistake does not diminish the risk of causing precisely that same harm. Neither, for that matter, is that harm diminished where an employer announces a policy of demoting those who, say, help a particular candidate in the mayoral race, and all employees (including Heffernan), fearful of demotion, refrain from providing any such help. . . . The upshot is that a discharge or demotion based upon an employer's belief that the employee has engaged in protected activity can cause the same kind, and degree, of constitutional harm whether that belief does or does not rest upon a factual mistake.

"Finally, we note that, contrary to respondents' assertions, a rule of law that imposes liability despite the employer's factual mistake will not normally impose significant extra costs upon the employer. To win, the employee must prove an improper employer motive. In a case like this one, the employee will, if anything, find it more difficult to prove that motive, for the employee will have to point to more than his own conduct to show an employer's intent to discharge or to demote him for engaging in what the employer (mistakenly) believes to have been different (and protected) activities. We concede that, for that very reason, it may be more complicated and costly for the employee to prove his case. But an employee bringing suit will ordinarily shoulder that more complicated burden voluntarily in order to recover the damages he seeks."

Justice Thomas, joined by Justice Alito, dissented. Justice Scalia passed away before the disposition of the case.

CHAPTER 17

RELIGION AND THE CONSTITUTION

1. THE ESTABLISHMENT CLAUSE

B. GOVERNMENT RELIGIOUS EXERCISES, CEREMONIES, DISPLAYS, AND PRACTICES

2. RELIGIOUS SPEECH AND DISPLAYS ON PUBLIC PROPERTY

Page 1651. Add after Van Orden v. Perry:

Town of Greece v. Galloway
572 U.S. ___, 134 S.Ct. 1811, 188 L.Ed.2d 835 (2014).

Justice Kennedy delivered the opinion of the Court, except as to Part II–B.[*]

The Court must decide whether the town of Greece, New York, imposes an impermissible establishment of religion by opening its monthly board meetings with a prayer. It must be concluded, consistent with the Court's opinion in *Marsh* v. *Chambers*, 463 U.S. 783 (1983), that no violation of the Constitution has been shown.

I

[The practice of inviting a local member of the clergy to deliver an invocation at the front of the board of supervisors meeting room began in 1999 in this town of 94,000 near the border of the city of Rochester.]

The town followed an informal method for selecting prayer givers, all of whom were unpaid volunteers. A town employee would call the congregations listed in a local directory until she found a minister available for that month's meeting. The town eventually compiled a list of willing "board chaplains" who had accepted invitations and agreed to return in the future. The town at no point excluded or denied an opportunity to a would-be prayer giver. Its leaders maintained that a minister or layperson of any persuasion, including an atheist, could give the invocation. But nearly all of the congregations in town were Christian; and from 1999 to 2007, all of the participating ministers were too.

Greece neither reviewed the prayers in advance of the meetings nor provided guidance as to their tone or content, in the belief that exercising any degree of control over the prayers would infringe both the free exercise and

---

[*] The Chief Justice and Justice Alito join this opinion in full. Justice Scalia and Justice Thomas join this opinion except as to Part II–B.

speech rights of the ministers. . . . The town instead left the guest clergy free to compose their own devotions. The resulting prayers often sounded both civic and religious themes. . . . Some of the ministers spoke in a distinctly Christian idiom; and a minority invoked religious holidays, scripture, or doctrine. . . .

Respondents . . . attended town board meetings to speak about issues of local concern, and they objected that the prayers violated their religious or philosophical views. . . . After respondents complained that Christian themes pervaded the prayers, to the exclusion of citizens who did not share those beliefs, the town invited a Jewish layman and the chairman of the local Baha'i temple to deliver prayers. A Wiccan priestess who had read press reports about the prayer controversy requested, and was granted, an opportunity to give the invocation.

[Respondents sued,] . . . alleg[ing] that the town violated the . . . Establishment Clause by preferring Christians over other prayer givers and by sponsoring sectarian prayers, such as those given "in Jesus' name.". . . They did not seek an end to the prayer practice, but rather requested an injunction that would limit the town to "inclusive and ecumenical" prayers that referred only to a "generic God" and would not associate the government with any one faith or belief. . . .

The District Court on summary judgment upheld the prayer practice. . . .

. . .

The . . . Second Circuit reversed. . . . [T]he Court now reverses the judgment of the Court of Appeals.

II

In *Marsh* v. *Chambers*, . . . the Court found no First Amendment violation in the Nebraska Legislature's practice of opening its sessions with a prayer delivered by a chaplain paid from state funds. The decision concluded that legislative prayer, while religious in nature, has long been understood as compatible with the Establishment Clause. As practiced by Congress since the framing of the Constitution, legislative prayer lends gravity to public business, reminds lawmakers to transcend petty differences in pursuit of a higher purpose, and expresses a common aspiration to a just and peaceful society. . . .

Marsh is sometimes described as "carving out an exception" to the Court's Establishment Clause jurisprudence, because it sustained legislative prayer without subjecting the practice to "any of the formal 'tests' that have traditionally structured" this inquiry. . . . The Court in *Marsh* found those tests unnecessary because history supported the conclusion that legislative invocations are compatible with the Establishment Clause. The First Congress made it an early item of business to appoint and pay official chaplains, and both the House and Senate have maintained the office virtually uninterrupted since that time. . . . When *Marsh* was decided, in 1983, legislative prayer had persisted in the Nebraska Legislature for more than a century, and the majority of the other States also had the same, consistent practice. . . . Although no information has been cited by the parties to indicate how many local legislative bodies open their meetings with prayer, this practice too has historical precedent. . . .

Yet *Marsh* must not be understood as permitting a practice that would amount to a constitutional violation if not for its historical foundation. . . . [Instead,] *Marsh* stands for the proposition that it is not necessary to define the precise boundary of the Establishment Clause where history shows that the specific practice is permitted. Any test the Court adopts must acknowledge a practice that was accepted by the Framers and has withstood the critical scrutiny of time and political change. . . . A test that would sweep away what has so long been settled would create new controversy and begin anew the very divisions along religious lines that the Establishment Clause seeks to prevent. See *Van Orden* v. *Perry*, . . . (Breyer, J., concurring in judgment).

The Court's inquiry, then, must be to determine whether the prayer practice in the town of Greece fits within the tradition long followed in Congress and the state legislatures. Respondents assert that [it] falls outside that tradition and transgresses the Establishment Clause for two independent but mutually reinforcing reasons. First, they argue that *Marsh* did not approve prayers containing sectarian language or themes, such as the prayers offered in Greece that referred to the "death, resurrection, and ascension of the Savior Jesus Christ," . . . and the "saving sacrifice of Jesus Christ on the cross,". . . . Second, they argue that the setting and conduct of the town board meetings create social pressures that force nonadherents to remain in the room or even feign participation in order to avoid offending the representatives who sponsor the prayer and will vote on matters citizens bring before the board. The sectarian content of the prayers compounds the subtle coercive pressures, they argue, because the nonbeliever who might tolerate ecumenical prayer is forced to do the same for prayer that might be inimical to his or her beliefs.

A

. . .

An insistence on nonsectarian or ecumenical prayer as a single, fixed standard is not consistent with the tradition of legislative prayer outlined in the Court's cases. . . . The Congress that drafted the First Amendment would have been accustomed to invocations containing explicitly religious themes of the sort respondents find objectionable. . . . The decidedly Christian nature of these prayers must not be dismissed as the relic of a time when our Nation was less pluralistic than it is today. Congress continues to permit its appointed and visiting chaplains to express themselves in a religious idiom. It acknowledges our growing diversity not by proscribing sectarian content but by welcoming ministers of many creeds. . . .

. . .

. . . *Marsh* nowhere suggested that the constitutionality of legislative prayer turns on the neutrality of its content. . . .

To hold that invocations must be nonsectarian would force the legislatures that sponsor prayers and the courts that are asked to decide these cases to act as supervisors and censors of religious speech, a rule that would involve government in religious matters to a far greater degree than is the case under the town's current practice of neither editing or approving prayers in advance nor criticizing their content after the fact. . . . Government may not mandate a civic religion that stifles any but the most generic reference to the sacred any more than it may prescribe a religious orthodoxy. . . .

. . . There is doubt, in any event, that consensus might be reached as to what qualifies as generic or nonsectarian. . . . Once it invites prayer into the public sphere, government must permit a prayer giver to address his or her own God or gods as conscience dictates, unfettered by what an administrator or judge considers to be nonsectarian.

· In rejecting the suggestion that legislative prayer must be nonsectarian, the Court does not imply that no constraints remain on its content. . . . If the course and practice over time shows that the invocations denigrate nonbelievers or religious minorities, threaten damnation, or preach conversion, many present may consider the prayer to fall short of the desire to elevate the purpose of the occasion and to unite lawmakers in their common effort. That circumstance would present a different case than the one presently before the Court.

. . . Prayer that reflects beliefs specific to only some creeds can still serve to solemnize the occasion, so long as the practice over time is not "exploited to proselytize or advance any one, or to disparage any other, faith or belief." *Marsh*,. . . .

. . .

The prayers delivered in the town of Greece do not fall outside the tradition this Court has recognized. A number of the prayers did invoke the name of Jesus, the Heavenly Father, or the Holy Spirit, but they also invoked universal themes, as by celebrating the changing of the seasons or calling for a "spirit of cooperation" among town leaders. . . .

Respondents point to other invocations that disparaged those who did not accept the town's prayer practice. One guest minister characterized objectors as a "minority" who are "ignorant of the history of our country," . . . while another lamented that other towns did not have "God-fearing" leaders. . . . Although these two remarks strayed from the rationale set out in *Marsh*, they do not despoil a practice that on the whole reflects and embraces our tradition. Absent a pattern of prayers that over time denigrate, proselytize, or betray an impermissible government purpose, a challenge based solely on the content of a prayer will not likely establish a constitutional violation. . . .

Finally, the Court disagrees with the view taken by the Court of Appeals that the town of Greece contravened the Establishment Clause by inviting a predominantly Christian set of ministers to lead the prayer. The town made reasonable efforts to identify all of the congregations located within its borders and represented that it would welcome a prayer by any minister or layman who wished to give one. That nearly all of the congregations in town turned out to be Christian does not reflect an aversion or bias on the part of town leaders against minority faiths. So long as the town maintains a policy of nondiscrimination, the Constitution does not require it to search beyond its borders for non-Christian prayer givers in an effort to achieve religious balancing. . . .

B

Respondents further seek to distinguish the town's prayer practice from the tradition upheld in *Marsh* on the ground that it coerces participation by nonadherents. They and some *amici* contend that prayer conducted in the intimate setting of a town board meeting differs in fundamental ways from the invocations delivered in Congress and state legislatures, where the public remains segregated from legislative activity and may not address the body except by occasional invitation. Citizens attend town meetings, on the other hand, to accept awards; speak on matters of local importance; and petition the board for action that may affect their economic interests, such as the granting of permits, business licenses, and zoning variances. Respondents argue that the public may feel subtle pressure to participate in prayers that violate their beliefs in order to please the board members from whom they are about to seek a favorable ruling. In their view the fact that board members in small towns know many of their constituents by name only increases the pressure to conform.

. . . On the record in this case the Court is not persuaded that the town of Greece . . . compelled its citizens to engage in a religious observance. The inquiry remains a fact-sensitive one that considers both the setting in which the prayer arises and the audience to whom it is directed.

. . . As a practice that has long endured, legislative prayer has become part of our heritage and tradition, part of our expressive idiom, similar to the Pledge of Allegiance, inaugural prayer, or the recitation of "God save the United States and this honorable Court" at the opening of this Court's sessions. . . . It is presumed that the reasonable observer is acquainted with this tradition and understands that its purposes are to lend gravity to public proceedings and to acknowledge the place religion holds in the lives of many private citizens, not to afford government an opportunity to proselytize or force truant constituents into the pews. . . .

The principal audience for these invocations is not . . . the public but lawmakers themselves, who may find that a moment of prayer or quiet reflection sets the mind to a higher purpose and thereby eases the task of governing. . . . To be sure, many members of the public find these prayers meaningful and wish to join them. But their purpose is largely to accommodate the spiritual needs of lawmakers and connect them to a tradition dating to the time of the Framers. . . . The prayer is [also] an opportunity for them to show who and what they are without denying the right to dissent by those who disagree.

The analysis would be different if town board members directed the public to participate in the prayers, singled out dissidents for opprobrium, or indicated that their decisions might be influenced by a person's acquiescence in the prayer opportunity. . . . Respondents point to several occasions where audience members were asked to rise for the prayer. These requests, however, came not from town leaders but from the guest ministers, who presumably are accustomed to directing their congregations in this way and might have done so thinking the action was inclusive, not coercive. . . . Nothing in the record indicates that town leaders allocated benefits and burdens based on participation in the prayer, or that citizens were received differently depending on whether they joined the invocation or quietly declined. In no instance did town leaders signal disfavor toward nonparticipants or suggest that their stature in the community was in any way diminished. A practice that classified citizens based on their religious views would violate the Constitution, but that is not the case before this Court.

. . . Courts remain free to review the pattern of prayers over time to determine whether they comport with the tradition of solemn, respectful prayer approved in *Marsh*, or whether coercion is a real and substantial likelihood. But in the general course legislative bodies do not engage in impermissible coercion merely by exposing constituents to prayer they would rather not hear and in which they need not participate. . . .

. . . Nothing in the record suggests that members of the public are dissuaded from leaving the meeting room during the prayer, arriving late, or even, as happened here, making a later protest. . . . Should nonbelievers choose to exit the room during a prayer they find distasteful, their absence will not stand out as disrespectful or even noteworthy. And should they remain, their quiet acquiescence will not, in light of our traditions, be interpreted as an agreement with the words or ideas expressed. Neither choice represents an unconstitutional imposition as to mature adults. . . .

. . . The inclusion of a brief, ceremonial prayer as part of a larger exercise in civic recognition suggests that its purpose and effect are to acknowledge religious leaders and the institutions they represent rather than to exclude or coerce nonbelievers.

Ceremonial prayer is but a recognition that, since this Nation was founded and until the present day, many Americans deem that their own existence must be understood by precepts far beyond the authority of government to alter or define and that willing participation in civic affairs can be consistent with a brief acknowledgment of their belief in a higher power, always with due respect for those who adhere to other beliefs. . . .

* * *

The town of Greece does not violate the First Amendment by opening its meetings with prayer that comports with our tradition and does not coerce participation by nonadherents. . . .

Justice Alito, with whom Justice Scalia joins, concurring.

. . .

Apparently, all the houses of worship listed in the local Community Guide [from which a clerical employee in the town's office of constituent services compiled the list of clergy to offer prayers] were Christian churches. . . . There are no synagogues within the borders of the town . . . , but there are several not far away across the Rochester border. . . .

. . . [R]espondents do not claim that the list was attributable to religious bias or favoritism. . . .

. . .

. . . The prayer took place at the beginning of the meetings. . . .

. . . I do not understand this case to involve the constitutionality of a prayer prior to what may be characterized as an adjudicatory proceeding. The prayer preceded only the portion of the town board meeting that I view as essentially legislative. . . .

II

. . . [T]he narrow aspect of the principal dissent . . . is really quite niggling. . . .

A

First, the principal dissent writes, "[i]f the Town Board had let its chaplains know that they should speak in nonsectarian terms, common to diverse religious groups, then no one would have valid grounds for complaint.". . .

. . .

Not only is there no historical support for the proposition that only generic prayer is allowed, but as our country has become more diverse, composing a prayer that is acceptable to all members of the community who hold religious beliefs has become harder and harder. It was one thing to compose a prayer that is acceptable to both Christians and Jews; it is much harder to compose a prayer that is also acceptable to followers of Eastern religions that are now well represented in this country. Many local clergy may find the project daunting, if not impossible, and some may feel that they cannot in good faith deliver such a vague prayer.

. . .

B

If a town wants to avoid the problems associated with this first option, the principal dissent argues, it has another choice: It may "invit[e] clergy of many faiths.". . .

If . . . such a rotating system would obviate any constitutional problems, then despite all its high rhetoric, the principal dissent's quarrel with the town of Greece really boils down to this: The town's clerical employees did a bad job in compiling the list of potential guest chaplains. For that is really the only difference between what the town did and what the principal dissent is willing to accept. The Greece clerical employee drew up her list using the town directory instead of a directory covering the entire greater Rochester area. . . . (I would view this case very differently if the omission of [the] synagogues [on the Rochester side of the border] were intentional.)

. . .

... Many local officials, puzzled by our often puzzling Establishment Clause jurisprudence and terrified of the legal fees that may result from a lawsuit claiming a constitutional violation, already think that the safest course is to ensure that local government is a religion-free zone. . . . [A] unit of local government should not be held to have violated the First Amendment simply because its procedure for lining up guest chaplains does not comply in all respects with what might be termed a "best practices" standard.

III

While the principal dissent, in the end, would demand no more than a small modification in the procedure that the town of Greece initially followed, . . . the logical thrust of many of its arguments is that prayer is *never* permissible prior to meetings of local government legislative bodies. . . .

The features of Greece meetings that the principal dissent highlights are by no means unusual. . . . [I]f prayer is not allowed at meetings with those characteristics, local government legislative bodies, unlike their national and state counterparts, cannot begin their meetings with a prayer. I see no sound basis for drawing such a distinction.

IV

The principal dissent claims to accept the Court's decision in *Marsh* v. *Chambers*, . . . but [its] acceptance . . . appears to be predicated on the view that the prayer at issue in that case was little more than a formality to which the legislators paid scant attention. The principal dissent describes this scene: A session of the state legislature begins with or without most members present; a strictly nonsectarian prayer is recited while some legislators remain seated; and few members of the public are exposed to the experience. This sort of perfunctory and hidden-away prayer, the principal dissent implies, is all that *Marsh* and the First Amendment can tolerate.

[To Justice Alito, *Marsh* and the congressional practice on which it was based were not nearly that narrow.]

V

. . . I am concerned that at least some readers will take [the dissent's] hypotheticals as a warning that . . . today's decision leads . . . to a country in which religious minorities are denied the equal benefits of citizenship.

Nothing could be further from the truth. All that the Court does today is to allow a town to follow a practice that we have previously held is permissible for Congress and state legislatures. In seeming to suggest otherwise, the principal dissent goes far astray.

Justice Thomas, with whom Justice Scalia joins as to Part II, concurring in part and concurring in the judgment.

Except for Part II–B, I join the opinion of the Court, which faithfully applies *Marsh* v. *Chambers*. . . . I write separately to reiterate my view that the Establishment Clause is "best understood as a federalism provision," . . . and to state my understanding of the proper "coercion" analysis.

I

. . . As I have explained before, the text and history of the Clause "resis[t] incorporation" against the States. . . . If the Establishment Clause is not incorporated, then it has no application here, where only municipal action is at issue.

. . .

II

Even if the Establishment Clause were properly incorporated against the States, the municipal prayers at issue in this case bear no resemblance to the coercive state establishments that existed at the founding. . . .

. . .

. . . At a minimum, there is no support for the proposition that the framers of the Fourteenth Amendment embraced wholly modern notions that the Establishment Clause is violated whenever the "reasonable observer" feels "subtle pressure," or perceives governmental "endors[ement].". . . [W]hatever nonestablishment principles existed in 1868, they included no concern for the finer sensibilities of the "reasonable observer."

Justice Breyer, dissenting.

As we all recognize, this is a "fact-sensitive" case. . . .

. . . In essence, the Court of Appeals merely held that the town must do more than it had previously done to try to make its prayer practices inclusive of other faiths. And it did not prescribe a single constitutionally required method for doing so.

In my view, the Court of Appeals' conclusion and its reasoning are convincing. Justice Kagan's dissent is consistent with that view, and I join it. I also here emphasize several factors that I believe underlie the conclusion that, on the particular facts of this case, the town's prayer practice violated the Establishment Clause.

First, Greece is a predominantly Christian town, but it is not exclusively so. A map . . . shows a Buddhist temple within the town and several Jewish synagogues just outside its borders. . . . Yet during the more than 120 monthly meetings at which prayers were delivered during the record period (from 1999 to 2010), only four prayers were delivered by non-Christians. And all of these occurred in 2008, shortly after the plaintiffs began complaining about the town's Christian prayer practice and nearly a decade after that practice had commenced.

. . . The inclusivity of the 2008 meetings, which contrasts starkly with the exclusively single-denomination prayers every year before and after, is commendable. But the Court of Appeals reasonably decided not to give controlling weight to that inclusivity, for it arose only in response to the complaints that presaged this litigation, and it did not continue into the following years.

Second, the town made no significant effort to inform the area's non-Christian houses of worship about the possibility of delivering an opening prayer. . . .

. . .

Third, . . . in a context where religious minorities exist and where more could easily have been done to include their participation, the town chose to do nothing. It could, for example, have posted its policy of permitting anyone to give an invocation on its website, . . . which provides dates and times of upcoming town board meetings along with minutes of prior meetings. It could have announced inclusive policies at the beginning of its board meetings, just before introducing the month's prayer giver. It could have provided information to those houses of worship of all faiths that lie just outside its borders and include citizens of Greece among their members. Given that the town could easily have made these or similar efforts but chose not to, the fact that all of the prayers (aside from the 2008 outliers) were given by adherents of a single religion reflects a lack of effort to include others. . . .

Fourth, the fact that the board meeting audience included citizens with business to conduct also contributes to the importance of making more of an effort to include members of other denominations. . . .

Fifth, . . . the Constitution does not forbid . . . efforts to explain to those who give the prayers the nature of the occasion and the audience.

The U.S. House of Representatives, for example, provides its guest chaplains with . . . guidelines . . . designed to encourage the sorts of prayer that are consistent with the purpose of an invocation for a government body in a religiously pluralistic Nation. . . . The town made no effort to promote a similarly inclusive prayer practice here.

. . . The question in this case is whether the prayer practice of the town of Greece, by doing too little to reflect the religious diversity of its citizens, did too much, even if unintentionally, to promote the "political division along religious lines" that "was one of the principal evils against which the First Amendment was intended to protect.". . .

. . . I conclude, like Justice Kagan, that the town of Greece failed to make reasonable efforts to include prayer givers of minority faiths, with the result that, although it is a community of several faiths, its prayer givers were almost exclusively persons of a single faith. . . .

. . .

Justice Kagan, with whom Justice Ginsburg, Justice Breyer, and Justice Sotomayor join, dissenting.

. . . [O]ur Constitution makes a commitment . . . that however . . . individuals worship, they will count as full and equal American citizens. . . .

I respectfully dissent from the Court's opinion because I think the Town of Greece's prayer practices violate that norm of religious equality. . . . I agree with the Court's decision in *Marsh* v. *Chambers*. . . . And I believe that pluralism and inclusion in a town hall can satisfy the constitutional requirement of neutrality; such a forum need not become a religion-free zone. But . . . [t]he practice at issue here differs from the one sustained in *Marsh* because Greece's town meetings involve participation by ordinary citizens, and the invocations given—directly to those citizens—were predominantly sectarian in content. Still more, Greece's Board did nothing to recognize religious diversity: In arranging for clergy members to open each meeting, the Town never sought (except briefly when this suit was filed) to involve, accommodate, or in any way reach out to adherents of non-Christian religions. So month in and month out for over a decade, prayers steeped in only one faith, addressed toward members of the public, commenced meetings to discuss local affairs and distribute government benefits. In my view, that practice does not square with the First Amendment's promise that every citizen, irrespective of her religion, owns an equal share in her government.

I

[Justice Kagan offered three "hypothetical scenarios in which sectarian prayer—taken straight from this case's record—infuses governmental activities"—(1) "a party in a case going to trial," where the judge "asks a minister to come to the front of the room, and instructs [those] present to rise for an opening prayer" that references Christian scripture, (2) an election official on election day asking everyone there to join him in similar prayer, and (3) "an immigrant attending a naturalization ceremony" told by a presiding official "that before administering the oath of allegiance, he would like a minister to pray for you and with you[,]" which also turned out to be in sectarian language.] I would hold that the government officials responsible for the above practices—that is, for prayer repeatedly invoking a single religion's beliefs in these settings—crossed a constitutional line. I have every confidence the Court would agree. . . .

. . . [I]f my hypotheticals involved the prayer of some other religion, the outcome would be exactly the same. . . . [T]he question would be why such government sponsored prayer of a single religion goes beyond the constitutional pale.

One glaring problem is that the government in all these hypotheticals has aligned itself with, and placed its imprimatur on, a particular religious creed. "The clearest command of the Establishment Clause," this Court has held, "is that one religious denomination cannot be officially preferred over another." *Larson* v. *Valente*, 456 U.S. 228, 244 (1982). . . . By authorizing and overseeing prayers associated with a single religion—to the exclusion of all others—the government officials in my hypothetical cases (whether federal, state, or local does not matter) have violated that foundational principle. They have embarked on a course of religious favoritism anathema to the First Amendment.

And making matters still worse: They have done so in a place where individuals come to interact with, and participate in, the institutions and processes of their government. A person goes to court, to the polls, to a naturalization ceremony—and a government official or his handpicked minister asks her, as the first order of official business, to stand and pray with others in a way conflicting with her own religious beliefs. Perhaps she feels sufficient pressure to go along—to rise, bow her head, and join in whatever others are saying: After all, she wants, very badly, what the judge or poll worker or immigration official has to offer. Or perhaps she is made of stronger mettle, and she opts not to participate in what she does not believe—indeed, what would, for her, be something like blasphemy. She then must make known her dissent from the common religious view, and place herself apart from other citizens, as well as from the officials responsible for the invocations. And so a civic function of some kind brings religious differences to the fore: That public proceeding becomes (whether intentionally or not) an instrument for dividing her from adherents to the community's majority religion, and for altering the very nature of her relationship with her government.

That is not the country we are, because that is not what our Constitution permits. Here, . . . all participate in the business of government not as Christians, Jews, Muslims (and more), but only as Americans—none of them different from any other for that civic purpose. Why not, then, at a town meeting?

II

. . . I agree with the majority that the issue here is "whether the prayer practice in the Town of Greece fits within the tradition long followed in Congress and the state legislatures."

Where I depart from the majority is in my reply to that question. The town hall here is a kind of hybrid. Greece's Board indeed has legislative functions, as Congress and state assemblies do—and that means some opening prayers are allowed there. But much as in my hypotheticals, the Board's meetings are also occasions for ordinary citizens to engage with and petition their government, often on highly individualized matters. That feature calls for Board members to exercise special care to ensure that the prayers offered are inclusive—that they respect each and every member of the community as an equal citizen. But the Board, and the clergy members it selected, made no such effort. Instead, the prayers given in Greece, addressed directly to the Town's citizenry, were *more* sectarian, and *less* inclusive, than anything this Court sustained in *Marsh*. For those reasons, the prayer in Greece departs from the legislative tradition that the majority takes as its benchmark.

. . .

Let's count the ways in which [the practice in Nebraska's unicameral legislature, upheld in *Marsh*, and the practice here] diverge. First, the governmental proceedings at which the prayers occur differ significantly in nature and purpose. The Nebraska Legislature's floor sessions—like those of the U.S. Congress and other state assemblies—are of, by, and for elected lawmakers. Members of the public take no part in those proceedings; any few who attend are spectators only, watching from a high-up visitors' gallery. (In that respect, note that neither the Nebraska Legislature nor the Congress calls for prayer when citizens themselves participate in a hearing—say, by giving testimony relevant to a bill or nomination.) Greece's town meetings, by contrast, revolve around ordinary members of the community. Each and every aspect of those sessions provides opportunities for Town residents to interact with public officials. And the most important parts enable those citizens to petition their government. In the Public Forum, they urge (or oppose) changes in the Board's policies and priorities; and then, in what are essentially adjudicatory hearings, they request the Board to grant (or deny) applications for various permits, licenses, and zoning variances. So the meetings, both by design and in operation, allow citizens to actively participate in the Town's governance—sharing concerns, airing grievances, and both shaping the community's policies and seeking their benefits.

Second . . . , the prayers in these two settings have different audiences. In the Nebraska Legislature, the chaplain spoke to, and only to, the elected representatives. . . . The same is true in the U.S. Congress and, I suspect, in every other state legislature. . . .

The very opposite is true in Greece: Contrary to the majority's characterization, the prayers there are directed squarely at the citizens. Remember that the chaplain of the month stands with his back to the Town Board; his real audience is the group he is facing—the 10 or so members of the public, perhaps including children. And he typically addresses those people, as even the majority observes, as though he is "directing [his] congregation." He almost always begins with some version of "Let us all pray together.". . . In essence, the chaplain leads, as the first part of a town meeting, a highly intimate (albeit relatively brief) prayer service, with the public serving as his congregation.

And third, the prayers themselves differ in their content and character. *Marsh* characterized the prayers in the Nebraska Legislature as "in the Judeo-Christian tradition," and stated, as a relevant (even if not dispositive) part of its analysis, that the chaplain had removed all explicitly Christian references at a senator's request. . . .

But no one can fairly read the prayers from Greece's Town meetings as anything other than explicitly Christian—constantly and exclusively so. . . . About two-thirds of the prayers given over this decade or so invoked "Jesus," "Christ," "Your Son," or "the Holy Spirit"; in the 18 months before the record closed, 85% included those references. . . . Many prayers contained elaborations of Christian doctrine or recitations of scripture. . . .

Still more, the prayers betray no understanding that the American community is today, as it long has been, a rich mosaic of religious faiths. . . . The monthly chaplains appear almost always to assume that everyone in the room is Christian. . . . The Town itself has never urged its chaplains to reach out to members of other faiths, or even to recall that they might be present. And accordingly, few chaplains have made any effort to be inclusive; none has thought even to assure attending members of the public that they need not participate in the prayer session. . . .

C

Those three differences, taken together, remove this case from the protective ambit of *Marsh* and the history on which it relied. To recap: *Marsh* upheld prayer addressed to legislators alone, in a proceeding in which citizens had no role—and even then, only when it did not "proselytize or advance" any single religion. . . . It was that legislative prayer practice (not every prayer in a body exercising any legislative function) that the Court found constitutional given its "unambiguous and unbroken history.". . . None of the history *Marsh* cited—and none the majority details today—supports calling on citizens to pray, in a manner consonant with only a single religion's beliefs, at a participatory public proceeding, having both legislative and adjudicative components. . . .

. . .

Everything about [the] situation [in Greece] infringes the First Amendment. . . . That the Town Board selects, month after month and year after year, prayer givers who will reliably speak in the voice of Christianity, and so places itself behind a single creed. That in offering those sectarian prayers, the Board's chosen clergy members repeatedly call on individuals, prior to participating in local governance, to join in a form of worship that may be at odds with their own beliefs. That the clergy thus put some residents to the unenviable choice of either pretending to pray like the majority or declining to join its communal activity, at the very moment of petitioning their elected leaders. That the practice thus divides the citizenry, creating one class that shares the Board's own evident religious beliefs and another (far smaller) class that does not. And that the practice also alters a dissenting citizen's relationship with her government, making her religious difference salient when she seeks only to engage her elected representatives as would any other citizen.

None of this means that Greece's town hall must be religion- or prayer-free. . . . What the circumstances here demand is the recognition that we are a pluralistic people too. When citizens of all faiths come to speak to each other and their elected representatives in a legislative session, the government must take especial care to ensure that the prayers they hear will seek to include, rather than serve to divide. No more is required—but that much is crucial—to treat every citizen, of whatever religion, as an equal participant in her government.

And contrary to the majority's (and Justice Alito's) view, that is not difficult to do. If the Town Board had let its chaplains know that they should speak in nonsectarian terms, common to diverse religious groups, then no one would have valid grounds for complaint. . . . Or if the Board preferred, it might have invited clergy of many faiths to serve as chaplains, as the majority notes that Congress does. . . .

But Greece could not do what it did: infuse a participatory government body with one (and only one) faith, so that month in and month out, the citizens appearing before it become partly defined by their creed—as those who share, and those who do not, the community's majority religious belief. . . .

III

How, then, does the majority go so far astray, allowing the Town of Greece to turn its assemblies for citizens into a forum for Christian prayer? The answer does not lie in first principles: I have no doubt that every member of this Court believes as firmly as I that our institutions of government belong equally to all, regardless of faith. Rather, the error reflects two kinds of blindness. First, the majority misapprehends the facts of this case, as distinct from those characterizing traditional legislative prayer. And second, the majority misjudges the essential meaning of the religious worship in Greece's town hall, along with its capacity to exclude and divide.

. . .

. . . The majority thus errs in assimilating the Board's prayer practice to that of Congress or the Nebraska Legislature. Unlike those models, the Board is determinedly—and relentlessly—noninclusive.

And the month in, month out sectarianism the Board chose for its meetings belies the majority's refrain that the prayers in Greece were "ceremonial" in nature. . . .

. . .

. . . When the citizens of this country approach their government, they do so only as Americans, not as members of one faith or another. And that means that even in a partly legislative body, they should not confront government-sponsored worship that divides them along religious lines. I believe, for all the reasons I have given, that the Town of Greece betrayed that promise. . . .

2. THE FREE EXERCISE OF RELIGION

Page 1727. Add at end of section:

Burwell v. Hobby Lobby Stores, Inc., 573 U.S. ___, 134 S.Ct. 2751 (2014). Finding it unnecessary to reach a First Amendment Free Exercise claim, a bare majority of the Court held that a proper interpretation of the Religious Freedom Restoration Act of 1993 (RFRA) did not allow regulations of the United States Department of Health and Human Services (HHS), adopted pursuant to the Patient Protection and Affordable Care Act of 2010 (ACA), to require closely held corporations to provide health insurance coverage for four FDA-approved contraceptives to which the family owners had sincere religious objections based on the fact that those contraceptives, unlike sixteen others, may operate after the fertilization of an egg. In doing so, Justice Alito's majority opinion understood RFRA, as amended by RLUIPA, "to provide very broad protection for religious liberty." From this starting point, the Court went on to hold that (1) closely held corporations are "persons" who can "exercise religion" within the coverage of RFRA, in significant part because that protects the religious liberty of the individual corporate owners; (2) the contraceptive mandate "substantially burdens" the exercise of religion; and (3) assuming, but not deciding, "that the interest in guaranteeing cost-free access to the four challenged contraceptive methods is compelling within the meaning of RFRA,"

RFRA's least-restrictive means standard was "not satisfied[,]" either because the Government itself reasonably could assume the cost of providing those contraceptives for employees who wanted them, or because HHS could provide to closely held corporations the same accommodation it had decided to provide for nonprofit corporations with religious objections—namely, having the group-health-insurance issuer exclude that coverage from the employer's plan and provide separate payments for contraceptive services for plan participants without imposing any cost-sharing requirements on the eligible organizations, its insurance plan, or its employee beneficiaries, thus requiring the issuer to bear the cost. In the majority's view, either alternative would be less restrictive of the religious liberty of the closely held corporate owners than the contraceptive mandate.[2]

There were four dissenters. Justice Ginsburg, joined by Justice Sotomayor, would have held that RFRA—particularly in light of the Woman's Health Amendment to the ACA that added minimum coverage requirements for preventive services specific to women's health, and in light of the Senate's rejection of a "so-called 'conscience amendment,'" which would have enabled any employer or insurance provider to deny coverage based on its asserted 'religious beliefs or moral convictions' "—did not extend any protection to for-profit corporations claiming a religious exemption from a generally applicable law. Those two Justices faulted the Court for failing to distinguish between nonprofit religious organizations, which "exist to serve a community of believers," from for-profit corporations whose owners sincerely hold religious beliefs, because the for-profits operate in a work "community . . . embracing persons of diverse beliefs."

Justice Breyer and Justice Kagan thought it unnecessary to decide whether RFRA extended to for-profit corporations. Instead, they joined the remainder of Justice Ginsburg's dissent, which would have held in any event that "the connection between the families' religious objections and the contraceptive coverage requirement is too attenuated to rank as substantial"—largely because the linkage is "interrupted by independent decisionmakers (the woman and her health counselor) standing between the challenged government action and the religious exercise claimed to be infringed. Any decision to use contraceptives made by a woman covered under Hobby Lobby's . . . plan will not be propelled by the Government, it will be the woman's autonomous choice,

---

[2] In a concurring opinion, Justice Kennedy thought it "important to confirm that a premise of the Court's opinion is its assumption that the HHS regulation here at issue furthers a legitimate and compelling interest in the health of female employees." He further explained his position as follows:

"Among the reasons the United States is so open, so tolerant, and so free is that no person may be restricted or demeaned by government in exercising his or her religion. Yet neither may that same exercise unduly restrict other persons, such as employees, in protecting their own interests, interests the law deems compelling. In these cases the means to reconcile those two priorities are at hand in the existing accommodation the Government has designed, identified, and used for circumstances closely parallel to those presented here. RFRA requires the Government to use this less restrictive means. As the Court explains, this existing model, designed precisely for this problem, might well suffice to distinguish the instant cases from many others in which it is more difficult and expensive to accommodate a governmental program to countless religious claims based on an alleged statutory right of free exercise."

informed by the physician she consults." They also joined that part of the dissent that affirmed the Government's compelling interests in helping women "avoid the health problems unintended pregnancies may visit on them and their children" and securing "benefits wholly unrelated to pregnancy, preventing certain cancers, menstrual disorders, and pelvic pain." Finally, all of the dissenters concluded that "none of the proffered alternatives would satisfactorily serve the compelling interest to which Congress responded."